PN
1998.3
.F75
C4
1990

Clagett, Thomas D.,
1956-

William Friedkin

DATE DUE

WILLIAM FRIEDKIN

Films of Aberration, Obsession and Reality

by

Thomas D. Clagett

McFarland & Company, Inc., Publishers
Jefferson, North Carolina, and London

British Library Cataloguing-in-Publication data are available

Library of Congress Cataloguing-in-Publication Data

Clagett, Thomas D., 1956–
    William Friedkin : films of aberration, obsession and reality /
by Thomas D. Clagett.
        p.   cm.
    Filmography: p.
    Includes bibliographical references and index.
    ISBN 0-89950-262-8 (lib. bdg. : 50# alk. paper) ∞
    1. Friedkin, William — Criticism and interpretation.   I. Title.
PN1998.3.F75C4   1990
791.43′0233′092 — dc20   89-43693
                                                              CIP

Manufactured in the United States of America

McFarland & Company, Inc., Publishers
  Box 611, Jefferson, North Carolina 28640

For Francis and Naomi Clagett, my parents,
and
Stephen Hedstrom and A. J. Langguth, the better writers

Contents

Acknowledgments

In late December of 1973, I stood in a line with nearly one thousand other eager patrons outside the National Theater in Westwood, California. A film entitled *The Exorcist* had just opened. The idea of an examination of the film's director, William Friedkin, and his work began rolling around in my head. What follows is that study, but it could never have evolved without some very kind and generous help: the staff of the Eileen Norris Cinema Theater at the University of Southern California, namely, Dana Knowles, Daniel Wolf, Kiki Morris and particularly Richard McKinney for his lewd comments; at the Director's Guild of America, David Shepard, special projects officer, and Selise Eiseman, education coordinator; Lin Ephriam, who kindly introduced me to Billy Friedkin; Ted Rich, vice president in charge of post-production at Mary Tyler Moore Enterprises and my former employer, who always understood that an interview with one of Billy's associates could be made available to me at a moment's notice and never objected to my sometimes hasty departures; Gloria Gunn, post-production supervisor, Patricia Kudish, Ted's assistant, and my friends who covered for me during my absences; Jave McWilliams, Dianne Marcinizyn, Ronni McGann, and Patsy Titus, whose skills at their typewriters and word processors saved me innumerable extra hours; Toni St. Clair Lilly, Billy's assistant, whose help and patience never faltered; and Joe and Jan St. Amant for their tireless researching.

I also must thank the score of individuals who freely and graciously gave their time and shared their thoughts to make this study a richer, fuller and, I hope, more insightful and rewarding experience. In particular, I wish to offer a special thanks to Randy Jurgensen whose contribution was invaluable. And, of course, Billy.

Finally, and most importantly, I thank A. J. Langguth, my mentor and a professor of journalism at the University of Southern California, who initially and then continually encouraged me; and I thank Steven Hedstrom, my friend, who mercilessly demanded in rewrites the best I could give.

Introduction

A film sense is a difficult gift to define. It's like pornography—you know it when you see it. Visually telling a story, layering it with style, drama, and themes partly make up a film sense. Another part is passion, possibly the most important, for it cannot be learned. It's the human part.

William Friedkin, the Academy Award–winning director of *The French Connection*, has that film sense, that passion. This is a critical examination of Friedkin's work, beginning with his television documentary days in Chicago in 1955 through his latest feature film, *The Guardian* (1990). Interviews and biographical information are used to take us from one project to the next, thereby discussing the background, circumstances and sources of each project. However, the focus is always the analysis of the films themselves. Therefore, chapters are devoted to each specific film chronologically to examine more clearly Friedkin's filmic progress by exploring the genesis and influences of the project as well as examining the film itself aesthetically, dramatically and thematically.

The first chapter begins with Friedkin's television documentary work, and specifically *The People Versus Paul Crump*, which sets forth the thematic preoccupations of many of his films. (Friedkin has attempted occasionally to diverge into previously, for him, untested and unfamiliar filmic waters.) Chapter 2 continues with his subsequent television documentary work in Chicago and his move to Hollywood with David Wolper Productions. It also includes Friedkin's perceptions of his initial work on sound stages with actors and his introduction to Alfred Hitchcock. Chapter 3 concerns *Good Times*, his first feature film, which starred the pop singing duo Sonny and Cher. This film served as Friedkin's introduction to what is often referred to in Hollywood vernacular as "The Big Time." *The Night They Raided Minsky's*, Chapter 4, follows. It was another step up the Hollywood ladder for Friedkin since it was a United Artists film, a major studio production. Chapter 5, *The Birthday Party*, based on Harold Pinter's play, was Friedkin's dream project—at that time. Chapter 6, *The Boys in the Band*, is based on Mart Crowly's successful Off Broadway play about gay relationships that established Friedkin as a filmmaker willing to tackle controversial topics. Friedkin's claim to fame, *The French Connection*, which concerns Chapter 7, about street-smart cops and suave drug pushers, thrust Friedkin

to the apex of his career. Following this is Chapter 8, *The Exorcist*, one of
the top money-making films of all time and one of the most controversial.
With carte blanche because of his extraordinary successes, Friedkin re-
made the H. G. Clouzot film *Wages of Fear* under the new title *Sorcerer*,
the topic of Chapter 9. Much maligned, *Sorcerer* may well be Friedkin's
most physical as well as his most personal film. After the thrashing he took
on *Sorcerer*, Friedkin's career began a downward spiral. His next film, *The
Brink's Job*, Chapter 10, was a safe, innocuous picture about the buffoons
who robbed the Brink's in Boston in 1950. Returning (briefly) to controversial topics, Friedkin directed *Cruising*. Chapter 11 examines this film about
the ambiguities and blurred meanings of sex and aggression within the
framework of a murder story set in the gay leather subculture. In an apparent effort to make a mainstream comedy, Friedkin made *Deal of the Century*, an unfunny and unredeemed film about arms dealers, discussed in
Chapter 12. Chapter 13, *To Live and Die in L.A.*, finds Friedkin back on the
gritty streets with tough Secret Service agents. *Rampage*, a film about the
death penalty that brings Friedkin's career full circle since his first film,
Crump, concerns a man on death row and is the topic of Chapter 14. The
final chapter finds Friedkin returning to the horror genre with *The
Guardian*.

Friedkin's latest work is simply that, and therefore any study of his
career and films remains incomplete. But the body of work of this talented
filmmaker deserves examination. His unique vision—fatalistic, violent,
realistic—has resulted in some of the most contentious and compelling successes and failures in American films.

"After his father died, Billy's mother told him, 'We got no money to make you a doctor so the best thing to do is get into records, TV or movies.'"

— Fat Thomas

1

The People Versus Paul Crump

"You're talking about *Rosebud* when you're
talking about Billy.... Here's young Orson
Welles trying to find himself."
— Bill Butler

I.

The electric chair sits inside a steel chamber like some ancient god
demanding human sacrifice. The head strap looks like a death mask —
leering, toothless. William Friedkin's taut documentary, *The People Versus
Paul Crump,* not only gave Friedkin that most important, sought-after and
elusive of Hollywood realities known as "The Big Break" but saved Paul
Crump's life from the electric chair.

The opening image in *Crump* reveals a jail cell and its three prisoners.
A cold, stark reality permeates the scene, accented by the sound of one of
the three playing a sad harmonica. The second leans against the bars; the
third sits. None faces the others. The harmonica player and standing
prisoner move away, leaving the third, who we will soon recognize as Paul
Crump, utterly isolated. Quickly, visually, the shot evokes feelings of emptiness, boredom, aloneness. And in the background throughout, stretching
across the concrete wall, the shadow of a uniformed guard, unmoving,
always present. The cliché of "men living in the shadow of the law" is nearly
obliterated by the deathly quality of the harsh black-and-white photography
wherein shadows hang more like shrouds.

On screen, John Justin Smith, a reporter for the *Chicago Daily News,*
speaks to Jack Johnson, Warden of the Cook County Jail.

Smith:	Warden, Paul Crump has been up to the brink of doom and back down again six, eight times, something like this?
Johnson:	It's been eleven times, I think, for Paul on dates and about forty continuances in relation to his case over a period of eight years. This in itself is mental torture.

1

> These men live from day to day and, of course, with
> this pressure, I'm inclined to think that they die daily
> with it.

A close-up of Paul Crump, a stocky, clean-shaven black man, fills the screen, and over this Smith reports: "For nine years Paul Crump has tried to tell his story. Either nobody listened or nobody cared or nobody believed."

What was referred to as "the most daring daylight robbery in recent years," "climaxed by a vicious assault and murder," took place on a Friday morning, March 20, 1953, at the Chicago Stockyards. More than $17,000 was stolen, and Ted Zukowski, captain of the Libby, McNeill, Libby plant guard and a family man with four kids, was shot and killed. The weekly clockwork of two guards, paymaster and credit union rep moving up the back staircase to the cafeteria where the employee checks were cashed was a ritual familiar to hundreds of employees.

The film bolts forward like a lethal charge of electric current. A re-enactment of the robbery-murder, the trench-coated assailants racing down the back stairs, guards in pursuit, a masked bandit pushing the gun into Zukowski's face, firing. Zukowski, hands to his face, blood running between his fingers. Crump's story of his first arrest where he and Eugene Taylor, who shortly before had admitted to Crump that the Libby robbery was his "score, his caper," were busted outside Hudson Tillman's house. That Tillman, a known drug user, had a personal animosity against Crump. Tillman fingered Crump not only as the trigger man but as the fifth member of his gang — a gang identified by witnesses as consisting of only four men. Crump's alibi — a girl named Fay he claimed to have been with during the time of the robbery, who testified at his first trial on his behalf but then left town due to public ridicule before Crump's second trial. A second arrest where Crump was sweated, beaten and interrogated until he "knew the part they wanted me to play." Crump's lawyers' appeals. The Supreme Court decision. A date of execution.

According to Friedkin, he met Paul Crump through a friend, a chaplain at the Cook County Jail, Father Serpling, who told him Crump might have been railroaded into prison.[1]

"It was a highly dramatic story — a man who'd been on Death Row for eleven years," said Friedkin. "It took me a long time to get up the nerve to go down to the jail and meet the guy. I was twenty years old."

Four years earlier, Friedkin had graduated from high school and had no desire to attend college. He answered an ad in the *Chicago Tribune* that offered opportunities for young men in television. He went to the wrong address (two television stations sat across the street from each other) but was still hired and started in true show-business fashion, in the mailroom at

WGN. That was 1955. About a year later, Friedkin was promoted to floor manager, and over the next eight years, he says, he directed more than two thousand live TV shows—documentaries, news, panel shows, quiz shows, variety shows—six, seven shows a day, forty shows a week, for fifty weeks a year.

But live television wasn't film; it was pushing buttons on a studio monitor. Making films was what Friedkin wanted, having been greatly influenced as a teenager by Orson Welles's *Citizen Kane.*

So Friedkin enlisted the aid of Bill Butler, one of the cameramen at WGN who also wanted to make films. (Butler would later become one of the top cinematographers in Hollywood, with credits such as *Jaws, The Conversation,* and *Rocky II, III,* and *IV.*)

According to Butler, he and Friedkin moonlighted on a documentary for the Protestant Church Organization entitled *Walk Through the Valley.* Friedkin combined five different cases of juvenile delinquency that the organization had on file.

"We had no written script, per se," admitted Butler. "It was our job to go into institutions like Cook County Jail and hospitals, and show the ministers taking care of teenage problems and counseling and visiting the sick and dying.

"Billy would find locations to shoot these events, and then we'd make the shooting script up as we went along, invent it out of our imagination. It was as good a script as anybody today would get off paper. The proof was the fact that it took first place in its category at the San Francisco Film Festival, and that was our very first film.

"We were also quite a ways into the film when the organization realized they they were getting a lot of bills from camera rental houses, editing charges and things they hadn't even thought about, and nor had we.

"They asked us if five hundred dollars would be enough to make the film. We said certainly. We really didn't know, of course, but we were willing to give it a try. We weren't charging anything for our services. We took the money and bought film because you don't get much credit from Kodak."

But now the organization was in a panic, Butler said, being a couple of thousand dollars into a film they had not planned to spend more than five hundred on.

"When we both had to show our faces," he went on, "they said, 'What are you guys doing with our money?' Billy was so cool and handled it so well.... With the heads of this group putting all this pressure on him, making me feel like we were guilty as sin, Billy simply pointed out that if they'd take the film to any local television station (even WGN since we were shooting it on weekends and our time off) and present it to them, they'd be most happy—inasmuch as it was a religious contribution and tax deductible—to pick up the bills and show the film."

Eventually the organization did just that, but there was still a minor problem: how to end the picture. According to Butler, the hero of the story— a street kid who had since straightened out—was killed in a knife fight under the El train tracks when he tried to pull this boy he knew out of a rumble. The hero fell backward and laid there looking up at the tracks.

"We just didn't know how to get off the stage with this. We'd snuck into the editing facilities of the educational station that night since no one was using them because we didn't have any equipment to edit the film ourselves.

"Now this night, after whatever medical show the station was running was over, a man came in with a reel of film and dumped it in a trash can. Here we were, trying to put a film together that's shorter than the one he's just dumped out. That act alone was depressing. We thought, 'My God, is that what happens to your films?'

"But the guy leaves, and we wonder, what's he throwing away? We pull this reel out of the trash and find that it's a medical film where as each doctor is introduced, his picture has optically been placed in the center of an enlarged eye. Now the eye closes, the doctor disappears. The eye opens again, and it's just a regular eye that closes again before opening to reveal another doctor.

"We thought *wow!* In go the scissors—clip—out comes the eye and into our film in five minutes. It's our ending: the kid's eye going shut.

"That's an example of how we just took whatever was in front of us and made film out of it. . . . You just know in your mind what you're trying to do. It's taking opportunity and turning it around. . . . We still didn't know what we were doing."

While Butler continued with his day job at WGN, Friedkin went to prison.

"So I met Paul Crump and he shook my hand," said Friedkin. "He stared right into my eyes, and people seldom do that. Most of the time you meet somebody and say, 'Hi, how are you?' But Crump looked directly at me and held my hand very tight, and I really felt a great sense of communication from this guy, and I sat down and listened to his story.

"In those days in Chicago, a black guy who was accused of murder was virtually guilty with or without trial, and it occurred to me that this guy may have gotten a really bum rap. So I set out not only to learn how to make a film utilizing his story but to make a film that would be kind of a court of last resort to try to save him from the electric chair."

According to Friedkin, WGN was not interested in a documentary on Paul Crump, so he took the idea to Red Quinlan, at that time the general manager of WBKB, the local ABC affiliate in Chicago, who had been trying to hire Friedkin away from WGN. Quinlan agreed to finance the project, though he still couldn't lure Friedkin over to his side of the street.

So Friedkin began moonlighting again with Butler. Friedkin said they would "do a full week's work at WGN and then on weekends and evenings we'd make the *Crump* movie." Crump's date of execution loomed six months away.

According to Quinlan, an appeal had been filed in the Supreme Court, and if it was rejected, "they were going to burn Crump pretty quick, and then the whole thing would be moot."

It took Friedkin and Butler six months to make the film, both admitting they still did not know how to do it. According to Friedkin, they rented the Arriflex 16 camera, which had just come out, and a Nagra tape recorder from Baron's Cine Rental, and set to work filming Paul Crump's story, still hazy on how to get sync sound between the camera and recorder.

Admittedly, it was the most amateur kind of filmmaking, Bill Butler said, "but we took the court records and filmed what they said as best we could with amateur people we'd recruited from universities and black people from the community who wanted to work on it. Then we went to the recordings we'd made of Paul of what he said happened at those same hours and recorded that on film.

"We were at our best when we were telling our story with pictures. A case in point was when the robbers arrive in the car, run through the puddle of water and stop under the fire escape where a welder is working and sparks fly down on the car. Both of us have a great eye. . . . We're both seeing the same vision. That's the reason we worked so well together. We'd see a fire escape and see a composition. We'd just punch the other person in the ribs and say, 'Look.' He'd look up, see the same shot, and we wouldn't have to talk about it. We were that much in sync.

"But it was Billy's sense of editing that made the difference. He's one of the best editors around, frankly. That's one of the reasons that that sequence works well. It's a creative sense of editing, not one where you're forced to cut because the actor made a turn and you must match it."

That "sense of editing" was honed using borrowed editing equipment sitting in Friedkin's room in a little apartment where Butler recalled the two of them "arguing until four A.M. over a *cut!* And Billy's mother is trying to sleep in the next room. I mean we were putting it together with spit and paste." Yet, that "spit and paste" became, in Red Quinlan's opinion, one of the finest documentaries ever made, even if Friedkin did double its $7,000 budget.

"It was all money I had hidden anyhow," Quinlan said. "New York didn't know I had it. I told my controller to set it up as the Project J Fund — J for justice — and not report it to New York. So we had enough money to do those things if we wanted to. If I had to get approval from New York every time I went to the bathroom, I'd never have gotten anything done around that station.

"So the controller would come in from time to time and say, 'Bill is running over budget.' I'd say, 'How much?' He'd tell me, and I'd say, 'Why that son-of-a-bitch. I'll get ahold of him.'"

But Quinlan had complete faith in Friedkin, though the young rogue filmmaker disappeared from Quinlan's sight for months. "He avoided me because he was getting rumors that I was getting impatient to get something on the air."

And what of those cost overruns?

"If it was a one hundred thousand dollar budget he was doubling, that would be serious," Quinlan said. "But with a low number like seven thousand dollars and then you looked at the film, it was a miracle he could turn it out for fourteen grand."

As far as Bill Butler was concerned, the real miracle was that William Friedkin was still alive.

They were shooting inside the Cook County Jail, Butler recalled. "We moved from the infirmary down a little hall, and we looked through the window, and here was a dead man on a stretcher. We weren't really supposed to get into that area, but it was another room, someplace different, though it was safe enough because all of it was locked off. We couldn't get out. There was one guard with us, and we really wanted to get away from him. And guards, being what they are, get tired of your filming and monkeying around and start not to pay too much attention to you after a while. So he either sat down or perhaps even left us alone. I don't remember. But he was in the other room, and we had worked our way off to get away from him.

"We saw a plastered wall that was textured, and we figured if we backlit it—run a light down by that wall—we'd get a great shot of Paul. (I'm only after an image.) So I told Billy, 'Have Paul against this wall, and let's do something against it.' I didn't know *what* 'something' any more than Billy knew because we're editing in our heads. We're saying we can use a shot here of that, a shot here of this, and at the same time wondering if we can use the dead body in the room there for something. This is all just off the ends of our fingers, so this particular moment occurred when we were trying simply to make a picture against this wall.

"I'm trying to get the little hand sun gun, which is all we've got, raking back against this wall, and I've got a great image, a good close-up.

"Suddenly, I get a little signal from Billy (we didn't need much), and this little signal meant to be casual but be ready. I knew something was going to happen.

"So I'm a little away from Paul. Billy goes down to talk to Paul, and they're whispering, talking about a very touching intimate thing, I guess. And suddenly Billy starts to slap him. Just started slapping the daylights out of him. It so shook Paul up. I mean Billy's got Paul in a very intimate, trusting mood, and he just starts to slap the shit out of him. Paul could have killed him. There're no guards around. I mean the guts to do this is beyond belief. I said to myself, 'What am I doing out here with this fool?' You can't believe it. He had me out on the South Side of Chicago at four A.M., and at that time it was a totally black neighborhood, and I'm in black bars with a camera and light, taking pictures. I should be dead by now. Talk about living on the edge of disaster. You've got the man."

Butler said they needed a shot of Crump crying because he had broken down on his own and began sobbing during an earlier tape recording of his story. "So Billy slaps the daylights out of Paul, and Paul, immediately, is so shook-up about it, he starts to cry. We turn the lights on and shoot. End of story."

When asked about the incident, Friedkin said, "Oh, that," showing just the faintest smile, and he looked away with almost boyish embarrassment.

"Billy's outrageous," Butler said, "and when you act outrageous, a lot of people don't realize that you're trying for an end result that you think is worth it. You can argue whether the end justifies the means or not. I simply know there's a lot in Billy's gut that he wants to get out.

"All the directors I've worked with—and I've worked with a lot of them—were trying to say something, trying to get something out of their gut, and as a cameraman it behooved me to try to find out what it was. I think in Billy's case I had a great empathy for where he was, what he was trying to get at.

"I really would hate to try to put into words what it is because . . . we can say things like this that would be true about him: He is a street person. He understands what those street people are about. Most people do not. Most people have such a poor understanding about what it means to be a wino on the street . . . what it's like to be a man coming out of prison. Or a man in prison, locked up as a criminal. Or a man who has grown up all his life with criminal friends, making the kind of deals they have to make, relying on one another. Billy understands. He has spent time in prison with people like Paul Crump. He has spent time on the street with people, understanding them."

"Once you've had that experience, you can't say life is sweet and cute," said Paul Hunter, a writer who worked with Friedkin on several television projects in Chicago, including another documentary on capital punishment. "The characters in Billy's films are losers. They aren't happy. I mean, who is happy in reality? Billy's pictures reflect his own view of reality."

"Maybe Billy's trying to say that there's a lot to life, a lot more than just what we are willing to look at," said Butler. "A few trips into Cook County Jail, into the black ghettos, into the kinds of lifestyles and places and ways that people have to live or do live that we don't know about—maybe it's important to him that we all go there because he's been there. Maybe he sees something in that that he thinks is important."

Butler believed there was something else important to Friedkin.

"When we were doing the *Crump* film," he continued, "I was very curious whether Billy thought Paul was guilty or innocent. . . . He didn't know, he couldn't tell. He couldn't cipher through all of the bullshit and the truth to find the truth. . . .

"I think Billy was looking for the truth. I honest-to-God believe that he was the typical example of the young man looking for truth. Not 'a truth' but *The Truth.*' I'm saying only as a personal observation that the people that I find that do that, because I spent some time doing the same thing, tend to destroy themselves. To some extent these people are self-destructive. Billy certainly was that. . . ."

But cinematically speaking, "the pragmatic truth that we deal with from day to day . . . that's what Billy likes to deal with," continued Butler. "Obviously his strongest films have dealt with stories that were real people in real situations. Even *Birthday Party* is about reality and pragmatic truth, though it's kind of far-out for some people. . . . I think the most fantasy oriented was probably Sonny and Cher's *Good Times.*"

Friedkin says his first impetus toward filmmaking was "a study of people in dramatic situations. Not films about the justice system or political system in this country . . . films about people.

"Another early documentary Butler and I made was on Red Grange, the football player, and I don't know what leads me from one character to another, but it's usually a person in a dramatic situation. *Birthday Party* was something else. *French Connection,* which is really the most personal thing I've done, was able to combine the documentary aspect of my work with the concern about these characters."

Friedkin added that while *American Graffiti* reflected George Lucas's youth, "I've never done a film to this day that has reflected my youth."

So what does attract Friedkin to characters who he says are living without alternatives?

"I tend to look more on the darker side of things," he said, "so I would tend to try to find stories that were more dramatic and therefore more suspenseful."

While Friedkin laughingly, and solely, attributes his attraction to the darker side of life as "possibly being a Russian Jew . . . I guess Woody Allen is Jewish, too," he is much more loquacious on the topic of being a filmmaker. "Gut-level reaction. If it doesn't get me viscerally, I'm out. . . . People want to see movies because they want to be moved viscerally. That's why they came there.

"There's a very famous story that Herb Gardner, who wrote *A Thousand Clowns,* told me about Alfred Hitchcock. Herb was hired by Hitchcock to write a script. He gets out here and finds that Hitchcock has drawn the whole picture out. It's all in cartoons. All he wants Gardner to do is write captions for what the people say. Gardner says, 'Jesus, I can't do this. I'm a writer. I'm not a cartoonist.' He's looking at these boards, and he sees in one frame a shot of a guy being pushed off the Verrazano Narrows Bridge. He's being choked and goes over the bridge, and two frames later, that same guy is sitting in an outdoor café on Fifth Avenue. Gardner couldn't make sense out of this, and he had a meeting with Hitchcock and said, 'That's the same guy in these two scenes?' 'Yes.' He said, 'How do we get from the guy being pushed off the Verrazano Narrows Bridge to him sitting in a café?' Hitchcock said, 'The crew goes there.' He said, 'Wait a minute. How do we get the audience there is what I mean.' Hitchcock said, 'Mr. Gardner, the audience will go wherever I take them, and they'll be very glad to be there, I assure you.'

"If I have a philosophy in a nutshell about what you're trying to do as a filmmaker, that would be it.[2]

"As a filmmaker, your primary job is that of a storyteller. You can do it with your own technique. And making film is putting your impressions on film, what you feel. That's all we give a shit about. Break rules when they get in your way. Trust your imagination."[3]

To a film director, talent is imagination. And imagination is talent. And as far as Quinlan was concerned, "Billy had the talent. He was a film buff as a kid . . . going to movies all the time. He saw *Citizen Kane,* what, two hundred times."

Friedkin has lost count himself.

But in Quinlan's opinion, "You learn from the masters. The stuff is out there for you. Billy didn't go to film school. He went to school every time he went to a movie—checked the lighting, pacing, mood, technique. The famous fast-cutting technique he used in *French Connection,* you can clearly see there's an umbilical cord going directly to that *Crump* film. He's done it. He's taken that technique to its farthest limits. In most cases, real great filmmakers don't have to go to any school to learn it. They just pick it up.

"Billy happened to have done a documentary treatment of a subject that was in the headlines. He was looking for headlines. By doing it, he learned a lot of things. I don't think Billy was trying to do films to elucidate his search for inner self or any of that bullshit. Crump was the hottest thing he could think of. It was full of action, and he figured he could reenact it, and I, too, liked it as a concept."

Ironically, *The People Versus Paul Crump* never aired because Quinlan refused to run it.

"It was too controversial," Friedkin said. "It named names of police officers that beat a confession out of Crump. And the lawyers for the ABC network saw it and thought it was libelous. It might possibly still be considered so today."

According to Quinlan, "Crump's lawyers did a complete turnaround and said Crump will be saved if we don't muddy up the waters; Mayor Daley and the governor will agree that they should burn him, so please, for Christ's sake, don't run it. I called all the liberals I could find in town, put them in a studio, and said, 'Watch this, give me your opinion.' (Now I was still going to make my own judgment.) The poll ran about sixty–forty. Billy was brokenhearted, of course, because it was fine work and a real shame not to run it. I was persuaded by these sentiments of the lawyers and a lot of the liberals in town that it might be better if we didn't run it."

"But we heard that the night before they were going to throw the switch on Paul, the governor stayed up all night," Butler said. "We don't know whether he viewed the film or people who worked for him viewed it. No one would tell us. But we know we finished the film like a day or two before he was to go to the chair. And the day he was to go to the chair, they didn't throw the switch.

"I didn't realize that you could take a tiny piece of sixteen-millimeter film and two amateurs who had shot one documentary before that and still didn't really know what they were doing, and put together a film that had that kind of impact, that kind of power."

Governor Otto Kerner commuted Crump's sentence to 199 years in 1962. Crump has since been turned down for parole at every hearing.

"I'm now contemplating making a videotape recording which would be an update on the case and an attempt to get him paroled. I'm working with his lawyers and others on this," Friedkin said.

II.

The image of Paul Crump crying, his face contorted in anguish, his body rocking violently, serves as the focus and climax of a film best described as pressure cinema. Crump's world is reduced to a daily existence of life or death, black or white; a world where every second does not simply count but becomes precious. It is an undeniable truth for Crump, as certain as the fact that he was sentenced to die in the electric chair.

To tell the story, Friedkin restages the crime, tells us the court findings, and reenacts Crump's version of what happened to him. In restaging the events, Friedkin relies on a simple cinematic technique: Follow the action. The immediacy of the action energizes the screen with foreboding and realism, and, in an early scene, a touch of irony as cattle move across the shot with wranglers on horseback herding them along. Cows and cowboys? They pass out of frame and reveal a dented sedan that accelerates toward us. But what about these beasts in a dense urban locale? It's the Chicago Stockyards, after all. Still, a bizarre image. But the car traveling steadily, inexorably, is what now seems out of place. It pulls to a stop at a brick building where a welder works overhead on a fire escape. Sparks fly down on the hood of the car. Four black men wearing heavy coats and sunglasses emerge from the vehicle and move off. These men don't belong here; they are more alien than the cattle initially appeared.

Down a long corridor lit alternately in sections, these figures move toward us like dark apparitions filling the frame, eclipsing the entryway. A tabby cat in the foreground scats. They board a freight elevator, pull the screen door closed, and rise out of frame, a diagonal slash of light emanating from the base of the elevator growing thinner until it disappears.

A feeling of dread builds, and all we can do is watch, already knowing what is coming and anxious for some kind of relief. It is as if we were accomplices in the crime, as if we had pistol-whipped our way to the money. And like robbers, we want to get away, escape, once the payroll is stolen. The fast cutting as the robbers flee adds speed and movement, emphasizing more the tightness and claustrophobia inherent in the staging of the action; they race past us down fire stairs, clutching steel pipe railings that appear to have grown out of the concrete.

Then the sudden appearance of the guard, the masked gunman raising his pistol, multiple explosions, the guard with his hands to his face and blood running between his fingers — all photographed in tight close-ups. Friedkin builds the robbery sequence slowly but with an ominous edge. He escalates the pace with the robbery, the escape becomes frantic, and the murder seems to happen in less than a heartbeat. By following the action, Friedkin conveys an immediacy. His staging here, as throughout the film, is organic, framing the action through window slits, steel bars and doorways. It accents, by extension, a picture of confinement.

In telling Crump's side of the story, Friedkin maintains his visceral cadence by confining the action to Crump's world, which is small and limited to his immediate surroundings, what he is familiar with — riding in a car, his bedroom, bars and jail, for example. It's not unlike the world Orson Welles built in *Citizen Kane.* The enormity of Kane's wealth and power becomes a giant prison that he shuts himself into because of his childhood unhappiness. He never recovers from it. It's a dark, lonely, frightening world Kane lives in, as does Crump.

A young woman named Fay was Crump's alibi. He claimed he was asleep with her in bed at the time of the robbery. She testified at Crump's first trial on his behalf but left town before his second trial because of "public ridicule," according to Crump. Both Crump and Fay were married at the time — though not to each other. Friedkin stages Crump's search for Fay — the night before the robbery — at a revival meeting and later in a bar. The remarkable aspect of these two scenes is that rather than walls and ceilings emphasizing a claustrophobic atmosphere, Friedkin populates them with faces. At the revival, a chorus of black joyous faces belt out a song of blessed life. While Crump cannot locate Fay while scanning the room, the happiness and exuberance of the song, combined with clapping hands, a lively piano player, and the almost overwhelming envelopment of the revivalists shot mostly in close-ups, may also be taken as partially responsible for Crump's exit. In contrast, the dark smokiness of the bar, with its slow jazz saxophone music, reveals pool players and bar patrons; hard, scarred faces; disheveled, inebriated faces; down-and-outs; lost hopes. Fay, too, appears in close-up. Her head rests on a pillow, smiling, and Crump's face descends slowly into frame, and they kiss. Undoubtedly, it serves as a lovely memory of tenderness and passion for Crump. And Friedkin films it as such, yet one cannot help but notice the dinginess of the room and the harsh light cast on the two lovers.

Friedkin also forces our perspective directly to Crump's as his world shifts from frightening to ugly. When Crump is arrested a second time, the police apprehend him at his mother's house. Crump had spent the three previous days in custody but was released for lack of evidence and "an airtight alibi" with Fay. In the meantime, Hudson Tillman had confessed to his role in the robbery and fingered Crump as the killer, possibly out of retribution/anger/spite over Crump's admitted dalliances with Tillman's sisters and other "bad blood" between the two men. When the police roust Crump from his bed, Friedkin frames the action from Crump's point of view. We are looking up into the stern faces of large, heavyset detectives leveling guns. Then another trench-coated detective, his mouth a hard straight line, silently pushes through the crowd and flashes his badge.

To those who would cry manipulation, yes, it definitely is. But *all* films manipulate. In Friedkin's case, his style, his choice of angles and perspectives, are designed to be the most realistic and therefore the most direct in conveying action, moving the story and involving us viscerally. That he succeeds is testament to his ability. For example, the ugliness of Crump's jailing and beating make us witness not only to Crump's lowest despair but the crux of Friedkin's want of "gut-level reaction" as well as a glimpse of regeneration.

Crump speaks of his treatment by the Chicago police as "something to come out of one of Hitler's dialogues." Friedkin adds an exclamation point with the image of Crump pushed into a dark little cell. Crump looks up at the graffiti-inscribed walls and sees, as do we, a Star of David and next to it a Nazi swastika. The camera angles down as the face of a prisoner in the next cell can be seen through the bars. In voice-over, Crump says the inmate asked him what happened. Crump responds, "I says, 'I don't know. They come in and handcuffed me behind my back.' He says, 'Well, baby, you're going to get it.'"

The brutality of Friedkin's reenactment of Crump's beating, because of the powerful statement of the close-up in which most of it is shot, startles and repels. Clenched fists and mean glints in the eye. Hands cuffed behind a chair, the links stepped on to bend Crump's arms back in an unnatural position. Crump's face, sweaty, eyes clamped shut in pain. Blows landed on Crump's body. The impact of these images serves much the same purpose as the close-ups on the electric chair that Friedkin cuts to after Crump's sobbing. Friedkin moves the camera over the chair's black contours, shiny arm bands, leg cuffs, and straps with a deliberate slowness, as if in intimate caress. Yet, the savageness, explicit and implicit in the beating and the chair sequences, fascinates. The intensity and rawness that Friedkin captures in these images have a seductive power that simultaneously repels and attracts because of his application of light and shadow that allows us to experience the horror and reality of his vision.

Friedkin has stated that "the American cinema is a kind of lean, hard, story-oriented cinema, just as American literature is. Scott Fitzgerald had a piece of paper stuck on his wall that said, 'Action is character.' Whatever the characterization is that you're doing is best fulfilled in the action line of the film. American cinema is based on the action line."

Put another way, action reveals character. While Friedkin succeeds admirably in generating action in *Crump,* Crump's actions reveal a man whose mistakes lead him to a point of no alternatives, as Friedkin shows us and Crump admits. That admission is the direct correlation to the *other* half of Fitzgerald's dictum, specifically, "Character is dialogue." As Butler pointed out, he and Friedkin placed Crump in front of the camera so we could size him up for ourselves. Crump may not be the most eloquent of speakers, but the condemned man's version of what happened in his own words adds an aural bite to Friedkin's corresponding images.

Crump states he was strung up by his hands, which were pulled behind his back, and "I hung there I don't know how long. I didn't think I was going to ever get down. . . . And I started praying out loud . . . I started saying the Hail Mary. . . . One of them [a policeman], I don't know who it was, one come up to me, and he hit me in the stomach, and he told me to stop praying. He says, 'You black son-of-a-bitch. What do you know about God? You should be in the jungle.' And then he said, 'What would the white Mother of God want to do with a black son-of-a-bitch like you?'"

Crump choked back tears through most of this and at the end broke down sobbing. When he begins crying, Friedkin cuts to a close-up of Crump, his face in anguish; he rocks back and forth banging his shoulder against the wall. To this point in the film, Crump's voice maintained a certain flatness while telling his story, rising to a combative swing at the mention of Hudson Tillman and the first "sweating" by the police, then finally crumbling, recalling the loss of hope at the hands of his interrogators. The emotions pouring out of Crump at this moment on screen (due to Friedkin's slap) and aurally (Crump's vivid recollection), combined with Friedkin's close images, achieves a visceral effect that validates Friedkin's concepts for the reasons he says he makes movies. It's the pressure point, the heart of the picture—in the making of it as well as the film itself. As Bill Butler said, Friedkin is outrageous, he's living on the edge. The thought comes to mind that Friedkin may have felt time was running out for him. He needed Crump crying on film, and he took a chance. Crump's control of the situation has crumbled on all levels. He doesn't simply relate his story; he bares his soul. It's not method acting; it's gut level.

Not every moment in *Crump* has this edge. When Friedkin directs his camera into trash cans and street gutters where newspaper headlines proclaim "Convicted Murderer a Changed Man" and "Doomed Slayer Waits an Eternity of Time," the impact, somewhat lessened due to its obvious staginess even for the early 1960s, is still potent visually and symbolically— Crump's case had a change of venue to the city dump. However, tremendous self-control must be exerted in suppressing a groan when Friedkin cuts to another newspaper report on Crump that suddenly drops out of frame to reveal a traffic sign: No Outlet.

Truly surprising, though, is Friedkin's ending of the documentary. It awkwardly loses sight of and diminishes Crump's story as well as Friedkin's dark, gritty imagery. Friedkin sets the scene against a barren landscape, save three leafless trees standing cold against a threatening gray sky. John Justin Smith, the reporter who has acted as narrator throughout the film, walks in silence. As he passes a church hall, the irony of children happily singing a song with lyrics like "Everybody must love Saturday night" give him pause. Cutting to a close-up of Smith, we hear, in voice-over, Crump's sobbing, followed by Warden Jack Johnson's early statement that "capital punishment is not a deterrent in any sense and certainly cannot be called punishment." Finally, Smith passes a construction site where black children play in the rubble.

Previously, Friedkin has not allowed much open sky, much room to breathe, in this film. Pressure and confinement have been his points of reference because they are Crump's. Only one other moment stands in contrast to this confinement. After Eugene Taylor informs Crump that Hudson Tillman has more than his share of the stolen money, Crump agrees to take Taylor to Tillman's house and force Tillman to give up the loot. Friedkin establishes a wide shot of the house. Crump and Taylor pull up, exit the car, and suddenly police burst out of the house and push the two black men against the wall. Intentionally or not, Friedkin has chronicled Crump's last moments as a free man with the "openness" of the scene. It is an openness we can appreciate with an ironic twist, since Crump will now always appear boxed-in, trapped.

But in the film's final moments, Friedkin appears lost in the wide outdoors. Allowing him the benefit of the doubt, we can swallow the implication that the autumnal loneliness Smith walks through while pondering Crump's predicament may be an abstract visual correlative to any man's death diminishing every man. We may even accept the irony of the children's song since Crump, presumably, will die before enjoying the festivities of another Saturday night. But that somehow Crump and the children playing with their toys in some construction site are to be equated is too much to ask. It has the unsettling look of a grandiose social comment done poorly by an Ingmar Bergman imitator. And if no connection with Crump is intended, why include it at all?

Paul Crump admits that he's a small-time crook, that he "did some capers." But he is adamant that he never killed anyone. He has tried to "work up tremendous indignation and anger and bitterness" over his situation but cannot because in his philosophy "what goes around comes around. . . . They didn't get me for those things, but they got me for this . . . ."

Friedkin's film succeeded in saving Paul Crump from the electric chair, but it also succeeded in letting us see a human being. In Friedkin's iconography, he's a man living on the edge, without alternatives. That Crump faces death Friedkin undoubtedly sees as the ultimate drama and visceral experience. Crump's thoughts on death are important here not only for their content but for the series of images Friedkin marries to them. Friedkin begins with shots of Crump in church, assisting other inmates in the hospital, smiling, maybe even laughing, and concludes on Crump alone in his cell.

"There's no getting away from it," the death row convict said.

> You can escape for a few moments in reading. I've managed to do so in my writing to a degree, but it's always there, just like the bars that surround you. It's like the cold steel that you feel your arm fall up against accidentally when you're trying to relax. And you think, cold, cold death.
>
> Then you think about the fellows upstairs that are in here with you. You think about their troubles because their troubles are your troubles. And when one of them get turned down, you're turned down. . . . And when a person die, when a man is executed, you die, too, because you know the process. You been in the death cell. I've been down there, and I know the deathly hush of it. I know the, the horror of seeing people that you've come to know and like, who you have did things for . . . small things, if it's just giving a cigarette or they given you a cigarette.
>
> You see them preparing to go through this ritual of taking your life, and it all seem like part of a macabre dream, a nightmare. But you know it's not a nightmare because you can feel the beating of your heart. You can hear its pound in your head. You can hear it's going to break out. It freezes you up from your heart to your throat. And you think over all of this, well, is this torture, this mental torture, this physical torture, would it actually prove anything to anyone? What would be gained out of it?

Study after Velasquez's Portrait of Pope Innocent X, 1953, by Francis Bacon. Coffin Fine Arts Trust Fund, 1980, Nathan Emory Coffin Collection of the Des Moines Art Center.

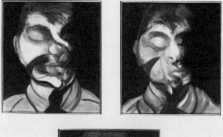

Three studies for Self-Portrait, 1972, by Francis Bacon. Private Collection. Courtesy of Francis Bacon.

And then, after twelve-oh-one, when you know that the man is dead, you find that there is no feeling other than a, a numbness within you and the knowledge, I mean, that, someone you know is gone. That there's a vacuum in life. That there's a, well, you can call this fellow's name as you often do accidentally if you have been intimately associated with him and he'll never answer. *Never* answer.

I, ah, you start thinking in terms of their parents, the effect of them waiting out these long, anxious hours and praying. And you wonder about prayer, and you wonder about God, and you wonder if perhaps if man's more or less taking over the role of God, if he hasn't completely destroyed everything that you have been taught that God believe, that God stand for. And this will make you a little cynical. And this will make your fight to sustain a belief in mankind a little harder, a belief in God a little more harder.

And the thing that affects me most is that after a week or so is past, nothing is changed. After the headlines have died down, nothing is changed. Another fellow will come in for murder. Another fellow will be sentenced to death for murder. And it just go on and on and on in this vicious, barbaric circle. It confuses you so until you don't know whether you're in a nightmare or whether or not you're really living.

I found that I have to reach out at night. I work hard and exhaust myself so I can sleep. And then before sleeping, I have to reach out and grab two of the bars and hold them. I guess this is my way of, of holding on to reality. Of holding on to, ah, my sanity, um, the possibility that I won't just slip away and, and be no more. . . .

A grainy black-and-white close-up of Crump fills the screen, his face down in a pillow. His strong black hands are clenched around two steel bars of his cell. A deathly silence envelops the image as his hands slowly relax, then sag.

A sad image and a frightening one, considering the story Friedkin has filmed. Yet there is an exhilaration to it, a regeneration, a redemption. Friedkin has cited the work of the artist Francis Bacon, and in particular a catalog entitled *Francis Bacon, Recent Paintings 1968–1974,* as "telling you more about myself than I or anyone else could." In the catalog, Bacon is quoted in an interview referring to the famous Isenheimer altar as "one of the greatest paintings of the crucifixion, with the body studded with thorns like nails, but oddly enough, the form is so grand it takes away from the horror. But it *is* grand horror in the sense that it is so vitalizing. . . ."[4] To paraphrase Bacon, *Crump* may be seen as a purging experience from which we may draw strength to a fuller reality of existence. Bacon also states that "death can be life-enhancing,"[5] that it is only the consciousness of death in life that gives death its power. Friedkin, then, finds the facing of death akin to "living on the edge." Certainly, the lives of the cops and the criminals who figure so prominently in Friedkin's films easily give life to Friedkin's danse macabre.

Also, Bacon's stylistic attitudes are evident in Friedkin's films. According to *Recent Paintings,* Bacon's portraits and triptychs, for which he is probably best known, present "the single human being, alone and flayed by a haunting series of circumstances . . . the imagery of the rapid motion, the contorted body . . . the head in violent motion. . . ." Consider Paul Crump crying. "The grotesque, even sadistic, content of Bacon's art," the catalog states, "realized through the masterful application of paint, lies at the heart of his aesthetic achievement. It is possible to feel excitement at the traditional bravura of the paint handling, and horror at the rawness of the subject."[6] Friedkin relies on light, shadow, speed, and movement to tell his story as a filmmaker. But it is the way he uses these elements to excite and frighten, to elicit response from the audience, that reveal his view of life and reality; his films, like Bacon's canvases, are his mirror.

2
A Year with Wolper, and a Moment with Hitchcock

"Billy was a hotshot, very sure of himself and cocky."
— David Wolper

After *Paul Crump*, Friedkin remained in Chicago making documentaries for about two more years, with Quinlan sponsoring him and Butler in a film deal that they could do whatever they wanted to do. One project was an entertainment documentary that Paul Hunter was also involved with. According to him, it was a look at "various aspects of Chicago in song and dance, but it was not your technicolor musical. It was gritty." (About ten years later, that last word became an accolade often used to praise *The French Connection*.)

Hunter explained the gritty entertainment: "We went to Clark Street. We shot in sleazy bars all night long. A lot of the mood and feeling in that early bar scene in *French Connection* with the black singers was shot by us in feeling and mood way back then. I remember Butler writhing on the floor with a hand-held camera. We shot from nine to six in the morning. Then we went to the lakeshore and shot some stuff on a yacht that was pretty with this lovely girl, Lee Barry, who sang this song, 'Shangri-La.' Just different aspects of Chicago. It was both scary and beautiful.

"Billy was experimenting. I don't think he was being innovative for its own sake." Hunter recalled the night they were "in the editing room with this documentary at two A.M. Everybody else had left. There was no rush on the show; Billy just wanted to work. I didn't help; I just watched and looked. And I remember thinking, 'Your job in editing would have been so much easier if you hadn't shot so damn much stuff.' He shot like he was going for a record on a four-minute sequence. He said to me, 'Always remember, when you get into the editing room when you're through shooting, you better have choices. Not simple coverage, but choices. The worst thing you can do is go into the editing room and find out you're missing something or something isn't as good as it should be!'"

19

Hunter added that though they did quite a lot of filming "shooting off the cuff," it was not done "as carelessly as it sounds because Billy always knew what he wanted to do." Also, "Billy had a budget of nothing but spent money like he didn't care. Quinlan would say, 'Billy, what are you doing?' Billy would shrug and say, 'You guys can afford it.'"

The long hours filming and the late nights editing were still better and more exciting than television as far as Friedkin and Butler were concerned. The "new methods," the "experimentation," the "days of invention," as Butler called them, were closing fast for these two mavericks. Television soon found its formulas, and the commercial powers of Wall Street began to take over because the advertising agencies had discovered how to do programs cheaply, Butler ruefully recalled. Television got less and less exciting.

When *The People Versus Paul Crump* won the top prize at the San Francisco Film Festival in 1962, Friedkin said, the producer David Wolper contacted him and invited him to work with his production company because he'd seen *Crump* and was impressed. Wolper had a number of films entered at the festival that didn't win.

"But I wasn't quite ready," Friedkin recalled. "I knew every inch of Chicago, every scene there, the jazz clubs, the basketball teams. Though I thought one day I would go to Wolper."

And Wolper meant Hollywood.

Butler remembered times when he and Friedkin would sit in Chicago dreaming of Hollywood: "We thought, Hollywood can be had. You can come to Hollywood and tell them you're the greatest thing on earth, and they'll believe it if you just do it right."

Ultimately, Quinlan was the catalyst: "I told Billy when I got fired in sixty-four to get his ass out of Chicago and the only place to go is Hollywood. All I knew was the eager, boyish Friedkin who wanted to be a big success. He was very certain about whatever he did, and that's the first sign of youthful insecurity. Anybody who knows all the answers at twenty you just know is going to be a little smarter at forty, but they don't know that. You recognize that in everybody. I just chalked it up to his style, his personality. Cocky, I'm sure. But with Friedkin, you knew where he was coming from. He had that wellspring of creative strength and power within him, and he can tap that as long as he lives while other guys are tapping an empty water bucket."

When Friedkin finished *The Bold Men,* his first documentary for Wolper Productions, he screened it for David Wolper and Mel Stuart, one of Wolper's top-line producers. After the lights came up in the projection room, "they absolutely destroyed me," Friedkin said. "They tore me apart. Mel Stuart took off his shoe and threw it at the screen. And I'll never forget what Wolper said. He just sort of spun it out, mixing his metaphors, 'There comes a time when the white hot light goes on and the bullshit falls away like bricks on the ground. This is the worst piece of shit I've ever seen.

This is despicable. I'd like to tear your eyes out.' That was the Wolper technique."

Wolper, whose producing credits for the past thirty years include over 550 documentaries, the Oscar-winning *The Hellstrom Chronicles,* and the Emmy-winning miniseries *Roots* and *Roots: The Next Generations,* admits that he would "scream out loud" when "something didn't work" in a film, but "if you didn't accept criticism in my place, you wouldn't be around very long. We were competing with the networks. We had to have something more. . . . I was raised on the philosophy that documentary was to inform *and* entertain."

The three documentaries Friedkin directed during his short tenure at Wolper Productions were one-hour specials contracted by the 3M Company. According to Friedkin, Wolper would sell 3M a title rather than a concept, "and then it was up to the filmmaker to build a show out of it. It was a great place to work in that respect. It would take you a couple of months to travel around and film, plus you're writing the script as you're filming." *The Bold Men,* for example, took Friedkin around the world.

Though Friedkin succeeds in taking the audience where he wants to take them with this globe-trotting, that audience may not necessarily be glad to be there. In other words, Friedkin's self-professed philosophy falls flat. He can whisk us anyplace he chooses, but we are not happy to witness timid and tired scenes of race-car driving, rodeo riding, and oil-fire fighting. Even Van Heflin's gravel-voiced narration cannot breathe life into a flaccid montage of surfers and acrobats and human cannonballs. Shortly, the film has the unfortunate effect of leaving an audience not in awe of the boldness of these men but secretly hoping to witness some mishap. Or the words "The End." It's not unlike the film *Terror in the Aisles* (1984), a compilation of moments from horror films. Lumping the shower murder in *Psycho,* the bloody alien birth in *Alien,* and a shark attack in *Jaws* together has no visceral impact other than making the viewer long for the whole film, not unrelated scenes strung together. In *Bold Men* we watch "daredevils" perform a 1965 version of state-of-the-art stunts, but instead of gut tightening tension we yawn "so what." In both examples we are removed from the action; *uninvolved.*

Further complications compound the problem. Fred Kaplan, who assisted Bud Smith, the film editor on *Bold Men,* said, "We had to stretch it out because it came in under the one-hour format. It happens many times in television. We put in extra footage." That "extra footage" is sometimes synonymous with "padding." In other words, a lion-taming sequence feels longer, much tamer.

In fairness, while the mostly lackluster presentation offers little in visual excitement, particularly in comparison to *Crump,* the film's visceral theme is markedly Friedkin. As the documentary opens, Van Heflin states it is about men who risk death because to them it's a way of life. Friedkin's fascination with that life-enhancing quality of death, that living on the edge, is reflected by the welder working high up on the girder of a skyscraper, the cliff diver in Mexico, the bullfighter who says he's not afraid of death but life scares him. All are examples of men who flirt with death. Sad to say, as Friedkin presents them, their collective stories cannot match the title.

Fortunately, Friedkin's second documentary focuses on the streets he knows well. *The Thin Blue Line* opens with an arresting image swaying across the screen: a close-up on a policeman's badge. Over this we hear, "This piece of tin is a target. Out on the street we don't know what we'll be up against." We pull back to reveal a big graying bear of a policeman watchful of the beat he patrols. Conflict, tension, and suspense are *immediately* established, pulling the audience into a potentially dangerous situation where "we don't know what we'll be up against." Conversely, the sky divers and trick sharpshooters in *The Bold Men* practice their stunts and acts to a show-level performance; it's like watching a circus act without the pizzazz.

Though episodic in structure, *Thin Blue Line* does not have a staccato, jarring flow. Friedkin again follows the action rather than setting up his camera and recording a feat. He tells a *story*, albeit an abbreviated one.

One sequence details a heroin bust in Los Angeles. The stakeout and surveillance of "Eddie," a twenty-nine-year-old gas station attendant by "Paul," a narcotics cop, quickly leads to a heroin buy and the seeds of *The French Connection*. At the police lab, the smack is tested for potency. The unwrapping, sprinkling the powder into test vials, the examination under a microscope—the mechanics all performed in close-up detail. In *Connection* a similar scene is done, but with more chilling effect. The three-piece-suit heroin dealers test the potency of their "USDA Prime" smack with glee, pleased with the knowledge they will get rich off other people's weaknesses. Friedkin shows us two different angles of the same thing, one from each side of the law. In both cases, the heroin tests out as lethally potent. In *Thin Blue Line*, the police react with relief at having it in their possession since Eddie would sell to *anybody; Connection*'s dealers congratulate themselves on their high-grade purchase since they too will profit from selling to anybody.

When Eddie is sentenced, Van Heflin informs us that he will be sent to Chino State Prison for five years. It seems hardly enough to Paul, the cop, since Eddie sold to children, Heflin states, adding, "Narcotics possession is a frustrating battle for law enforcement. They are losing." Here, another foreshadowing of *Connection* in which the drug dealers receive abbreviated sentences and Heflin's line about "losing" relates to Doyle and Russo, the detectives who busted the French connection, who are then transferred out of narcotics.

Friedkin fills the screen with a close-up of the crook of Eddie's arm. On it, the tattoo of an insect. It disguises the needle tracks of an addict. Like a Frances Bacon portrait, its rawness horrifies and excites. The image conjures up thoughts of infected needles, abuse, violence, insignificance, death. It's frightening because we know of people who exist for the fix; it's exhilarating because Friedkin states so much with that single stark image.

In another sequence, this time in Chicago, Friedkin focuses on a graveyard-shift police dispatcher. He sits at his desk, and a call comes in from a hysterical woman. She cries that a burglar is in the house, send over a car. Her husband has a gun, he's going to check. The dispatcher tries to coax the address out of her. She's becoming more hysterical. Her husband is downstairs, gunshots are heard, she's screaming her head off. Then another policeman's voice is heard over the telephone saying everything is okay. Friedkin stages this scene with the dispatcher sitting on the far side of an office with his back to the camera. All the action and movement within the scene is in the dialogue. Friedkin performed an interesting reworking of F. Scott Fitzgerald's dictum with this scene in which action became dialogue.

While stretches in *Line* tend to bore (training sequences, for example, but necessary for the reordering of actuality that is documentary), Friedkin improved his narrative problems and, as with *Crump*, previewed things to come.

In his final film for Wolper, *Mayhem on a Sunday Afternoon,* Friedkin adhered to a cohesive single element story, namely, the Cleveland Browns football team. He forces us into the tackles; we feel the impact. He lets us peek at the players off the field, the emotional highs at scoring a touchdown, the drudgery and monotony of bus travel from city to city, game to game, the ever-present threat of injury, even death. It was a losing season for the Browns that Friedkin chronicled. In *Line* he depicted beleaguered police forces attempting to stem an onrushing wave of crime. *Crump* shows us a man who has lost everything but the will to live. Friedkin has an affinity for the underdog.

He also enjoys a black brand of humor that occasionally complements his dark images and worldview not unlike Raoul Walsh's in *White Heat,* which Friedkin has said may be his favorite film. In it there is a scene where James Cagney as gangster Cody Jarrett has a stooge locked inside a car trunk. The stooge mumbles he has no air to Jarrett, who's standing by the car. Jarrett says, "I'll give you a little air," pulls a gun, and fires into the trunk. There's a certain black aplomb, originality, and humor to it. In *Mayhem,* Heflin says, "This was the first football . . ." and a human skull rolls into frame. It was supposed to represent the skull of a thirteenth-century Danish pirate who was executed by the British. There's a surprise and simplicity to this deathly humorous imagery. A segment in *Bold Men* (interestingly enough!) recounts an incident in Paris, circa 1930s, about a man who thought he could fly. He jumped from a plane wearing a Batman-style outfit. After he plunges out of sight, Friedkin cuts to a close-up of the bleached skulls and bones of animals. Then boots enter the shot, and he reveals a modern skydiver whose drop point is the animal boneyard. Not only is the image of "Batman" attempting to take flight humorous in dark fashion, but Friedkin arrests attention with that transition to the skulls. A fleeting thought is that "Batman's" body was never recovered but his bones have been discovered. But Friedkin, with that cut, simultaneously establishes humor and maintains the core of the documentary—flirtation with death, the same core that is explicit in *Line* and *Mayhem*.

But visualizing a theme was not Friedkin's problem; telling a story was the difficulty. Realizing this, Wolper counseled Friedkin on improving and sharpening his visual storytelling technique. So, after the screaming, Wolper said Friedkin would "go out and shoot it or get it or redo it according to the way I wanted it."

And Friedkin admits that Wolper was usually right. "Most of us who were working there were self-indulgent. I was. I had an inflated idea of myself based on a couple of little documentaries I had made that were well received. There were others like me who thought we were geniuses at documentary when we had everything to learn.

"And Wolper, who outwardly at that time had this incredible reputation as being a representative of taste and dignity and classical subjects, carefully researched and presented, basically that was a facade. Basically, Wolper was interested in getting ratings for his documentaries and reaching the broadest possible audience even though he was the critics' darling. The shows they made were wonderful, very important, but the thinking was all on a gut level, and the idea was to beat into the people who made the films there that you had to come in under budget and that you had to clarify everything that you meant and that the focus of your work had to be clear and not diffused because at that time the New Wave French cinema had just become popularized over here and all of us were imitating Renoir and Truffaut.

"But at Wolper they beat the shit out of us. Especially me. They destroyed me, but I think whatever filmmaking abilities I've retained today came out of that experience."

And Friedkin did not only have his films torn apart as if they had no clarity, no purpose, no focus, no point. Fred Kaplan recalled an experience while they edited *The Bold Men:* "Theodore White was down the hall doing *Making of the President: 1964,* and Billy was in an editing room shouting and using his foul mouth. He was upset about the cutting or something. Well, White went into that room and chewed out Bill. He said, 'Can't you keep a civil tongue in your mouth?' He went on and on, getting mad at Bill. Bill apologized to him, and White stormed out. Bill still used his foul mouth. He just didn't yell as loud. It's part of his personality."

Yet criticism was not always a losing battle for Friedkin. When they took *The Bold Men* to the dubbing stage, where sound effects, music and dialogue are mixed together and married to the sound track of the picture, Mel Stuart was there. Kaplan said, "Things started happening. Film broke, and Mel would call out, 'Kaplan, get that film!' He was very foul-mouthed also. And he would purposely keep yelling and keep yelling. He was just showing off to the mixers as if to say, 'I can yell at this guy and you can't. Isn't it great'?"

"And once in a while, Friedkin would come in and yell at me too to make a joke of Mel. He'd imitate Mel.

"So later, Bill and Mel got into an argument over which should it be over some sequence in the film—leave in the music and not the effects or have the effects and not the music? Something like that. It became a tremendous argument. Mel threatened to fire Bill. Bill said, 'Go ahead and fire me.' The foul language was just pouring like crazy. To me, this was par for the course. I see them do this at Wolper all the time. But the mixers couldn't believe it. They'd look at me, and I'd shrug my shoulders. They were awed at watching these two men carry on like children.

"Finally, Mel jumped up on top of a chair so he could look down at Bill, and Bill very quickly jumped up on the mixers board so he towered over Mel. Mel was shocked. Now he was looking up at Bill! Mel just broke into a laugh, jumped down, and said, 'Okay, Bill, it's yours.' And Bill got his way."

Friedkin said that during his year-and-a-half residence at Wolper Productions, "I just lived, ate and breathed filmmaking."

He also used to play poker one night a week in the office, Wolper said with a sly smile. "Billy used to claim I'd give him his check on Friday and take it away from him Tuesday night, which was true. He plays a lot of poker."

Ten years later, one of Friedkin's biggest gambles, *The Exorcist*, paid off handsomely, and Friedkin's devotion to filmmaking (in some circles this may also be known by the Hollywood invective "perfection") was again demonstrated to Kaplan when his former editor on *The Bold Men*, Bud Smith, hired him to check foreign-language prints of the picture at the MGM lab.

"Bill had four to five other guys checking, too, and we had to make sure the sound was perfect, the changeovers were perfect, every frame was perfect. It was an ordeal," Kaplan said, adding that each print had to be viewed at normal speed. "So I'd be watching the film, and on a few occasions I'd hear the door open. Naturally, I had to have my eye on the screen. That's how critical it was. Finally the reel came to an end, and I looked around and there's Bill. He said something like, 'Kaplan, glad you didn't take your eyes off that screen.' He came up to me, shook my hand and said, 'Hi Freddy, how are ya?' He made me feel like I hadn't seen him in ten days as opposed to ten years. But he was a character. Another time at Todd-AO [a dubbing facility in Hollywood] while he was talking to us, he unzipped his pants, reached in, and began pulling his shirt down but still talking. . . . He used to do it all the time while we were working at Wolper."

In between filming documentaries and adjusting his clothing, Friedkin was offered another directing job: the final episode of the *Alfred Hitchcock Hour*. Wolper gave Friedkin a leave of absence to do that show.

Entitled "Off Season," Friedkin called the story a "conventional little Hitchcock thriller with a twist at the end." It was written by Robert Bloch, who also wrote *Psycho*.

According to the book *"Alfred Hitchcock Presents": An Illustrated Guide to the Ten Year Television Career of the Master of Suspense*, the story concerns a trigger-happy policeman named Johnny Kendall who is fired from his city job and is

> forced to take a position in a small resort town checking on va-
> cant summer homes during the off season. His long suffering
> girlfriend Sandy accompanies him and quickly finds work as a
> waitress. Johnny is told the previous deputy was fired for carry-
> ing on with unidentified women in one of the vacant homes.
> Later, Johnny sees the vengeful ex-deputy hanging around Sandy
> and begins to suspect the two of them may be having an affair.
> Believing the pair to be together one night, he straps on the gun
> which he has been prohibited from wearing, and, finding that
> one of the homes has been broken into, enters to hear the deputy
> and a woman carrying on in the dark. In a rage, he shoots the
> deputy then kills the woman as well, only to discover she is not
> Sandy at all, but the sheriff's wife.[1]

As with most of the original series, this episode is not readily available in any format except haphazardly on those stations that carry syndicated reruns of old television series.

Friedkin was hired because Norman Lloyd, producer of the series, saw the *Paul Crump* documentary. Lloyd was impressed and told Friedkin there was more suspense in the first five minutes of *Crump* than in any *Hitchcock Hour* they'd done all year. The episode starred John Gavin (a former U.S. ambassador to Mexico), who had the right of refusal on the director. He met Friedkin and concluded that "whatever his inexperience, I was perfectly delighted to give him a chance. . . . The directors of those shows, whatever their talents or abilities, were under great pressure to bring the shows in on time." (They had five days to shoot.) In Gavin's opinion, Friedkin ac-complished this "creatively and decisively."

Before he began shooting, Friedkin received a word of advice from

Lloyd. "He told me the most important thing you should do, being a new director, is when you go down on the set, make sure everything's carefully planned. You have your first shot in mind. You know exactly what it is. It's a simple shot, and you get it in one take. It'll be a very important emotional thing for you.

"Well, I was about thirty-five takes into the first shot when all these guys in black suits started to appear from Universal. They couldn't believe what was going on because I was going for perfection and I wasn't getting it. Finally, I moved on, and the thing started to move along on time. . . . It was the first thing I'd done on a sound stage with actors. I started getting a sense of what I was doing." Learning quickly and deciding "to feel my oats a little bit," Friedkin shot an elaborate camera move that followed the action, in this case, Gavin and his costar Indus Arthur, through a small room. It took awhile to light the set for this, but an entire scene was filmed in one take. The standard television style is usually an establishing shot of the actors on the set followed by their close-ups; nothing innovative. The next morning, Norman Lloyd came to the set after seeing the dailies, which included Friedkin's setup, and praised it, saying the entire series should have been done that way all along.

By his own account, however, Friedkin's most memorable experience was with Alfred Hitchcock. "He was going to read this introduction off an idiot card, you know, where he says, 'Good evening' and all that bullshit.

"Norman Lloyd came down on the set and asked me if I'd like to meet Hitchcock. I said, 'Sure.' Hitchcock and Lloyd came over to me, and I was standing there trying to figure out how to direct this fucking show which I was faking completely. Lloyd said, 'Mr. Hitchcock, this is Mr. Friedkin.' Hitchcock gave me this limp handshake and said, 'Mr. Friedkin, you're not wearing a tie.' I thought he was kidding. I'd heard all about the great Hitchcockian humor. I said, 'Yes, that's right. I'm not wearing a tie.' And he said, 'Usually our directors wear ties.' And he turned and left, and that's all he said to me.

"So I made this show, and I think it's terrible. I hate the fucking thing. The one admirable thing from it was Hitchcock, who always used to go to the cutting room with Lloyd and change the director's cut all the time, didn't change my cut at all. He just let it stand.

"But now some seven years go by, and I hadn't seen Hitchcock in these seven years. I'd made *The French Connection* and was at the awards ceremony for the Director's Guild of America. I'd just won the DGA award for *French Connection*. Hitchcock was in the audience getting an honorary award and was on the aisle. We were all in tuxedos, and I had just accepted the award and was starting back up the aisle. As I went by him, I had on one of those snap-on ties, and I snapped my tie at him and said, 'How do you like the tie, Hitch?' He looked at me and stared. He didn't remember, but

I did. It was part of my motivation for seven years. I said one day I'm going to get back at this pompous asshole, you know, who comes up to a kid on the fucking set and says, 'I see you're not wearing a tie.' That is probably a key to my character, you know.

"The biggest satisfaction—I mean, to me Hitchco—I've seen—I've liked three or four of his films—*Notorious* is a great movie in my opinion. *Psycho* is a masterpiece; flawed. *Vertigo, Rear Window*. I think this guy has made some incredible movies. But I don't think he's God, and I don't give a flying fuck about him, and I'm not a worshiper of his, nor have I ever set out to emulate him. I certainly have learned things from looking at his films, but I've also learned things from looking at the films of Hubert Cornfield and Dario Argento and other films of people nobody's ever heard of. And Joseph H. Lewis and Otto Preminger. And Preminger's considered an asshole.

"But I'm glad that people deify directors because I make more money that way. If guys didn't deify directors, I'd be working for a living."

Shortly after he completed his *Hitchcock Hour* episode, Friedkin was offered another Hollywood Big Break: directing a feature film. He was still under contract to Wolper, so he had to negotiate a deal. According to Wolper, Friedkin "owes me a picture for twenty thousand dollars. I have the contract in my desk drawer." A big smile crossed his face, and he said, "I'm going to collect one day."

When asked if he had any words of advice for Friedkin upon his departure, Wolper said, "I was pissed off. I think he needed to do a few more things. He was out here such a short time. But having a company that was bringing young people up, I was used to it. It's a momentary annoyance. You invest time, money and energy in somebody. I didn't think he was ready, but it was up to the producers to make the decision."

Friedkin was on his way to another Hollywood reality known as "The Big Time."

3
Good Times

"Hollywood was paying Billy to direct a picture so he could learn how. You don't know
until you do it, and that's where you learn
where the mistakes really are."
— Bill Butler

I

"To get into movies, Billy might very well have killed someone," Bill
Butler said. He emphasized this, adding that Friedkin was "deadly serious"
about directing a feature film. Ironically, Friedkin's killer instinct led him
to *Good Times*, a whimsical fairy tale starring Sonny and Cher, the popular
pop singing duo of the sixties, in their screen debut. In the film, Sonny (playing himself) goes to see Mordicus (George Sanders, Academy Award winner for *All About Eve* in 1950), a film tycoon, saying he and Cher want to
make a movie together. When Sonny balks at Mordicus's ideas, Sonny is
given ten days to come up with something better. What follows are a series
of sketches that Sonny and Cher dream up as possible story lines for their
movie-within-a-movie that include a Western routine, a Tarzan spoof, and
a private-eye skit.

The Hollywood Reporter called the 1967 release "the most impressive
directorial debut since Francis Ford Coppola's *You're a Big Boy Now.*" The
Los Angeles Times stated that it had moments of Woody Allen brillance.
Friedkin says, "If I could, I'd burn the negative."

Sonny Bono said he hired Friedkin to direct this "Walter Mitty"
because he liked Friedkin's hard documentaries and "just instinctually
thought he was a winner."

"We spoke the same language," Friedkin said. "I liked him, I liked their
music and thought he was a really clever if not brilliant guy who really, at
that time, had his finger on the pulse of the youth of this country in terms
of the emerging pop scene. . . . We had a similar sense of humor, and we
liked each other and wanted to work together."

Lindsey Parsons, the film's producer, added that this picture was

29

Friedkin's great opportunity. "Billy was determined to make a good motion picture, but he was also determined he was going to please them. He had their absolute confidence, and at the same time they were his road to success. He had to make a picture *they* wanted."

"There was no script," Friedkin said. "We hired a guy out of New York called Nick Hyams, who'd written a letter to Sonny describing what he thought the film should be."

Hyams turned out to be "a total sham," Bono said. "He would spend weeks writing *a* scene, and then it would be a scene where I wanted a cigarette and the car would be in the living room so I could push the cigarette lighter in the car. It was just folly."

And to complicate matters more, Steve Broidy, the executive producer of the picture described by Friedkin as "the king of low-budget pictures before Roger Corman was gleam in anyone's eye," was told all was going well by Bono. Actually, "We'd been faking," Bono said. "We acted like we had the script, but everything was behind. The script wound up being written, no matter whose name is on it, by me and Billy."

"We brought in a couple of other guys but to no avail," Friedkin said. "It was hard for them to understand what Sonny and Cher were all about. So we got together at Sonny's house, he lived in Encino, and we'd sit around all day and night and bat around ideas."

"He'd come over in this little black Ford. We called it the Batmobile," Bono said.

According to Friedkin, the approach finally settled on was to treat the picture as though it were the only picture Sonny and Cher would ever make, to do everything in it that they would like to see. A "wouldn't-it-be-fun-if" approach.[1]

When they finally had about twenty-five pages, they decided to have them typed, Friedkin said. "Sonny got a typist through the phone book. A woman came over, and we gave her these pages. She goes in the kitchen to type them out. Hours go by. She's supposed to be a fast typist. Pretty soon we're working on other stuff, and one of us says, 'What the hell, what is this? Where are these pages?' So Sonny goes into the kitchen, and he comes back out a few minutes later with pages she's typed, and she's typed a hundred pages. Sonny says, 'You're not going to believe this.' He starts reading some of it to me. The typist decided to interpolate our script. She put herself in it as a character—a typist who is hired by Sonny and Cher to come to their house and type a script for their movie. We thanked her very much. We laughed our ass off and realized we were in some kind of trouble here. We threw all that out, and about two weeks before the film started, we finished the script. We really winged the film."

Friedkin did attempt to give the other writers he'd brought in screen credit, since they had contributed gags, according to Parsons. "I said we've got a Writer's Guild and they're going to tell us who gets it," Parsons said he told Friedkin. Tony Barrett, who was hired to write the private-eye sequence by Parsons, who felt it "needed an expert and Barrett had done a great many of the private-eye shows for Four-Star Productions," utlimately received sole credit. However, as far as Parsons was concerned, *Good Times* "was one of those pictures I wouldn't have fought over a screen credit on except for the residuals."

And writer objections were not the only emotional battles Friedkin had with Parsons.

"When I suggested George Sanders to play the big motion picture mogul, Bill rejected it immediately," Parsons said. "But pretty soon he came around to it and thought Sanders was the only man in the world to play the part, only this time it was his own idea. (I could see that he was modeling Sanders on Steve Broidy himself, satirizing him. I don't know if Broidy was aware of it or not. Billy was trying to burlesque the motion picture industry.)

"And Bill, at that period of his life being very young (he was twenty-three), was inclined to reject any suggestions from anybody who was six months older than he. I just wanted to steer him in a direction to get a complete picture. But I must say, in all my career, and I've produced over three hundred pictures and three television series, I've never had a good director yet I didn't want to fire at least two or three times during the course of the picture."

Like Quinlan and Wolper before him, Parsons had no doubt that Friedkin's ego probably kept him buoyed him up and that he was talented, saying that "When you've been in the picture business long enough, you can detect a phony very quickly." And just to reassure himself, Parsons said he viewed two of Friedkin's documentaries, again.

And there was Cher, who "didn't really want to make a movie and could give a shit," Bono said. "The closest we came to a hang-up was that Billy depended on me to talk to Cher as far as creatively communicating with her. Sometimes when she wasn't able to communicate, it was tough for Billy. He'd lose his temper with her or yell at me. And as you get to know Billy, you know when he's serious and when he's just yelling."

Friedkin's initiation into "The Big Time" did not end with script and cast difficulties.

According to Friedkin, Parsons hired Robert Wyckoff as the director of photography. "Bob Wyckoff was a nice guy, trained in the Hollywood mold. He was a hack. . . . For example, there was one shot of Sonny in the Western sequence, riding along on a hill, supposedly in silhouette. We went out to Bronson Canyon. I get out to the location about a half hour after the crew has arrived, and I see a battery of brute lights, I'd say maybe a dozen. Each one has two or three guys standing around it. Each light is pointing up into this little hillock. Wyckoff is there. I'm looking at this, at trucks, at honeywagons.

"The budget of the movie is supposed to be five hundred thousand dollars. I see all these lights and people and trucks, and I said, 'Bob, I told you that this shot is a silhouette. I never mentioned it, but it just seemed to me to be obvious that we'd just shoot it in a natural light. We're here. It's five, six o'clock when the sun is down. What are you doing with these lights pointing up into the hill?' And he said, 'Trust me, it'll be a silhouette. I'll expose it for a silhouette. I have to use these guys, and I've got all this equipment.' I said, 'Why?' He said, 'Because the studio makes me do it.' I said, 'We have no studio deal. This is an independent production.' (We were renting offices at Paramount Studios.) He said, 'I have to use these guys. Trust me, you'll get what you want.'"

Parsons recalled that a bulldozer had been sent up on a flatbed truck because somebody thought maybe a new road would be needed. He couldn't believe it. "I told them this is a Los Angeles City Park. You can't touch a blade of grass here! The studio production manager sent out all that equipment. It wasn't even ordered, but it was billed to us by Paramount. That's the way they operate."

Parsons sympathized with Friedkin, saying that when you're used to four or five guys following your direction and then you find you've got eighty-five people helping you, it's pretty hard to concentrate; it may throw you.

"It was a little picture that should have cost fifty thousand to one hundred thousand dollars," Friedkin said. "It cost about eight hundred thousand dollars to shoot maybe a little over half of it with these guys who were turkeys, just jerks. And I couldn't control them because it was my first feature. The burden was on me to just move faster and get out. And of course, you can't move fast with this kind of a crew," which, as far as Friedkin could tell, appeared to drag with it every piece of equipment not in use at Paramount Studios.

"I wasn't used to working that way at all," Friedkin said. "Not in documentaries, not even on the *Hitchcock Hour*. But they expected me to move. By the time the crew lit and overlit and did this shit, there was no time for the actors or for anything creative."

"Billy didn't want to cheat on the production value," Bono said. "We weren't going to back off on that. That put us behind schedule and caused big, big fights with Billy, because he was responsible for the time, and Broidy. Huge fights right on the set because this whole picture was personally financed by Broidy. Billy will go in with every intention of being honorable and will deliver, but he will not sacrifice the product to deliver it on time. The problem with Billy is he wants to feel real comfortable with what he gets, and if he doesn't, he'll keep going after it until he does. In that particular aspect he didn't shoot it like the nine-day wonder it was supposed to be."

So, with Broidy angry, the production running out of money, and only half a film shot, Friedkin's reaction is not altogether surprising. "I said to Broidy, 'Look, this fucking Hollywood crew and this whole goddamned thing is bullshit. And I'm not even getting stuff I like.' And Sonny backed me on this. I said, 'We're going to close shop. We're through. Shut down. We got enough film. Now, I'm going to film the rest of it with a nonunion crew. I'm going to bring Bill Butler out here, and we're going to go out into the streets and film the rest of the picture.' He said, 'You're crazy. You'll never get away with it.' I said, 'That's it. I don't even want to stay here if you're going to keep pumping your money into this goddamn thing.' And Sonny said, 'I hate the fucking experience too.' So I said, 'If you want us to mess with this goddamn thing, you just walk away and let me finish it.'"

It should also be noted that according to Parsons, there was really no way Friedkin could be removed because Sonny and Cher had an implicit belief in his ability to direct them. If you fire the director in that situation, the star would go with him.

Butler, who was still living in Chicago, said Friedkin called him and told him that *Good Times* "doesn't have our look," that "it looks like a Hollywood film shot in a studio, and I can't get it any other way working under the Hollywood system." Friedkin asked Butler to come out the next morning, and he did.

By Friedkin's estimate, he and Butler bootlegged almost half the film for $35,000. This half consisted mostly of Bono's songs, which Butler said they shot much the same way they did *Crump*, "off our fingertips." He said Bono would write a song at night and record it. Then "Billy and I would listen to it, go out to find locations for that song the next day and dream up how we were going to shoot it that afternoon or evening. We shot one down at the Los Angeles Music Center at night with a minimum number of lights. John Alonzo was around then, and he shot with us just to get the experience." (Alonzo's future cinematography credits would include *Chinatown* and *Blue Thunder*.)

Bono said he and Friedkin would go to clubs such as the Whiskey A-Go-Go to watch bands and their light show. These performances and materials gave Friedkin new inspiration. Butler said, "We threw the camera out of sync, used streaking lights and solarization and what were then new techniques that at least gave the film some life. We shot about five songs—quite a bit for the picture—and gave it a loose, nice feeling. If the whole film had been that way, I suspect Billy would have had a pretty unusual film.

"Frankly, there were too many corny segments in it. He knew it was corny, but he was trying to push the corniness over to the point where it would be funny and enjoyable, but it was tough to make it under the circumstances he was shooting under."

Tough as the shooting was, Friedkin's problem did not end when the shooting wrapped.

"I have a complete vision of the entire film, and I try to shoot it," Friedkin said. "I adjust to the conditions of the location at the time, and then for some reason I get it in the cutting room and it doesn't work. It takes on a life of its own, and I have to go and find it in the cutting room.

"*Good Times* didn't work when I brought it in. I had to rework it and rework it. I don't know if it works now, but it was a disaster when it came in. The dailies looked good, but it didn't cut. The pace was off. This has been true of every film I've made. I plan them carefully, but then they come into the cutting room like terminal patients. Then I start operating. So it must be that I work on different conscious levels that are not clear to me at the time."

"It wasn't a formula-type picture," according to Mel Shapiro, the film editor.

Friedkin said Shapiro "had no idea what I was doing because it wasn't all that clear to me. He assembled the picture according to his own feelings about it, which I hated." Friedkin decided to start from scratch.

"He wanted the dailies reconstituted," Shapiro said, which meant pulling the picture apart *completely* and putting it all back into the takes as originally shot by Friedkin. This is a drastic measure on any film and one Shapiro did not feel was completely called-for, adding that "often we'll reconstitute trims — the parts of the scenes not used in the film — so a director can see what's missing or what he'd rather have." Shapiro offered to leave the film, believing Friedkin was not satisfied with his work, "but Billy wouldn't hear of that." So they set about taking the film apart, Shapiro believing it was the only way Friedkin could get control of it.

"It became a process of rebuilding," Friedkin said, "but as I was destroying his assembly of the film, I was also realizing my own concept of it as I had shot it was not all that great anyway, and I had to rethink that as well."

When Parsons saw the completed film, he was astonished at how quickly it moved. "In fact," he said, "it was short of the footage we agreed to sell it to the ABC television network for, so that we had to cut together twelve minutes of junk in order to fill it out to meet the minimum network requirement of ninety minutes."

Meanwhile, Broidy moved fast too, according to Friedkin, selling the film to Columbia at a profit.

"When I saw it, I knew the picture wasn't going to work," Bono said. "By the time we had finished and released it, the country was off Sonny and Cher. We were considered corny, so our box office wouldn't be to teenagers. Little kids liked it. The market we'd had was gone because it was a real clean picture. My music was passé too."

"Acid rock and the Rolling Stones had just come in when we released this tender little whimsical picture," Friedkin said, adding an exclamation point to his statement, recalling one of the promotion tours the advertising department at Columbia Pictures asked Sonny, Cher and him to do. "We went to Austin, Texas, for the opening. There was to be a parade from the motel where we were staying to the governor's mansion, and there were more people sitting in the parade cars than there were on the street. There was a little black kid running alongside our limousine, pointing at us and laughing his ass off."

Paul Hunter, a television writer and associate of Friedkin's during the latter's days at WGN in Chicago, said he took Friedkin's mother, Rae, to the premiere in Chicago. Hunter was aghast, saying Friedkin did better with a few thousand dollars on his documentaries. "But Billy's mother was proud of him. Everything he did was the best, the finest, the greatest." (Friedkin's mother died the day after he finished *The Boys in the Band* several years later, Hunter said. Friedkin established the Rae Friedkin Clinic with a grant to Reiss-Davis to further work with retarded children.)

Critical response to *Good Times* was generally favorable, but Friedkin said, "I still couldn't sit down and read the shit. I was pleased that others were impressed and that it looked like I had a future as a filmmaker. It occurred to me at that point that reviews were meaningful in situations like that. But so were the reactions of others like your peers."

Howard Koch, then head of Paramount Studios, "saw it and loved it," Friedkin said, and introduced him to Blake Edwards *(The Pink Panther* series, *10, Victor/Victoria)*, who asked him to make films for his company. Friedkin declined. Steve Broidy and Parsons sent Friedkin a couple of scripts after *Good Times*, but according to Parsons, "Billy said they weren't what he wanted to do."

II

Both Friedkin and Bono agree that *Good Times* is less a film than a television show. Specifically, Bono considers it the prelude to his *Sonny and Cher Comedy Hour* variety series, which aired on the CBS network from 1971 to 1974. Friedkin disparingly says his film has "a TV look" and none of the youthful vigor and vitality that Richard Lester brought to *A Hard Day's Night* (1965), which starred the Beatles. Granted, Lester successfully combined his own brand of frenetic filmmaking with the Beatles's naturalness and achieved an expressionistic spontaneity, while Friedkin's dark visceral seductiveness, displayed with harsh intensity in *Crump*, has little comedic connection. Friedkin was, and continues to be (see *Deal of the Century*), out of his element with straight comedy.

Yes, the humor in *Good Times* is puerile, the dream sketches sophomoric, and the story an adolescent fairy tale—when studying the film two decades after its release.

In 1967, however, it very much reflected the persona of Sonny and Cher, especially since they played themselves. The shtick that would imbue their variety series four years later was very much on display in the film, with Sonny's buffoonery kept in check by Cher's earthiness. When Sonny would say he had a great idea and explain it in detail, Cher would listen patiently and respond with a matter-of-fact "It stinks." Wearing leather, bell-bottoms, and long hair, they symbolized a generation of flower children who, in sixties jargon, "did their own thing." In *Good Times,* Sonny and Cher "do their own thing" by wearing their own style of clothes and ad-libbing their dialogue in shared scenes. Even in their fantasy episodes they never step out of themselves as they play characters such as Jungle Morry, the worst Tarzan in the world, and his bored mate, Zora; Sheriff Irving Ringo waiting for "high noon" with Nell Belle, his beehive-hairdo-bedecked dance-hall-hostess girlfriend; and the poor man's Sam Spade hired by Baby, the gum-chewing Veronica Lake–wigged "mysterious woman," and wooed by the sultry songstress Samantha (Cher in a dual role).

By way of conveying the promise of the title, the sketches are peppered with sight gags. In the Tarzan spoof, Sonny swings from tree to tree but loses his grip on a vine and crashes to the jungle floor. He wears a small sundial as a wristwatch. The bamboo treehouse he and Cher live in looks compact on the outside, but when we cut inside, it's a palatial avant garde interior with marble floors and elevators. As the town sheriff in the Western skit, Sonny can't keep his bullets from falling out of his gunbelt. The detective parody finds Sonny wearing a trenchcoat, trench hat, and trench shoes. He also has a dozen pistols strapped across his body when he opens the coat for Cher's inspection. But Friedkin and Bono did not stop with just poking fun at Tarzan movies, *High Noon,* and film noir. They also satirized the movie industry in the same broad visual fashion. In an early scene, Sonny tells Mordicus, the charmingly sinister film mogul, that he and Cher don't want just to sing in a movie—"We want to do something different, we want to do a story." "Ah, an astute observation," Mordicus says, adding he has already chosen a screenplay for them to do. He holds up a script twice the size of Tolstoy's *War and Peace,* entitled *Rags to Riches.* Sonny wonders how much it weighs. They balance it in their hands and agree on "about ninety minutes." Though these visual gags and "in" movie jokes may prompt groans, they are directed and delivered with a casual offhandedness that usually overrides their hoariness. Speaking of hoariness, what should have been a leadened moment of banality—a shot of monkeys in the Tarzan spoof shooting craps, with human ethnic accents dubbed over their antics—is actually very funny. This brand of comedy and humor works because it is *unexpected*. You can forgive a hackneyed moment if you don't see it coming three days beforehand.

Friedkin does admit that "there are a couple of good little sequences" in the film but adds that there's also "a couple of nice turn of phrase in Hitler's speeches." In fairness, one can easily surmise Friedkin's droll remark, though laced with discontent for the film, is the product of hindsight since he made this statement almost fifteen years after directing *Good Times*. As mentioned earlier in this chapter, part of Friedkin's objection to the film is its "TV look." True, Friedkin did have much of the action centered in the frame as is the wont of television productions. (They are, after all, meant for viewing on the smaller television screen as opposed to the wide screens of the movie houses.) But all of Friedkin's filmic background to this point was in television. Even *Crump* was made for television viewing. Though *Good Times* isn't the film of fierce intensity that *Crump* is (nor was it intended to be), Friedkin's first feature film does have the loose style and naturalistic feel of his earlier work.

Unfortunately, this tends to work against him in the musical segments where that style appears pedestrian. Friedkin either stages Bono's songs in a room with Sonny and Cher singing to each other or lays the music over montages. While Friedkin's use of solarization and psychedelic optical effects make some of the montages visually interesting and (at the time) innovative, the use of the songs themselves tend to drag the momentum of the film. For example, during an argument near the end of the movie, a tearful Cher tells Sonny he shouldn't be forced to make Mordicus's movie if he doesn't want to. Sonny exits to cool off while Cher sings that Sonny's "just a guy who gives me all he has to give, and I couldn't live without him." The song begs Cher's love for a *long* five minutes while Friedkin and Shapiro, his editor, show us Sonny riding around town on his motorcycle thinking and Cher sitting and walking and pondering and singing. (Friedkin was not a complete novice to filming musical interludes either. According to Bill Butler, he and Friedkin had shot a concert series for the Television Academy in Chicago as well as a number of short films and television programs that were musical in content.)

When Friedkin does manage to liven things up in a musical segment, the screen bursts with choreography, camera movement, high-kicking dance-hall girls, flying bodies, and snappy editing. This all happens during the performance of the title song in the saloon during the Western skit. Though the young director does tend to get crane-happy in this sequence to the point of overuse, there is still a naturalness to the excitement; no camera tricks or jerky Lesterlike editing. Friedkin laments *Good Times*'s "lack of vitality" in comparison to Richard Lester's Beatles films. But rather than attempt a limp, obvious copy of *A Hard Day's Night,* Friedkin fashions his film around Sonny and Cher's innovative, independent style and corny, wholesome humor.

The real failing of the film, however, was out of Friedkin's hands. Within the year *Good Times* was shot and released, the Sonny and Cher fad had faded as fads tend to do. Witness the rise and demise of disco with *Saturday Night Fever* and the short-lived *Urban Cowboy* craze. Friedkin's attempts at being current quickly became dated.

But not before producers and studio executives of the time offered this neophyte feature film director other scripts because they thought highly of his first effort. In Hollywood vernacular, Friedkin's telephone was ringing. But just as Sonny ultimately turns Mordicus down, opting not to make a film at all and thereby maintaining his personal integrity rather than selling himself out simply because the offer exists, so too art imitates life, in this case, Friedkin's. Rather than jump at the first feature offer, he waited, selected.

Ironically, Friedkin directed a television pilot entitled *The Pickle Brothers.* According to Gerald Gardner, he and cowriter and coproducer of the show, Dee Caruso (their credits include *Don Adams Screen Test* and *NBC Follies*) had Friedkin specifically in mind. They'd heard good word-of-mouth on *Good Times* and felt they "needed a youthful and energetic director." *The Pickle Brothers* was designed to capture the spirit and magic of the Marx Brothers, which appealed to Friedkin, Gardner said, adding that though Friedkin told him he no longer did television, this project was special. "He told me later, 'I am willing to direct every single episode if it is picked up.'" The ABC network decided not to include it on its schedule.

Friedkin's next feature film project had nothing to do with his having directed *Good Times.* Nor would the making of the picture have any connotations of good times.

4
The Night They Raided Minsky's

"I've always thought that comedy is not Bill's forte because he is really heavy. If he failed with any part of that picture, it was probably the comedic end."

—Bud Yorkin

I

At the end of the opening credit sequence in *The Night They Raided Minsky's,* Raymond Paine (Jason Robards) and Chick Williams (Norman Wisdom) perform a comedy routine before a lowbrow audience in Minsky's Burlesque House, circa 1925. Paine, dressed in a dapper gray suit and flat straw hat, squirts seltzer water down Williams's baggy pants. The dopey grin Williams wears refuses to droop. Over this, the credit "Directed by William Friedkin" appears and remains until an exasperated Paine says to Williams, "Hey what's the matter with you? You ain't got no feeling?" Credit sequences do not happen by accident. Each credit "card" is deliberately placed at the discretion of the producer or director. (One of the most effective placements of a directorial card was Sam Peckinpah's in his 1969 film, *The Wild Bunch,* when Pike Bishop looks into the camera and says, "If they move, kill them.") It is doubtful Friedkin had much creative input regarding the main title credits. He had left *Minsky's* soon after delivering his cut of the film, months before they would have been composed. However, that Friedkin's credit falls where it does would seem an appropriate filmic comment, considering his own thoughts on his second feature film.

"I really didn't understand it when I made it," Friedkin said.[1] "I had no vision whatever. I found as I got into the project that it's basic—I might have totally misread its intent—but it had nothing more nor less than a TV sensibility about it. Norman Lear's concepts were, in *my* opinion, naive and simplistic and not very funny anymore. It was a series of one-liners. He had structured his screenplay like a burlesque show where everything was a

39

series of one-liners, including the characterizations. I tried to do combat
with that and get changes in the script. I did get several but not enough.
The script is terrible. And the only way to have saved that film was to kind
of Richard Lester it up with a lot of shtick, which I hate doing. Without content, form is meaningless.

"And what Lear had hoped that I would do was to go out and shtick
the picture up. Richard Lester-type-stuff—flip focus, weird cutting—all the
kind of thing he did in *A Hard Day's Night*. Lear saw that in me, I guess,
not because of anything he'd seen in my work but because I was a young
director for a story about older people in burlesque."

Though Norman Lear was unavailable for comment, Bud Yorkin,
coproducer with Lear and a director himself *(Start the Revolution Without
Me, Twice in a Lifetime)*, said he knew Friedkin from his days with David
Wolper and had hired him to shoot the opening sequence of his film *Divorce
American Style* (1967). This sequence shows a man carrying a briefcase to
a hilltop overlooking suburbia. He opens the case, pulls out a baton, and
begins conducting as if he were before an orchestra. What he's "conducting," though, are domestic arguments, which we hear as we cut to different
houses. Lear did not ask Friedkin to direct *Minsky's* because of *Good Times,*
however. Yorkin said, "Texture, ambiance, flavor, feeling. Bill can put that
on the screen. That's a rarity, and that's what the picture needed. We were
talking about a period, an essence. I felt that if he felt he could do it, he
would do as good a job as anyone."

Knowing nothing of the history of burlesque or the Lower East Side
of New York, Friedkin set about researching. He spoke with many old
burlesque comedians to get a sense of what burlesque was like and
discovered "it was a breeding ground for American humor, and it influenced
American humor even to this day, none of which was reflected in Mr. Lear's
script." Friedkin also went to the movies, specifically a Rouben Mamoulian
early sound film entitled *Applause*. (Mamoulian's films include the 1932 version of *Dr. Jekyll and Mr. Hyde, Golden Boy*, and *Silk Stockings*.)

"*Applause* was one of the most extraordinary films I've ever seen on *any*
level, whether you're interested in backstage theater story or burlesque or
not," Friedkin said. "But it is absolutely the inspiration for *Minsky's*, which
doesn't come anywhere near this film. If anything, it's a slim copy of the
effects and atmosphere and texture that Mr. Mamoulian brought to the
screen for all time in that film.[2]

"So whereas some of his other films influenced me a great deal more,
I have to admit that I stole from that one . . . . I really stole stuff out of there.
Anyone who has seen both films will recognize exactly what was taken,
spiritually and literally."

Andrew Lazslo, the cinematographer whose credits include *Southern
Comfort* and *Streets of Fire*, added that Mamoulian's 1929 film was so

The Night They Raided Minsky's. Raymond Paine (Jason Robards, right) in a burlesque sketch with second banana Chick Williams (Norman Wisdom).

remarkable because it had technical wizardry in it that they just didn't have a right to have because they didn't have the right film, the right lab technique, the right lenses, and *still* these shots were in the film. "We were amazed that some of the things we had concocted and were going to put in *Minsky's* were already in that film."

"But all of these things are colored by the fact that I hated the script," Friedkin said. "Nevertheless, I directed it because they paid me seventy-five thousand dollars, which was a lot of money in those days. It was a United Artists picture that put me into the mainstream. I was directing a mainstream film. And on the advice of my agents and because I liked Yorkin and Lear and thought they would be helpful and supportive of me, I took the picture. As I got into it, I found that Lear and I were completely at odds and Lear was *anything* but supportive of me. . . . I felt and said to him a number of times along the line that he should have directed the film himself, that that's really what he wanted to do, but that he could not direct it through me. That film is neither his film nor my film. It is a hybrid.

"Directing is communicating with people, that's all. I tried to deal with the material and the talent as best I could, and because I didn't believe in the script very much, I was not all that successful in achieving the rapport with the actors.

"If you love the material as I did with *French Connection* and *Exorcist,* for example, you can achieve that rapport because actors and crew people come to you with very important questions pertaining to how they're supposed to conduct their work and their business, and if you're not sure yourself what to do with this material, it's hard to give them a direct answer. So I may not have been as decisive or as forceful or as visionary on that film as a director should be in order to achieve what is really either an interpretation of someone's script that he has a feeling for or his own vision." As Orson Welles once said, "A director has to function like a commander in the field in the battle. You need the same ability to inspire, terrify, encourage, reinforce and generally dominate. So it's partly a question of personality, which isn't so easy to acquire as a skill."

Friedkin said, "I had a marvelous cast, except for Britt Ekland, who can't act but who is a very good-looking woman. Lear and I saw a film which she had made with her then-husband Peter Sellers called *The Bobo.* Sellers loved her and helped her to do some nice work on film, and I thought she had a great little talent, and I think perhaps she did and maybe does, but she was miscast playing the part of an American little girl wanting to make it as a burlesque actress.

"I couldn't help her much. She really didn't understand it, and I frankly didn't understand it, so we faked it. The whole picture was faked from beginning to end. It's not a film I like."

Friedkin's consternation was also fueled by his relationship with

Norman Lear. "On many occasions I said to Lear, 'You better fire me, or I should quit.' And he said, 'No, no, let's just get it done and do what we have to do.' I mean Lear would not let me quit; wouldn't fire me. We were antagonistic virtually every day on the film. . . . I did the best I could with the picture but did it really with half a heart."

Though he has been told by individuals he respects, such as the rock and roll songwriting team of Jerry Lieber and Mike Stoller ("Kansas City," "Hound Dog"), that *Minsky's* is a classic, Friedkin maintains that they are wrong. "It's unwatchable as far as I'm concerned. I've glanced at it a few times on television. There are nice moments in it. The music of Charles Strouse and Lee Adams is evocative of the period, highly reflective and beautiful. And the dance numbers that Danny Daniels choreographed I think are absolutely of the period."

While Yorkin believes the comedic elements of the film were more suited to his abilities, he is adamant that Friedkin still captured a mood, essence, and nostalgia he would never have done.

Friedkin does not agree and adds that "I wanted to do it a lot darker I think, too, than Lear wanted to see it. Lear wanted a piece of froth. Perhaps he wouldn't admit to this. Perhaps he would say that he wanted something meaningful."

Froth or meaningful, Lear's source materials for the script, cowritten by Arnold Shulman, Sidney Michaels, and Lear, was based on the book by Rowland Barber, which is about the bawdy side of burlesque. According to Friedkin, "The characters were great raucous people onstage, and offstage they were pricks. It was a sordid, seedy world, and we didn't catch that in the film."

The production designers, William and Jean Ekhart, whose credits include numerous films and plays, agree that the look of the picture was not sufficiently exploited. In Jean Ekhart's opinion, the opening sequence showing young Rachel making her way through a crowded street packed with people, peddlers, and pushcarts, and finally stopping below the Minsky Theater marquee was too brief. "My thought is that should have been the thread that ran through and connected all the disparate elements—the street and the theater both. The grubbiness of the street and the basement of the theater with the made-up, half-dressed women was the quality that the movie should have had."

William Ekhart added that he felt part of the problem was that Friedkin wasn't expressing himself. "I think that's what Lear got nervous about. There was no concrete expression of plan."

The key to Friedkin's difficulty with the picture is best expressed by Danny Daniels, the choreographer on the film. "Bill saw the script the way somebody who would do *The French Connection* would see it. *Minsky's* was just another world. Directing the burlesque sketches was completely

outside his realm of experience. Burlesque sketches are bigger than life . . . .
I don't know whether he understood the musical theatricality of it, but in
my experience over the years, I found that people who aren't involved in
musical theater literally don't understand it at all. Some directors talk like
they understand it, but when they start to do it, they just have no idea as to
what's going on on stage. They haven't a background in it. The best example
is Peter Bogdanovich and *At Long Last Love*. The audacity of somebody ex-
pecting to come in and do a musical that's never done musical before! They're
complicated. They're difficult to do. They require great skill and background
and experience. Anybody who is a director and intellectual and has a lot of
book learning and directorial experience can't suddenly divorce himself
from that background and come to work on a musical. It's another world."

Daniels wouldn't elaborate with examples of what a novice director to
musicals would need to know. "It's the same as saying, 'What do you have
to know to do an appendectomy?' You have to understand the musical part
of it and how it is married to the action, particularly in films. You should
have background in dance and music and a vocabulary of the musical tricks
that have been used. You can't give crash courses."

By way of comparison, Friedkin says, "*The Exorcist* came off. I understand it; I knew what it was about."

Daniels said that due to Friedkin's lack of understanding of burlesque
routines, the "quality of bigness" that they require, "it got to the point where
Norman Wisdom, who I knew would give the burlesque material the kind
of quality in the acting that it needed, would come to me and say, 'Danny,
Jesus, this guy doesn't understand these sketches and for Christ's sake do
something about it.'

"Lear was watching and knew what was going on. I had a conversation
with Lear, and he said, 'Danny, why don't you direct the sketches?' I said,
'Well, Norman, you're going to have to get Billy to okay it.' I wasn't about
to pull the rug from under him. So Lear talked to Billy, and Billy came over
to me and said, 'Danny, I'd like you to do this.' I said, 'Fine.'"

When it came time for the staging of the musical numbers for the
cameras, Daniels said, Friedkin "didn't understand the linking up of the
music with the action on stage." Again and again, Lear intervened, and
Daniels was given a free hand to insist on getting the shots that he wanted.
"When Billy found out, he was kind of sore about it, and I don't blame him.
But it gets difficult when you're telling the director what you want when
the fact of the matters is you know better than he does . . . . You pretty much
know the way you want it on camera, and you don't want somebody telling
you this is the way it should be shot when you know it should be shot the
other way . . . ." One area of contention was Ekland's strip at the end of the
film. "There was one low angle shot I was in love with and I wanted it. The
camera does a truck-dolly shot as Ekland comes forward doing some low

***The Night They Raided Minsky's*. Rachel (Britt Ekland) performs her climactic striptease.**

movements, and you were looking up. It was hard to get because they had to pull chairs out of the theater and that was the big magilla because it was going to take an hour. Bill didn't want to do it, and I did. I don't know if it was an arbitrary thing on his part or he was trying to be stubborn for the sake of being stubborn, but I wanted it, and I had Lear's backing."

One thing Friedkin succeeded in banning from the set was spangles. Speaking in a pleasing Southern drawl, Anna Hill Johnstone, nominated for her costume designs for *Ragtime* (1981), said that Friedkin did not want her to use any spangles on the costumes for the chorines. "This kind of floored me. Burlesque and spangles had always gone together in my mind. And he didn't want me to use any red. He just thought it would be an interesting show without them. I groaned and carried on, but it was a challenge." But, she adds, "I think we finally broke down and snuck a red dress in toward the end."

This request of Friedkin's to Johnstone would be akin to his telling the art director to throw out the seltzer bottles. What point would be served?

"I've been in this business a very long time," Johnstone said, "and every now and then it happens: I get a very young person who is trying to do

something different, and I'm sure I was the same way when I was Billy's age.
. . . He doesn't want to do history as it was. And I think that's part of youth.
It's very stimulating. That's what I meant when I said I was groaning
because I had no passion for feathers *but* the variety I could get by *not* using
spangles! I guess I believe if a director's got an idea, let's explore it."

Her "exploration" resulted in the chorines bedecked in feathers and
nets, and one costume had mirrors on it.

And Friedkin did not stop at spangles. He said, "*Minsky's* was all sched-
uled to be shot at Universal Studios on the old sets for *Thoroughly Modern
Millie.* The Lower East Side of New York is in New York. We shot it there.
It's all about feeling." But he reiterated that that feeling didn't come off.[3]

In Ralph Rosenblum's book *When the Shooting Stops . . . the Cutting
Begins,* he recounts, among other things as the editor of *Minsky's,* something
he refers to as the "New Look"[4] the film was to have and even says it was
"essentially a Richard Lester Look." Rosenblum also writes that "the producer, the director, and the people at United Artists were excited by the
prospect of the 'New Look,' although what it was and how it was going to
be accomplished no one knew."[5]

According to Friedkin, whatever the "New Look" was, "we weren't getting it across to each other."

"No one could define that 'New Look,'" said Andrew Lazslo. "We tried
to get a 'New Look,' and it was a different look. It was a look Lear called
the 1925 'Look' presented to today's audiences. You can't define it. It was
certainly on everybody's mind."

Lazslo explained that the intention of the so-called 1925 "Look" was "to
introduce some element that would separate *Minsky's* from the films cur-
rently then playing in the theaters. . . . Billy, Norman Lear, and myself all
agreed from the beginning that the interior of the theater would comprise
one look, all the exteriors would comprise another look, and such things as
the interiors of the delicatessen, homes, and other stores a third look.

"In the theater, what we did everyday twice—once in the morning just
shortly after we arrived and once in the afternoon shortly after lunch
break—was to fill the theater with smoke. We'd let the smoke settle out so
that you couldn't tell that is smoke. You shouldn't have been aware of it
because it wasn't the usual swirling, rolling type smoke. It was a sort of an
atmosphere."

The remaining "atmosphere" or "look" of the film was achieved with
settings, costumes, and performances, according to Lazslo, but not with
documentary realism. He insists the "look" was not a starkly realistic one
(it isn't) but an "honest preparation" to involve the audience, coupled with
a nostalgic ambience that enhanced the tone and texture of the film.

But what about all the hand-held camera work in the opening street
scene and especially in the backstage theater scenes?

Lazslo, whose background is one of rehearsing, blocking, and painstakingly executing a shot, readily admits the hand-held footage added a "freshness inasmuch as at that time most of the studio-made films had such a rigid format of tripods, dollies, and camera cranes."

Both Lazslo and the Ekharts recalled that Friedkin had wanted to shoot the entire film with hand-held cameras, "grabbing shots and moving quickly" as his background had taught him. But dialogue and stage production numbers would have to be done with stage-of-the-art equipment, Lazslo said, adding that shooting exclusively with hand-held cameras was a technique the audiences weren't used to, that they had to keep the tastes and desires of the audiences in mind.

"Billy had made reference early in production to the fact that everything would be done completely differently, that the rules were going to have to be broken," Lazslo said, noting that one of the first things Friedkin objected to was the use of his camera equipment that was brand new and the very best available. "I had no objections to breaking a few rules, but I reminded Billy that one has to know the rules before one can break them. He mentioned the fact that the Beatles were such a wonderful new phenomenon with what they were doing with music. It was a new way to go. I sort of agreed but also reminded him that this didn't do away with Beethoven, Mozart, and Chopin. After that conversation, it seemed to me that we didn't see eye-to-eye much."

Rosenblum states in his book that his intercutting of black-and-white newsreel footage with Friedkin's original film was his "grasping for an inspiration"[6] to improve a film that had "no pace, no suspense and not a moment of believable dialogue."[7] This integration permeates the film, not only augmenting various scenes (a huge smokestack topples over, and a log roller tumbles into the water—the black-and-white—juxtaposed with a fight scene in a penny arcade—the color), but especially in the opening sequence where Rosenblum says he spliced pieces of black-and-white footage made from Friedkin's original color footage, achieving the effect of "stock footage bursting into Technicolor."[8] Though the editor admits he "became self-conscious about the number of times we used this trick. . . . Lear was captivated by it [and] insisted on employing it more times than I thought was necessary. . . ."[9]

According to Bud Yorkin, the inclusion of black-and-white footage was all Lear's idea. (This visual concept had been incorporated earlier in an unproduced script written by Lear and Yorkin, entitled *Playboy*. They open the story in black-and-white on a woman driving through Chicago looking for the Playboy Building. As it comes into view, the script calls for the film to dissolve into color.)

Andrew Lazslo said he would "take credit for that [color trick]." However, he only wanted a few shots of black-and-white film to fade to color. "I think that extra footage looks pretentious. I felt once we got into the color, we should have stayed in the color and forget about a reoccurring gimmick. As far as the title sequence is concerned, I think it's the most difficult sequence in the picture to sit through." And the slapstick of seeing someone punched in the face and then cutting to a smokestack collapsing Lazslo did not approve of either. "I can't see the necessity. Ralph thinks it did something wonderful, but I think it interrupted the picture."

Daniels, too, felt the editing of the picture was a problem, but for a different reason. "Ralph said something very strange in his book. He gave the dance numbers an oblique compliment without any reference to me, as though they kind of just magically appeared on the screen—as though they dropped in out of heaven and came in front of the camera, and then he could edit them as he wanted. Lear thought Rosenblum was a genius, but I wasn't very happy about the way he did the editing. For example, if I did a number that was two minutes long, it was chopped up into forty-second segments and spotted through different segments of the film to give it pace. This, I think, did help the pace, but it was detrimental to the choreography. Here's one corner who doesn't think Rosenblum's a genius."

Friedkin's observation of *Minsky's* as a "hybrid" seems even more appropriate at this juncture. It must also be remembered that filmmaking is a collaborative effort. Editors, choreographers, cinematographers, and all the other production artists enhance the director's vision of the film. Sometimes, that vision goes cockeyed.

Yorkin said that Friedkin's first cut of *Minsky's* "just missed. It was all there, but it needed more." Rosenblum says that he and Lear screened the picture for David Picker, an executive vice president of United Artists, who said afterward, "In all my years in film, this is the worst first cut I've ever seen."[10] (Before anyone envisions the spectre of Friedkin's experience on *Good Times* enveloping *Minsky's,* the story goes that *The Godfather Part II* was completely recut after a disastrous preview. And that film won the Academy Award for best picture.)

But, back in the projection room after running Friedkin's cut, Yorkin said, "It was just Norman, Bill, and myself in there, and we were quite outspoken. What the hell, we knew each other well. I said I was disappointed. I think Norman felt that way."

Shortly after this screening, Friedkin left for England to shoot *The Birthday Party.* Meanwhile, *Minsky's* had to be "resuscitated," according to Rosenblum, "finessed" according to Yorkin.[11] By Rosenblum's account, he had to recut the film completely. This necessitated rearranging and altering scenes, intercutting old newsreel black-and-white footage throughout, and employing Handel's "Hallelujah Chorus," "the use of which is always a sure sign that a film is in danger," he adds.[12] Yorkin said Lear reshot theater audience reaction "because Billy didn't shoot enough of those people," black-

and-white footage was incorporated as well as the color trick, and the burlesque routines were reedited because "Billy hadn't cut [them] quite right."

Regardless of whose version one accepts, what is clear is that for better or worse, *Minsky's* needed a lot of work in the editing room and reediting a picture is a long and tedious job. But aside from Yorkin's comment about Friedkin's not having enough coverage on the theater audience, neither the editor nor the coproducer dispute the fact that the director *did* shoot the script.

"It was not an easy screenplay to do, either," Yorkin said. "It's one of the most difficult things Billy's ever approached. He can jump into *Birthday Party,* which he knew like the back of his hand. He knew every essence of the play, every nuance. Of all the pictures Billy has done outside of *Sorcerer, Minsky's* was about the most difficult. *French Connection* was physical; *Exorcist* was his own vision, his control. *Minsky's* was not. It may well be that Billy could never do something for someone that he hasn't really developed."

Yorkin says comedy is not Friedkin's strength cinematically. Friedkin has stated that Yorkin "probably would have made a classic out of *Minsky's.*" One can only guess that David Picker at United Artists must have felt the same way since he asked Yorkin to take over directing *Minsky's* from Friedkin. Yorkin has just returned from Europe, where he was shooting *Start the Revolution Without Me,* when Picker made his offer, Yorkin said. "UA was very upset. I said I'm not about to do it, and some of the problems Billy was having was that it was a tough picture for anybody."

Some of the problems included only ten days to dress and shoot the street scenes because the tenement area they were going to use was going to be torn down, claustrophobic conditions inside the theatre since it was not a set with movable walls as on a sound stage, and the death of Bert Lahr during the filming, forcing script changes and deleting parts of scenes already shot with him, which were now unusable.

"Both Billy and Norman are perfectionists," Yorkin said. "Dealing with people like that, you reach a point where you have to say, as Fred Astaire said to me, 'I respect you, but I may disagree with you. If I attack you, I won't attack you personally. I'll attack what you're doing or the material. Let's have that free-wheeling association, and you deal with me that way.' Norman does this same thing. But that didn't make it any easier for Billy, who was doing his first major picture."

Friedkin had total selection of the cast, which he said was originally to be Alan Alda and Joel Grey. "We were going to go younger because it was about younger guys. We had them signed, and they were being fitted for costumes."

Johnstone said that at one point in preproduction she was fitting Tony Curtis for costumes. "When you're a costume designer, you can't do anything until you get the body. We were close to my deadline to get the people. I was just swamped with having to get it delivered on time."

But, with the film's shooting schedule conflicting with Alda's and Grey's stage commitments, the producers of their plays "told us to forget using them," Friedkin said. "Lear and Yorkin had worked with Jason Robards on *Divorce American Style,* liked working with him, and suggested him to me." Friedkin thought Robards would be terrific, and Norman Wisdom, whom he saw on the Broadway stage in *Walking Happy*—which Daniels choreographed—"is burlesque," but, he hastened to add, "it was a handpicked cast all doing what I thought inferior material."

However, Yorkin said, "It may not have been cast properly, and Billy just didn't have the touch. That was a very tough role for Jason Robards to play. He's not a song-and-dance man. He's O'Neill, not *Minsky's.*"

"Robards was drunk about one-third of the time through the shooting," Friedkin stated. "We'd have to peel him off the wall to do his part. We had to revise his part many times because he was just drunk. We shot some of his scenes drunk. A little bit of it is in the film. When the guy's drunk, there's nothing you can do. He'd go off on a binge and stay out all night and come in the next morning unable to work. The script would have to adjust." (Robards declined to comment on this picture.)

"There's a scene in the film," Friedkin said, "where Norman Wisdom, who I loved working with, is trying to explain to Britt Ekland what burlesque is all about in a series of pantomines. We ad-libbed that scene one morning. It wasn't in the script. We had nothing to shoot that morning because Robards didn't show up, so we shot that little scene. It's the only scene in the picture that I care about." Wisdom, too, enjoyed this scene "because of the freedom I was allowed. I could adjust it to my own style, making many suggestions, most of which Mr. Friedkin accepted, and if he didn't, then I deleted without argument. It was, as we would say in England, a piece of cake."

While Friedkin had a difficult time working with Robards, Danny Daniels recalled that while rehearsing Robards and Wisdom on the "Perfect Gentleman" musical dance sequence for two weeks, he was aware he was "working with an actor, not a song-and-dance man, and I think he approached it from the actor's point of view. I think he gave it a character it wouldn't have had otherwise, and I thought it was quite wonderful. He was very determined to get the musical end of it right, though. Now Wisdom, it just rolled off of him like water off a duck. He's been doing this since he was a kid. Robards was singing the words like he was doing a scene."

Lazslo remembered an important aspect about the "Perfect Gentleman" sequence. "The way we had designed and scheduled the shooting was that all the musical numbers, particularly that one, would be done without an audience of extras. Then, when we brought the audience in, we would redo the number in long shots taken from behind and over the audience onto the stage and also from backstage and behind the performers onto the audience.

"So what happened was, we shot without an audience first, and then we filled the theater and had five cameras rolling. Even though this audience was comprised of professional extras, nevertheless, seeing a stage performance, particularly this type by Robards and Wisdom, the audience responded. Their response in turn had a reaction on the performers. Just as soon as we made these long shots, I immediately went to Billy, and he was aware of it too—these performances were vastly different from the performances in the tight shots. Right there and then he decided to cover the performances again, and almost everything we did without an audience in tight shots was cut."

There was an issue of coverage of a different sort with Britt Ekland. Danny Daniels said, "I staged the strip with Ekland looking into the wings and her dress dropping, but all her emotion in the face and the things she was experiencing at the time were things Billy got into with her.

"Now, Britt and I worked on the strip for two or three weeks. I taught her how to bump and grind. We are on the stage after all this preparation. There is a theater full of extras screaming and carrying on as they are directed to do. Britt had done the first part of the strip, and now she's up to the point where she's going to drop her dress. She then said, 'Where is my double?' Or words to that effect. I said, 'What are you talking about?' She said, 'Well, I'm not going to show my boobs here.' I said, 'Britt, what are you talking about? We've been doing this for three weeks.' I never asked her to do the thing full-out when we rehearsed it. She'd always be dressed, and she'd drop the garment, but she had a blouse on or something underneath. I called Bill up and said, 'She doesn't want to drop her dress now. What the hell are we going to do?' He tried to talk her into it. Bill called Lear. But she was absolutely adamant. Lear said, 'We'll have to get a double.' So Billy postponed this sequence until later in the day. A call was put in to the casting people, and three hours later they sent some girls down. Well, all these people—extras, crew—are waiting, and I'm down in the basement auditioning girls by telling them to take their clothes off so I can see their boobs. So I picked a girl who I thought had the best-looking breasts. I rehearsed her downstairs with the bit of just reaching out her arms and dropping the dress. Bill staged it when the extras had gone. We did the thing with Britt doing everything except that. Then we put the double in. It was such a quick glimpse anyway. She could have done it. Today she probably would, but in that day it was a little too much." Daniels then added, "While Britt was doing her strip, I was doing it on the other side of the camera. My wife always said watching me was a better show than watching her."

"My early films are very disposable," Friedkin said. "Like many film-makers, my early steps were not always inspired."[13]

II

Critics sometimes have to guess at who is responsible for what in films. In the case of *Minsky's*, Andrew Lazslo was credited for the "droll trick of conjuring up period film from old newsreel clips" by *Playboy*[14]; the *Los Angeles Times* praised Friedkin's sense of editorial timing, saying, "He knows precisely how long to stay with a production number or a character so as never to lapse into the merely corny;"[15] the *Hollywood Reporter* attributed the blending of newsreel footage and the infusing of color into shots introduced in black and white to Pablo Ferro, the film's visual consultant and second unit director; and the *New Republic* attacked Friedkin, saying he "bombarded [*Minsky's*] with inappropriate techniques — a melange of fake-documentary, classy TV, and traces of Richard Lester."[16] With disagreement in the production ranks on which ideas were whose and since critics must make understandable stabs by crediting, Friedkin's statement that *Minsky's* is a hybrid rings too true. And since Friedkin admits to having "no vision" with *Minsky's* and stole from *Applause*, any further discussion of his contribution might be negated. However, in spite of this and the stage routines directed (excellently) by Danny Daniels, the antagonism between director and producer, and the editor's self-avowed conquering of a "silly, uncohesive musical" that he made "attention-holding for close to ninety-nine minutes,"[17] some of *Minsky's* still retains a markedly Friedkin style; his "look."

The film opens with a brief title-card introduction and simultaneous voice-over reading by the old-time crooner Rudy Vallee, informing the audience in a vaudeville manner that "the film you are about to see is based on really true incidents that actually happened," that "in 1925 there was this real religious girl, and by accident she invented the striptease. This *real* religious girl." Black-and-white images of Model A's motoring down busy avenues, a dancing horse, pudgy chorines, acrobats balancing high above the street, and many other impressions of fun and frolic whisk by, finally giving way to a bustling market street packed with people, peddlers, and pushcarts that pops to color. There is a close-up on Rachel (Britt Ekland) riding wide-eyed on an elevated train into the "big city." Her perspective gazing out the train window at the tenement-lined street bursts from black-and-white to color, as does the sequence of her making her way down that street. She drinks in the flavor and atmosphere of a new world, crowded yet exciting; bleak gray skies but a bright colorful experience punctuated by more color shifts visually suggesting her innocence.

Friedkin shoots Rachel's arrival in his documentary style of following and revealing action. Rachel's discovery of so many faces, vegetable stands, clothing merchants, and finally the Minsky's Burlesque Theater, is *our* discovery. We become participants instead of merely spectators. And the attention to detail—from the ripening yellow of bananas to the furrows in the face of a beshawled crone haggling over a head of lettuce to the Minsky's marquee proclaiming "The Poor Man's Follies"—meshes with Rachel's (our) point of view on the marquee lowering to reveal Professor Spats (Bert Lahr) smoking a cigar, a white carnation in his lapel and grinning from ear to ear. He looks like a cherubic little devil about to befriend this female Candide.

The cramped spaces of crowded backstage corridors add a claustrophobia to Friedkin's cinema of immediacy as he pushes us into the theater atmosphere. Chorines bounce out of dingy dressing areas separated by hanging sheets; props carried by stagehands rush by. The stage with its narrow runway is dissected with curtains and backdrops suspended by miles of rope. Friedkin makes this atmosphere a character itself. For example, there is a scene in which Paine storms through the backstage door into the wings. Williams can be seen doing a solo skit out on stage. Paine passes so close to the camera (us) that we're backed against the wall. There's no more room as he charges by. Seething over a practical joke pulled on him by Williams that has made him late for the the performance, Paine says he's going to get "that little runt." A nervous Billy Minsky (Elliot Gould) tells him his problem is with Williams, not the show. We weave around Paine, who deftly maneuvers through the obstacle course of stacked props and stretching chorus girls as he dons his costume and makeup and tells Minsky to stop worrying. Stepping into the glow of a red stage light, Paine checks his makeup in a small mirror. Williams can be seen performing in the reflection. Paine is bathed in a red glow; the object of his anger occupies the same reflected space as his face. As he did in *Crump*, Friedkin utilizes the organic setting to accent visual statements.

Not surprisingly, the finest Friedkin moment is also the only one he says he cares for. During the lull between the afternoon and evening shows, Williams takes Rachel up on the stage where she performs her biblical dance for him. Stagehands and musicians watch her flit and float. Finishing the dance, she looks up, with the warmest smile. Williams, enamored by her beauty and wholesomeness, is the only person who doesn't walk away as if nothing had happened. He goes to her, and as the stage empties but for these two lonely figures, Friedkin slowly pulls the camera back. The darkened theater begins to envelop the stage, swallow it up, like an era drifting lovingly, sadly into memory. Friedkin foreshadows the finale of the film, the death of burlesque, with this poignant bittersweet image. The scene continues with Williams showing Rachel what burlesque is, since her dance isn't. He shows her how to shimmy; he gets his foot "caught" in a bucket and can't pull it out; he opens a prop door and "crashes" into a brick wall. Watching these pratfalls, Rachel glows with wonder and enjoyment while Williams's crush grows. Unfortunately, this wistful moment was sabotaged by the editor's splicing block. In comes ersatz sweetness: a black-and-white shot of a little boy sharing his lollipop with a little girl. This piece of ridiculousness bludgeons us. Did the filmmakers think an audience too dull to understand without this blatancy?

Aside from Friedkin's impressionistic immediacy of New York's Lower East Side and the backstage moments where he feels comfortable seeking movement in the shadows and clutter of the theater, the remainder of his (apparent) work is perfunctory, in the TV sensibility he states he so detests. For example, there is a flatness to the delicatessen scene in which Paine and Williams need a diversion to get Rachel away from Trim Houlihan (Forrest Tucker), an Irish gangster who has only a sexual interest in her. We can see waiters and customers in the background, but for such a cramped setting—a claustrophobic atmosphere—Friedkin shows none of the visual interest he demonstrated in other crowded moments. It may be due to the point of the scene. When the waiter delivers Houlihan a bagel, the Irishman objects, saying an order of bagel is not one bagel but two. The balding waiter disagrees—"new policy." Paine interjects that the waiter is cheap. Suddenly the bagel question escalates from verbal disagreement to slapstick, the waiter throwing bagels on the floor and Houlihan tossing off his clothes and jewelry, both trying to prove it's principle, not possessions, that are important. Their diversion successful, Paine and Williams manage to slip Rachel away amidst the pratfalls. The intended burlesque quality of this scene (as with most of *Minsky's* scenes) falls as flat as Friedkin's staging. In other words, scenes that appealed to Friedkin's sensibilities worked. Those that didn't seemed to have been shot with the TV sensibility of hurry up, shoot, cut.

Also, that "burlesque quality" was an obvious problem for Friedkin. The story asks us to accept that an innocent Amish girl comes to New York to dance Bible stories at Minsky's Theater, loses her virginity, finds true love, and invents the striptease all on one day. To make this whimsical farce work needed a lighter touch than Friedkin's gut-level instincts. His sense of comedy relies on cynicism, not the broad physical absurdity that is slapstick—the core of the deli scene.

Yet many of Friedkin's dramatic moments lack punch as well. When Rachel prepares to give herself to Paine, Friedkin's close-up of their first kiss is sparkless. We are not spectators or voyeurs or even involved. The seediness of Paine's hotel room, complete with a Murphy bed that slowly drops out of the wall when this single-minded rogue twists the latch, fails to elicit any inspiration from Friedkin. In *Crump*, when Fay and Crump kiss, there is an intimacy to the moment because of the dire consequences we already know will befall Crump. With *Minsky's,* one almost expects the kiss to end with Rachel or Paine's sitting on a whoopee cushion. This doesn't happen. Instead, Rachel's bearded orthodox father (Harry Andrews) has come roaring after her, having traced her to Paine's room. Paine scrambles to keep the bed upright in the wall while frantically searching for a place to hide. Though Ralph Rosenblum credits himself with saving this scene with the "shameless crutch"[18] of using Handel's "Hallelujah!" every time the bed begins to descend, the repeated hallelujahs become annoyances. They are like the repetitious use of black-and-white footage that serves to interrupt rather than, in Rosenblum's words, "mercifully sublimating the original material."[19]

The characters, too, present a problem. They function as devices rather than examples of change. Williams remains the doleful comic, Rachel's father is fanatically zealous, Houlihan's a big dumb gangster, Billy Minsky chomps cigars. These and most of the other characters in the script, though admittedly credible, lack humanness. In Friedkin's words, they are "one-liners." We do glimpse a touch of humanity in Paine when he tells Williams that women want bastards and that's why he gets them. "You're decent, devoted, and dependable," Paine tells Williams. "Good qualities in a dog, disastrous in a man." This firmly believed truism Paine sees skewered by Rachel when she takes the stage at the film's climax. In his eyes, Rachel violates her own sweet innocence, a trait alien to himself, with her strip. She's no longer different from the other women to Paine. It is in the sad disappointment on his face, watching her bump and grind across the stage, that we are witness to a rogue reformed.

But, amazingly, through the mish-mash of "looks"—the slapstick of the script, editorial gimmickry (the *only* way the "Lester look" would have worked since Lester's Beatles films rely heavily on editorial fiat), the 1925 period "look," and Friedkin's style—a theme emerges. In spite of all the cross purposes, Friedkin shows us a childlike innocence through Rachel. This innocence and its loss is the heart of *Minsky's,* no matter how inadvertently it happened. When Rachel bumps and grinds across the stage, tentatively and awkwardly at first, we see the only change in her character from the innocent abroad to celebrity showpiece. Rachel represents not so much a person but an ideal—that America's innocence was to be stripped, so to speak. When Rachel dropped her dress, society dropped the blindfold. Bawdy was now bare.

Ironically, the *visualization* of this theme utilizes the best of Friedkin's documentary style, the incorporation of black-and-white footage and the color trick. As already discussed, the arrival of Rachel at the start of the film evokes a time, atmosphere and feeling of newness. The newsreel footage establishes the festiveness of the 1920s, a more innocent, nostalgic America when fun was dancing in the streets and the latest women's fashion included the full-length bathing suit. Rachel's fresh unblemished appearance personifies that innocence as she leaves her prim black-and-white life and enters a new colorful world, every sight an enticement.

The climax of the film begins with uniformed policemen pouring into Minsky's Theater. Vance Fowler (Denholm Elliott), the snooty leader of the morals committee who wants to close the theater down because of its overt suggestiveness, believes Rachel will be performing "the dance that drove a million Frenchmen wild" because Paine has told him that Rachel is actually Mademoiselle Fifi, the hottest cootch dancer around. Paine wants to embarrass Fowler publicly. What better way, Paine believes, than to make Fowler think Rachel will do an indecent dance when she will actually dance Bible stories. Of course, Paine does not let Rachel in on the joke. With policemen swarming around, the distraught older Professor Spats goes to young Billy Minsky and tells him, "This is degrading." Spats begs Minsky to let him go out on stage and do his act. The people in the audience, he says, "They'll remember me." Minsky has his reputation with the uptown audience sitting in his poor-town theater on his mind and impatiently tells Spats to "leave me alone." A sadly touching moment, the first death toll for the old guard vaudevillians.

Rachel strips off her clothing partly by way of exerting her independence from her father but mostly because he calls her a whore. When she bares her breasts—it's an accident; she reaches her arms out to Paine whom she sees leaving the theater, and her dress drops—a new era of morality is born, and Rachel becomes an instant celebrity. Amid the newshounds and flashbulbs, Rachel is escorted out to the police paddy wagon. She smiles brightly, basking in her newfound popularity but, more importantly, unaware of her notoriety in the American psyche and society. The color trick begins. However, Rachel's warm smile appears dulled by the coarseness of black-and-white, the sparkle in her eyes dimmed.

We cut to the faces of the lowbrow audience reprised from earlier in the film. But now their fleshy faces are in black-and-white too. Though they are laughing, the only sound heard is a mournful tune. The innocuous gaiety of the times presented at the outset, exploding into the freshness of color and life, has been reversed, shrouded into a harsh, grainy black-and-white, ruddy faces turned deathly gray. One can't help but think that had the color trick and use of black-and-white been used *only* as the frame of the film, *Minsky's* would have been much more ironically effective.

The final images harken back to Friedkin's shot of Williams and Rachel alone on the stage. A forlorn Spats slowly crosses the lonely stage and picks up a seltzer bottle, an integral tool of old vaudeville. He sets it on a stepladder and exits. We cut to a high-angle shot of the empty theater, the lights lowering, enveloping the theater into a blackness—the end of an era. The closing credits roll.

This was all constructed from Friedkin's original film by others. He had the footage but not the vision. ("Hey what's the matter with you?" Paine says under Friedkin's credit. "You ain't got no feeling?") Friedkin has said that if he were to make *Minsky's* today, "with the influence I've picked up as a director, I would make it much differently, much better. And I would have found the words and the way to express myself to enforce my vision on it."

Several years and six films later, Friedkin would attempt to do that with another film about the loss of innocence, where "criminals" are cheered and adored by the crowds. The film is *The Brink's Job*, his only other period piece. But first Friedkin had to go to *The Birthday Party*.

5
The Birthday Party

"He wanted to do it, and he did it. You might
say it's easy for him to do because he made a
lot of money. No. He did it before he had the
money."

— Paul Hunter

I

When he was eleven years old and living on the North Side of Chicago,
Friedkin sold soda pop at Wrigley Field. He says he had "permission" to
work because the local ward committeeman secured jobs for children as a
payoff for getting their families to vote Democratic. "That was my earliest
brush with corruption in the political system." Friedkin says his father
never made more than $50 a week. He died when Friedkin was very
young.[1] The world Friedkin knew also included seeing "cops shoot guys in
the stomach," and though he says his curiosities went beyond that, "My influences were right there in the streets of Chicago, and that's what I know."
So, is it surprising that Friedkin asks the question "What am I doing trying
to make *The Birthday Party?*"[2]

One critic called Harold Pinter's 1958 play a "comedy of menace." Two
men, Goldberg and McCann, who work for a mysterious "organization," arrive at an English boardinghouse to take away Stanley, who is apparently
hiding out there because, also apparently, he ran out from this same "organization."

According to Friedkin, "My mother said, '*Birthday Party?* What the
hell is that?!' You know, my aunt, people I respect, would say, 'I don't
understand this picture.' I'd say, 'Hey, it's a picture about irrational fear.'
They'd say, 'Aw bullshit! Where's this who-what a cockamamie jive?' I mean
that's what people in my neighborhood said to me, and they were right. I
thought the play was fantastic. It wiped me out—five people who were
possessed of irrational fear and take it out on each other."

But Friedkin refers to his film of the play as "inept," adding, "I don't
think I was completely familiar enough with its nuances and tones. It's the

58

film of mine that I would find most difficult to watch today. It has a fine script by Harold Pinter whose mysteries are now reasonably clear to audiences, whereas they seemed befuddled by what he was doing when he wrote it in 1957. Twenty years later, it's rather conventional avant garde theater. And I don't think it should have been filmed, not by me, anyway. I'm not happy with it."[3]

But at the time, Friedkin believed he had to make the picture. "I swear to you, I thought *The Birthday Party* was going to make me a millionaire, make me so successful. People were going to be standing in line."[4]

"Nobody came," said Edgar Sherick, executive producer of this film as well as *Mrs. Soffel* (1984) and *The Taking of Pelham One Two Three* (1974). "The first day we did one hundred ten dollars worth of business. It was the worst opening day I'd ever had." He added that he did not believe that it was Friedkin's fault or anybody else's fault. "But I was proud. I think it's marvelous that that document exists because I don't think that play will be done any better. . . . Interestingly enough, we had a terrific full-page ad for the opening in the *New York Times.*"

Sherick said Friedkin did not attend the opening. "Billy Friedkin was not a name at the time. By then, *Minsky's* had opened, but Pinter, were he here, would have commanded attention. [Pinter lives in England.] I wrote to him and asked him to come over when the picture was premiering in New York. I was surprised. I got a letter from him in which he said he was very busy with work and couldn't make it. It wasn't a dismissal. It could have very easily been the fact. But I know that when he had plays open or even revivals, he had made it to New York to see how they went."

Though Friedkin had expected the picture to make him a millionaire, Sherick did not know what to expect. "It was a different world than what it is now. There seemed a broader range of acceptance then. Certainly I expected to make money, or we wouldn't have commissioned the picture. But I didn't make the picture just to make money. I made it for the same reason I make any film. I make it because it intrigues me, and I expect that if it intrigues me and the crystal rings true, that ultimately the film will be well done and make money. So making money is the last part of the chain under which I have always structured a venture.

"But I was quite shocked at the fact that nobody came to see it. Later we put it into sixteen millimeter. We took it out of release. There was no point in spending any more money. It was not a successful picture, but that's life."

When asked if he and Friedkin had any discussions about the film at this point, Sherick said, "I don't know what he felt. I think by that time Billy had gone beyond the picture." He smiled at a thought and said, "Billy said to me, 'Edgar, no matter what else you do in life, you will be immortal because your name is on *Birthday Party.*' By the time *Birthday Party* was finished, he had forgotten all about it *and* my immortality. To a young man like Billy, *Birthday Party* was the most important thing in the world—this month. So when it was done, it was done. On to the next thing."

Sherick could not recall when Friedkin "made that wonderful statement to me, but he was talking about his deep belief that he was making a document for the ages, which is terrific, by the way. I love that kind of intensity and dedication. And I went right along with him. I was waiting for immortality." Sherick laughed, looking heavenward.

Sherick had seen *Good Times* and thought it "quite good, unusual." He was certain Friedkin would translate *The Birthday Party* to the screen effectively. "Consistency is the hobgoblin of a small mind. The fact that Billy did *Good Times* well only indicated to me he would do the other well because he *wanted* to do it. If he wanted to do it and he was talented, why would I say he did a musical and therefore he should only do musicals?"

But talent and desire weren't the only forces driving Friedkin to examine irrational fear. Joe Wizan, an agent with the William Morris Agency at its Los Angeles headquarters when Friedkin arrived from Chicago (Wizan is now an independent producer), represented Friedkin and recalls him being "the most confident guy. The day before he shot the *Hitchcock Hour,* I said to him, 'Are you nervous?' He said, 'I can do this standing on my head!'"

Wizan was responsible for putting together the deal with Friedkin and Sherick, who was then president of Palomar Pictures, a subsidiary of the American Broadcasting Company. According to Wizan, Friedkin obtained the rights to a play from Pinter "for a dollar or something. Also, Pinter saw some of Billy's work and loved it." Sherick wryly recalled that "there wasn't a long line standing there to get the rights, either."

To make the film, Friedkin's approach was to rehearse it as a play for three weeks. "On Friday of the third week, we had this hall where we were rehearsing, and to an audience of one, we gave the play—Harold. One performance before lunch and one after lunch. And at the end of this performance, we were all very eager about what his reaction was going to be, the actors and myself. He had few notes, and he stood up, and he took off his glasses and said, 'Well, certainly some very interesting work is going on here. Of course, you're not doing my play.' And we all died.

"Then he read from his notes, and his notes consisted of six words that were wrong in the course of this two-hour-and-fifteen-minute play. He cited the words and what they were to be, and we laughed. 'Is that all, Harold?' And he said, 'Yes, that's all, but they have to be right. I mean, if you want to do my stuff, it's got to be verbatim.' Of course, we understood and set out to do that."[5]

There were two instances of irony to Pinter's "verbatim" dictum. The first had to do with two lines of dialogue. Friedkin said that he discovered that when Pinter first wrote the play, the Lord Chamberlain, who in effect ruled the British theater, decreed you could make no reference to either the queen of England or to the Crucifixion. "And so there were two lines in the play that were deleted that Patrick Magee, who's a great actor and who's in the film and knew this play, remembered. . . . They were lines in which one of the questions was 'Who hammered in the nails?' And the other line was 'Who drove in the screws?' These two lines refer to the Crucifixion and this man's and mankind's guilt in the Crucifixion of Christ.

"And Magee told me about those lines right in the middle of shooting. I said, 'Jesus, where the hell are these lines in the scene? They're great.' They weren't in the filmscript. So I called Harold, woke him up, and said, 'Harold, those lines! Magee told me about those lines that you had to cut.' He said, 'What?' I said, 'Who hammered in the nails? Who drove in the screws?' He said, 'I never heard those lines.' I told him they were in the original version. He said, 'Wait a minute I've got the original playscript. Let me find it.' He left the phone for about fifteen minutes. He came back and said, 'I've got the damn scene here, and those lines aren't in it.' I said, 'Oh, shit.' He said, 'Wait a minute. Do you really like those lines? You think they work?' I said, 'Work? They're fantastic! They're the best lines in the scene.' He said, 'Keep it.'"[6]

The second irony was with another line in that same scene, "What about the Albigensenist heresy?" According to Friedkin, "The Albigensian heresy refers to a religious movement in France during the Middle Ages, which Magee pointed out to Pinter, who didn't know a damn thing about the Albigensian heresy, but he heard Magee, who was his close friend, talking one night in a bar about the 'Albigensenist' heresy. He put the line in the play. . . . And Magee said in rehearsal, 'Listen, Harold, as long as we're going to do the definite version of this thing and keep it on film forever, why don't we get the thing right? It's the *Albigensian* heresy. Not the Albigensenist.' Harold said, 'Patrick, it's been wrong for ten years. Let's just leave it and get on with it.'"[7]

"Billy was very much in command of every aspect of the production," Sherick said. "Plays are subject to the interpretation of the directors and actors of the times."

The actors included Robert Shaw (*Jaws, A Man for All Seasons*), a friend of Pinter's; Patrick Magee (*A Clockwork Orange*), a drinking buddy of Pinter's; and Sidney Tafler (*The Lavender Hill Mob*), Pinter's suggestion when Zero Mostel was not available, according to Sherick. Mostel was the original choice of both Friedkin and Pinter to play the part of Goldberg, "a great comic role," Sherick said. Tafler's performance, as well as those of the other actors, are believable admist the absurdities.

However, once a film is shot, it must be edited, and for any number of reasons, whole scenes and parts of scenes are pulled out. The most common reason for deletions is to shorten the running time. For this reason, *The Birthday Party* was subjected to the splicer, and a scene in the third act of the play was eliminated from the finished film. (It had to do with a local girl named Lulu who returns to the boardinghouse after Stanley's birthday party to confront Goldberg for taking advantage of her.) Sherick could not recall any serious discussions on what went in and what went out of the film. "It was just too long. . . . I've never heard anyone get up in a theater and say they were upset because the picture was too short. I wish *Birthday Party* could have been shorter. There was no music in it, and I didn't disagree with that decision. But it was so internal, it got claustrophobic, which was one of the things you wanted it to do, but it was claustrophobic to an excessive degree. . . . That house is like a little world in which all these characters move and live. To that end Billy was successful.

"But then to say it's long is kind of nonsensical because the next part of the statement should be 'And I believe the following should be eliminated.'"

While most critics did not pick up on what had been deleted, Stanley Kauffmann, in the *New Republic* did, specifically the scene where Lulu, the local girl seduced by Goldberg, does not return after the party.

"Unfortunately the picture did not get great notices," Sherick said, "because critics are ready to jump on something easy. To them it was more the rendering of a play than it was the creation of a motion picture. I remember Judith Crist liked it. I think she liked Billy."

For the most part, critics were enamored with Pinter's dialogue, but the filmic technique was more often than not cited as the problem. The *Saturday Review* said the acting is there, the words are there, but the movie isn't. Practically all the rest take exception with Mr. Friedkin's "gimmicky" direction — *Variety, The Hollywood Reporter, Playboy, Today's Cinema.* And *Holloway's Movie Guide* calls it the "first of the black absurdities which proliferated in the 60's to general disadvantage." When told of Holloway's criticism, Sherick said, "That guy's pretty tough." When asked if he knew what Pinter thought of the film, Sherick said, "I don't know. I'm not sure what his attitude was toward it. Robert Shaw [who plays Stanley] and I worked together later on *The Taking of Pelham One Two Three*, and we were very good friends, but we never discussed *Birthday Party* much. It came up once or twice but was dismissed."

The Birthday Party was not designed to be an expensive film. "Five or six hundred thousand dollars," Sherick said. "Maybe seven." Though Sherick admitted to having certain creative disagreements with Friedkin, he quickly added that he did not believe it was "my place to say. . . . It's very difficult to shoot a picture in a room, basically. And Billy was very inventive in his setups. There was no doubt you were dealing with a major force. You knew if this guy hung around long enough, he'd have a terrific career, if he didn't self-destruct on the way. . . . Two other things about Billy: Instead of sitting around between takes like everyone else does on a set, he had a basketball hoop put up (they don't play basketball in England) and shot baskets to relax. I've never seen anybody else do it. And he took extensive notes. He prepared his work not only for each day but his overall impression of the piece. I liked that. I like a man who has enough respect for his own thoughts to write them down.

"I also named Max Rosenberg and Milton Subotsky to be the producers, which I think was a very good move. Max is a literate man, and he's had a lot of experience producing small pictures. They were horror pictures, but what's the difference? The mechanical process of producing a picture is a picture. He and Milton were two of the leading horror producers in London. Max got on famously with Pinter; got on atrociously with Billy, as I did also."

By this time, it should come as no surprise that Friedkin's arrogance was the issue. Sherick illustrated his difficulty with this aspect of Friedkin's character by relating "an allegedly true incident." He said Friedkin blatantly refused to run a sneak preview of the film in London "and was rather nasty about it." (Shortly after the release of *The Exorcist*, Friedkin emphatically stated he would never sneak a picture, that 20th Century–Fox Studios wanted to sneak *The French Connection* and he refused. However, Friedkin *did* sneak *The Brink's Job* in Long Beach, California. The reason was to get a balance for the picture audience-wise: did they want comedy or drama?) Sherick believes that people change and that it's "a long drink of water between *Exorcist* and *Brink's*." But, as far as *Birthday Party* was concerned, he and Friedkin got into a heavy argument over sneaking the film. Sherick said, "I was deeply upset and hurt by that. I felt there weren't a lot of people around who wanted to make *Birthday Party* and it took somebody with my vision and my position. Max went in to Billy after this argument and asked him why he did it. Billy said, 'I just wanted to see how mad I could get him.'"

Though Sherick says he knew Friedkin had to mature, to learn to contain "that terrible, overwhelming anger and not let it explode at innocents, people trying to help you," arrogance was not his major impression of Friedkin. Rather, it was his "terrible dedication and great talent. . . . I think he's also just come off a bad experience with Norman Lear. I do not think he had a good experience on *Minsky's*. So I think he may have been a little wounded and a little bit suspicious or uncomfortable or protective. He was very smart, very wunderkind! He was constantly into subjects you weren't even sure you were interested in, and the conversation flew from one subject to another.

"I remember walking with him all over London. He was very alert and excited. He must have sensed at that time that all that was open in front of him in terms of expressing himself. His interest was in the aberration of human nature. He was not interested in the human condition as it related to the nuclear family. He was interested, as many filmmakers are and as Pinter was on a different level, in the aberration of the human condition. That's what he gravitated toward, and you can see it in his ensuing work.

"He was a very angry young man. Don't ask me what he was angry about because it was none of my business. But he was angry in a good, pro-ductive way. Most artists are not cut from the common placid bolt of cloth. Billy was able to bring all these energies to his work. He found a means of expressing them. The most important picture he made is *French Connec-tion.* (He hasn't been too successful of late, but that is meaningless. I can remember when Sidney Lumet made ten lousy pictures in a row.) But Billy sensed the aberrancy of society, the emerging violence. It's that stuff with Doyle and 'picking your feet in Poughkeepsie.' It had a sense of where we were going. Billy was ahead of his time with *French Connection.* You can be ahead of your time and be right and be ahead of your time and be wrong."

While working in England, Friedkin had come upon another story dealing with the aberration of society and human nature, more so than *Birthday Party*'s deviations, a book entitled *The Murders on the Moor* by Emlyn Williams. Friedkin said that it "would not be an exploitation melo-drama, even though some of the sadistic atrocities will be indicated." He also believed "that the film should present a case against our permissive society which allows people to feed on pornography and sadism in maga-zines, books, and films."[8]

According to Sherick, the story was about "a man and a woman who worked in an office, who got together, attracted young children out onto the moors, took pictures of them in sexual positions, tortured them, killed them, and buried them in shallow graves. When they were caught, it was shocking because, I guess, we were not as inured as we are today by these horrible mass murders."

Friedkin wanted to make a film out of this material, and Sherick agreed to produce it. Sherick said he recognized a real dedication to the macabre in Friedkin. He said it was also "the only time in my entire experience that my management overruled me." One can easily surmise that Sherick's management believed that this was probably one of those cases of being ahead of your time and being wrong. (However, Friedkin would later do films about heinous murders growing out of an aberrant society: *Cruising,* released in 1980, and the unreleased *Rampage,* made in 1987.) And, as Sherick pionts out, "Billy is interested in violence, and *Birthday Party* is essentially a very violent play. Harold Pinter is a violent man. There is a deep, brooding anger in his plays. *Birthday Party* is a story about an ominous threat that comes onto a lower-middle-class house that presents itself in a tangible shape. It's a very threatening piece of work. Goldberg and

McCann, whatever they are, are threatening characters. And the threat of violence hangs over the piece. Even Stanley is a latently violent character. Billy liked that."

When asked if he ever discussed this particular interest of Friedkin's with him, Sherick replied, "Nathaniel Hawthorne, in his short story *Ethan Brand,* says that Brand goes out to look for the essential sin, the cardinal sin. He searches all over. He comes back and realizes that the cardinal sin is for one man to look into another man's soul. I'm not going to look into Billy Friedkin's."

II

The artist Francis Bacon finds the color of blood on pavement "invigorating . . . exhilarating." He says, "In all the motor accidents I've seen, people strewn across the road, the first thing you think of is the strange beauty—the vision of it, before you think of trying to do anything. It's to do with the unusualness of it."[9]

Friedkin's fascination with *The Birthday Party* is not unlike Bacon's perception of traffic accidents. Characters collide, but rather than blood and glass strewn across a highway, fear spills out into a claustrophobic, fatalistic world—the strange beauty of a world one cannot control. From this stems the fear of the unknown, irrational fear to Friedkin, a visceral fear. He reflects his attraction for this with a realistic style that presents Pinter's very human characters and their mundane existence not through stagebound confines but in a tiny, cluttered cinematic space. It is not so much the downstairs of a boardinghouse as it is the external trappings of dire, nonspecific, internal torment.

At first, Pinter's examination of the human condition is humorous in an unsettling way. As the film begins, the banalities exchanged by Petey (Moultrie Kelsall) and his wife, Meg (Dandy Nichols), who operate the boardinghouse are ordinary enough. Petey has just entered from setting up two more deck chairs outside. He sits to read the paper as Meg calls out from the kitchen offscreen, "Is that you, Petey? Petey, is that you? Petey?" Finally, Petey answers, "What?" "Is that you?" she calls. "Yes, it's me." "What? Are you back?" It is obvious Petey is back, and his attitude suggests his responses are quietly, stiffly conditioned to Meg's dingy banter. Common, ordinary dialogue, that is Pinter. He's writing about nothing, really, but it's funny in its human context. But just as it begins to feel as though "real life" may wear thin, Stanley (Robert Shaw), the sole boarder, appears from his upstairs bedroom, unshaven and unkempt in his pajamas. When Meg tells him two men are coming to stay for a night, Stanley's peaceful, quiet, uneventful existence is altered psychologically and physically. His wariness of two unseen strangers forces his brow to wrinkle and sweat. Stanley is hiding from something. His past? The "organization"? Himself? We do not know. To Pinter, that is not the point. To Friedkin, all that matters is that Stanley is scared.

The bizarre little universe of the film becomes pressured with the arrival of Goldberg and McCann. They represent a threat to Stanley's safe, snug, mentally crippled world. But before these two inquisitors begin their browbeating, another person from the "outside" enters Stanley's world (mind)—nonthreatening, unassuming Lulu (Helen Frazer), a local girl. Her very presence imbues the action with a triteless normalcy; maybe she's a hope for Stanley. She invites him for a picnic; she fancies him; or is it that she is simply lonely? No matter to Stanley. He's already slipping. The seams in his psyche strain under the added presence of "outsiders."

Lulu's purpose may also be to reveal Stanley's emotional emptiness as well as reinforcing (or restating) just how far he's removed himself from the outside world. When Lulu asks Stanley if he ever leaves the house, he does not answer. One can see him retreating further into himself as Friedkin builds the pressure by forcing perspective and framing angles with furniture, hanging pictures, roof beams, even Stanley's rigid posture—weighing heavily, grimly, seeming to sink into his clothing. Abruptly, Stanley asks if she would rather go away with him. "But where would we go?" "Nowhere," he answers. "There's nowhere to go. So we could just go. It wouldn't matter." She says, "We might as well stay here." "No. It's not good here." Frustrated, Lulu gives up and leaves, saying, "You're a bit of a washout, aren't you?" Stanley's world is again normal to him. By now, we feel as trapped in that room as Stanley is in his fear.

It's unity of space, that claustrophobia. The hues of grays and browns in Edward Marshall's production design, captured in Denys Coop's rich photography, make it almost comforting after a while. Like a cocoon. True, the talk, talk, talk is incessant throughout, but that's Pinter. And to "open up" the play and move scenes outdoors—and therefore outside the confines of Stanley's mind and sanctuary—would dissipate the tension Friedkin establishes. Even the moments outside at the very beginning of the film have the Friedkin stamp, which is consistent with the film. He quickly establishes a bleak lonely world with the image of four solitary deck chairs standing in contrast to a cold, gray sky. Then Petey, wearing a woolen sweater, enters the shot and sets up two additional chairs. Empty chairs for empty people living absolutely isolated lives. This image and the following one under the main title credits were not part of Pinter's original play. The cut to the credit sequence looks odd, almost out of focus. It soon becomes clear, however. This blurry image is a reflection in the rearview mirror of a moving car. We rush forward obliquely and cannot clearly see where we have been. Strange and unsettling, too, is the sound of paper slowly tearing.

What does this mean? Already Friedkin has the audience wondering, cocking their heads, as he visually and aurally draws them into the mental labyrinth of Pinter's exasperating, invigorating prose.

The more mundane dialogue works well in contrast to the series of non sequiturs that roll out during the Goldberg-McCann interrogation of Stanley. The audience, as well as Stanley, is lulled into a comfortable rut by the ordinary daily prattle. But when the charming, urbane Goldberg and a dour, hostile McCann launch into their psychological pummeling about things for which there are no answers, Stanley's mind, as well as the audience's, takes a verbal beating. Goldberg and McCann fire off questions and accusations like a malevolent "Who's on first?" version of Abbot and Costello.

"Why did you leave the organization?" McCann asks.

"What would your old mum say?" Goldberg says.

"Why did you betray us?" McCann leans in.

"You hurt me. You're playing a dirty game." Goldberg draws closer to Stanley.

"That's a black and tan fact," McCann says.

> *Goldberg:* Who does he think he is?
> *McCann:* Who do you think you are?
> *Stanley:* You're on the wrong horse.
> *Goldberg:* When did you come to this place?
> *Stanley:* Last year.
> *Goldberg:* Where did you come from?
> *Stanley:* Somewhere else.
> *Goldberg:* Why did you come here?
> *Stanley:* My feet hurt.
> *Goldberg:* Why did you stay?
> *Stanley:* I had a headache.
> *Goldberg:* Did you take anything for it?
> *Stanley:* Yes.
> *Goldberg:* What?
> *Stanley:* Fruit salts.
> *Goldberg:* Enos or Andrews?

This interrogation escalates with a twist on F. Scott Fitzgerald: Inaction is character, and character becomes brutal, physical dialogue.

"Is the number 846 possible or necessary?" asks Goldberg.

Stanley says, "Neither."

"Wrong!" Goldberg shouts. "It's only necessarily necessary! We admit possibility only after we grant necessity. It is possible because necessary but by no means necessary through possibility. The possibility can only be assumed after the proof of necessity."

"You contaminate womankind," McCann says.

> *Goldberg:*   Why don't you pay the rent?
> *McCann:*   Mother defiler!
> *Goldberg:*   Why do you pick your nose?
> *Stanley:*   I demand justice!
> *Goldberg:*   Why did the chicken cross the road?

"He wanted . . ." Stanley falters.

"He doesn't know!" McCann says.

"Which came first?" Goldberg asks.

"Chicken? Egg? Which came first?" McCann drills.

Both start asking, "Which came first? Which came first? Which came first?"

Stanley screams, and Goldberg calmly says, "He doesn't know. Do you know your own face?"

"Who are you?" McCann asks Stanley.

"What makes you think you exist?" Goldberg asks.

"You're dead," says McCann.

"You're dead," says Goldberg. "You can't live, you can't think, you can't love. . . . There's no juice in you. . . ."

They stand over Stanley, who's crouched in his chair. He looks up and savagely kicks Goldberg in the stomach. Goldberg falls. Stanley and McCann circle each other, holding chairs as weapons. Suddenly a drumbeat is heard, and Meg enters in an evening dress and, holding the drum, momentarily diffuses the tension, saying, "I brought the drum down. I'm dressed for the party." She is oblivious to any problem here.

Ironically, the birthday party of the title is Stanley's, only Stanley insists it is not his birthday. The entire proceedings of the film are focused on breaking Stanley down. Internally, Stanley's cracks are widening. The visual manifestation is best exemplified in an earlier scene when Meg gives Stanley his birthday gift: the toy drum. He stands and begins tapping it gently, marching around the table. The beat quickly turns erratic, uncontrolled, his expression savage, possessed. Can Stanley's daily routine and rituals be so easily interrupted in this frightening way by the introduction of a boy's toy? One wonders. And after Goldberg and McCann have whipped Stanley into a state of near-catatonia, poor Stanley slips into a giggling breakdown during the birthday party game of blind man's bluff.

Freshly shaved and dressed the next morning, Stanley is but a shell. Escorting him out of the house, Goldberg and McCann continue their intimidation, only now in soothing tones. They tell him, "We'll watch over you," "Advise you," "We'll make a man out of you," "And a woman." Mind games are played by everyone in this skewered little world. Meg does it to Petey because she's dingy. Stanley does it to Meg because she's gullible. Lulu and Goldberg do it to each other as verbal sexual foreplay at the party. Goldberg and McCann do it to Stanley because they've been hired to do so.

McCann plays his own game of solitaire by ripping newspaper into neat, tidy strips. (The tearing sound at the beginning of the film from inside the car!) The most frightening moment of mental combat comes at the end of the film when Petey attempts to stop Goldberg and McCann from taking Stanley. Goldberg studies Petey a moment, then says insidiously, "Why don't you come with us, Mr. Boles? . . . There's plenty of room in the car."

Certainly, the brainteasing here has a correlation to the much longer version of the good cop–bad cop interrogation methods used by police investigators. One acts friendly, the other mean. For Friedkin this foreshadows Popeye Doyle's "pick your feet in Poughkeepsie" harangue in *The French Connection*. Even Paul Crump said of his interrogation by the Chicago police that they drilled him "until even I knew the part they wanted me to play."

Friedkin conjures up a few visual moments to tease the audience too. During the party, all the lights are turned out, plunging the screen into a deep blackness. McCann shines a flashlight in Stanley's face. The scene's use of black-and-white not only intensifies Stanley's outward appearance of mental collapse, but the sharp edge to the photography makes the sequence appear otherworldly, as if Stanley had died and it's his soul emerging from the darkness. But he isn't dead. The high angles looking down from the far corners of the ceiling also force perspective for the audience: We want out of this madness but are trapped, like Stanley, in this ever-shrinking space accented by the limited movement of the camera, as well as Stanley's own crumbling psyche. This same sort of cinematic thinking was incorporated in *Citizen Kane*. Odd angles and camera moves were used by Orson Welles to establish mood and, as in *The Birthday Party*, to reflect a character's mental makeup. The opening of *Kane* pulls us closer and closer to a single lighted window high in Kane's Xanadu home. The light goes out, and we dissolve to Kane's bedroom, his prone figure silhouetted in front of the large bedroom window. Welles's opening shots show us the many possessions of a man who has everything, yet he has retreated into isolation. Outside the huge glass is nothing but the dark. Inside is nothing but Kane's dark shape, unmoving.

Given the comic absurdities in the vernacular of the ordinary, the irrational fears unleashed in spasms of violence are terrible and unexpected. Consider Stanley's kicking Goldberg in the stomach. Finally, Stanley *acts*. The savagery of the action startles since Stanley has appeared so meek. Earlier, McCann had struck Stanley a blow, sending him to his knees, when Stanley had touched him, pleading that he was not the someone Goldberg was after. But Stanley's action against Goldberg comes far too late. Poor Stanley's fears of the outside, anything beyond his mental reach, have consumed him. As Goldberg states, he is a "juiceless" man. When Stanley finally cracks at the party and stands tittering uncontrollably over Lulu, we catch a glimpse of what he may have once been: a composite of Goldberg's urbanity and McCann's dementia. More importantly, we see a portrait of Stanley, his face in motion, gleefully grotesque in the light. Will he lash out at Lulu or giggle himself into submission? It has been said that the subject of Francis Bacon's portraits is "most often the single human being . . . flayed by . . . circumstances." Sherick stated that Friedkin "was very much in command" on this production.

With Friedkin's noted interest in irrational fear and violence, *The Birthday Party*'s intensities were well suited to his skills of establishing realistic terror in a fatalistic world. When we meet Stanley, his physical size would have us believe he might be a fighter. He claims to be a pianist. Somehow (we're never sure how), his fears have beaten and overwhelmed him into hiding rather than setting him into action. Stanley's single act of aggression against Goldberg is but the last hurrah. Though Stanley and McCann then menace each other with chairs, Friedkin's composition of the moment utilizes an angle to include the ceiling, compressing the action within the frame, limiting space even more. Stanley's world closes in.

An intriguing aspect of Pinter's play and of many of Friedkin's films is the poised knife. In *The Birthday Party*, there is no holy order to the world, no rhyme or reason to the lives we watch. This builds the levels of tension and suspense. People are trapped: Meg and Petey in their dull lives, Stanley by his unknown fears, McCann in his violent ignorance, even Goldberg, who begins to unconsciously tear down his personal facade, saying he always did what he was told, never sick a day in his life, kept his eye on the ball. He sounds like a cog in a machine, but the cog sounds worn. The irony is that he has come to make a new man of Stanley, reintegrate him. Stanley has broken down on himself, while Goldberg needs to remind himself that he is worthwhile.

It's funny and tragic at the end of the film when Petey calls out in a whimper to the emotionally empty Stanley, "Don't let them tell you what to do." Yet the psychological violence of this film is as astonishing and visceral as Paul Crump's interrogation. There's a random quality to it. The threat is ever-present, like a knife waiting to fall. But hanging on it, building the tension, is what Friedkin excels at in visually telling his story. It provokes immediate gut-level reaction. You don't know when the knife will fall. In *The French Connection*, when Popeye Doyle is walking home and suddenly a couple of shots ring out, a woman walking past him falls dead, and all Doyle knows is that someone is trying to kill him. No warning. During the interrogation in *Birthday Party*, Stanley finally realizes Goldberg and McCann are a threat more ominous than he originally thought. They mean to do him harm, to take him out of his sanctuary. So he lashes out in an attempt to save himself. Or is it simply an involuntary reaction? No matter.

A psychological death awaits him even worse than the one he's already subjected himself to.

The surprise is a violent one, a latent one. The audience reacts. Friedkin has succeeded. He has drawn us in to a kind of twilight zone where there is really no sanctuary. Stanley merely exists on the edge, as do Doyle and Crump. In their own fashion, all three are playing a kind of jump rope on a razor. Doyle's obsession is to catch the bad guys. Crump's is to save his own life. Stanley wants to be left alone. The difference, though, is that Stanley is a traffic accident that has already happened. The fascination in this aberration for Friedkin is not watching Stanley fight the fight, as Doyle and Crump do, but how, or if, Stanley crawls away from the accident.

6
The Boys in the Band

"I had no particular desire to make a film
about homosexuals. It was just the best script
to come to me at that time."
—William Friedkin[1]

I

With *The Birthday Party* relegated to the "nickel and dime business"
of the college circuit, as Edgar Sherick called it, and finding little interest
from producers for *Murders on the Moor,* Friedkin's exploration of human
aberration in such physically violent terms would have to wait. Enter Mart
Crowley, whose play *The Boys in the Band* had become an Off Broadway
success. Like *Birthday Party, Band* deals in psychological brutality. But
unlike Pinter's play, the birthday party in Crowley's story is thrown by seven
homosexuals for their gay friend Harold. An unexpected guest arrives—the
former college roommate of the party's host, who may or may not have a
yen for the gay life. Between the pot and the booze, the bitchy backbiting
humor turns ugly, ominous. A humiliating "truth" game ensues, with the
guests telephoning the one person they have ever loved and telling him so.
Guilts and revelations are exposed.

As Michael, the host, tells his straight friend Alan, "It's like watching
an accident on the highway—you can't look at it, and you can't look
away."

Crowley said he wrote the play in the summer of 1967, which was a
very low ebb in his life. He'd been fired from a number of film jobs in
Hollywood. Once the play became a hit, however, major film companies approached him about purchasing it. Paramount Studios lost out because they
had fired Crowley the year before. "It was, in fact, the very same man who
had dismissed me who came to buy the play," Crowley said. Big-name stars
were also interested in it, such as Warren Beatty and Kirk Douglas,
Crowley added, "but I decided that I wanted to produce it, and everyone
else thought I was nuts, and no one would come across with the money."

(Crowley says his friends also thought he was nuts when he told them what his play was about in the first place.)

Finally, the CBS television network, which was developing films through their Cinema Center Films wing, put up the money, gave Crowley his producer deal, agreed to use the original cast, and allowed Crowley the choice of director with their approval.

Crowley said he knew he would need help and went to Dominic Dunne, a producer at Four Star Productions who had befriended him when Crowley wrote a television pilot for Bette Davis that was shot but never sold.

With Dunne keeping "a paternal eye out for the production as executive producer," Crowley said he still needed to find a director. (Robert Moore, who had directed *Band* on the stage, had no filmic background.) "It had been by accident that I had seen *Birthday Party*," Crowley said. "It was a little coincidental because 'Birthday Party' happened to have been one of the titles that I would have used for *Band*. I had read about this play, and I thought, 'Oh shit, there's my title gone.'" But he thought *Birthday Party* was exceptionally directed particularly since it was not, in Hollywood terminology, opened up. Crowley's idea for filming *Band* was not to breathe air into it by putting in scenes in parks and automobiles, dramatizing the other ends of the "truth" game telephone conversations or flatly photographing the play. "I wanted the camera to whiz around the room and to be on everybody almost simultaneously, and you get into these people and into the ambience and claustrophobia. I also thought all that could be promoted by what I did with the screenplay, which was to pull some of the opening lighter sections out onto the terrace at night and then have the rainstorm pending, which later pushes everybody back into the living room, sopping wet, disheveled, uncomfortable, and really trapped."

In Crowley's view, Friedkin had injected an "infinite visual variety" into *Birthday Party* while maintaining a literal translation as well as extracting performances of extraordinary quality. "And I knew Pinter had said some very wonderful things about Billy's work."

Another coincidence was that Dominic Dunne knew Friedkin because Friedkin had filmed *The Pickle Brothers* for Four Star Productions. Crowley said he and Friedkin met, "hit it off as great as any two people can, and he more or less agreed totally with what I wanted to do."

Was Friedkin hesitant about translating another play to film?

According to Crowley, Friedkin was not. "I began to discuss pictures with him that had been made in a certain way that had influenced me. The Hitchcock film *Rope* influenced the writing of the play."

Friedkin had also seen *Rope,* which was loosely based on the Leopold and Loeb murder case. In *Rope,* two men murder their friend, put his body in a chest, and then serve cocktails and dinner to his parents off it. "*Rope*

had a Greek unity to it," Crowley said. "It takes place in the time it takes
to play, and Billy and I decided *Band* would roll that same way, too. We
started to make the picture . . . and little by little I began to see that Billy
had a temper and that certainly it was beginning to reflect itself on the
set."

William C. Gerrity, first assistant director on *Band* who would repeat
those chores on *The French Connection,* said, "A lot of guys had problems
with Billy because they thought he thought he knew everything, or at least
presented that facade. I got along with him because I called him on it a couple of times and said, 'Maybe I know my job just as well as you know yours.'
Maybe that helped our relationship."

"There were times you didn't know when he'd be set off," said Peter
White, who played Alan, the straight friend. "I can remember him getting
furious at crew members. He was very impatient. He wanted things his
way."

So how did Friedkin communicate with the actors, all of whom were
the original cast members from the stage play?

According to Frederick Combs, who played Donald, the host's lover,
"When we began, we needed confidence because we were stage actors
predominantly about to appear in our first film, as opposed to Billy, who
worked with actors and actresses who've made their livelihood in film."

"Any expression that's exaggerated that might do well on stage
becomes overexaggerated on film, especially in a close-up," Gerrity said.
"You don't, as they say, 'shoot your wad in the first scene.' Theater people
are used to a continuous performance, so they build. In film, it's more
difficult. So it was more demanding on Billy to get a credible job from
them."

While Hitchcock was famous for referring to actors as cattle, White
said Friedkin used to comment that "he'd rather work with tree stumps than
actors. . . . I think he was intimidated by the fact that we had been with
this play a long time and knew it an awful lot better than he did. Also, we
had Bob Moore directing us on stage, who is a strong actor's director. Billy
wasn't. He was a technical director."

"I really didn't realize it until we were in production," Combs said. "It
was a new experience for me to see my director suddenly consumed by the
technical problems of putting it on. In the theater we don't have that. Billy
became obsessed by *how* a scene was going to be worked out, how dailies
were coming out, what the lighting for the camera would be, different
setups. On stage, as actors, we're used to the director spending all his time
trying to make the moment come true, to make us comfortable in the part.
When Billy first met with us, he explained we were going to have a rehearsal
period of two weeks. This made us feel even more comfortable with him.
The trick with most actors is, when in doubt, tell them how wonderful they

are. Billy was very supportive in that area. He made us play realistically for the camera instead of playing up; let the moment happen instead of over-doing it."

Explaining Friedkin's film technique, Gerrity said that as opposed to some directors, Friedkin "likes to do the majority of things on the set like setting up the shot from the inception of saying what lens he wants to use, how he's going to do it with a dolly or whatever, and the background action. Now, until Billy and I had a meeting of the minds where he allowed me to function with my background action, which is my job so he could concentrate on his principles, he would've liked to do the entire world by himself. Some directors would come to you and say, 'I don't have too much. Would you help me?' Billy's line was 'I know it, and I can do it, and I don't want to make mistakes.' I had to confront him at times and say, 'You can't do it all by yourself.'" Gerrity cited the scene where Emory walks his poodle while cruising the street hustlers, sizing them up and picking one out as Harold's "present." It was a street scene filmed during the Christmas rush. "I had about fifty or sixty extras to line up, and Billy was saying 'Come on, we gotta go.' I'd been waiting for the cameraman for about an hour. Billy said, 'We gotta go, now.' I said, 'Well, I'm not ready.' He said, 'We're going.' I said, 'You'll have to go without me because I'm not ready, and neither is my background.' He said, 'Well, I'm not going to wait for you.' I said, 'You waited an hour for the cameraman, you can wait ten minutes for me.' So I took a little walk. We cooled off. But Billy is not one to apologize outwardly to anybody, but I think later on he did. It was under the pressure of this whole thing and Christmas time and the nervousness and the streets of New York packed with shoppers that created all the havoc."

Speaking of havoc, Friedkin fired the film's first cinematographer, Adam Hollander (who photographed *Midnight Cowboy* the previous year), either after the first week, first day, or first twenty minutes—Crowley couldn't remember exactly. And no one could recall the exact circumstances, but Gerrity said one of the major causes was over a scene in the apartment. "Billy wanted to get back against the wall with a very wide angle lens. Adam said he didn't know where he was going to put his lights. Billy said to find a place. Adam said he couldn't. It went back and forth. Finally, Adam and his crew went."

When it happened, Combs said, the cast "began to wonder, what does this mean, he messed up the picture? When things weren't done technically, we saw Billy flair up on the set and always toward the technical crew. He got very short sometimes with a few of us, but it was over in a flash. It was almost like he knew it was better to get off the actors."

"Billy was hard," Gerrity said. "He likes complete consistency of quiet on his set, and sometimes in New York you do get a noisy set. I don't blame Billy. I agree with any director who needs that total concentration."

But the buildup of tension needed release. Gerrity believed Friedkin broke his own tension. "He would have a basketball net set up someplace and throw off some of that energy by throwing the ball through the hoop." (Recall that Friedkin did the same thing in England during *Birthday Party*.) However, relieving tension on the set was another matter. Gerrity recalled an instance where Friedkin "came to me and said, 'Tell me when you're ready after the cameraman lights the set.' I told him okay and got it all lined up with the cast and the crew that when he was about to come up the stairs, I'd be behind the camera. As he reached the top of the stairs, I said, 'Cut. That's beautiful. Let's print that.' I thought Billy would have a fit. He thought I'd shot a scene without him. But then when everybody laughed, it was a good moment. Those kind of things were necessary."

Considering Friedkin's previous dealings with producers (the tirades with Mel Stuart at Wolper Productions, Edgar Sherick's recollections on *Birthday Party*), his dealings with Crowley were quite congenial. Crowley said he had a reputation himself at that time. "I would turn on somebody and wipe the floor up with them. I think that Billy had heard some of these stories about me, and when we started the picture, he came up to the hotel room one night after rehearsal or shooting some tests—maybe Adam Hollander was fired during the tests—and he said, 'We gotta make a pact with each other. Whatever we feel, no matter how intensely we feel about it, let's not blow our tops at each other in front of everybody.' I said, 'Great. I promise to keep the lid on. I'll wait until we're back in the office.' He said he'd do the same, and we really stuck by this. The fact was that we really didn't have any terrible scenes, even behind closed doors. And I never saw him blow up at people on the stage in front of me, but I heard stories. I mean, why would anybody make them up? Sometimes at the dailies I couldn't go or he couldn't go, so we'd watch them at different times. But I heard there would be things about the sound or the camera operator wouldn't follow somebody or the focus puller wasn't right. I heard these stories about how he would jump up in the middle of dailies and scream and rant and rave like a maniac. I heard this from people I trusted. But I never saw it. Sometimes the atmosphere between us got kind of thick. Especially in the cutting room. Later on, he didn't want me around during the dub at all."

Upon its release, the *New Yorker* called *The Boys in the Band* "a theater piece that has lost its theatrically satisfying form."[2] *Variety* said it "drags," but added there is a "perverse interest."[3] The *Los Angeles Times* hailed it as "unquestionably a milestone" because of its unabashed use of four-letter words not uttered in films before; however, "the events seem contrived," and "the anguish somehow diminished."[4] *Time* believed the film "suffers slightly from 'opening up' the work to include exteriors and reaction shots" but concluded by saying, "If the situation of the homosexual is ever to be understood by the public, it will be because of the breakthrough made by this humane, moving picture."[5]

"Billy really didn't have the sense of humor that Robert Moore did on the stage," Crowley said.

Peter White recalled that people left the play laughing and it would hit them several hours later what they'd been laughing at. "The film was much more honest, much more depressing, than the play."

"I thought it was almost disastrous when I saw a cut of it because I thought he brought up all the melodrama and let the comedy go right out the window," Crowley said. "He brought out a real dark underbelly. There was probably that underbelly there to be brought out, but what I wanted to do with the play was to try to hold down the sentimentality and melodrama, the turgid unhappiness of it all, and try to mask it with at least a surface veneer of humor. Billy began to scrape that veneer and just gouge into whatever was down below." For example, Harold refuses to play the "truth" game and sits off in a corner thumbing through a book on the films of Joan Crawford. Friedkin subtly adds an ingredient of black humor by allowing the audience a peek at the photo on the cover of the book, which shows Crawford with a terrified look on her face, the back of her hand covering her mouth, as if she is aghast at the degeneration of the party. This visual commentary is not comedy. (Recall Bud Yorkin's statement that comedy is not Friedkin's forte.) As Crowley said, Friedkin exposes the darkness of the play. Many of Harold's bitchy comments in the film's second half become throwaway lines. His dryly saying "I for one need an insulin injection" after listening to Emory's pitiful tale of unrequited love loses its punch, for Friedkin prefers to linger on the "accident," the Truth in the aberration. Crowley admits there were "things on the stage that could never be translated onto the film with the same impact. The dance with Alan approaching, that sense of it all happening at once is still okay in the film, but it didn't build up this hysteria in the audience because on stage they could see the banana peel and they saw the fucking slip, too.

"I just felt the play at its worst is in its most sentimental moments. Fortunately, through a lot of editing that was necessary, even though it's a two-hour movie, half an hour of the script is cut because of length. Just that very pretty visual opening of introducing the nine people coming from different directions takes up enough time to knock out quite a few pages, thank God."

Friedkin's montage introduction is masterful in its *visual* simplicity, underscored with Cole Porter's camp classic "Anything Goes" establishing a light, breezy mood. Dozens of open jars of salves, creams, and ointments reflected in a mirror crowd a bathroom sink. The camera pans to reveal a hand soaping a hairy leg. This, we will later realize, is Harold (Leonard Frey), a self-described "thirty-two-year-old, ugly, pock-marked Jew fairy." Michael (Kenneth Nelson), wearing tight pants and a blazer, shops only at the finest stores in Manhattan. Poor Donald can't afford books, so when he enters Doubleday's bookseller carrying a package wrapped in Doubleday's paper, his friend Bernard (Reuben Greene), who works there, pulls a quick swap with a larger package that Donald scoops up. At a gym, Hank (Laurence Luckinbill) plays basketball. Larry (Keith Prentice) moves about his photography studio, snapping pictures of women for a fashion layout. A troubled-looking Alan steps off an airplane. Effeminate Emory purses his lips at Cowboy (Robert La Tourneaux) while "shopping" for Harold's present. "Heaven knows, anything goes!" It's cinematic, presenting the characters in *action,* a Friedkin trademark; the kind of "opening up" Crowley wanted.

Crowley also recalled eliminating many of the self-pitying speeches and many of the jokes. "Some good stuff had to go with the bad."

There was also an important structural addition to the film. Shortly after the arrival of Alan, a rainstorm forces the "boys" off the terrace and into the apartment where the telephone "truth" game begins.

Combs said he personally would not have stayed to play the game, so he had to invent internal reasons for his character to remain there in the original play. However, with the rainstorm there was a physical reason to stay, and Friedkin's ideas of the lights and decorations falling apart and crashing down with the partygoers forced inside were "very actable— almost like he had been an actor. For an actor it's tremendous because you can then place a lot of trust in the director."

Also, understanding the subject matter builds trust. According to Combs, there was very little conversation, if any, about Friedkin's beliefs or perceptions of the material, but he added, "I knew at the time Billy was doing some research, if it was nothing more than going to Fire Island for the weekends and just watching groups of homosexuals."

White recalled hearing the same thing.

"That seemed very admirable because I would always assume that as an actor I would do my research work. The same with a director," Combs said.

Friedkin made *Band* "a bit more decadent," White said, and recalled the sequence that begins with the rainstorm and everyone's rushing to clear the terrace, getting wet, some laughing and others griping, to illustrate his comment. A stoned and grinning Cowboy walks through the apartment, holding a sheet of red cellophane wrapping paper in front of his face while he surveys the couples dancing to Burt Bacharach's "The Look of Love" and Harold sprawled on the couch, giggling. The cellophane drops from Cowboy's hands and floats languidly to the floor. He crawls under the glass coffee table and is entranced with his distorted reflection in a colored crystal egg, which he toys with as Friedkin slowly pushes in to a close-up on him.

We have a tendency to forget, Combs said, that in the late 1960s, when the play was produced, and in 1970, when the film was released, "homosexuality was not a popular bandwagon to crawl onto." When he read the play in 1968, Combs thought it was dated, "but the rest of the country didn't think so. People seem to forget that Mart never said that it is the universal homosexual experience. It was a section out of life at a certain time, that's all. I was impressed with Billy for having the courage to direct it and being secure enough in his own sexuality so it's no big deal."

But what of Friedkin's vision of Crowley's story?

Combs recalled that Irving Lee Penn photographed the cast for a *Look* magazine layout. "He met with each of us for about a half hour before he photographed us separately. He said he wanted to get the true inner feeling of us. We eventually came to find out what he meant when we saw the pictures. They looked like they were pictures taken just before we were to be electrocuted. It didn't take long for me to understand that Mr. Penn obviously thought that we were such tragic figures. I felt very upset by that. The photographs were indeed sad and forlorn pictures, and I had a feeling that in the last half of our film that happened also. When you have a camera coming down on you and that scene is just total despair, you finally think, 'Well, why not just go out and kill yourself?' That was someone's conception of how they saw it, and I would assume it was the director's."

"I can understand Billy's evolution into this more macabre and morbid frame of mind," Crowley said. "There's a kind of dark beauty to it . . . . And you can see there's not a lot of laughs there . . . . He probably has grown to identify with Francis Bacon, who I find just a terribly tortured genius. I hope Billy doesn't see himself that way."

II

The aberration that Friedkin dissects in *The Boys in the Band*, using camera rather than scalpel and shadows instead of anesthetic, is a brutality coupled with enormous tenderness, neatly summed up by Michael when he says, "You show me a happy homosexual, and I'll show you a gay corpse." The "boys" in *Band* are very much aware of their fears. They need no Goldberg and McCann to dredge them up, for these "sons without a mother," as Proust called homosexuals, confront their fears every time they look in the mirror. And it is through the mirror that Friedkin explores the dark underbelly of Crowley's story. Friedkin is looking for the Truth: What do these eight men know? Why are they the way they are? Because homosexuality and expletives had not been so pointedly and openly dealt with in a mainstream picture before (Michael and Donald bandy words like "cunt" and "prick" around as backhanded terms of affection), Friedkin's

The Boys in the Band. The "boys" in *Band:* Starting at left, Hank (Laurence Luckin-bill), Donald (Frederick Combs), Emory (Cliff Gorman), Cowboy (Robert La Tourneaux), Larry (Keith Prentice), Michael (Kenneth Nelson, seated on couch), Harold (Leonard Frey), Alan (Peter White), and Bernard (Reuben Greene). This is *not* a scene in the film.

style appears more effective. We are not *aware* that we are witness to an accident because he stages the story not to make a collision obvious but rather to present normalcy in an askew world where collision will be inevitable.

Through the opening montage, with the exception of Emory's bla-tancy, the "boys" all seem "normal" enough; an unthreatening world. Then the perverse fascination begins—appropriately enough, since it is also a social world presented in the film—with eye contact. Donald tells Michael he was raised to be a failure because it pleased his mother and upset his father; failure is all he feels comfortable with in his life. Donald's oblique eye contact with Michael tells him, and us, that is why he is with Michael. Friedkin cuts from Donald's look to Michael's reaction. The looks tell all. Shortly, Michael bemoans being gay without flatly stating it: amidst all the one-night stands, the booze and traveling around the world, "the only place I've ever been *happy* was on the goddamn plane. . . . Waste, waste, waste." He gazes at the portrait of himself while uttering those last three words.

Certainly the dialogue explains the character, but by framing Michael within his own portrait—an unchanging mirror, a constant reminder of yesterdays never to return—Friedkin reveals a dying soul. Even Alan, who Michael says wouldn't show any emotion even in a plane crash, evokes sympathy—and suspicion in Friedkin's vision. Alan breaks down crying while talking to Michael, practically begging him to let him come over; desperate, he needs to talk. After Alan hangs up, he clasps his hands together, revealing his gold wedding band. By holding on this image a few extra beats, Friedkin visually plants doubt in the viewer's mind regarding "straight" Alan's reason to see his friend.

What we quickly discover, through Crowley's biting realistic dialogue and Friedkin's direct style, are not deviates but human beings filled with passions, doubts, guilt. Especially guilt. When Michael is lambasted at the end of the party by Harold, it's a significant moment of truth, for Michael, a pessimist who sees the world (his world?) only in hopeless terms. "You are a sad and pathetic man," Harold tells him. "You're a homosexual, and you don't want to be. But there is nothing you can do to change it." And Emory, initially the flaming stereotype, reveals the pain behind the lisp when he talks about the dentist he fell in love with while he was still in high school. Emory told him he wanted him to be his friend and then later, at the prom, heard several girls giggling over his "funny secret." At this moment, Emory is as helplessly human as anyone we have seen in a Friedkin film since Paul Crump. Cynical Harold says he would gladly sell his soul for some "skin-deep, transitory, meaningless beauty." Hank and Larry are battling lovers. Larry wants to be free to see other men. He loves Hank, but Hank insists on a one-to-one relationship. It's not a titillating freak show. Their fears are universal and understandable. Michael does not like what he is, Emory's feelings are trampled, Donald can't lift himself from failure, and Harold fights a self-inflicted battle with his own narcissism.

And Friedkin records it all coolly, almost dispassionately, as if he were a silent and unseen guest at Harold's party. Curiously, that impartiality evokes tremendous involvement, for it passes no judgment. As his documentary work taught him, Friedkin simply records the facts. Plays have no profound imagery. The audience watches the actors, and there is a spontaneity to it. In films, the camera totally controls what the audience sees. When Friedkin moves his camera and covers numerous angles, the edited scene appears seamless. For example, near the start of the film, Michael, arms loaded with packages, is trying to get into his apartment where the telephone is ringing. He can't get the key in the lock, and that ringing becomes an incessant irritant. Quick jerky movements in close-up on the keys in his hand, Michael's face, and the lock effectively build the tension, not unlike the interrogation scene in Crump with close-ups on fists and faces.

The Boys in the Band. Emory (Cliff Gorman, left) greets Bernard (Reuben Greene) while Hank (Laurence Luckinbill) looks on.

This moment also prepares an audience for the claustrophobia to come, for the visual structure of the film is like a funnel. When the partiers perform a Rockettes highstep to the song "Heat Wave" before Alan's unexpected late arrival, Friedkin glides the camera around them, isolating faces and body movements. We feel we are part of the chorus line. But, as with Michael's fumbling for his keys or everyone's dancing on the terrace, there is a cramped, claustrophobic feeling. Friedkin narrows the funnel once the boys are forced inside the apartment after the cloudburst. When a hostile, drunken Michael starts the "truth" game, his apartment becomes terribly stifling; everyone is damp, drunk, and sweaty, which adds to the closeness. One gets the feeling you can smell them. Sets of track lights are switched on, which suddenly gives the uncomfortable appearance of a police station interrogation. Darkened ceilings and rain-splattered windows further compress the action. It is like being trapped in a Francis Bacon painting where "there is always his immense coiled vitality and the discovery of unexpected insight . . . and, as time goes by, there is a certain calm. We are still absolutely walled up in our own madness, but after a while it seems acceptable."[6]

The Boys in the Band. **A drunken Emory (Cliff Gorman) prepares to call his one true love during the "truth" game.**

We have become comfortable in the shadows Friedkin shoots from, while witnessing doubt escalate as to Alan's sexual preference, Hank and Larry's edging toward physical violence, and the fissures widening in Harold and Michael's love-hate relationship.

It is also at this moment, when the "truth" game begins, that Friedkin is at his most effective. While Pauline Kael in the *New Yorker* objects to Friedkin's "long see-the-suffering-in-the-face close-ups,"[7] it is the close-up that is *the* statement of movies. The screen is filled with what may be the most intense image possible, whether it be a kiss or looking down the barrel of a gun. That Friedkin uses close-ups during the "truth" game when the guests call the one person they have ever loved adds emphasis to the caller's vulnerability. For example, when Emory telephones the dentist, we feel his bittersweet joy when he says, "Del, is this really you?" And his sadness, admitting, "You wouldn't remember me. I'm just a friend. A falling-down drunk friend." As Friedkin pushes in for a close-up, aided by Arthur Ornitz's beautifully dark photography, he isolates the caller in a crowded, claustrophobic room, just as Francis Bacon enhances "the drama of absolutely isolated lives" in his portraits.[8]

The Boys in the Band. Alan (Peter White) waits pensively for his old college friend
Michael to answer the telephone.

By admitting their innermost secrets and fears, the boys strip away the
layers, revealing truth in this game that Donald states is like murder—
"somebody gets killed." It's death in the psychological sense; brutally baring
the soul in close-up, exposing a tenderness within. Bernard refuses to admit
to the mother of the man he calls why he's calling and then drinks himself
into a stupor to hide his shame. Hank and Larry reach an understanding
that they may be able to live with and go up to the bedroom to be alone
with each other. And Alan, goaded by Michael, who believes him to be a
"closet queen" who was secretly in love with a mutual male college friend
of theirs but couldn't admit it, calls his wife and makes amends to her.

Michael is left stung at this revelation in his life where he was convinced he was entirely, faultlessly correct in his appraisal of Alan. It is here
Harold tells Michael that he will always be a homosexual, "always, until the
day you die." Brutal, yes. But there is an honest tenderness in Harold's
words, delivered matter-of-factly. That Friedkin stages this moment with
Harold first approaching Michael, who stares out a window silently crying,
and then isolates the two of them in frame adds to their unspoken yet

implicit closeness. A collision, yes. Michael and Harold's cynical barbed views of the same world whip us and the other boys along. While Michael hates himself and tries to drag everyone else down with him, Harold sums up his outlook as he enters the apartment and is presented with Cowboy, his present. Michael demands to know "What's so fucking funny?" over Harold's whiny laughing, to which Harold responds, unintimidated, "Life. Life is a goddamn laff-riot."

While the film itself acts as a mirror for examining ourselves, the mirrors in the film serve organic purposes. They reflect the implied narcissism in the gay lifestyle. Michael combs his hair numerous times early in the film, before a mirror. Harold's physical appearance is his main topic of interest. Upon cleaning up his bloody lip after his brawl with Alan, Emory checks his face in the reflection and says, "I'm not ready for my close-up, Mr. De Mille." But in the strictly visual sense, Friedkin utilizes mirrors to "open up" the story. In the scene where Michael fumbles for his keys and bursts through the door, he runs past the camera, which pans him into his apartment. He dashes around the corner out of sight into the kitchen to answer the telephone. But we see him reflected in the living room mirror. We notice it only *because* of his sudden reflection in it. Friedkin stages the shot with Michael disappearing off one side of the screen and reappearing in the reflection on the other side. The director simultaneously "opens" the film but also emphasizes the impending claustrophobia since we are only allowed to glimpse a tiny fraction of the kitchen. He "opens it up" while closing it in.

Conversely, in the scene where Alan calls Michael the second time, Alan stands in a phone booth, the lights of the city reflected in the glass all around him. Yet Friedkin frames the shot so that Alan's reflection is unseen in the four walls of glass. And when he hangs up, we cut outside the booth to include a flashing yellow warning light in the foreground. We pan with Alan until the light disappears out of frame, but then he crosses in front of the headlights of a car. There's a prism effect, resulting in a red spiraling light zeroing in on him as if he were a target. It is also implicit of the random violence in Friedkin's films. When Harold opens Michael's birthday gift, we are in close on Harold. We never see the gift, but Harold says it's a photograph of Michael with an inscription. It's something personal, and the tension between the two men is momentarily dissipated. Friedkin frames them both in separate close-ups, a stylized claustrophobia exposing their tenderness, relieving the unhappiness. But only momentarily. The tension builds again, and no one knows when it will explode or who will be hit with the verbal shrapnel. It's a roller coaster ride created by Crowley's scathing dialogue and Friedkin's technique of moving in for the kill.

7

The French Connection

"I know about people in cities. I remember
stories about Chicago that haunt me, and I
used to see cops shoot guys in the stomach
and holster their guns, and you'd never read
about it in the newspaper."
— William Friedkin[1]

I

"The French Connection has a street language no one can write,"
Friedkin has said of his Academy Award–winning film. But before he began
shooting, Friedkin ("a street kid filmmaker" according to assistant director
William C. Gerrity) also realized that the story, based on Robin Moore's
book, "needed a flavor." That flavor took the form of Eddie Egan and Sonny
Grosso, the two detectives who actually made the French connection bust
in 1962 and on whom Gene Hackman and Roy Scheider based their characters. "Egan's and Grosso's nicknames were Popeye and Cloudy," Friedkin
said. "Some names are like poetry. That triggered me."[2]

Philip D'Antoni, the film's producer (he did *Bullitt* in 1968), knew the
detectives and also knew Friedkin because they played basketball together
at the Paramount gym. When D'Antoni and Friedkin decided to make the
picture, the producer introduced the director to the detectives. Friedkin
then strapped on a .38 pistol and spent months going around with Egan,
Grosso, and Randy Jurgensen, another detective who helped bust the
French connection.

Jurgensen said Friedkin wanted to "check out the details" before
shooting the film. The three detectives took him to shooting galleries. One
was on 126th Street. "Afterwards, Billy said, 'My God. To think I live six
minutes from here.' He'd never seen that." What Friedkin saw were "the
dregs of life," Jurgensen said, where "twenty or thirty human beings are in-
jecting themselves with heroin in squalor that I could not describe to
you . . . . No matter where you think you've seen needles in people, you have

86

not—under the tongue, swollen veins in the vagina, between the toes. Now, Billy went right in like he was a detective. He was, if not the second man through the door, the third when we went in."

Friedkin said he intended *French Connection* as a police procedural film. "There was no script to the picture. It was all ad-libbed dialogue from my experiences and later, the experiences of Hackman and Scheider with the actual cops."[3]

When asked about his battle with Ernest Tidyman over screen credit—a credit Tidyman won in arbitration with the Writer's Guild as well as winning an Academy Award—Friedkin dismissed his writing as inconsequential.[4]

"His script was a fucking joke," said Thomas Rand, the film's location manager who goes by the moniker Fat Thomas. "We used to shake our heads about it. It was not a cooking script. It wasn't moving. Tidyman had the basic stuff from the book in it."

Tidyman chose not to answer questions regarding Friedkin or the film.

D'Antoni had urged Friedkin to read Moore's book before meeting Egan and Grosso. Friedkin said he read eight pages, fell asleep, saw D'Antoni the next day and told him, "Let's make it."[5]

Though Friedkin insisted the film was "calculated to entertain,"[6] Jurgensen believed Friedkin accomplished much more. "Billy exposed that a police officer's problems are not only dealing with crime in the street and dealing with the public but dealing with a system that physically chokes him off from doing his job. He shows the frustration of Doyle, his removal from the case, priorities in other areas. The audience was so for Doyle and Russo because they saw that these guys are not invincible, that they are human."

D'Antoni added that the energy in the picture "is unbelievable. Some say it comes from the city of New York. That's bull. I've seen pictures done in New York that don't have it. Some say it's because of Gene Hackman. That's a lot of bull because Gene, while a terrific actor, at many times lacked the energy. Billy would just get it out of him."

"Each actor requires a different technique," Friedkin said. "Hackman and I fought almost all through *French Connection*. I provoked him because he hated Doyle. He backed away from the brutal aspect of him. Scheider responded to encouragement and to his character. But I became an object of a lot of Hackman's antagonism."[7]

Gerrity recalled there were times Friedkin tried to overdirect Hackman. He cited the scene "where Hackman watches the Frenchman eat in a little restaurant. God, it must have been zero degrees. Gene had only a coat and his Popeye hat on. Billy said to him, 'Now, Gene, remember, it's cold here. You gotta act cold.' Gene said, 'No, Billy. Tell me.' Billy was about to start telling him but realized he was being put on because everybody was freezing their butt off at that moment."

The French Connection. Popeye Doyle (Gene Hackman, left) and Cloudy Russo (Roy Scheider) "interrogate" a pusher (Alan Weeks) before arresting him.

There was also the scene in which Doyle and Russo grill the black pusher in the alley, D'Antoni said. "They worked that for the better part of a day or two, and it was horrible. Billy and Gene were both upset. They were both separately and secretly telling me how terrible each other was in the thing. Now Billy, like a lot of people, has a certain stubborn streak in him. I think that stubbornness rubbed against Gene."

"It was the first time I had ever worked with Hackman, and it was the first scene we came to shoot," Friedkin said. "I had staged the scene as it usually takes place, in a police car — not on the street — with the two detectives flanking the suspect.

"I wrote out the interrogation scene, which was based on actual interrogations that I had seen Egan and Grosso do.[8] . . . I tried to give the scene the Pinteresque flavor of the interrogation in *Birthday Party*. . . . And thirty-two takes later, the scene was stiff, didn't work, couldn't get it to happen. Scheider would be pretty good, then Hackman would blow."[9]

Fat Thomas said, "Gene was still coming from Wheaton, Illinois, you know."

Friedkin said Alan Weeks, who played the dealer, "was getting slapped around. Real blood was coming out of his face because they were slapping him up. And he was saying, 'It's okay. Hit me. Go ahead, you can still hit me.' Lumps in his face. The scene's no good. Hackman and I had given each other long looks. We lost the light. We got no shot. The scene was pathetic. Went home. I thought, 'Jesus, I'm through. I'm going to be fired off this picture.'"[10]

"Remember," D'Antoni said, "Billy had lived and died with this project for over a year, and now it was finally starting up. He had to go through certain adjustments like any director during the first week."

Friedkin said that later that night he realized what was wrong with the scene: "It's not Harold Pinter. This is a street show. I've got to let them improvise the scene. I can't restrict them to this car and this tight shot." So he gave the actors a whole courtyard, a notion of the scene, and just let them wail on it. "That's the way you see it in the picture. One take. Two cameras. I chose the best moments and got that wonderful tag line from Hackman, 'Not only am I going to bust you for those two bags back there, but I'm going to run you in for picking your feet in Poughkeepsie.'"[11]

Hackman knew that line because Egan used it all the time, Friedkin said. "The Egan-Grosso interrogation technique is very simple. They get a guy who is obviously into something because we're all into something, so we feel a certain guilt. There are questions we all have the answer to, like what's your name and address, and there are some for which we don't have answers. . . . So Grosso would say, 'What were you doing in that bar?' And the guy'd say, 'Huh?' And Egan would say, 'Have you ever been in Poughkeepsie?' The guy knows he's never been there, but he's thinking,

'How come this guy wants to know if I've ever been in Poughkeepsie?' It's a double-talk kind of thing."[12]

But even with that first scene "in the can," as they say in Hollywood, Hackman was still, in the words of Fat Thomas, "coming from Wheaton."

Roy Scheider said that Hackman "kept wanting to humanize Egan, but Billy would say, No, this man is a pig. He's as rotten as the criminals he's chasing.'"[13]

Between what Fat Thomas called the "New York–type dialogue and bullshit and Egan's lines that everything is shit," and Friedkin "molding an unbelievable performance," according to Scheider,[14] Hackman became Popeye Doyle.

And Hackman, who was voted the Academy Award for his performance, was not Friedkin's first choice. The director said he spent two weeks trying to rehearse Jimmy Breslin, the New York–based writer, for the part of Doyle. "He was the vision I had of this cop. A big fat slobbering guy trying to run down the street, tripping over himself. There were only two problems that I found in trying to work him into the part. One, he was the worst actor I ever saw in my life, and two, he had never driven a car. He couldn't drive."[15]

Fat Thomas chuckled, recalling that when Egan heard Breslin was going to play him in the picture, "he almost died. He was in a horror. He couldn't sleep. He wanted Newman, Redford, or Mitchum."

Egan, according to Jurgensen, his friend for twenty years, is totally disorganized. "But as a cop on the street, he had no equal. Eddie Egan lived and breathed his job. Not wardrobe. Not relationships. So Hackman's tie's not on straight and looks like he's got a five o'clock shadow? That's Eddie Egan." And Owen Roizman, the cinematographer whose next project would be *The Exorcist*, recalled that while they were filming in the subway station, a man walked by dressed exactly like Frog One—Charnier—Doyle's nemesis. "He had the umbrella, the little black hat, and the black overcoat. Very debonair. Egan looked at him and said, 'That guy's dirty.' He took off and followed him."

D'Antoni said that he told Richard Zanuck and David Brown at 20th Century–Fox Studio, the financiers of the film, that he and Friedkin were thinking of going with unknowns with the exception of Jackie Gleason, who was seriously considered to play Doyle, but scheduling problems prevented it. "I should mention that Zanuck and Brown also felt the film was the kind that could stand on its own. We didn't need major casting. Eventually we saw Hackman and thought he'd be great because of his rough, slightly overweight look. Of course, he came in with just the opposite feeling. He'd lost about twenty pounds. He was wearing a new jacket. Looked slick as hell."

Also, Hackman was not the only actor to have difficulties with

Friedkin. Fernando Rey and Tony LoBianco, who play Frog One and Boca, respectively, "hated Billy," D'Antoni said. These two actors had a scene together in Washington, D.C., and when they returned, "both whispered in my ear how they would never work with Billy again. He was insulting to them. He told them they couldn't do the scenes right. What Billy did was simply to whip them into a frenzy. I knew because Billy told me on the telephone that day what was going on down there. It was Billy's way of getting them up to a certain level of energy."

Scheider states that on a Friedkin movie set "everyone is on edge. He believes you get the best work out of people that way."[16]

D'Antoni calls Friedkin's method "a trick, a ruse," but adds, "it works."

Nine scenes of character exposition did not work for Friedkin, however. He admits they may have added another layer to the film but discovered in the editing room that they "stopped the action cold."[17] As Fat Thomas said, "Billy don't make long movies. He don't want people getting sore asses." Among the excised scenes was one in which Frog One approaches a nun, puts his arm around her, and we discover she is his daughter. Another was set in Moochie's bar where Doyle goes one night and gets drunk. The purpose of the scene was to show that Doyle had a friend in life, namely Moochie, who was played by Fat Thomas. A third deleted scene followed the tail end of the Moochie scene; Doyle wakes up hungover on the bar, goes outside, and sees the girl on the bike wearing boots. According to Roizman, "Doyle stopped her, saying, 'What are you doing riding that bike there? You're on the wrong side of the street.' He's doing this big number on her, and she's standing there very fluffed, and then he gets on the bike and starts riding it around his car. He's on the handlebars backwards and clowning for her. It was a roar in dailies. At first I thought Billy was wrong to take those scenes out. I thought the picture could have used them, but it still works. Billy knows how to edit. When we shot *French Connection*, I never thought the picture would move along that quickly. Nobody had any idea how good that picture would be. Nobody."

Friedkin has said he made both *Connection* and *The Exorcist* instinctively. "You must trust your instincts and your imagination. You sail with them or die with them. The more experienced you get, the harder it gets. But something will dictate to you as you work that the colors, the casting, et cetera, feel right or wrong. It's finding the active frame."[18]

There are plenty of active frames in the celebrated chase scene in *Connection*. Friedkin said, "I had a tonal feeling of what New York looked like through that chase. And I never would have done the chase if it were not possible for a car to catch an El train. It wasn't scripted originally. D'Antoni and I walked fifty-four blocks of New York one day until we figured out all the details of the chase. The guy tries to kill Doyle, jumps on the El train. Doyle grabs a car . . . and the first crash you saw should have been a near miss. It was all filmed one shot at a time, but it was shot at speed. Even in the close-ups on Hackman through the windshield you can see the reflections of the tracks from above.

"I made one long run of twenty-six blocks with Bill Hickman, the stunt driver, so I could film Hackman's point of view. I told Hickman he had no guts, he was chickenshit. I kept getting his goat. He told me to get in the car and he'd show me some driving. I trusted nothing would happen, and it didn't. It wasn't for the sake of art."[19]

Jurgensen added that he was in the car lying down in the back so that if anything happened, he could take action such as identifying himself as a police officer in case other policemen got involved, thinking the car was running from a crime. Roizman said the only difficulty he had in photographing the sequence was "trying to make it all look like it was happening at the same time. We had snow and rain and sun and overcast over the five-week period we shot it. Everything, the elevated train, too, was shot with available light. It was a matter of movement, choosing the right lenses and trying to keep some kind of matching control on our lighting because we were going in and out of dark and light areas."

"And fifty percent of the effectiveness of the sequences comes from the sound and editing," Friedkin said. (Jerry Greenberg won the Oscar for best editing.) "Individual frames or shots or still photographs from the chase are unimpressive. The manner in which all the elements are combined, and how sound effects orchestrate the scene, make it effective. And a piece of music influenced the cutting of the chase called 'Black Magic Woman' by Santana. I just cut it to that tempo. There's like nice, sliding, long sort of guitar trills and licks, and the thing sort of moved along nice to that, and then there's some hard stuff and it slows down. The imagery will lay right up against that music."[20]

To draw a comparison, Friedkin said that a play like *Boys in the Band* relies for its effect "essentially on good dialogue, verbal effects, the verbal interplay between characters, whereas my concept of a good film is more of a visual thing.

"*The French Connection* had twelve reels, six of which have no dialogue at all. It works a lot better for me because it's a story told in pictures. A guy can look at that in Thailand and figure out what's going on. Maybe they chase each other with donkey carts or something, but they understand the chase. So you want to look for essentially visual things."[21]

Part of that visualization was a texture, according to Roizman. "We wanted the picture to have a pulse, tempo. Therefore we did most of it hand-held. That was Billy's idea, and I agreed. I'd say sixty to seventy percent of it was hand-held. It was also faster to do it that way. It keeps things from getting too stagey, too. You grab the camera and shoot. A lot of it doesn't look like it because I had a very good operator who was real steady with the camera. But we didn't want it too steady. That's also to make the audience uneasy. They can feel the same thing that is felt on screen. You just shake a little bit. We didn't want it to look like documentary but to look real, like it was happening."

What's the difference?

"With a documentary, you visit an event and photograph it," Roizman said. "In a film, you stage an event. You may photograph it to look like you visited it and you filmed it at the time, but that's the art of making a film that looks like that.

"Additionally, lots of times we used long lenses. You can lay back with a long lens and make something look much more realistic than if you get in close with a wide-angle lens. So we just laid back as an observer from the viewpoint of the cops.

"In fact, Billy wanted to do the picture all from the backseat of the car originally. He wanted to be behind Doyle and Russo so that we never saw what they were going into. We always discovered it with them. When they'd get out of their car, the camera would move with them on their backs through the situation. We did that for a day and knocked our brains out trying to make shots that seemed exciting to us while on screen they were going to be boring. Billy was smart enough to see it wasn't going to work.

"'Real' is the word that best describes what he wanted, what we all wanted. And not 'pretty' real. The picture was definitely stylized to go for the dirtiest areas we could find. A street picture. The locations picked were the scrungiest."

Fat Thomas said, "As you know, the picture's all action. What you needed was all those good locations."

Of course, but were there difficulties in finding those "good locations"?

"For the big shoot-out at the end of the show," Fat Thomas said, "we were going to go on Welfare Island, which is—what do they call it now? Roosevelt Island? But the building we were going to use was crumbling, and we were a week away from shooting. The state finally turned us down. They owned the property and were afraid people would get hurt. See, the building would never hold a Mitchell Panavision camera. And Billy said, 'You'd better not come up here, Fats, you'll go through the goddamn floor.' So I really had to go to work, and I found a place. At one time it was the bake shop for the city prison system. I happened to know about it because a friend of mine was up there doing time and I used to go visit him. When Billy seen it, he was enthralled.

"Billy said to me when we started, 'I'm not looking for anything like that *Cotton Comes to Harlem* where they made Harlem look like a fucking country town.' So I took him out to these places like Ridgewood where I come from. That's where we did the surveillance scenes because the hospital that Egan and Grosso were working out of at the time when they had the surveillance on 'Patsy' Fuca (the character Boca is based on) was St. Catherine's. Fuca had his candy store he was selling the junk out of across the street from the hospital. When Billy and I went by it, the candy store was still there, but the hospital was down. So we went up to Ridgewood, which Billy dug because there was a button factory across the street from the deli we decided to use in place of the candy store. The people we dealt with to get permission to shoot on their property were very nice. They hear 'Hollywood' and go berserk and all that horseshit."

This overall look is what *Life* magazine called, "an expedition through the jungle of the city to something that seems like the grungy heart of its darkness."[22]

"It's all because Billy did his homework," Jurgensen said. "I was on tour with the picture in a midwestern state. It was in an American WASP area. They could go anywhere for one hundred miles in any direction and not possibly see the shooting galleries or those bars. Yet, while discussing that picture after it was shown, a woman in her fifties said to me those scenes were real, and she knows they were real and she knows that happens. I said to her, 'Have you ever been to a bar like that? She said, 'No.' I asked if she'd ever encountered people like that. She said, 'No.' I said, 'How do you know it's real?' She said, 'I'm telling you, it's real.'"

In the bar scene, Doyle and Russo shake down the black patrons. Running his hand under the length of the bar counter, Doyle comes up with a hatful of illegal drugs and pills ("What is this, a fuckin' hospital?" he observes), all the while berating the customers with "Get your hands on your fucking head" and "We're going to keep coming back until you clean this place up." He mixes all the narcotics with beer in a cocktail shaker, asking, "Anybody want a milk shake?"

Fat Thomas was laughing. "That was all cops in that bar scene. It was shot down at Roy's Bar. It ain't there no more either. They tore it down because the neighborhood is getting so dilapidated. But see, we had to use nonunion help like that. We couldn't find any rugged-looking black guys that were in the Screen Actor's Guild. There just weren't any at the time. Anybody over forty was either a Shakespearean actor or a fag."

"*The French Connection* is an impression of what happened," Friedkin said. "Film is not real time. It's a cinematic language. Impressionistic paintings give us reality, but they don't perpetuate it. Hieronymus Bosch gave us nightmare visions out of his imagination. No one can re-create life exactly."[23]

But Friedkin did try. Gerrity, the assistant director, recalled that Friedkin wanted the Brooklyn Bridge tied up with traffic for the climax to a scene where Doyle and Russo are tailing Boca. "We had no permission to do this, of course. I said to Billy, 'This is rush hour, kiddo. We can't do this. We'll be in trouble.' He said, 'I don't care what it is. I don't care how you do it. I want this bridge tied up, and I want them stuck in traffic, and I want to see the heavy get away.' So we took two of our cars, faked them to be broken-down, and created such a traffic jam that we had traffic backed up from Brooklyn to Queens and, I think, everyplace else. The cops didn't take too lightly to that."

In another instance, Friedkin re-created an actual incident from the original case, namely, the scene in the subway terminal with Doyle and Frog One stepping on and off the subway train, with Frog One finally eluding him.

Art imitated life as well in the scene where Doyle stands outside in the cold, watching Frog One and Frog Two eating in a posh restaurant. Jurgensen said he, Egan, Grosso, and Friedkin were sitting in a diner one day eating a cup of soup and a hamburger. "It was pretty run-down. Billy fit right in. He asked us if we eat like this all the time. We said, 'Hey, this is how we live. This is what we do. And the sons-of-bitches we're chasing, you should see how they live.' Bang. That's in the movie. It was never in the script."

And neither was the gunshot that climaxes the film. Friedkin says he did it in the dubbing room on the day before he left as a joke. "It simply means that the movie ends with a bang. . . . A number of studio executives asked, 'What the hell is that shot?' I said, 'It's possible that Doyle has become so crazed he's firing at shadows. Another possibility is that his partner in the room offstage put a bullet in the dead federal guy to take the onus off Doyle for having shot the guy.' I ad-libbed about three or four possible explanations, none of which were in my mind when I put the gunshot in . . . .

"But I must say that the whole idea behind *French Connection,* and *The Exorcist,* too, is for the audience to draw their own conclusions, whatever they may be . . . . I had as many people who saw *The French Connection* tell me it was a put-down of cops as told me it was the most accurate, realistic story of a cop. I got citations from police organizations, and I was accused of being a Fascist by the Italian press.

"All I tried to do is make the picture, just tell the story straight as I saw it. If you just tell the story straight as you see it, people will put another handle on it. But you've got to leave a lot of things in there, build a lot of things in that'll cause people to do that. If they're talking about what something means in a movie, usually you've got a movie people will want to see. Example: the obelisk in *2001: A Space Odyssey.* What the hell is the obelisk? And that's why I put the gunshot in at the end of *French Connection.*"[24]

"On the other hand," D'Antoni said, "there's an ending to *French Connection* which no one ever sees. Billy felt it would be a marvelous scene in which Doyle goes totally berserk. I didn't necessarily agree, but we had enough time, so we got it both ways: one from an acting point of view and one from a cinematic point of view.

"After Doyle accidentally kills Federal Agent Mulderig, it was Billy's idea to shoot with a nine-millimeter lens from Doyle's point of view so that everything was in total distortion."

(This "distortion" amounts to affixing a fish-eye lens on the camera and achieving a cheap horror-movie effect out of place with the rest of Friedkin's vision.)

"It was to show that Doyle had gone crazy," D'Antoni said. "But more than literally crazy, it was to be a wavering drunken kind of movement. Then we shot it in the straight form you see it in. This was the correct way to do it. That other one wasn't realistic, and Billy agreed. It was the symbolism that Doyle had gone totally off the wall. I think we'd said it without saying it."

Friedkin said he now has a different idea for the ending. "Two junkies sitting on the East River at seven o'clock in the morning on a wintry day, nodding off, and a barge is going down the river dumping all this heroin, all this shit, into the East River, which is what they were doing at the time with all the confiscated stuff that had reached its final disposition in court. Now as we all know, a lot of bags didn't get dumped. They got sold back onto the market, but police procedure was to dump all this stuff, and that image of these two guys, just nodding out, seeing thirty-two million dollars worth of heroin in the East River. . . . It reminded me of *The Treasure of the Sierra Madre,* which I thought would have been a gas."[25]

However, an irony lurks behind all of Friedkin's procedural research, battles with Hackman, and ending things with a bang: He almost never got to make the film. D'Antoni explained that "Billy's reputation at that time from *everybody* that knew him professionally was that he was very artsy-fartsy. I went to several studios, and all of them turned down Billy out of hand because they thought there was no way Billy Friedkin could do an action film."

"It stems from the old Hollywood mechanism of always casting everybody in the role that they most recently did. Prior to doing *Bullitt* I had worked with Sophia Loren, Elizabeth Taylor, and Melina Mercouri. I was known as a glamour TV producer. Then I do two or three movies about cops, and I'm an action producer. It was the same thing with Billy. I had finished *Birthday Party* and was in the middle of *Boys in the Band.* That's what people were reacting to."

Obviously, had any of these production executives seen *The People Versus Paul Crump,* they would have realized *The French Connection* was a natural progression for Friedkin.

According to Friedkin and D'Antoni, National General Pictures eventually gave them the go-ahead and "reluctantly" allowed Friedkin to direct. Several writers were brought in — among them, Alex Jacobs, who wrote *Hell in the Pacific,* to do the script.

"But all the concepts leading up to it were too intellectual," Friedkin said.

"We thought they were awful," D'Antoni said. "We had to start all over again."

That's when they hired Ernest Tidyman, a crime reporter for the *New York Times* who'd just written a book called *Shaft*.

"Billy and I worked with him because he'd never written a screenplay before," D'Antoni said. "In about sixty days, we had a screenplay. But now National General was having problems in the movie business. They rejected the idea of the movie, *not* the screenplay. They didn't have enough faith in Billy that he could make a movie for two-and-a-half million dollars—a budget that we wanted. They felt it should be done for a million, million and a half. This was when the movie *Easy Rider* came out and set everybody in Hollywood thinking every movie that came out should be made for that."

Considering the Hollywood mechanisms, it's puzzling that any film company at that time would say no to a young director like Friedkin since *Easy Rider* was made by Dennis Hopper, a young filmmaker as well.

"Again, I figured it was Billy's reputation out in Hollywood that he couldn't handle a hard-hitting subject," D'Antoni said. "Then we pulled away from National General and submitted the script to every other studio in Hollywood."

"Some twice," Friedkin said.

"Every place rejected it," D'Antoni said. "Some on the basis that the script was okay but it wasn't that unusual. Some places didn't like Billy as the director, and other places just didn't have the money. Billy was despondent. He really felt he was not going to get another job, that *French Connection* would never get made. *Band* had opened to mixed reviews, and no offers were coming in. We took a long walk around Manhattan, and Billy said to me, 'I'm not a director unless I'm directing. If I'm not directing, I'm not a director. I may never do it again.'"

Fat Thomas recalled a night he and Friedkin "were having dinner at Sam's Steak House on Sixty-fourth and First (it ain't there no more), and Billy didn't know what the hell to do. He was very close to taking a job with Random House as a book editor. I swear to God."

Meanwhile, D'Antoni said, he and Friedkin began to toy with developing a private-eye movie based on a story by English author Oliver Bleak (a pseudonym) as well as securing the rights to the Dick Francis mystery books. And then Richard Zanuck at 20th Century–Fox, who had liked the story initially but could not act on it because Fox was involved in a proxy battle, now wanted to meet with him immediately regarding *The French Connection*. "He told me Fox had enough money and how fast could we get the film going. I said we could organize it in about eight weeks, and I phoned Billy."

The French Connection. **Popeye Doyle (Gene Hackman) uses deadly force to stop Frog Two Pierre Nicoli (Marcel Bozzuffi), at the climax of the chase.**

The problem did not exactly end there for Friedkin. He said the film cost $1.8 million, "three hundred thousand dollars over budget. That's why Fox was trying to fire me almost daily."[26]

But success won out, in Hollywood terms, with *The French Connection* grossing more than thirty million dollars.

On its initial release, Fat Thomas said, "It took off like a skyrocket. Lowe's East State Theater had six performances a day and at midnight every night. Word-of-mouth is the best thing for movies. Before you know it, the whole town is looking to see a flick."

Jurgensen recalled that on opening night he and Friedkin were in the theater and it was packed. "When that scene came up at the end of the chase and Doyle shoots Frog Two in the back after the chase, a thousand people stood up and applauded. I was amazed."

Jurgensen explained: "The Frenchman loses his gun on the train and comes down the stairs, unarmed. Doyle is at the bottom of the stairs and represents the New York Police Department detectives, Narcotics Division, which I was a part of. Doyle says, 'Halt!' The Frenchman does not, turns around, starts up the stairs, and Doyle shoots him in the back.

"Now this was horrifying to me from my limited point of view as a police officer of twenty years. I went to Billy immediately and said, 'This is murder. You're having a New York City detective shoot this man.' Billy said, 'What are you talking about?' I said, 'Not only is he shooting this guy and he's unarmed, you got him shooting him in the back.' Billy said, 'Don't worry about it.' I said, 'I am worried about it. It's murder. Audiences are going to see this, cops I work with are going to see this. You've hired me to pick my brain. This is murder.' He said, 'Don't worry about it.' For three days we went round and round, with Billy listening to every sane approach I could think of to try to change the scene. I said, 'Let there be a second gun. Let him just pull it out so there will be danger to the detective. By rights, they should take this detective before a grand jury and indict him.' Billy just kept smiling.

"And then to add insult to injury, I see the poster ad, and it's Doyle at the bottom of the stairs, the Frenchman at the top of the stairs with his hands up in the air, no gun, and he's obviously being shot in the back. I thought, 'Oh, my God, I don't believe this.' So here's the audience applauding and Billy looked at me and said, 'Well?' From that day on, I realized I was just the adviser and Billy was the filmmaker."

II

Friedkin bloodies the Old World charm of Marseilles, France, with a cold, brutal murder barely two minutes into *The French Connection*. A man who has been eyeing shipbuilding magnate Charnier's brown Lincoln Continental automobile too much stares down the black barrel of a pistol. There's the gunshot, and the man's face is covered with blood (in quick close-up) as he drops out of frame. The killer, Charnier's strongarm Nicoli (Marcel Bozzuffi), steps over the prone body, breaks off a piece of bread from the loaf the man carried, and chews it as he departs.

On the streets of Brooklyn Friedkin introduces us to narcotics detective Popeye Doyle, dressed in a bright red Santa Claus suit. Doyle is staking out a bar when he and his partner, Russo (posing as a hot dog vendor), chase a black drug pusher. When the pusher falls running through a vacant lot, Doyle pounces on top of him. Russo has to pull "Santa" off, shouting, "Don't kill him!"

The wry morbidity in both these scenes visually establishes the fatalistic cynical brand of Friedkin's humor as well as his street reality. They also present a world in chaos in which tranquil cobblestone streets are red with death and Santa Claus busts pushers for picking their feet in Poughkeepsie.

Friedkin gives new definition to the thriller genre; the gray shadings have never had such high resolution before. For example, back at the police station after they have booked the pusher, Doyle tells Russo, "Never trust a nigger." (The pusher had pulled knife and cut Russo's arm early in the fracas.) Russo tells Doyle the same thing could have happened with a white guy. Doyle responds, "Never trust anyone." We've seen Doyle in action, and we have just heard Doyle's philosophy on life. Friedkin has neatly, quickly personified Fitzgerald's dictum "Action is character, character is dialogue" in a cop as rough and callous as the streets he works.

Doyle's (and Friedkin's) New York City is a cesspool, ugly and sinister. But he's been hardened to it, desensitized. He and the street have become one—they are both comfortable in their anger. In a scene set against a bloody automobile accident, the victims are pried from their car while Doyle argues with his superior Simonson (Eddie Egan) for more time to work the case. An FBI agent assigned to the case named Klein (Sonny Grosso) runs over and tells Simonson he found "a set of works" (slang for the syringe paraphernalia of heroin users) on the white kid driving the sports car. Doyle desperately tries to convince Simonson that the deal with Boca and Frog One has not yet gone down.

Implicit in the scene, as explained by Randy Jurgensen, was that "the drug problem was not just a black problem but a white one as well; it was no longer isolated." Doyle's strenuous arguing with his boss climaxes in a fistfight between Doyle and FBI Agent Mulderig (Bill Hickman), who tells Doyle the last time he was "dead certain we had a dead cop." The scene serves a dual purpose. Friedkin believes the best American cinema is action-oriented—"If there are ideas embodied in it, they have to be by the way."[27] In other words, he lets the action tell the story and reveal characters; morality is less important than physical danger. Rather than have one of the detectives launch into a diatribe on the evils of drug use, Friedkin impressionistically depicts through image the underlying point, the idea "by the way," of the film.

Bodies splattered with blood pulled from the twisted wreckage of a street accident where drug use may have been involved is the visualization of Doyle's obsession to bust the drug czars. Klein makes his report to Simonson. We cut to two other accident victims covered by white sheets on the side of the road. Klein's report complete, we cut to a close-up on Doyle, positive in his resolve: "I say we keep sitting on Boca." Juxtaposing these images of violent death against Doyle's determination, Freidkin embodies the idea within the narrative while simultaneously maintaining the chaselike speed of the narrative.

Also, this scene, as well as the earlier one in the "drug" bar where Doyle and Russo roust the patrons and Doyle mixes up the drug "milk shake," serves to demonstrate that Doyle cannot lower his guard; neither his fellow officers nor the street sleaze can pierce his hardened armor. His savagery makes him intense, *believable.* No cop in film before, not even Harry Callahan in *Dirty Harry,* released that same year, had been so consumed in nihilistic obsession. Yet, through Friedkin's filmic street sense, we can watch Doyle's outrageousness and laugh at him ("I wanna bust him, let me bust him!" he pleads with Russo after they collar the pusher) *and* pull for him because he believes so intensely in what he is doing.

Like a bulldog, Doyle cannot let go. He knows he's on to something while he and Russo have a drink at a club: While sitting at the bar, Doyle eyes a table where several couples sit, dressed in evening wear and finery, passing money around, he says, "like the Russians have landed in Jersey." From Doyle's point of view we see the flashy smiles, flashier jewelry, and champagne. In the background, a Supremes-style lounge act belts out an up-tempo song. (The lyrics, "We're gonna fly to the silvery, fly to the silvery, everybody's goin' to the moon," sung by a black female group, serve as an ironic counterpoint. Blacks are represented as the main users of drugs for getting high. The song lyrics then become a metaphor for that, for "goin' to the moon.") But then their singing fades out along with all the bar sounds and is replaced by a high-pitched threatening music sting. A close-up on Doyle fills the screen as he looks closer, harder, at the group, positively identifying known "junk connections."

That sustained eerie note is like a burning fuse, and Doyle is the explosion. The tension Friedkin builds is almost unbearable. Given Doyle's earlier actions, we wonder if he might lunge at the table. Instead he shrugs. The sounds of the club return to the scene, and Doyle says to Russo, "That table is definitely wrong." It's just a hunch based solely on street smarts born of years of experience. He lives for his job. He works the case with proper police procedure. He and Russo tail the big tipper Boca and his wife to a greasy Italian deli they run. Since seeing Boca passing out more money in one night than he makes in a month and then stuffing thin boxes of something into newspapers, Doyle and Russo know (and Friedkin allows us to see with them) that Boca sells more than deli sandwiches.

Wiretaps and surveillance follow, and Friedkin, again, shows us impressionistically the drudgery of building a case. Doyle and Russo sit for hours in a dull gray concrete incinerator room playing cards while taping Boca's phone conversations. These two detectives get so punchy, they laugh uproariously over a conversation in which Boca argues with his wife over picking up a pizza.

Connection, therefore, is realistic in its depiction of cops and solving crime, as opposed to *Dirty Harry,* which panders to an audience. It makes the Scorpio killer an obvious maniacal extreme and Harry, always dressed in a pressed shirt, straight tie, and dapper V-neck sweater, a Nietzchean superman. And Harry's San Francisco locale glamorizes and romanticizes not only the city but its shootings, beatings, and knifings; it's a stylized slickness that tends to cleanse its ugliness. *Connection*'s New York is a decomposing landscape against a cold gray sky where junkies don't have enough sense to lie down and die. Yet Friedkin rivets our attention with the speed and economy of storytelling that he demonstrated in *Paul Crump*.

There are also cues from Francis Bacon. "Blood against the pavement is invigorating," and "only the consciousness of death in life gives death its power" because Friedkin presents a glimpse of a cop's life that, by the very nature of his work, makes him a constant target, living on the edge. (Randy Jurgensen said that until this film, he never realized in twenty years as a police officer that he was living the kind of life where he could be killed that quickly.) Nicoli tries to gun down Doyle who is carrying a bag of groceries home at midday. This triggers the chase. And as Doyle, Gene Hackman's doughy, dirty, unshaven face even resembles a Bacon portrait. Especially telling is the scene where he wakes up hungover in Moochie's bar. He raises his head, trying to pull himself together, to focus; his hair is awry, the lines of his face fractured and attempting to right themselves; flesh, shadow, and color in conflict. And with this portrait of a frayed human being plays Friedkin's cynical sense of humor in the sound of a radio commercial telling Doyle (and us) to "say good-bye to air pollution, commuting, and cold depressing winters" and come to Florida for "fresh clean air, warm sunny year-round weather, and a home you'll be proud to own."

For Friedkin, following the action means not only Doyle in a car chasing Nicoli on board the El train down twenty-six blocks of elevated rail and crashing into cars and narrowly missing a woman pushing a stroller but also generating suspense with intense inaction. For example, Doyle and his team stake out the brown Lincoln Boca had earlier left on a deserted side street. They wait. Finally a car circles the block three times and then stops. Several Hispanics get out and head for the Lincoln with crowbars. The next thing we know, Doyle's got half the police force blasting down the street, and they bust these guys, who turn out to be car strippers. When their car goes by the first time, we don't think anything of it. When it goes by the second time, it slows down as it passes the Lincoln. Something's up. Doyle's wondering too. On the third pass, Doyle's on the police radio. The car stops. Doyle's yelling into the radio to hit them. And Friedkin has built up so much tension and pressure that we're as distraught as Doyle when the bust turns out to be only small-timers. This and the chase are both effectively suspenseful sequences because Friedkin and Jerry Greenberg, his editor, establish a breakneck pace, and all we can do is hold on. We don't know where it's going, or more importantly, what's coming next. This suspense generates fear, and fear becomes a rush.

But Friedkin refuses to stop there. Fear and intensity complement each other in a moment reminiscent of Friedkin's lingering over the straps and cables of the electric chair in *Crump*. The director forces us to examine in chilling detail the testing of the heroin for potency. He fills the screen with extreme close-ups of the flame heating the mineral oil, a needle scraping the white powder, the mercury rising in the thermometer. This sequence, like the electric chair sequence, is composed of frightening images playing on our fear of death—the ultimate fear. Both the chair and the heroin are lethal. As a viscerally aural bonus to this moment, Harold (Pat McDermott), the stringy-haired chemist, watches the mercury rise, pronouncing the powder "U.S. government certified" to "junk-of-the-month-club sirloin steak" to "absolute dynamite, eighty-nine percent pure junk" with mounting reverence.

Given the relentless nature of this thriller that Friedkin imbues with what he calls the "muscular, visceral, storytelling sense of the American cinema best embodied in the work of Raoul Walsh, Howard Hawks, and John Ford,"[28] it is easy to forgive (or simply run with) its questionable moment. It concerns Doyle on a seven-story apartment rooftop, searching for Nicoli, who had just tried to shoot him. Doyle looks down and sees him running away from the building. Then we cut to Doyle on the street, chasing Nicoli. Both are on foot. Nicoli is maybe fifty yards ahead. One wonders how Doyle gained on him so quickly. But, then, quickly is how everything happens in this film.

We can see almost a foul choking stench rising up from the street. We stamp our feet with Doyle against the cold. We are as exhausted as he is after the El train chase. If realism is the heart of *The French Connection,* then irony is its soul. Doyle is a slob. His diet is rubbery pizza. It's probably the original dirt in his apartment. But he knows a criminal when he sees one, and he will not stop until he apprehends him. Charnier dresses impeccably. He lives in a seaside villa in Marseilles. Only the best will do. Sophisticated as he is on the outside, inside he's full of cockroaches, a drug dealer.

Friedkin revels in this irony. In the restaurant scene, Charnier and Nicoli sit warm inside, drinking fine wine, while Doyle watches them from outside in the cold, disgustedly pouring out coffee that looks like crankcase oil. When the heroin is tested, it takes place in Weinstock's (Harold Gary) richly furnished apartment, not a squalid shooting gallery. And in this same scene, Weinstock, the American buyer of Frog One's heroin, and Boca discuss the ramifications of purchasing the sixty kilos for half a million dollars versus the $32 million they can make selling it. It's played as a casual business transaction, nothing illegal. The whole time, Weinstock puffs on a big cigar. Conversely, when we pick up Doyle and Russo sitting in that concrete-walled room while tapping Boca's telephone conversations, papers are strewn about, Doyle's clothes look like he slept in them. Police work is cramped and uncomfortable, unlike the business of drug dealing. Yet, the smiles Weinstock and Boca wear have a reptilian curve, while the excitement and exuberance of Doyle and Russo on hearing Boca's rendez-vous telephone call is delightfully infectious.

In the end, Frog One escapes. Though the heroin is confiscated, Doyle misses his man. Doyle pursues Frog One from the moment he sees him, a game of cat and mouse. The sequence on the subway train, with the two of them going back and forth, stepping on and off the train, is a prime exam-ple of virtuoso visual storytelling. Frog One knows Doyle is tailing him. Behind his perfectly barbered countenance we can see Charnier trying to formulate a plan to lose Doyle. And Doyle watches every move, keeps pace with every step until Frog One, using his umbrella for a sleight-of-hand trick, finally catches Doyle outside when the train doors finally close. Frog One adds to Doyle's humiliation by waving good-bye as the train pulls out. This is doubly important because not only has Doyle been outsmarted by a *foreigner* in his own town (Doyle calls the Frenchmen "frogs," Italians "greasers," and all blacks "niggers"), but it compounds his frustration and serves to point out that he is *not* a supercop.

And Friedkin does not tell us this, he *shows* us. It is Friedkin at his gut-level best. He is not so much concerned with the right or wrong of the story as he is with the validity—the truth—of the image. It is his view of the world, his reality—harsh, bleak, and tough like the streets where he grew up ("I remember stories about Chicago that haunt me"). His world is populated with the faces of people who look as if they *belonged* in this gritty environment. The only message is what the audience cares to read into it.

If you accept his reality—his vision—you give it credence. If not, you still give it credence because you are, in effect, saying this vitiated reality is too much, too intense. Watching *The French Connection* is like Friedkin's shoving a .38 pistol in your face and saying, "Well, what do you think?"

8
The Exorcist

"I used to make up stories and scare the little
girls in my neighborhood."
— William Friedkin

I

On that spring evening in 1972 at the Academy Awards ceremony,
when *The French Connection* was collaring its Oscars, Charlie Chaplin, the
silent film comedian and reclusive star, was worried. He was accepting a
special Oscar and did not know how the industry that had ostracized him
because of his politics and dubious morals would receive him. Paranoia in-
fused the air backstage, so the story goes. As a measure of protection, all
the doors were suddenly shut and locked, guards were instructed to allow
no one through. Friedkin, who had earlier thanked the academy for his
award, was shortly observed trapped inside a double-glass entrance, banging his Oscar against the glass and yelling at the guards: "Don't you know
who I am? I just won an Academy Award; let me out of here!"[1]

Two years later, Friedkin would attend another Oscar ceremony.
Though he would have no gold statue to bang around, the film that brought
him to the awards again had assuredly made him known. Arguably the best
film of 1973 (and possibly the best American film of the decade), *The Exorcist* lost to *The Sting*, an entertaining fluff about two small-time con men
who outwit a big-time gangster. Friedkin lost to *The Sting*'s director, George
Roy Hill. Of its ten nominations, *The Exorcist* garnered only two: best
screenplay adaptation and best sound. It would have certainly been
awarded an Oscar for special effects but, according to producer William
Peter Blatty, veteran director George Cukor, a committee member of the
academy, lambasted the film, calling it "a disgrace." A resolution was passed
by Cukor's committee, Blatty said, that no film that year was worthy of a
special effects award and therefore no award would be given. But the film
was a major success financially, earning over $250 million, and created at
the very least a controversy, at most a phenomenon.

105

On August 14, 1972, Friedkin rolled his cameras on what many readers of Blatty's best-selling book thought was unfilmable. Three months later, on November 15, Pope Paul VI, in a General Audience, declared, "Evil is not merely a lack of something, but an effective agent, a living spiritual being, perverted and perverting. A terrible reality. . . . So we know that this dark and disturbing spirit really exists and that he still acts with treacherous cunning; he is the secret enemy that sows errors and misfortunes in human history. This question of the Devil and the influence he can exert on individual persons as well as on communities . . . is a very important chapter of Catholic doctrine which is given little attention today, though it should be studied again."[2] Without realizing it, the Pope was giving a credence and reality to Friedkin's vision.

The story concerns a twelve-year-old girl named Regan (Linda Blair) who is inexplicably possessed by a demon. Her mother, Chris MacNeil (Ellen Burstyn), an actress who is making a film in Georgetown, exhausts the medical and psychological possibilities before turning to Father Karras (Jason Miller). He refuses at first, his psychiatric training telling him that it cannot possibly be possession. But with the arrival of Father Merrin (Max von Sydow), Karras agrees to combat the demon with an exorcism.

The film opened on the day after Christmas 1973. Fundamentalist author Hal Lindsey and the Reverend Billy Graham said it was dangerous. According to Lindsey, "It sets the stage for an attack by Satan."[3] The Reverend Juan Cortes, a Jesuit at Georgetown University, said the picture is "not helpful to society" and that "you can't bring people to God by scaring them to death."[4] People rushed to priests demanding an exorcism because they thought they were possessed. Doctors, psychiatrists, and psychologists were divided, calling the film a "menace to the mental health of our community" as well as a "genuine aesthetic catharsis."[5] A leading member of the Church of Scotland wrote that he'd "rather take a bath in pig manure than see the film."[6] Friedkin recalled reading an article from a Catholic newspaper that a friend of his in the clergy sent him. "Some clergymen suggested that the story was a homosexual fantasy, that Karras and Merrin were in a male bond to physically torture this little girl. The girl stabbing the vagina was a gesture of female hatred, and the passionate involvement of these two men ends in death over the actions of this little girl and her vaginal problems. Presumably, anyone looking for this sort of thing is going to come up with something equally as far-fetched." He added wryly, "I must say it never occurred to me, but when the guy puts up such a convincing case, what can I tell you?

"I intended to make a picture that would first and foremost be an engrossing work of fascinating entertainment. The hullabaloo that's taken place is a big mystery to me, frankly."[7]

The genesis of the "hullabaloo" for Friedkin began in 1965 in the office of film producer Blake Edwards. Friedkin said after he made *Good Times*, Edwards hired him to direct *Gunn*, a feature film based on his *Peter Gunn* television series. "I hated the script. It was a hashing together of two of the TV shows. There were essential things Blake didn't know, like what city Gunn operated out of. He operated out of the Universal Studios backlot. The great private eyes come from a specific environment. Chandler, Hammett, San Francisco, Los Angeles. Blake had never bothered to find out who the hell Peter Gunn was. The whole thing was a concoction. I hated it, but I thought I should be very careful about trying to get changes in the script because, after all, it was Blake's creation and he was very protective of it.

"So I did try to get changes, and slowly they're coming. Finally Blake reached a point where he said, 'Look, I don't want to change the script anymore. I think the script is good enough. We've got a budget, you've got your locations. Go make your movie.' I said, 'Blake, I just can't. I don't understand the character. I don't know why this is. It's just a bunch of dialogue. It's a TV movie to me. I think it's awful. I think you got the wrong guy.' He said, 'Very interesting. The fellow who wrote the script with me happens to be in the outer office. Would you mind giving him your comments?' So Blake pushes a buzzer and in comes Blatty, who was like a ghost writer for Blake."

"Billy was only twenty-six then and with his horn-rimmed glasses looked like *Fiddler on the Roof*'s Tevye as a boy. But he wasn't about to ask God for any favors," Blatty said.

"Blake sits Blatty down," Friedkin said, "and says, 'Mr. Friedkin here has read your script, and I'd like him to tell you what he just told me about it.' I told him, at which point Blatty burst out laughing. And Blake, who was very serious, didn't understand that. The meeting was over, and that was the last I saw of Blake for a long time. But Blatty called me shortly after and said, 'I gotta tell you, the script is awful. It's as good as Blake wants it to be. You're the first guy that's ever told Blake the truth about anything for as long as I've known him. I really admire you for it, and even though my work is in there, you're absolutely right, and maybe we should work together someday.'"

Six years later, Blatty's book *The Exorcist* was a huge best-seller, and Warner Bros. had agreed to make the film as well as to allow Blatty to produce it. A number of directors were considered, according to Blatty, but were not available. For example, "Arthur Penn was teaching at Yale. Stanley Kubrick could produce for himself, thank you. And Mike Nichols said he didn't want to hazard a film whose success might depend on a child's performance." Blatty had submitted Friedkin's name on his original list to Warner Bros. because of their previous acquaintance. But Friedkin was rejected.

William Friedkin, director of *The Exorcist*, preparing for a take.

Blatty submitted his name again, but the studio executives were now pushing another director. Though Blatty has refused to name names, he has referred to this director as "Edmund de Vere,"[8] who, according to an informed source, "smacks pretty sharply of John Cassavetes."[9] At the urging of the studio, Blatty viewed "de Vere's" latest film and said he felt that he was watching a murder, "the victim in this case being pace. Entire novenas could be said during pauses in dialogue."[10] After the screening, Blatty went to dinner and a movie, a disheartened man. But the film was *The French Connection*. "The pace, excitement, and look of documentary realism were what *The Exorcist* desperately needed . . . Billy was hired."[11]

Initially, though, there was some worry on the part of the Warner Bros. executives as to whether Friedkin and Blatty could work together amicably, not argue. Friedkin and Blatty said they knew about the Warner trepidations, so they went into the first studio production meeting prepared. The meeting was to discuss the shooting schedule and budget. Friedkin suggested immediately that Green Goddess salad dressing would be good for the production crew. Blatty didn't agree. Friedkin said if they used the same salad dressing all through the filming they'd save $50,000. Blatty wanted a variety of dressings. Friedkin said no. Blatty said yes. The argument escalated to shouts, and Blatty stormed out of the meeting. According to Friedkin, "The studio guys didn't bother us too much anymore."

Friedkin said that *The Exorcist* was the most perfect script he'd ever seen and he wanted to shoot it word for word. However, of Blatty's first draft of the script, Friedkin recalled saying to the writer, "This is terribly interesting, but it's not the book."

(Friedkin has said he read Blatty's novel "for relaxation while mixing the chase in *The French Connection*"[12] and claims "the book took hold of me; I became physically ill.")[13]

According to Blatty, Friedkin objected to the cinematic trickery of his first-draft script, such as flash forwards, freeze frames, and flashbacks. "He felt that in a film which depended on whether or not the audience believes that the bed really is levitating, only disaster could result from drawing attention to cinematic mechanics."

He said Friedkin was also adamant that the film be faithful to the novel in every respect. "In fact, he was so fixated on the novel that when in my first draft I changed Regan's sculpture from the bird it had been in the novel to a bear, Billy demanded we go back to the bird. . . . Even slight dialogue changes he would cringe at."[14] However, in the Iraqi prologue, "if you look carefully, you'll see a little boy hawking lottery tickets with a red devil sketched on them. Two dogs fighting, one largely black, the other largely white. These and more are touches Billy added."[15] Also, certain subplots were excised from the script such as "red herrings that pointed to Karras, and even to Sharon [Chris' secretary], as being somehow involved in the church desecrations or in Denning's death" for purposes of pacing and time as well as adding nothing to the forward movement of the plot since "after the film had been playing for a month, the audience would know from the outset that the butler didn't do it."[16]

"I tried to make the film with no sense of style," Friedkin said, "with no sense of doing something that would ever remotely be classified as a horror film or a work of fantasy. I attempted to make it as realistic as possible. At the very most, I think it could be called a work of the inexplicable. By now, I accept that *The Exorcist* does belong in the horror genre. At the time I didn't. But I had an obligation to deal as straightforwardly as possible with it because of my attraction to this unusual but factual event.

"And I am totally convinced that the events upon which the film is based occurred. The film, of course, is not a literal depiction of those events. It's fictionalized. The actual version, even what you'd read in a newspaper account as I did in the *Washington Post* article written in 1949 about a fourteen-year-old Mount Rainier, Maryland, boy, would be just as disturbing

Director William Friedkin and producer-author William Peter Blatty on the set of
The Exorcist.

and inspiring and in many cases shocking because we don't understand what went on there."[17]

The production problems in making the inexplicable believable Friedkin termed "a nightmare."[18] This "nightmare" had its humorous as well as its costly moments.

Directing is communicating, Friedkin says, and it's accomplished "largely through actors. . . . So I try to envision the kind of person I want or don't want in any given role."[19] He did not want a known actor to play Karras. Both Jack Nicholson and Roy Scheider wanted the role, Friedkin said. And Stacey Keach had the role at one point. Then Scheider suggested that Friedkin see the play *That Championship Season,* written by Jason Miller, who was a friend of Scheider's, according to the director.[20]

The play's strong Catholic currents intrigued Friedkin, who was "not going to hire any actor who had not had a Catholic education."[21] He met with Miller, who had been trained to be a Jesuit at a Catholic university for three years and initially thought Friedkin wanted him to write the script. "He was extremely intelligent, and I thought he had an inherent sensitivity that I could photograph," Friedkin said. "I shot a test with him and Ellen Burstyn. They turned out great. I started to like him. Then Burstyn said, 'No way. He can't do it.' I asked Blatty what he thought."

"*I* wanted the part," Blatty said. "I told Billy I thought Miller was too short."

Friedkin said, "Then Ted Ashley at Warner Bros. told me, 'You have complete control. It's all yours. But Ellen Burstyn will play this part over my dead body. You can use Jane Fonda, Audrey Hepburn, Anne Bancroft, or Shirley MacLaine.'"[22]

"The first thought for Chris MacNiel, before Billy was involved, was Jane Fonda," Blatty said. "She thought it was, as she expressed it in her telegram, 'Rip-off capitalist bullshit.' I think she didn't want to play the part. Anne Bancroft was the next one. She was, I think, eight months pregnant and looking rather ill at the time."

"Carol Burnett was my first choice," Friedkin said. "But I got scared. I wasn't sure the audience could make the leap from her as a comedienne to a serious role."[23]

Blatty said he'd also thought of Shirley MacLaine because "that dimension of her personality and her screen persona was a plus in terms of the realism of the film. Billy suggested Ellen Burstyn, and that was right out of nowhere for me. I can imagine no greater performance from anyone. When I look at her, I see a lady who looks like she's got a little girl who is possessed. I didn't get that feeling from Carol Burnett or Shirley MacLaine."

Friedkin said he saw twelve-year-old Linda Blair in the last week of auditions. "I knew as soon as she came in she was right. But I've got to deal with her on a gut level, see if I can talk to her . . . . And she was the most pulled together, intelligent, sensitive youngster I've ever known. I got her alone and said, 'Did you read *The Exorcist?*' 'Yes.' 'What is it about?' 'It's about a little girl who gets possessed by the devil and does a lot of bad things.' 'What sort of bad things?' 'She pushes a guy out a window and masturbates with a crucifix and—' I said, 'Wait, what does that mean?' 'It's like jerking off, isn't it?' 'Yeah. Do you know about jerking off?' 'Oh, sure.' I said, 'Do you do that?' 'Yeah, don't you? Everybody does, don't they?' It was that kind of not being smartass. She was comfortable with herself, her body, her life."[24]

Blair said working on the film was "trying and difficult" and that she was very much like the part she played, "the innocent young girl going through all this who really didn't know." (Also, Friedkin initially did not believe Blair would be able to perform all the strenuous action the part called for and hired Eileen Dietz as her double. Dietz's onscreen presence amounted to less than thirty seconds.[25] According to Blair, Dietz was used for the slow regurgitation sequence during the exorcism, and she is the one we see grappling with Ellen Burstyn in the masturbation scene.)

In communicating with actors, Friedkin speaks "in terms of the emotional barometer of a character in a given production problem or acting problem. Once I establish this way of communicating, I can talk about a little hotter or a little cooler. I use musical expressions like allegro, andante, molto vivace. When I started out, I used to say, 'Oh, Jesus Christ, that's terrible. Could you read it like this?' But that's when I was casting wrong, when I didn't do the casting. Or if I had no communication with the actor."[26] (One cannot help but recall Bill Butler's story of Friedkin's slapping Paul Crump.)

Friedkin also says that "if you cast the part right, it comes down to a problem of pacing or the emotional intensity that the director wants to accelerate or decrease."[27] Friedkin has been known to accelerate intensity on the set by employing Howard Hawks's trick of firing off a gun after he says "Action." But as Marcel Vercoutere, the special effects man, says, "There is that longing deep down in Billy's heart that he wants total realism."

Vercoutere had a few insights on how that was achieved with the actors to Friedkin's satisfaction. On the second take of the scene, where Regan slaps Chris across the room after their struggle in the masturbation scene, "Ellen Burstyn smacked the wall, landed on her hiney, and didn't care for it *at all*. And the look on her face was a look to kill. Acting there had ceased. The first time I rigged the gag, everything worked perfectly, but Burstyn wasn't P.O.'ed. The second time I did it, I knew what Billy was after." Another example was when Regan bounces up and down on the bed. "What I tried to do was give the feeling that it was an invisible person shaking her. I put myself into the frame of mind that I was this invisible person reaching over the bed and thrashing her. I said to myself, 'Okay, now you're going to get it.' I'd give it sort of the touch of a personal thing." It took nine or ten takes, according to Vercoutere, to get Blair's reaction. "By that time, she had had enough, and she wants out. That's when Billy said, 'This is the one we want.' Now remember, at that point, she sincerely wants out, and she says so, 'Make it stop! He's trying to kill me!' It's in the movie. That's when the acting ceases and realism starts."

But the ultimate act of realism was attempted for the exorcism scene. Vercoutere said, "If Max von Sydow could have pulled it off, he'd have died on camera. He reached his climax of a dying man at the edge of death at about the point where he takes his nitroglycerin pills in the bathroom. Goodness knows, Max tried to go beyond that peak, and Billy tried everything he could to work with him. Max tried. To satisfy Billy, he would have damn near done it."

Friedkin said that a few days into shooting the exorcism scene he was afraid he was going to be forced to have Father Merrin die once he entered Regan's bedroom. "Max started blowing his lines. He said them in a way that was ridiculous, worse than a Sunday-night evangelist. We'd rehearsed it for weeks, and now the scene was awful. We spent two full days on one take. I told Blatty the takes were unspeakable and unprintable. There is a demonic curse on this film. This actor cannot perform this scene. We tried it again, and another day was lost. I told Blatty, 'I think we'll have to have Merrin die as soon as he enters the room.' Of course, I'd been saying all along not to cut a word, to stay faithful to the book. I told Max I'd bring Ingmar Bergman in to direct this scene. I tried shooting the scene with no crew on the set. In the meantime, Blatty rewrote the exorcism. Finally, I went to Max. His dressing room was monklike, with the words 'Help Me' written on the mirror. I threw the script on the bed, grabbed him, and said, 'What the fuck is wrong?' He said, 'I don't believe in God, and I don't believe in this!' I said, 'But, Max, you played Christ in *The Greatest Story Ever Told.*' He said, 'Yes. But I played him as a man.' That broke the ice. We hugged and went back and filmed the scene as in the movie." Blatty laughed, "We could have avoided the problems by casting Paul Scofield as Merrin. He wanted to do it, in fact. But I was outvoted."[28]

"No one gives a histrionic performance out of keeping with human behavior," Friedkin said. "That's why I cast it the way I did. The one mistake I sort of made in casting was Lee J. Cobb. I did it as kind of a crutch. I wanted one guy in there that the audience could relate to. I was going to cast Studs Terkel in the role of Kinderman. He would have been more real, and less an archetype."[29]

To this point in his career, Friedkin had achieved realistic performances by casting not only for ability but for a certain look, which is to say, the actor is not a "star," not immediately recognizable. Though Burstyn, Cobb, and Jack MacGowran in *The Exorcist,* and Hackman in *The French Connection,* for example, had all already been established in films for varying numbers of years, all added freshness *and* believability to their roles. Their intensity brought believability to Friedkin's realism.

And then there was Titos Vandis. According to Blatty, "Billy had told the casting agent, Juliet Taylor, that he wanted complete unknowns for the parts of Karras's mother and uncle. So Titos Vandis was cast as the uncle, and on the first day of shooting Vandis worked in the hospital scenes at Welfare Island where Karras goes to visit his mother. You'll notice he's not wearing his hat anytime in that sequence until the very last shot and it's partially obscuring his face. After the first day's shooting, Billy and I went to a sneak preview of a rough cut of Woody Allen's *Everything You Always Wanted to Know About Sex but Were Afraid to Ask.* In it there was a great deal of talk by Gene Wilder, who played a psychiatrist, about a man who had a physical relationship with sheep. And in walks Titos Vandis to Wilder's office. I felt Billy stiffening up, as if in the grip of rigor mortis. The first thing I heard him whisper was 'I'm putting a hat on that son-of-a-bitch tomorrow.' Not only was the face recognizable; it would be connected with, and only with, an actor who played a man who fucked sheep. That's why the hat is on in the last part of the scene."

One of the costly moments of the production "nightmare" was an early-morning fire that destroyed the entire set of the interior of the house, causing a six-week delay while it was being rebuilt.[30] Friedkin theorizes that a pigeon flew into an electrical box. Also, a ten-foot-tall statue of the demon Pazuzu was misplaced. It was shipped to Iraq for location scenes in a box fifteen feet tall. Because it was so big, it was placed in a different compartment of the plane and ended up in Hong Kong, causing a two-week delay. Location shooting in Iraq had already been delayed, so that instead of filming in the cool spring, Friedkin and his technicians shot in the blazing summer, 130 degrees in the shade. "We had to film from six to nine o'clock in the morning and in the late evening," Friedkin said; Max von Sydow's facial and hand makeup would melt otherwise.[31] Between these delays, trial and error on the demon makeup, and special effects and a host of other problems, *The Exorcist* took two hundred days to shoot, as opposed to fifty days of improvisation on *The French Connection*.[32]

The associate producer, David Salven, said the delays were no fault of Friedkin's. "We were just doing things that had never been done before. It was unusual circumstances." Studios, sometimes, aren't so understanding. "I remember one time when a couple of Warner Bros. executives said we're over schedule and over budget. It was around four million dollars to start and came in at about eleven million dollars, but the difference is that everything that went into the picture is up on the screen. Anyway, the studio guys asked Billy, 'What do you think we should do?' His answer was 'I would suggest you fire me.' Now how do you answer that? He was being Billy Friedkin. It's his plus side. He could say fire a grip or get rid of a truck or we won't eat lunch tomorrow. Instead, it's 'Fuck it. We're doing everything to the best of our knowledge and capability. Otherwise fire me.' That stops the meeting. It's either you're fired or how do you like the food in New York?

"Billy didn't change. He wasn't a humble, quiet guy on *Good Times* when he had nothing. He took the same chances then that he did on *Exorcist* when he had everything. He's a perfectionist. Sometimes I think people can go too far being a perfectionist. But sometimes it was perfectionism in relationship to his peers rather than to his audience."

Salven cited Friedkin's close scrutiny of each print of the film, which Fred Kaplan discussed in Chapter 2. Not only did the prints have to meet rigid quality requirements, but so did theaters. "A huge percentage of theaters in the *world* have mediocre facilities," Salven said. "We had a crew go around to the twenty-six theaters *The Exorcist* was going to open at to examine their projection and sound facilities, and a couple of places had to make changes or we weren't going to give them a print."

Friedkin also had theaters checked the same way for *The French Connection.* "I want people to see the picture in focus, you know? I shot it in focus," he said.[33]

Salven also said that innovation was very important to Friedkin. If certain effects, for example, "had been done a hundred times before and worked, he'd want to do something that hadn't been done before that would work a little better, even if at that time he didn't know exactly what it would be. There was also 'Don't say we can't do it. Let's try it.' Like the cold breath in the bedroom."

"In the old days," Friedkin said, "when they wanted breath to show in a room, they used to go down to the Glendale icehouse and build a stage. Well, the Glendale icehouse doesn't exist anymore."[34] So they built the set of Regan's bedroom inside a refrigerated cocoon. "Alan Snyder, who designed and engineered the cocoon, is dead now," Salven said.

Friedkin said, "At the end of each day's shooting, we had to turn the air-conditioning on to build it up for the next morning's shooting. We'd get in and shoot for four or five hours, and the temperature would go up because of our lights to twenty-five or thirty degrees, and there'd be no more breath in the room. We'd have to stop shooting, turn off the lights, and build the cold up some more. The entire set was balanced on a bowling ball, which permitted us to rock it back and forth when we wanted to. There were also three different beds which did three different things."[35]

The special effects man said that depending on the effect, or "gag," he could make the bed appear "to rock and roll and shake and shimmy and tap-dance." Originally the bed started off as a very tiny one. As more gags were added, the bed evolved into "a big four-poster, and with Linda Blair on it, it weighed about two hundred pounds. I had all my devices behind the walls. You could shoot under the bed, over it, anyway you wanted, and you couldn't see anything because the slot I had that levitated the bed—which was counterweighted in the back of the walls—had a window-shade roll covering it. As the bed went up, it rolled the wallpaper back on the wall again where the slot was, so you could take the bed up, look under it, and you'd see nothing. So we could do anything we wanted."

Anything as long as they could make the audience believe it.

"There is a very fine line as to how far realism can go, and that fine line is what Billy was after," Vercoutere said. "That was the reason we tested the exorcism effects and checked the makeup before we started shooting. That's what was worrying him—if they were believable."

Friedkin indicated that the first makeup for Blair was wrong. "The demonic mask had to come out of what Blatty wrote; some force outside her had to come from within. Something organic, self-inflicted."[36]

"From there on, Billy was totally confident he could pull it off," Vercoutere said.

But about three weeks into filming, Friedkin called all the department heads of the shooting company together. Vercoutere explained: "Billy said that if we were the audience eventually going to see the movie, what would be our opinion up to this time? Nobody was really open at first, but then Dick Smith, our makeup man, said he felt he was into it a little too heavy. I felt the same way. We were reaching our peak too early in the film with the heavier makeup and the thrashing of the bed. By the time we'd've gotten to the exorcism, there wouldn't have been any effect left."

An example of this reining-in evident onscreen was the bed levitating during the exorcism scene. "The thumping of one bed leg and then two legs was a little teaser," Vercoutere said, adding that earlier in the picture we see the bed shake but in this final scene it pounds violently before it goes up, and that was "Billy's idea—it was not originally in the script."

There were also times when Friedkin was not sure what he wanted. Or at least he did not know until he saw it. "For the scene when Father Merrin arrives at the house," cinematographer Owen Roizman said, "Billy wanted the shade on Regan's window to be down but with a shaft of light to be coming from the window."

The difficulty for Roizman in composing the shot was obvious. "You can't make a shaft of light through a shade. You have to have a sharp source of light. So Billy had drawn a sketch of what he wanted it to look like, with the light coming out, and it appeared below the window. We tried that. We made a little hole in the wall underneath the window, and it looked ridiculous. He saw it and said, 'That's terrible.' And I said, 'But that's what you've drawn.' He said, 'You've got to go beyond that. I expect you to go beyond that.'

"We spent two nights working on it. We did a rehearsal—fog and everything. It looked sensational. Then we said let's roll it. Just as we rolled, a wind came up and blew a lot of the fog out. We made the take, but it wasn't as nice as it had been in rehearsal. Billy said, 'Great. Print it. Let's move on.' And I said, 'Wait. Let's make another take. The wind came up and blew half the fog out.' Billy said, 'Oh, it was great. We got it.' He wouldn't do another take." (This shot of Merrin standing on the street silhouetted in the light was used as the poster art for the film. It establishes a sense of foreboding suited to the picture.)

Yet, considering Friedkin's desire for perfection, Roizman says Friedkin "likes a certain element of error. Now that may be strange to comprehend, but he's willing to accept flaws in the film. He'd like to see them. They're almost calculated."

Friedkin offers his own example, citing the scene where Karras comes to tape-record Regan's voice. "In the long shot, Karras reaches down to turn on the machine with his left hand. The insert is close on his right hand turning it on. I asked the dubbing mixers, who had worked on it for two days, if they noticed what was wrong with the scene. They didn't until I pointed it out. I did it on purpose." Friedkin has taken the deep-immersion concept of Slavko Vorkapitch, who used to be the best montage director in films, and applied it to this film: "If an audience is immersed, you can do anything."[37]

This particular scene with Karras is important, too, because it is the first time he meets Regan. It is also the first time the audience sees the demonic countenance of the little girl. The scene opens with the demon taunting Karras by saying, "What an excellent day for an exorcism." A strange greeting? Not to Friedkin, who said his attitude about the scene was twofold: "We needed some levity somewhere along the line," and "if one were spirited off by the Frankenstein monster, after you got over the initial shock of being in the presence of this thing, you'd soon be playing chess together;"[38] "familiarity breeds a certain relaxed quality."[39] (Conversely, in the 1935 film *The Bride of Frankenstein*, the villain introduced himself to the monster by offering it a cigar.)

Friedkin's point was that he did not want the audience to start feeling comfortable with the demon. "Every time out, I wanted to come in with something new like here's this weird way she's talking or here's some vomit or a little levitation shot, but nothing too long. Don't stare at the face too long because the more you're looking at it, the more comfortable you're going to get with it. The whole idea is to put you off guard. You are uncomfortable with that which you are least familiar.[40]

"Fear, the essential principle of fear, has something to do with having something standing behind you . . . like a cold chill on the back of your neck.[41]

"I was conscious of introducing all the major characters, except Karras, from behind. Everybody is sort of snuck up on or discovered. We come up behind them, almost like an unseen force."[42]

(We see Merrin on his knees at the archeological digs near Nineveh, his back to us. Chris lies on her stomach in bed reading her script when she suddenly hears a noise and turns toward us, revealing her face. Regan sleeps on her stomach, the camera looking down on her. We dolly along a set of bleachers until we pick up the lone figure of Kinderman, sitting on them reading a newspaper, his back to us. The camera pushes through a crowd to find Dennings, who turns around to face us. So why do we see Karras full face in a crowd shot? "Karras," Friedkin said, "is the person at whom the whole thing is directed." He is "seemingly successful in driving the demon out of the girl."[43])

Speaking of "unseen forces," Friedkin said, "It's easy to achieve special effects that are not convincing, like levitation. But it's quite another thing to get people to suspend disbelief, and that's what I tried for. Most people are willing to forget there's a camera or a projector or a screen and accept it as life."[44] Friedkin admits he thought the film "might become a comedy," however, because the special effects began to provoke laughter when they were shown in dailies.[45] While making Regan's neck bulge, projecting vomit, levitation, and Regan's head turning 360 degrees were all in the film, effects such as the demon's walking backwards on all fours down the stairs and its tongue hanging from its mouth two feet long were not used. Though Friedkin "chickened out on them" because "people wouldn't dig it,"[46] the effects were all believable. In other words, the ultimate illusion. "As a filmmaker I ask the audience, 'Did it work?'"[47]

Blatty said that though he first balked at the 360-degree head-turning with the argument that "supernatural" was not synonymous with "impossible," it was still obvious that audiences loved it.[48] But something Blatty did not love was the first vomiting scene, the scene where Karras initially meets Regan. After some verbal jousting, Karras calls the demon's bluff on whether or not it knows Karras's mother's maiden name. Regan responds by spewing a stream of vomit into Karras's face. Blatty said he "wanted the vomiting shot cut *way* down. Billy cut it somewhat, but there is still way too much. There is a difference between shock and revulsion. It made me queasy. Had she vomited, it hit his face, and we cut away, we'd have known exactly what happened—startle, shock, cut. How long one lingers on it changes the quality of the scene. I feel the same way about eels out of severed horses' heads dredged up from a river in Volker Schlondorf's *The Tin Drum.*" Blatty thought for a moment and added, "Of course, because a German did it, it's art."

Special effects man Vercoutere added another dimension to the vomiting scene, saying it was difficult for him because the pea soup kept freezing. "Remember, that bedroom set was a refrigerated cocoon, and the temperature was down to around ten degrees or lower so you could see the breath of people. But the soup had to be hot to make it steam. I had it in a stainless-steel container that was electrically heated, and I was supposed to hit Jason Miller in the chest. But I had a little too much elevation on my aim. First shot hit him right in the face. And I'll never forget the look he gave me. It was 'Why you dirty son-of-a-bitch.' But his reaction was so real. He was pissed. He didn't know what the hell was in my container."

Then Vercoutere chuckled and said that Friedkin did not like it. "It wasn't in the script. The script said it was supposed to hit him in the chest. And I thought I'd better give it a little more elevation because it might drop short due to the weight. You just can't go up in that cold room all day and practice. So I shot him in the chest for the next two takes. Then we saw all the dailies, and everybody saw the one where I nailed him in the face and said it was *it*. At the time, though, it was considered a missed shot."

The creation of the voice of the demon was not quite as messy. Friedkin asked himself, "What does a demon sound like? What inspiration do you get to portray a demonic voice? I came up pretty empty, so we spent a lot of time working with this." Luckily, the Reverend Thomas Birmingham, one of the technical advisers on the film, gave Friedkin a recording of an actual exorcism that took place in the Vatican. Friedkin says he copied the voice of the possessed young boy from the recording and combined it with his own voice, Linda Blair's voice, animal sounds, and especially Mercedes MacCambridge's voice at adjusted speeds and syntax.[49] The classic symptoms of possession, Friedkin said, "all involve this business of complete personality change, physical change, obscenities, supernatural occurrences. A characteristic always in a young person, male or female, is that the voice becomes deeper, matured beyond its years, and somewhat emphysemaic. The key word is 'emphysemaic.' The wonderful wheeze sound you hear is Mercedes MacCambridge. She smokes heavy. It sounds like she has three or four screaming animals in her throat. We recorded that very close up and then made a loop out of it."

After he dubbed in the voice, Friedkin felt something was wrong, and then it occurred to him that he "had to keep that demon presence alive, even when it wasn't talking, and that's when we decided to put that looped wheeze in there." He says Linda Blair mouthed the words as best she could. "Some of her stuff was very good. . . . When I started the picture, I thought, I'm just going to get a good ballsy masculine voice to do this thing. But then it occurred to me that if I could get a female voice that had a masculinity to it, it would be that much more believable. . . . And whatever effectiveness the voice has is in large part due to the way Mercedes MacCambridge dramatized it."[50] MacCambridge, incidentally, claims to have "swallowed eighteen raw eggs and a pulpy apple," resulting in self-induced regurgitation, and "had the crew tear up a sheet and bind me hand and foot" so she could properly dramatize (one supposes) the cries and vomiting sounds.[51]

But Friedkin says the vomiting sound was achieved by the fiancée of one of the sound technicians, and it was "rather humorous the way we arrived at it. She was with us at a recording session, sleeping, lying facedown on a couch because it was about two or three in the morning. He set a microphone up next to her and then ran across the room and leapt on her with his knees on her back. The sound that she made when she woke up is the sound that you hear in the film. Other sound effects included taking an old leather wallet filled with credit cards and cracking it close to a microphone to achieve the sound of bending bone in the head-turning sequence, and dragging rats backward over sandpaper for the scratching sound Chris hears up in her attic early in the film.[52]

Depicting horror in daylight is not a new concept. Hitchcock did it in pictures like *Shadow of a Doubt,* Friedkin said.[53] However, the horror in *The Exorcist* is contrasted with normalcy. Bill Malley, the production designer, explained that the interior house set "is a builder's colonial, a brick box, not an architectural gem. Regan's bedroom is a square box, so to make it interesting, you never move outside the perimeter of this sixteen by sixteen-foot room." Close it in, in other words. This is a natural way of inducing claustrophobia, and given a new unknown horror every time Friedkin takes us through Regan's door, it builds more tension. Another important facet of maintaining the normalcy and claustrophobia is keeping the camera at eye level. The crucifix masturbation scene, for example, was shot in close-up that way. This choice, according to Roizman, allowed audiences to put the image in their minds. "When you see a close-up of a hand holding a crucifix and a close-up of a face and the action of her hand, you *know* what she's doing." That the scene takes place in daylight in her room makes it all the more horrific because it is *not* ominous.

In the nighttime bedroom scenes, two lamps on either side of the bed were the only sources of light, and, Roizman said, that was how they wanted it to look. "Let's keep it real-looking, but 'pretty' real. We didn't want a horror movie. None of the underlighting-faces clichés. I said to Billy at the time that with the light coming from a lamp, rather than do a fashion type of lighting, I would cheat it so it was coming from a little bit below, and because of that, it went slightly ominous. The cold breath, too, had to look like it was being lit from the lamps. To show it, we had to use back lights, and when you use them, it starts looking theatrical. So we ended up having a guy hand-holding the light and aiming at the breath of the actors and moving with them and not shining it on other things. It had to look natural."

"Every scene was planned for its light and dark values, even down to the actors within a shot," Friedkin added. "I tried to alternate those values as much as I could."

Roizman, however, recalled that one of the major arguments he and Friedkin had was "how much we'd see of the actors' faces. I'd opt to keep them darker, and he'd always want to see them." He cited the scene where Karras is listening to the demon's voice on the tape recorder in his room. He had it lit so that when Karras answers the phone, his face is etched in the dark. "If it looks good and tells the story, you don't need to see the actor's face all the time. But Billy's theory was he had to see the face. Billy was an enigma that way."

Speaking of enigmas: The St. Joseph medal first found in the archeological digs by Merrin. It later figures in Karras's dream, gets torn from around his neck during the climactic struggle with the demon, and is ultimately given to Father Dyer by Chris. Much significance was attached to it by audiences, Blatty said. "Did Karras get possessed because it was ripped away from his neck? Was it a talisman that protected him up to that time?" When Blatty first saw the medal while watching the dailies of the Iraq prologue, it "was a surprise, and I asked Billy, 'What is the medal doing there?' And he said 'resonance,' which means Billy didn't know." Blatty grinned. Friedkin has varied explanations of the enigma of the medal, from "a workman dropped it"[54] (referring to the Iraqi digs) to "a talisman of good or evil" to "letting the audience have its own interpretation."[55] However, of the specific shot of the medal's falling through the air in Karras's dream, Friedkin contends it is as much part of the connective fiber between the images Merrin saw in Iraq—like the dogs and the clock stopping and the demon face he would see during the exorcism—as the dream itself, which is like a time warp. These are subliminal images that are on screen for literally only a second or two. "I used them on the theory that time doesn't exist. Another kind of time. It's fractured. . . . Critics say it's manipulation. I say that's great because absolutely, it's manipulation. I wish there was a better way to put it, but if it works, great. I treasure that word as a filmmaker."[56]

Music manipulates, too, and Friedkin said he wanted no scary music and no wall-to-wall music, which is to say, music that starts with one cut and ends with another. He wanted it to dissolve in and out, come and go at strange places, and be "like a chill presence that would never assert itself."

Originally, Bernard Herrmann was going to compose the music, but "he didn't want to work in Hollywood again," Friedkin said. He then hired Lalo Schifrin to compose a score and told him about the kind of musical influences he had in mind, which were the compositions of Anton Webern, Hans Werner Henze, and Kryzysztof Penderecki. But then Schifrin's score was "big, loud, scary, wall-to-wall noise," Friedkin said. "The references that I mentioned to him have to do with a very minimal kind of sound. It's surreal music. It's music that is like a cold hand on the back of your neck. It's texture. When I heard the score, I broomed it immediately right out of the recording session. Threw it away.

"It pained me to do it, but I would rather have Lalo Schifrin denounce me on the front page of the *Los Angeles Times* every day for the rest of my life than use one note of his score in my picture. It's nothing against him . . . . I was bound and determined to have the kind of music I originally intended. I then went over to Wallach's Music City and bought the albums by the composers I mentioned, picked out the sections I wanted, and that's the score for *The Exorcist*."[57]

(Lalo Schifrin chose not to comment for this study.)

However, the one piece of music that became the theme of the picture Friedkin found in the music library at Warner Bros. Friedkin also believes this selection, entitled "Tubular Bells," saved an otherwise lifeless scene in the film. The scene shows Chris walking down a quiet Georgetown street, the rust-colored leaves of autumn hanging on the trees. A group of children dressed as witches and ghosts for Halloween run laughing past her. "It was beautiful," Friedkin said, "but I felt everything stopped here and the only thing that could save it would be this weird sound coupled with this nursery-rhyme motif that would be vaguely disturbing."[58]

Something else that may have been vaguely disturbing to Friedkin was an ad-libbed moment during the sequence where Dennings is seen directing the big student demonstration for the movie-within-the-movie. Blatty has a cameo role as the producer (ironically), and he shouts at Dennings, who appears totally unconcerned, "Is the scene really essential?" Was this line indicative of the actual filming of *The Exorcist* since it did go over budget and over schedule? "No," according to Blatty, who added with a grin, "you must remember the scene was a great deal longer originally. Billy asked me to extemporize the character, and I did. In the last take I shouted a line to the director, which was 'We are two hundred thousand dollars over budget!' I think we *were* around that at about that time, and I guess Billy got too sensitive. We dropped the line."

What they did not drop, though, were a series of obscenities uttered by twelve-year-old Regan. "Our demon was real," Blatty said, "and since we were representing a reflection of ultimate evil, we could not, as Stanley Kauffmann has noted, simply have Regan say, 'Darn,' or have a Greek chorus enter and announce that Regan has done some very naughty things off camera."[59] The writer-producer said that the obscenities written originally for the exorcism scene "lacked authenticity" according to Father John J. Nicola, another technical adviser. "While he never suggested that we change what we had, he did point out that in actual cases the language was far beyond what we had." Blatty said he went to his office and wrote a string of the worst filth he could imagine, and Friedkin chose the worst of the obscenities for the scenes requiring them.[60]

While the demon's "language" had to be authentic, so too the medical jargon and procedures. Friedkin said he asked doctors what they would do if confronted with the symptoms exhibited by Regan. They told him they'd go through arteriography and pneumoencephalography. And if they didn't find it was a lesion in the temporal lobe of the brain, they'd remand the patient for further observation. If that didn't solve it, then psychiatry.[61]

The real deviltry in filmmaking for Friedkin is in exorcising those scenes that slow his pictures down. (At 120 minutes, *The Exorcist* is Friedkin's third longest picture.) While Karras and Merrin used the "power of Christ" to expel the demon, Friedkin relied on the editing, what he refers to as "the language of filmmaking."[62] Using the exorcism scene as an example, Friedkin said it was originally about twenty minutes long, though now it runs about eight minutes, "but I think people would have been falling asleep with the popcorn spilling off if I had gone any longer. I love speed on screen, and I wish the exorcism was faster." He says he also shot three and a half hours of usable film when he went to Iraq. (The Iraqi prologue lasts eight minutes.) Included in his usable footage were scenes of men stab-bing themselves and putting daggers to their throats, which, though darkly appealing, would "mess up this story" if included.[63]

Malley, the production designer, recalled the scene in which Merrin walks down the open corridor behind the row of praying men. "If you just had panned to the right, there was a gorgeous brick minaret. We thought about shooting it, and Billy said it was too much of a phallic symbol. Then Billy said, 'Will people say, "Did that enhance the story, or is it just a postcard shot?"'" Though Friedkin resisted that temptation, he did include shots of Merrin walking through a bazaar where people are making shoes. "It's all natural lighting, the sun pouring through these holes in this cave, and it doesn't belong in the movie, but it's just so beautiful. I had it out, and the scene played a lot better, moved a lot faster. I went to bed one night, and, Christ, I got up and called the editor. I said, 'Put those damn shots back in.' He said, 'Why? They fuck up the scene.' I said, 'They're gorgeous. You know, if they'll believe any of the rest of this stuff, they'll believe this shot.' It means nothing, I assure you. I love it. The sound is so nice. It has nothing to do with the picture."[64]

However, there were some deletions that Blatty says still cause *him* "to bleed varying quantities of blood."[65] One concerned the omission of an early medical examination of Regan. Blatty said, "Any craftsman seeing that picture has got to get a case of the giggles when you go to the party scene and there's Regan, laughing. She's happy. She urinates on the rug. A minute after that, she says, 'Mother, what's wrong with me?' And Chris says, 'It's nerves, like the doctor said—' What doctor?—'you keep taking your pills.' What pills?! Movies are magical, and you don't have to do exposition on everything, but this was just unacceptable. In fact, I think a New York reviewer talked of the horrendous construction of the screenplay and logical gaps and nonsense like that."

Another deletion concerned what Friedkin called a "showstopper," ac-cording to Blatty, in the sense that it stopped the story cold to pause for a "theological commercial."[66] "It was the scene in which Merrin and Karras converse in the hallway after they perform the first rite of exorcism," Blatty explained. "Karras asks, 'Why this little girl?' Merrin tells him the purpose of the possession of her was to make everyone surrounding her despair of their own humanity and decide that even if there really was a God, that he couldn't love anyone as bestial as we are.

"The audience is longing to hear that! The audience wants to know 'Why am I being subjected to all this bestiality; what is the point?' It's part of the message of the film. They think it was just a series of shocks with no point at all otherwise; it was just Halloween."

Friedkin said that that message was implicit in the film. "I trusted the audience to understand this implicitness. I shot the scene, but then I pulled it out in the editing."[67] (As with the bloody accident scene in *The French Connection*, ideas embodied in Friedkin films must be "by the way.")

"There is a message implicit in the film, but not the one expressed on the staircase," Blatty said. "It is the most fundamental and crude idea that there is a transcendence, that there is a conflict between the forces of good and the forces of evil. That the selfless act of love performed by Karras at the climax of the film on behalf of a complete stranger—he's never met Regan—argues there is more to man than molecular structures; the essence of this other reality about man is essentially good, loving. That's implicit.

"But at least half the people who see the film completely misconstrue this. They don't understand what's happening on the screen. It beggars my imagination. Billy and I were keenly aware of this problem before the scene was shot, and we spent a great deal of time going over it in the effort to be absolutely certain that the climax was obvious to even the meanest intelligence."

When asked why he believed many audiences missed this point, Blatty answered that he thought that their "senses have been numbed. They are in a certain state of shock where they were focused on one some thing, and I don't know what."

Friedkin said some audiences might misconstrue the triumph of good over evil "because it's within them to begin with. One thing you cannot exorcise is the deep-seated tenets within people who come to see a movie that deals on such a primitive level with their emotions. Karras's deed is understandable to anyone who has read *A Tale of Two Cities*."[68]

(It is unfortunate that Friedkin chooses to equate Karras and Sydney Carton of *A Tale of Two Cities*. True, good does conquer evil in *The Exorcist*. Even two of the most venomous attacks on the film admit that; Vincent Canby, in the *New York Times*, says that "God triumphs over the devil,"[69] and Pauline Kael, in the *New Yorker*, calls Karras "a modern Christ who dies to save mankind."[70] However, Sydney Carton's decision to die in Charles Dickens' novel is one he *prepares* for; Karras's sacrifice is a spontaneous reaction with no regard for the consequences to himself.)

A third omission was the ending. Blatty explained that originally the film was to end with Father Dyer, Karras's friend, and Kinderman reprising the playful discussion Kinderman and Karras had earlier in the film about going to movies together. Blatty believed this suggestion of "carrying on" would provide a lift for the audience. "Even the audience that understood the climax of *The Exorcist* wanted to walk out and cut their throats. You feel depressed. And you want to give the audience not a logical reason for thinking everything's okay but a visceral one, an emotional reason. You do it with the tones and the textures and the conversation and the music. It's the ending of the novel I wanted."

Though Friedkin did shoot this scene between Dyer and Kinderman, part of the reason he pulled it out was that "it was wrong to end upbeat. It would have been gratuitous."[71] He adds, "I'm very conscious of making a movie that will enter the minds of those who see it, that will grow in their minds and alter and affect them."[72]

Blatty is less . . . obtuse. "Billy didn't know what he had. He thought it should be cut down to two hours because he didn't think any audience would sit still for longer than that."

The final image in the film shows a lonely Dyer, clad in black, looking down at the stone stairs Karras had died on earlier. Dyer turns and walks out of frame, and we fade to black. It seems somehow incomplete, awkward. "It sure is," Blatty said. "But to think it was contrived and shaped that way would be misguided because the continuation of that scene as it ends now is with Dyer turning, walking to the curb, and Kinderman pulls up. Billy didn't shoot that scene thinking he would end the picture there. Let's face it: It seemed more arty to end with the priest on the steps, looking like Ingmar Bergman trying to figure out the meaning of the last movie he made. But it's very hard to argue with a picture that enormously successful."

Blatty adds, with a chuckle, that a Warner Bros. executive "who shall remain nameless" stated at the first public screening of the film in Los Angeles, "'Well, we've got our *Cleopatra.*' He predicted a worldwide gross of twenty million dollars." (As screenwriter William Goldman has stated of studio executives, "Nobody knows anything.")[73] Blatty also said that same executive told him two yers later, "Don't tamper with success" when Blatty and Friedkin wanted to shoot a new ending for the film for its re-release in 70mm. Though Friedkin was anxious to return to Georgetown to film the new ending, Blatty said, adding that it "would definitely, absolutely give you a nice glow," it would have cost $400,000. However, the Warner executive decided against it because he believed it "might destroy the film's success," Blatty said. "This is a know-nothing attitude because it springs from a point of view which doesn't understand why the picture was successful to begin with." At the time of this writing, Blatty, in the true show-biz vein, still refuses to reveal exactly what constitutes the new "surge of joy" ending.

Audience response to *The Exorcist* was not much different from the reaction to the original *Frankenstein* when it opened in November of 1931. Parents and civic groups called that film too horrifying for children, saying it should play only to adults. (Shortly after it opened, *The Exorcist* was banned to people under eighteen years of age in Washington, D.C., and Boston.) There were also reports of people running screaming from the theaters *Frankenstein* played at, and exhibitors started keeping supplies of smelling salts on hand.[74] At Mann's National Theater in Westwood, California, where *The Exorcist* opened in the last week of December 1973, the manager, Harry Francis, said he and his staff indeed carried pocketfuls of smelling salts. "We'd also have to throw kitty litter down to absorb the vomit as well as keep watch for the phonies who'd show up to act sick for publicity." He added that Friedkin had food catered in for the theater's late-night employees for the first two weeks of the film's engagement.

"All the furor and hype about people getting ill and fainting," Blatty said, "would leave you with the impression that it must be due to some lurid content or violence in the film. Well, I was there many times when people got faint, and it was always at one time: when the blood spurted out of Regan's neck during the arteriogram, which is carried out by actual doctors at NYU Hospital."

Friedkin said, "When people got carried out of *The Exorcist,* I say they got what they paid for.... They went in to be shocked and scared."[75]

(One wonders if Friedkin wanted audiences to be certain to know who "shocked and scared" them when he took his first possessory credit, "A William Friedkin Film," on *The Exorcist.* Or maybe it was just an ironic twist that when he began shooting, he told the *New York Times,* "I don't take credit on my pictures, a film *by* so-and-so. If it's a film *by* somebody instead of *for* somebody, I smell art.")[76]

Critical response was splintered, but ironically, a contemporary review of *Frankenstein* that appeared in *Film Weekly* mirrored and encapsulated what many of the negative reviews of *The Exorcist* said: "The film has no theme and points no moral, but is simply a shocker beside which the Grand Guignol was a kindergarten.... It is the kind of film which could only induce nightmares."[77]

Blatty chuckled when he said, "When I wrote *The Exorcist,* I had no sense of writing something to frighten, only to fascinate."

Friedkin stated matter-of-factly, "We never talked about scaring people."[78]

II

It has been described as "a vision, distorted, tortured ... and honest ... made available to an audience hungry for intensity."[79] Though it could have been written about *The Exorcist,* it was said of the work of the artist Francis Bacon. His trademark 1953 painting, "Study After Velazquez's Portrait of Pope Innocent X," at first glance appears to have captured the look of a man in the throes of electrocution. (See Chapter 1.) But no. It is that Papal authority overcome by some horrific vision, his face cadaverous and mouth agape in a mute black scream. Bacon says he "wanted to make the scream into something which would have the intensity and beauty of a Monet sunset."[80] One cannot help but focus on Bacon's visual manifestation of the scream, the mouth forever frozen in horror. It's the ghastliness of this image, just like the Isenheimer painting of the Crucifixion with the body

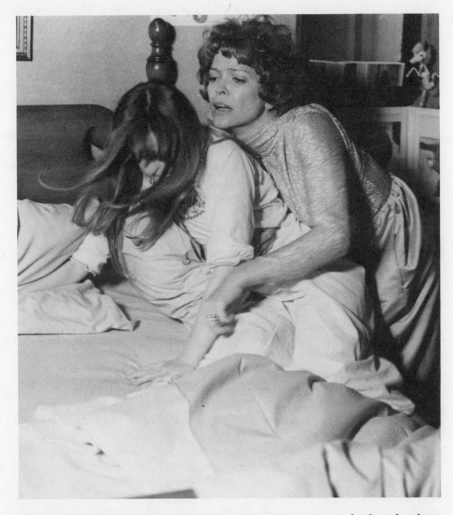

The Exorcist. **Chris MacNiel (Ellen Burstyn, right) tries to calm her daughter Regan's (Linda Blair) convulsions.**

studded with thorns that Bacon admires, that, strangely enough, transcends the horror, becoming vitalizing, fascinating, attractive in its ugliness. This perverse edge of entertainment, visceral in its impact, is the very essence of Friedkin's vision in *The Exorcist*.

Regan's writhings and contortions, her neck bulging, eyes rolling back in her head, and her vomiting are grotesque, violent acts. But unlike Stanley in *The Birthday Party*, whose breakdown is caused almost exclusively through verbal violence, Regan's aberration carries more impact, more reaction, and therefore involvement for an audience because it is *visual*.

Friedkin focuses the perspective of these moments from the point of view of the priests or her mother or whoever is in her bedroom.

And that bedroom, as with every place else in the film, is a very *natural* setting. No horror-movie Gothic mansion up on a hill. The crucifix masturbation scene, in particular, best expresses this perverse edge of entertainment coupled with Friedkin's sense of realism. The lead-in is a very tense scene between Regan's mother, Chris, and Kinderman, the police inspector. He has come to see Chris about the death of Burke Dennings, her friend the movie director, who he believes was killed and then pushed from Regan's window. Dennings was found at the bottom of the M Street stairs, which run next to Chris's house, with "his head turned completely around." At this moment, Chris suddenly realizes to her horror that her daughter *may* have committed murder. (The previous evening, driving home from a conference with doctors, Chris passed a crowd of people and an ambulance at the foot of those stairs. Entering Regan's room, she found her asleep, the window wide open, curtains fluttering.)

During the entire scene of Chris and Kinderman's talking and drinking coffee, there is a deathly quietness. No tick of a clock, no refrigerator hum, no other presence. Only their voices and the occasional clink of a cup set in its saucer. The eeriness heightens our senses. Chris's edginess becomes ours. Moments after Kinderman leaves, Friedkin electrifies the tension with a loud crash and Regan's cries of "No, no!" Another voice, deeper and masculine, shouts "Do it!" Chris races upstairs. Running toward Regan's bedroom door, the look on her face seems to say, "Oh my God, what now!" She throws open the door as we cut inside the room to reveal her look of frightened awe as books, papers, records, and toys fly uncontrollably around the room.

Then we see Regan's bloodied face, a blood-smeared crucifix she holds poised above her, and a guttural voice coming out of her mouth, commanding, "Let Jesus fuck you!" Regan forces her arm down (it's as if she were fighting the movement), and we cut to a side angle of her bloody thighs and the crucifix jabbed between them like a knife stab. Chris lunges for the crucifix, and in the struggle, Regan grabs Chris' head and pushes it into her pelvis, shouting, "Lick me, lick me!"

Pulling Chris' head back, she slaps her so hard that Chris slams into the far wall. From Chris's point of view we see her secretary Sharon (Kitty Winn) and the housekeeper rushing up the stairs. Regan telekinetically jams a chair against the door, slamming it shut. Chris looks up and sees a tall heavy bureau advancing across the floor at her, the wood moaning. She crawls out of the way in time to see Regan sitting on the bed, her head turning backward to face Chris, telling her in *Dennings' voice,* "Do you know what she did, your cunting daughter?"

Chris's cry of despair climaxes the scene because now she knows

Regan murdered Dennings. Visually a story point is accomplished as well as presenting perverse entertainment. Regan's actions and words are repellent, but Chris's shock is our shock because of Friedkin's realistic handling. The scene is a pivotal moment in the film, too. Chris is almost at wit's end. She's exhausted the medical and psychiatric possibilities of what's afflicting Regan. And now Regan, whose physical appearance has not changed drastically to this point, commits a vile act that attacks and defiles God, her mother, the sanctity of the home, her own sexuality and physical being.

Friedkin also enhances the reality of the scene by not underlining it with piercing music as Hitchcock did with the shower murder in *Psycho.* He allows the dialogue, sound effects, and images to carry the impact and horror, and thereby the realism. Admittedly, Hitchcock made audiences believe the Janet Leigh character was stabbed to death in the shower without ever showing the knife implanted in her body. In Friedkin's vision, though, the inexplicable violence to Regan—being thrown up and down on her bed like a rag doll, the vomiting, masturbating with a crucifix—must be graphic because making the unbelievable a reality is integral to the perverse entertainment.

And Friedkin knows how to build up to that shocking realism. First, Regan complains to her mother that her bed shakes. In this scene Chris wakes to a ringing phone. Switching on a lamp, a black-and-white photograph of Regan is revealed. That it is black and white adds an element of stark apprehension to the photographic reflection of Regan with her hands clasped together to her mouth. She appears to be hoping, praying. Or maybe pleading. When she urinates on the floor at her mother's house party, the aberration becomes visual (seeing is believing). Regan's screams while her bed shakes and thumps with her and Chris on it viscerally startle. Later, when doctors are called to the house, they find Regan being thrown and jerked up and down on the bed by unseen forces. She suddenly backhands one of the doctors, who drops to the floor, and she shouts in her guttural tone, "The sow is mine" and "Fuck me." Friedkin escalates the intensity with each new horror and violation, culminating in the masturbation scene, probably the most intense moment in the picture because of the nature of the defilement. We accept and believe; we are compelled to watch because Friedkin's perverse edge of entertainment also lies in fascination of fears unknown made real.

For Friedkin, turning fear into reality was an influence from his youth. Suspense films such as *The Wages of Fear, Diabolique,* and especially *Psycho* had great effect on him. Friedkin describes *Psycho* as "a dull sort of story" for most of its first hour, "but the audience is so expectant. They know they're coming in to see this horrific suspense film, and they're not getting it. They're getting edgy, and then suddenly [Hitchcock] whacks them.... I've wanted to make a film where I could do that...."[81]

Unlike Hitchcock's *Psycho,* Friedkin immediately establishes a sense
of foreboding with his first image. A sunrise in black and white fades —
seemingly burning — to color, the white orb dissolving to a hot, searing, oppressive orange. One can almost feel the heat, or is it an edginess? We cut
to the Nineveh archeological site, standing in shimmering waves of heat
against a cloudless blue sky. Workers with picks chop into the earth, the
digging sounds become louder, intense. That foreboding becomes sharper
when Merrin visibly shakes at discovering the amulet of the demon Pazuzu.
Sitting in the cafe, Merrin, with trembling hands, takes a nitroglycerin pill
for his heart (he may be kindly, but he is an old man near death). A
cacophony of hammering assaults his ears (and ours) as blacksmiths forge
a twisted piece of iron. The sound overwhelms, hypnotic in its piercing
rhythms. Merrin stops as if transfixed, the sound possibly indicative of the
rapid pounding of his heart. He glances over at the smiths as their clanging
ceases, and one of them wipes his brow, turns, and we see one eye white
in blindness.

Foreboding gives way to tension. Merrin tells the curator of antiquities'
office that he has to leave — "There is something I must do." Rounding a corner, Merrin is nearly run down by a galloping black horse pulling a carriage.
Inside is an old, withered woman veiled in black, a premonition of death.
A feeling that something is coming, something terrible, Friedkin ac-
complishes visually. He has the edge as he pulls the string, tightening the
gut of the audience. Merrin returns to the archeological site and climbs
through the ruins, looking, searching. A shadow passes over his face. He
turns and confronts the huge ugly statue of Pazuzu, its mouth wide in a
wicked grin. Black and white dogs fight viciously, winds blow and howl
across the parched earth, separating Merrin and the demon, each standing
on raised mounds as if preparing for confrontation. The fight of the dogs
becomes more intense; the demon statue erect and solid against the winds
while Merrin's shape, though bent and frail, stands in defiant determination,
action revealing character.

The sense of something terrible coming has given way to a sense of evil,
dark and ugly against the setting sun; that fear exists not only in the dark
but in the bright light of day. Friedkin then dissolves to the barking of
neighborhood dogs in the damp gray dawn over Georgetown, and the
bedroom of Chris MacNiel, who hears strange scratching sounds coming
from her attic. Friedkin has not "whacked" the audience yet. He's taken us
to a peak, revealed the forces of good and evil in a frightening world, a
universe out of control, and then drops off much like a roller-coaster ride
and starts up again to the next peak.

Leaving her bedroom to investigate the attic sounds, Chris looks in on
Regan and finds her with the bed covers thrown off, sleeping soundly, yet
the bedroom window is wide open. Chris shivers from the cold. Friedkin

teases. The tension begins (again). Something isn't quite right here. Chris informs her Teutonic butler, Karl, that there are rats in the attic. He states it is clean, "no rats." Chris says, "All right, then we have clean rats." Karl does not accept this. It becomes exasperating, this argument. Tension again; the world askew, tilting.

At the Georgetown University location where Chris is filming a movie (a make-believe world within the film itself; a reflection of a reflection), the director, Burke Dennings, is shooting a campus protest scene. Placards read Keep Classes Open as well as Close the School. A protester shouts, "Let's get the Defense Department off this campus," and then Chris pushes through the crowd, grabs the megaphone, and says, "Wait a minute, the kids who want to get an education have a right, too." Contrasts within contrasts. Peaks of tension, peaks of chaos. All goes smoothly—in Friedkin's vision.

Friedkin has stated he believes the events the film is based on actually occurred. In depicting the "unusual yet factual," he and scriptwriter Blatty have retained the physiological and psychological possibilities to explain the possession. These, too, are used to suspenseful and brutal effect. Regan screams and struggles against an injection, spitting in the doctor's face, calling him a "fucking bastard." An arteriography follows, with blood squirting out of Regan's neck and the tube for the dye inserted. She whimpers and cries. No irregularities are found in her X-rays, but then the doctors are urgently called to Chris's house. They find Regan being thrown about violently on the bed; she slaps one of the doctors. Chris screams, and Sharon pulls her from the room.

More tests prove unhelpful, and a psychiatrist is brought in to attempt hypnosis. Regan, while in a hypnotic trance, brutally attacks the psychiatrist with a viselike grip on his groin. Screaming, Regan is pulled from the panicked doctor. As each medical and psychiatric possibility is eliminated, the suspense factor rises as we witness the demonic possession escalate, resulting in Friedkin's achieving audience acceptance and belief.

This same acceptance and belief must be acquired by Chris, as well. As the various medical treatments are exhausted, Chris remains firm in her resolve to protect and save her daughter. No hysterical clichés here. Her pain at seeing her only child in such dire straits never slips into hopelessness. Yet Chris's actions, ironically, are presented as at least a partial reason behind Regan's possession and also explain some of Regan's early symptoms. The swearing, for example, Regan could have picked up from her mother, as demonstrated in the scene in which Regan eavesdrops on Chris, who tries to contact her ex-husband, who's living in Rome. It's Regan's birthday, and "he doesn't even call his daughter, for Christ's sake. . . . He doesn't give a shit." But it is Regan's sullen despair implied in an earlier scene over her belief that her mother may marry Dennings and the implied guilt in the telephone scene that she is somehow responsible for

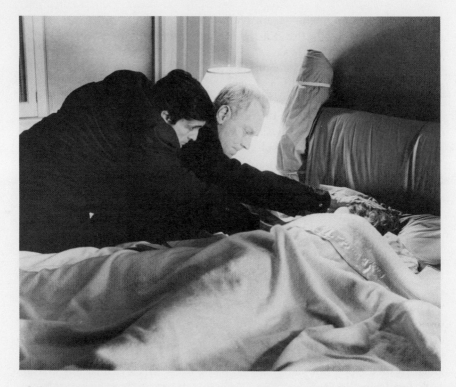

The Exorcist. **Father Karras (Jason Miller, left) and Father Merrin (Max von Sydow) anoint Regan (Linda Blair) during the exorcism.**

her mother's anger that has made Regan susceptible. Yet, it is Chris's scream at the revelation of Regan's heinous act of murdering Dennings that becomes not her final cry of despair but her first step toward Regan's ultimate recovery.

She is convinced Regan "needs a priest; she's already seen every fucking psychiatrist in the world," she tells Karras. After Karras's initial examination, he tells Chris he's not sure what it is; however, "she says she's the devil himself. Now if you've seen as many psychotics as I have, you'd realize that's the same thing as saying you're Napoleon Bonaparte." Chris replies, "You show me Regan's double—same face, same voice, everything—and I'd know it wasn't Regan. I'd know it in my gut. And I'm telling you that that thing upstairs isn't my daughter. Now I want you to tell me that you know for a fact that there's nothing wrong with my daughter except in her mind! You tell me that you know for a fact that an exorcism wouldn't do any good! *You tell me that!*" Chris is presented, at the very least, as an agnostic, but the intensity of her fervor at this moment convinces us, without doubt, that she *believes* her daughter is indeed possessed.

The diabolical "whacks" begin in natural, commonplace settings. When Regan urinates at her mother's party after cryptically telling one of the guests, an astronaut, that he's "going to die up there," Chris apologizes, moving Regan quickly out of the room. Chris bathes her, puts her to bed, and then Regan asks, "Mother, what's wrong with me?" Downstairs, the housekeeper scrubs the carpet, and Chris comes down to see how she's doing. Suddenly, Regan cries out; crashing sounds follow. Chris races back upstairs to find her daughter crying hysterically as her bed shakes and rocks and pitches. Chris jumps on the bed with her, and Regan screams, "Mother, make it stop!" By the time we witness the cross masturbation scene, Friedkin has taken us from short strange teasers like the attic scratchings to Regan's traumas and violent vulgar actions.

Screams heighten the suspense of many scenes, capping them emotionally, viscerally. In Karras's dream, the St. Joseph medal falls with a hypnotic grace through the air. As it drops onto stone, the sounds of Karras's breathing are obliterated by Regan's screaming, and we cut to her spitting on a doctor. Friedkin uses sound as a character. We are lulled momentarily by the quiet, and then the scream startles. It becomes that "cold hand on the back of your neck" Friedkin calls fear. The contrast from serenity to chaos in the dream scene, for example, has the effect of whipping us instantly from a relaxed low to a visceral high.

Also, the use of light and dark qualities from scream to scream and scene to scene is effective for its ironies. As in the previously described sequence, the silver medal hits a black stone, and we cut to Regan in a brightly lit examination room. The irony here is the contrast of a symbol of goodness (the medal) falling onto blackness, juxtaposed with Regan's ugly act in the sterile light (the medical office). A moment of normalcy such as students playing tennis is contrasted with Inspector Kinderman talking to Karras about the strange death of Dennings and the desecrations in the church (shown earlier) where a statue of the Virgin Mary had bloody appendages attached to its breasts and groin. Even in the daylight horror of the masturbation scene, a darkly shaded image caps the moment before cutting to the brightness of the following image. Chris crawls to Regan's bedroom door but can't get out. Friedkin frames a claustrophobic close-up on Chris as she's wedged herself between the door and the chair blocking it, the shadow of the chair across her face.

Her anguished cry echoes over the cut to Karras walking toward us against a gray-gloss sky that fills the screen. In this scene, Chris meets with Karras to ask for his help in exorcising Regan. Chris wears a pair of sunglasses. In her frustration in trying to explain to Karras (who sees the situation in psychiatric terms, not religious) that she has exhausted all other avenues ("Jesus Christ, won't somebody help me?"), she starts crying and removes the glasses to wipe her eyes, revealing a black bruise on her white cheek.

Friedkin's most inspired use of ironic contrasts is in the sequence of Merrin's arrival at the MacNiel house. Friedkin begins the sequence on Merrin moving away from us as he walks up a hill that is covered in dead leaves. A young bearded priest runs up to him and hands him a letter. Merrin does not open it; he knows it is his summons to Chris's home. This old man with the failing heart continues his walk up the hill. We dissolve to a close-up on the demonic face of Regan, its welts and cuts grotesque, green eyes wide, cracked lips moving in silent evil prayer (one guesses) to another dissolve showing Merrin's arrival at the house. He steps from the taxi and pauses momentarily, a black silhouette in the single shaft of light coming from Regan's window. Inside the house, Chris opens the door to reveal Merrin, a black silhouette standing in the doorway, wearing a black hat and black clothing. He looks like Charon, the River Styx ferryman, an image of death. Ironically, Merrin has come to save a life, not take it. These contrasts all add to Friedkin's chaotic vision *and* the sense of evil he established early on, in which beautiful visions took on ominous overtones: a deep blue sky with the statue of Pazuzu jutting into it and Chris's walk home on Halloween evening where children dressed as ghouls and witches gleefully run by her. And especially Regan herself, whose innocence is ravaged by the demon throughout.

Yet these attacks, verbal and physical, are not crude exploitation by Friedkin, though some critics (see Vincent Canby, *New York Times,* and Jay Cocks, *Time*) claim otherwise. Suspense is the focus, not serving up gratuitous shocks. Labeling *The Exorcist* "cheap shivers"[82] is akin to shrugging off Sam Peckinpah's epic of heroism, *The Wild Bunch,* as a bloody exercise in metaviolence. The point is missed. True, witnessing the aberration is part of the vision and entertainment, but it is coupled with catharsis and compassion. Blatty's story demands it. The ugliness of the possession is in direct contrast to the weakness of Karras turned to strength through self-sacrifice.

When we meet Damien Karras, he is on his way to visit his mother in New York City. In a subway terminal, a bum—dirty, unshaven, urine stains on his pants—begs Karras to "help an old altar boy." Karras only stares. His mother lives alone in a run-down tenement. Her joy at seeing her son feels genuine. "Dimmy, Dimmy," she says, her eyes welling up as she strokes his face.

But Karras is a man wracked with guilt. Not only is he a priest; he's a trained psychiatrist as well. He counsels other priests but believes he is losing his faith. The world is too cruel a place. When his mother dies, his guilt overwhelms him. (Seeing her in the Welfare Island Hospital, restraints on her wrists, Karras tries to comfort her, but all she could cry was "Why you do this to me, Dimmy?")

Yet these same guilts and inner conflicts are the stuff of heroes. In the face of personal adversity and doubt, he goes to do combat for someone he does not know. When he first meets Regan, she is strapped to the bed (this scene is the next time we see Regan *after* the masturbation scene), and the physical signs of possession are in evidence. The ugly welts and open cuts on her face, matted hair, putrid green eyes, and copious vomiting bear little resemblance to the sweetness of the little girl who enjoys sculpting funny-looking birds for her mother. Though he is not completely convinced it is a genuine possession, Karras secures permission from the bishop to perform an exorcism. To Karras's disappointment, the bishop believes "it might be best to have a man with experience." The bishop takes the matter up with the university president, who is also a priest, and they decide Lankester Merrin would be the best choice, having exorcised a demon years before in Africa.

When Merrin and Karras meet in Chris's house and shake hands, a loud unsuspected shout of *"Merrin!"* from the demon startles the household. With this, Friedkin again demonstrates the fact that Merrin and the demon are old nemeses—from their standoff in the ruins of Nineveh to Regan's demonic features growing more intense with Merrin's arrival to the demon's verbal challenge. And finally, during the climactic exorcism, an apparition of the demon statue appears in the room, visually laying to rest any doubts that indeed this is the demon Merrin had bested in Africa.

Merrin dies while performing the exorcism, and Karras tries frantically to pump life back into the priest with blows to his chest. Regan begins to giggle delightedly. Karras throws her to the floor and begins beating her with his fists, shouting at the demon to "take me!" A guttural lowing is heard. Karras looks up at the closed bedroom window; the curtains flutter, beckon. His features have changed to the demonic, and his first act is to attempt to throttle Regan. He has been the object of possession by the demon all along. (When Karras had come to see Regan a second time to record her voice, the demon says an exorcism would bring Karras and him together. Regan, then, is merely the catalyst.)

So when Karras forces himself away from Regan, his body shakes with inner conflict, and his features instantly revert to normal. He has the strength to be in control, but for how long? He realizes his weaknesses have made him vulnerable to the possession. In his mind he can see *no* other choice but to save everyone in the house rather than be a priest controlled by the devil. He is on the edge—no alternatives, another facet in Friedkin's iconography of aberration. Yet the implicit message remains; weakened spiritually, Karras battles supernatural forces to save a stranger. A reaffirmation of hope is born out of the aberration, the conflict between good and evil resolved by the ultimate act of love.

Though the *Christian Century* has stated that Karras's act "by our Protestant standards" was "a completely impossible solution,"[83] Karras's

The Exorcist. **Father Damien Karras (Jason Miller, left) tells Father Merrin (Max von Sydow) of the possession.**

choice is clearly not suicide. His choice is neither a good one nor a bad one, only a *right* one. It is the same principle of self-sacrifice that motivated Christ, who gave his life to save all men. This was also part of Blatty's point with the story. For example, the medal that Regan rips from Karras's neck in their titanic struggle is a St. Joseph medal. Joseph was Christ's human father, and a priest represents Christ on earth. Wearing a symbol of Christ's father around his neck becomes even more significant when we realize there is never any mention of Karras's father in the film, not even a *picture* of him at his mother's apartment. Karras's mother's name, incidentally, is Mary. Recall Chris's meeting with Karras: "Jesus Christ, won't somebody help me" has the impact of a statement rather than a hopeless sob of frustration. Most priests are commonly referred to as father. In the film, Karras addresses all the priests by their first names, or "Your Excellency" when he speaks with the bishop. But when he meets Merrin for the first time at Chris's house, he greets him as "Father," establishing a more paternal than reverent bond. Damien Karras is even bound to Jesus Christ by the first letters of their names: *D* and *K* are the letters that follow *C* and *J*.

Friedkin has said that "joyful poetry is about human frailty"; he calls that poetry a "celebration."[84] Certainly Karras sees the world and himself in worthless terms—guilt, remorse, lost faith. The film celebrates the impulse for good, love, redemption. Friedkin, like Francis Bacon, has no morals to preach.[85] Instead they show us "by the way" with their images. In *The Exorcist*, Friedkin shows us the horror overcome through struggle, a violent purging. But, more importantly for Friedkin, it is the "grand horror" of Karras's leap through the window and his torn body and blood on the pavement that transcends that horror, becoming vitalizing, invigorating. It's the same catharsis in which Bacon views the Isenheimer Crucifixion. Friedkin's image of Karras's triumphant scream of "No!" to the demon as he propels himself to the window has all the beauty and intensity of a Monet sunset as seen through the viewfinder of a fatalist.

9
Sorcerer

"You love to see me in the toilet."
—William Friedkin

I

At the climax of the 1948 film *White Heat*, the driven self-destructive killer, Cody Jarrett (James Cagney), stands atop a giant oil refinery storage tank firing his pistol wildly at the policemen below. Jarrett laughs maniacally and shouts at the heavens, "Made it, Ma! Top of the world!" Jets of steam and flame from ricocheting bullets erupt around him. He fires off a few more rounds. One of them ruptures a pipe valve, and Jarrett's world blows up spectacularly in his face.

Friedkin says *White Heat* is "better than anything I've put on film yet"[1] and that he "identifies with the criminal part of Jarrett."[2] One cannot help but wonder, metaphorically speaking, if Friedkin felt a closer spiritual kinship with Jarrett when his film *Sorcerer* opened. Friedkin, who was very close to his mother, was on top of the world. The Academy Award–winning director with the box office blockbuster of the year to his credit had signed a contract with Universal Studios. "They would have been happy to let me shoot a telephone pole if I'd wanted to,"[3] Friedkin said. But, instead he made his ode to the action-adventure film in which four criminals transport volatile nitroglycerin through treacherous jungle terrain. At a cost of $21.6 million of two studios' money, *Sorcerer* grossed only $9 million worldwide. Reviews were mixed but so too were the criticisms of *The Exorcist*. Damning to Friedkin was an uninterested public. The world had blown up in his face.

What happened?

Friedkin, who would take his second possessory credit with *Sorcerer*, said he wanted to make a classic. "There are remakes, and there are transformations. *Sorcerer* is a transformation which I want to stand up as the perfect example of the genre."[4] He had met French film director Henri-Georges Clouzot, whose film *The Wages of Fear* Friedkin particularly admired. "It had a great effect on me and a powerful theme: four men—strangers, enemies—sitting on a load of dynamite together. They have to cooperate, though they hate each other, to survive. That was a metaphor to me for the situation of the world—these different countries need each other. I thought I would take this theme with new characters and a different setting and do my version. It's like different versions of *Hamlet*....[5]

"We tried to make a film in which the action spoke for everything and everyone. The action my people perform is what they are. We tried to make this picture without any dialogue. That was originally the concept. I felt that most of the films I had directed were much too talky, like photographed plays, in a way. One of the things that motivated Walon Green, who wrote the script, and myelf was to try to tell a story using only filmic substance. In some cases, even having characters on screen who didn't speak the same language. They would have to communicate and solve their problems without words.... A film that could be seen in any country and understood.

"Another one of the experiments in *Sorcerer* was to see if an audience can get behind unrelieved killers and criminals; put four of the worst imaginable people together and see if the audience is as behind them as I am.[6]

"I know who my characters are. I try to cast them as close as I can to type, and then I think it's clear, but it isn't always clear to an audience. Everyone has a different approach. It's very personal. I present it to the audience and let them decide. There's no accounting for taste. I just don't want to load up my films with a lot of claptrap about why my characters do what they do. That's on soap opera right now. They sit there and tell you about themselves endlessly."

Walon Green, who had been recommended to Friedkin to write the screenplay by Bud Smith, Friedkin's film editor, said that in their initial meeting Friedkin told him he wanted to do "a full-out big outdoor action adventure. At first the idea was a Clint Eastwood film. We agreed it should be very hard in the way the original film was pretty hard and cynical. We didn't want to lose that. We didn't want any real sentiment in the film. Then we talked about some specifics. Billy said, 'I've always done a prologue in my films. That's how we'll bring this character into the story.' I said, 'Well, there's a problem. If you do that with one character, it'll be obvious that that's the guy who's going to make it. Maybe we should do it with three of them and leave one a mystery.' He said, 'Okay, let's do that. And let's go with different kinds of characters.' I said, 'I haven't seen an Arab terrorist treated as a personality in a film, except as a guy with a bomb in his hand.' Billy liked that idea.

"I wrote a ninety-page draft that Billy absolutely hated. When I reread it, I realized it was the way I would have written it for Sam Peckinpah. It was very broad and very expanded." (Green cowrote *The Wild Bunch* with Peckinpah.) Green said Friedkin wanted the story and characters "to

belong in the line of action. 'It's got to be organic,' he'd say. And I couldn't
use convenient plot devices like a telephone conversation or a line of
dialogue to advance the story. . . . We were committed to only an action
line, and I think sometimes his films tend to become too complex because
of that. He's doing too much to make a point that could be made with a line
of dialogue. It isn't worth the effort."

According to Green, "William Peter Blatty would have been Billy's first
choice as the writer, but Blatty is a religious guy, and he believes in God
and Billy doesn't. I wouldn't say outright Billy's an atheist, but Billy can't
believe in God the way Blatty believes in God."

("I'm probably an agnostic," Friedkin has said. "I believe that God and
the soul are unknowable. So why should I waste my time on something that
will never be revealed to me.")[7]

Green also says that "Billy thought I was an atheist. When he saw my
film *Hellstrom Chronicles,* he probably thought, 'If Green thinks insects are
going to take over the earth, he can't think much of Divine Notion.' That
intrigued Billy at that particular point in his life. *The Exorcist* has a certain
kind of darkness, but it's redeemable. For *Sorcerer,* Billy wanted to find
somebody who believes there is no redemption. But when I asked him why
hire me to write *Sorcerer,* he said, 'You're the perfect guy to write it because
you haven't written anything for a long time. And you're a leftist who lived
in Latin America, and you're into violence, and you see things darkly. That's
what I want—a sense of people in the Third World manipulated by these
international companies that aren't even there.'" (During his schooling in
Latin America, Green recalled, "a teacher asked, 'Where is and describe the
capital of Honduras?' [It's Tegucigalpa in the highlands.] Nobody knew.
There was a Honduran kid in the class, so the teacher asked him to tell us.
He answered, '2562 Commonwealth Avenue, Boston, Massachusetts.' That
was the headquarters address of the United Fruit Company.")

There were other significant influences on the screenplay. One was the
1957 David Lean film *The Bridge on the River Kwai.* "I saw *Kwai* about two
months into the writing of *Sorcerer,*" Green said. "It was so good, and the
writing was so right. For four days after seeing it, I couldn't do anything.
I thought, 'Oh, God, I'm fucked. I'll never come up to that.' Then I talked
to Billy about it, and he'd met David Lean in Europe. Lean had said to him,
'If I had *Kwai* to do over again, I would try to eliminate at least a third of
the dialogue.' So I said to Billy, 'Let's take the lesson of the master.' I went
back and took dialogue out. *Sorcerer,* I'll admit, doesn't deal with the issue
of character as well as *Kwai* does. On an action line, though, we tried to
make it as good or better."

Moments of verisimilitude and textural richness were important to
Friedkin. For example, Green said all the touches of detail in the
establishing shots of the Latin American town, such as the lizard hanging

on the bed netting, the man sleeping in the mud, even the crowing of the rooster, were all scripted. Also, the church robbery in the New Jersey prologue was based on the actual robbery of a church that was perpetrated by Gerry Murphy, an ex-convict, who played the leader of the gang in the film, Friedkin said.[8] (This scene was later filmed in a church three blocks from where the original robbery took place, according to Friedkin.)

Yet another major influence was Steve McQueen. According to Friedkin, the script was ultimately written for the actor "who loved the script and wanted to work with me. But he didn't want to leave the country for ten months. He'd just married Ali McGraw, and there was no part for her in the film. He said, 'Maybe there's a way you could write one in.' I said, 'No, there isn't.' And there wasn't." (Ironically, McQueen had seen Friedkin's documentary on Paul Crump years earlier, shortly after Friedkin had arrived from Chicago. Joe Wizan, Friedkin's Los Angeles–based agent at that time, had arranged the screening, and they all met to discuss a joint project. "Bill turned it down," Wizan recalled. "McQueen couldn't believe this young kid did that. Bill said to him, 'I'd love to work with you, but I don't like this project.'")

Green said they probably should have rewritten the part of Scanlon in *Sorcerer* at that point "because McQueen was ideal in a silent part like that, driving a truck, looking at this guy, keeping alert. He was not great with dialogue, but he had that absolute thing about him that his gears were whirling the whole time. I think McQueen could have made the film work in a much better way than Roy Scheider did because Scheider had to act in it. McQueen, in fact, was that kind of character, a guy who was bright but didn't express himself. He was clever, determined, and really on the move but couldn't articulate it. Didn't articulate it. The problem with Scheider was he was neither quite fish nor fowl."

"He was absolutely wrong for that part," Friedkin said. "The biggest casting mistake I've ever to date made. I think he did a damn good job, though. But nobody gives a shit about Roy Scheider in that part. Scheider is an interesting second or third banana. But he is not a star. I've told him that, and it's not a secret. . . . And most pictures don't need a star. *Sorcerer* needed stars, I'm afraid. The characters were written for people bigger than life. They required guys who bring with them the baggage an audience understands. McQueen, Clint Eastwood, Jack Nicholson. I went for months trying to get them, but none of these guys wanted to go away."

Casting major stars in a Friedkin film?

"It wasn't that Billy made movies before without stars because he wanted to," Green said. "You have to remember that suddenly he's made *The Exorcist* that was out grossing one hundred fifty million dollars, and the studios were kissing his ass. He says 'I want to make a movie with Steve McQueen,' and they go, 'Whoa, do it! We can't wait. Run, do it!'"

Most of the supporting actors, too, were not the first choice. "The only
character in *Sorcerer* that was cast as I wanted him to be was Amidou, who
played the Arab," Friedkin said. "He was my first and only choice. The part
was written for him. The rest of the people were all fifth, sixth, and seventh.
Well, no, Francisco Rabal, who played Nilo, the Mexican assassin, was
about second or third choice. But not Scheider and not Bruno Cremer, who
played Manzon, the Frenchman. I like Cremer, but that part needed Jean-
Paul Belmondo or Leno Ventura."

Green recalled that "Ventura said he didn't like the script and wasn't
sure he wanted to do it. Finally he said he'd do it if McQueen or Eastwood
did it."

Yet Friedkin was still determined to "go for a classic." He began location scouting in Ecuador with Green, who said they found "one of those
massive waterfalls that was pouring off this cliff. It was like a chimney. It
must have been three hundred feet across. Billy and I saw this while we
were driving on this very remote mountain road in the Andes Mountains.
We came around the bend, and there was a peasant shack with this guy with
one eye living in it. (I was Billy's translator before he started filming because
he didn't trust other people to do it.) So Billy said to me, 'See if you can get
us over to the river. Talk to this guy.' So I did, and the guy got his machete
and cut a path toward the river. Billy was saying, 'This is fabulous. This is
the greatest fucking location I've ever seen. We'll build the oil field right
there. Ask the guy if we can clear those trees to put an oil field in.' I said,
'Wait a second. Let me ask him who owns the land.' I asked, and the guy
said, 'I think *I* do. I live here.'

"Billy said, 'Oil wells. We want to put in oil wells over there' — and he
pointed off into the jungle — 'and over there we want to build a road.' When
we got to this huge Andean river, Billy said, 'And we're going to put a bridge
right across here.' The guy said, 'But there's nothing on the other side.' I
started laughing. Billy asked me what was so funny. I translated, and Billy
said, 'Explain to him it's for a movie.' The guy said, 'What?' I said, 'A movie.
Have you ever seen a movie?' He said no, but he'd heard of them. So Billy
said, 'Tell him we'll be back tomorrow with helicopters and the whole team
to survey this area.' I told him, and the guy just nodded, probably thinking
these two gringos escaped from somewhere. Then Billy said, 'Give him
some money. Give him what you've got and, here, take all mine.' We gave
this guy about three hundred dollars. The guy was blown away. (Billy's very
generous. He makes a lot of money, but on the other hand, he likes the
excitement of giving things. It gets him off.) Anyway, we left, and the
next morning three of the biggest helicopters in Ecuador land right in front
of his shack. All these people get out with survey equipment, tapes, draft-
ing boards, and we march into the jungle to build this road that won't go
anywhere. And this guy got very concerned. He kept saying, 'Please, tell

them there's nothing on the other side of the river.' I told him, 'I've explained it to them, but they don't care. They want to build a bridge here anyway.' He just shrugged his shoulders. We all gave him more money. That money is probably the only reason he knows what happened was real."

They also found a town, Green said, called Puerto Bolivar, "that was worse than the town in the picture by tenfold. When Billy saw it, he said, 'That's the town for the film.'" (Green added that Lino Ventura and others were very critical of the oil company town depicted in *Sorcerer*, saying that American oil companies don't really have these squalid towns. "Puerto Bolivar was owned by Texaco.")

Reality set in. Because of a proposed budget of $15 million, Universal canceled the picture, the director said. The major part of that budget figure reflected an inability to house people on distance locations for so long, Friedkin said. "It cost about one hundred thousand dollars a day to make this film. . . . A number of studios knew about this script and wanted to make it. Universal finally said they'd go in on a coproduction deal with Paramount Pictures because they jointly owned a foreign distributorship called CIC and they would share the foreign distribution."

Friedkin further explained that another reason for Paramount's participation was due to its parent company, Gulf and Western, which had interests such as nickel and sugar in the Dominican Republic. "They said if I could find locations there, they would make the film. What I found there was certainly quite a bit less than Ecuador, but they were usable."[9]

The town, for example, was Alto Gracia, which, Green said, "wasn't that bad a town" compared to Puerto Bolivar. Gaylin Schultz, the key grip, recalled that "Alto Gracia was full of chicken coops, period. When we landed there in helicopters, they thought we were gods. Most of them had never seen a helicopter before." Green said that John Box, the production designer on the film, whose credits include *Lawrence of Arabia* and *Dr. Zhivago*, had to "really do a number" on the town. (*Time* called it "some of the most squalid squalor anybody this side of a PBS documentarian has put on screen in a long time.")[10]

However, David Salven, Friedkin's first producer on *Sorcerer* (Salven was the associate producer on *The Exorcist*) did not believe the film "needed *that* village. You could have been in Pacoima [California], damn near, in a lot of ways. Salven said he disagreed with Friedkin's approach to *Sorcerer*. "It blossomed into this huge apocalypse. Billy was just getting caught up in it. . . . And I'm not saying never go on location, but I think Billy wanted to prove he could make *Sorcerer* once he'd gotten into it. He didn't want to back off from it and say, 'I failed.'" Friedkin fired Salven, who said, "You can call me the producer, you can call me God, but I'm still working for Billy. He would never want a producer who could literally say, 'No.' And that's not just Billy. That's Hollywood today."

Director Martin Scorsese *(Taxi Driver, Raging Bull)* has said creative producers can be particularly helpful. "When you're so close to a picture, you tend to lose perspective. You need somebody . . . to help you along. They act as a buffer between us and the studio, so that we don't feel the squeeze as much."[11] Friedkin felt that squeeze doubly in the roles of producer and director. "You come to the set feeling that every decision you've made from the beginning was wrong, and if you'd thought the thing out clearly, you wouldn't be in the jam you're in. It's an enormous difficulty to come to the set with any optimism, with any degree of creativity, when you're in that situation.

"You then have a clear-cut choice: Abandon the essential aims of this picture and simply finish it and do it cheaply, or bite the bullet and do it the way we thought we wanted to make it at the beginning, because that's the only way to give it to an audience."

Friedkin said that at any time both studios could have "pulled the plug" on the project. "They backed me, saying, 'We believe in you. We want to release the picture you want to make, so go ahead and do it.'"[12]

Ironically, fate, in the form of natural disasters, swooped down upon the production, making the location shooting as arduous a task as the journey in the film itself. "For example," Friedkin said, "originally the bridge sequence was planned to be over a gigantic raging river, and the river in the Dominican Republic, which had a history of never having diminished by so much as two to three inches in history, went dry. In the middle of production we had to shut down and find a verdurous area somewhere else in the world in November where it would remain green, the trees wouldn't be bare, and a raging river would be there when we were ready to shoot it in three or four months. It might be in Greenland or somewhere.

"John Box found a river that historically had not diminished by two or three inches in the entire history of the life of the river in Tuxtepec, Mexico. This location was even better than the one we had in mind. We built the bridge with all the supports, safety devices, and hydraulic ramps so we could raise and lower it, and then the water started to go down. It was seven or eight feet and really raging when we first looked at it. By the time we were ready to shoot the sequence, I don't think the water was more than eighteen inches. So we decided to add a rainstorm."[13]

Gaylin Schultz, the key grip (who's responsible for building camera mounts and other special behind-the-scenes construction), recalled that twenty-four-hour guards had to be posted at the bridge. "The superstitious locals were threatening to blow it up since they thought our building a bridge on their river was what dried it up."

Since nature was not cooperating with the river, there was no reason to believe it would supply Friedkin's rainstorm either. According to Mark

Johnson, the second assistant director (he has since become a producer and won the Academy Award for *Rain Man*), "We'd have two helicopters warm up, and then we'd indicate to forty Mexican greensmen half a mile up the river to start throwing rubbish into it. When we'd see the branches and all come down around the bend, the helicopters would take off. One would be situated above the bridge, the other off from the background. They'd get down as low as they could so they were just out of camera frame and then really kick the hell out of the trees and water and everything else. The special effects crew would start to sway the bridge, using the hidden cables. The stuntman in the truck would turn on the lights and make sure the windshield wipers were going, and then start across the bridge. At the same time there were eight or ten special effects men with hoses on towers, and they'd cover the place with rain. Every now and then, we'd do it and someone would notice the windshield wipers weren't on, so we'd have to shut the whole thing down and start all over again. Obviously, it takes a couple of hours to get ready."

Schultz added that he and his crew built pontoon floats to give Friedkin the flexibility to be along the river anywhere he wanted, parallel with the bridge. The key grip also bought every nitrogen bottle in Mexico City, 150 of them. "We had a system set up with gauges, pipes, and outlets, so the guys could plug in wherever their camera was and spray their camera lenses clear because of all the turmoil with the water and wind."

Then there was the matter of keeping the trucks on the bridge. Friedkin said this was accomplished by hooking the truck to the bridge with a small triangular device. "The truck could only move by fixed increments of about ten feet, and then it would start to drag its support. So each time the truck would make progress, we would have to stop and move the increment to another position. Then we had to line the entire bridge with nail studs to give the tires greater traction. Air was released in the tires so they would sink into the studs. But it was enormously slippery and dangerous and not really balanced." And the trucks did not always stay on the bridge. "In rehearsal and even during actual shooting, the truck went over five times. We almost had four people killed one day."[14] Friedkin was thrown from the bridge "a couple of times," according to Mark Johnson. Yet there was a moment of Friedkin-style humor. Bud Smith, who acted as both film editor and associate producer on *Sorcerer*, recalled that "John Box, who is a very serious man, went up to Billy after the truck flipped off the bridge for the third time and said, 'Billy, why don't you make a comedy?' Billy looked at him straight in the eye and said, 'There's nothing funny.'"

Another production problem Friedkin faced that he admitted tied directly into the escalating cost of the film was a bright blue sky. "I decided never to shoot this film if the sun was shining. . . . Once we got committed to going to that village in the rainy season and we found out that that particular rainy season there was no rain and the sun was shining every day, we were only able to get our shots early in the morning and late in the evening when the sun went down."[15] (This decision resulted in seventy-two days of downtime — the production crew on location does not film, so they wait, and get paid.) Bud Smith explained, "If it's real heavy overcast, it's more of a depressed feeling that you'd get; hot, humid. And with this heavy pressure, which is the ground heat coming up, the light is infinity. The further away, the better it looks. If it's overcast, a sea of green looks like it goes on forever, as seen in the opening shots of the mountains that establish the village. If it was hot bright light, you wouldn't want to look much further past your hand. The pressure of rain, overcast, and fog build a lot more tension than a bright sunlit day." "Also," Friedkin added, "John Box and his crew kept all the bright colors out of it in terms of clothes and design. We very definitely had in mind a bleak-looking film."[16]

Though Friedkin did not mention it, his first cinematographer, Dick Bush, who later photographed Blake Edwards's *Victor Victoria*, was equally responsible with Friedkin for almost the whole look of the film. Apparently, Bush and Friedkin had a "disagreement" over the lighting of the fallen-tree sequence. Bush wanted to use lights. Friedkin wanted natural lighting only. Over half of the film had been shot, with earlier "disagreements" already behind them, when Bush and his camera crew left the film. Bush said, "I found it impossible to get to know Mr. Friedkin to build up any relationship, which I find essential between a cameraman and a director. But I feel that rather than suffering any breakdown in relationships, it is essential for the director to be happy with the cameraman and vice versa, as they have to work so closely on a vital part of the film." Friedkin then had John Stephens, who had been shooting second-unit photography — close-ups on truck wheels, aerial shots, things that did not directly involve the actors — take over as the cinematographer.

To be fair, a few things did work in the jungle. The camera mounts and rigging for the trucks that Gaylin Schultz devised and built allowed Friedkin to place his camera *anywhere* in or around or underneath the trucks. For example, Schultz said, "Billy said he wanted a shot hanging off the side of the truck showing the outer rear tire of the truck hanging over the side of this very narrow mountain road it was going up. You could see the one wheel hanging off, and if the wheel next to it goes off, that truck would have been a memory. (That's one of Billy's favorite phrases, by the way.) Anyway, he wanted to start with that shot, track along to show the deep gorge below and then up to the driver." To accomplish this, Schultz constructed a basket tied in with cables that could be cranked to extend the basket five feet out from the moving truck. "It was dead positive. Nice smooth starts and stops." Bud Smith said that without Schultz's expertise "a lot of those shots of the trucks would never have looked so good."

Something else that worked in the jungle to Friedkin's satisfaction — and special effects man Marcel Vercoutere's relief — was the oil well explosion. "The derrick was ninety feet high," Vercoutere said. "The fire went up three hundred and fifty feet. And the explosion had to be big enough to block your view of the five men on the tower. When we set off the explosion, Billy looked at me and said, 'I believe that.'"

According to Vercoutere, Friedkin believed the oil fire, too, which Vercoutere manufactured by pumping thousands of gallons of No. 2 diesel fuel with two inches of liquid raw propane going up the center of it into the air. "When we set the fire off, you couldn't get within a football field of it. The ground was smoking for over another fifty yards in all directions. It had to be that hot to melt the derrick. See, if none of this had worked the first time, we'd have been in big trouble. For one thing, it would have involved a whole new derrick because we blew the deck right out of the first one."

"Billy had the whole rig flown in," Gaylin Schultz said. "There wasn't even a road to that location. Nobody even knew where the heck we were. Even the pilots were trying to figure out how they're going to get back there."

The entire sequence, Vercoutere said, from the initial explosion to the resulting fires, to the panicked reactions of the workmen, was outlined by Friedkin.

And then there were more misfires and planning problems. Schultz recalled that "Billy spent a fortune with electricians because one of them had an idea that he could create some real lightning effects. Real, not phony. Billy said fine and gave the guy carte blanche to do whatever he had to do. Well, it looked like one of those Oriental firecracker things. They set it off, and it was just one big short circuit. Billy shook his head, a little disgusted, and said, 'Call me when you're ready. I'll be in my hotel room.'" Vercoutere also remembered Friedkin's disappointment and John Box's embarrassment when Box initially revealed the two trucks to Friedkin. The teethlike grillwork and overhead and underneath exhaust pipes were fine. Even the dents and tears. But the chartreuse-and-blue color combinations had to go. "Billy said, 'Oh, paint them green. They're supposed to be army trucks.'"

Then there was the car crash for the New Jersey prologue. According to Johnson, that particular intersection they wanted to use was available to them *only* on the weekend because of the heavy factory business there. (Production crews and teamsters were paid quadruple time for working weekends.) Also, all the previously photographed point-of-view shots clearly showed the car approaching that intersection with its giant water tower and cobblestone streets. "Billy had outlined how he wanted the crash to work," Johnson said, "and the stunt guys couldn't come up with it. There were all kinds of excuses, like the road surface was not right, the cars weren't right. The bottom line was they just weren't ready, and they'd had plenty of time to prepare." Friedkin finally got the stunt the way he wanted it after bringing in Joey Chipwood, a stunt driver from Florida, and utilizing a ramp to flip the car. They crashed a dozen cars before the stunt was satisfactory, according to Johnson, who added, "I'm told that when Bob Rafelson was directing *The Postman Always Rings Twice* with Jack Nicholson, he wanted to find out exactly how that car crash was done and who did it because he thought that was the most spectacular crash he'd seen. He used it as a standard for the car wreck in *Postman*."

With all these location problems, particularly in the Dominican Republic, Friedkin did consider moving sets into studios. But he said that he and John Box agreed that "we would still be dealing with a studio sky"; in other words, unrealistic. It may have been easier, but not right, not perfect. Friedkin also claims "jungle madness. John and I were infected by the opportunity to go for perfection on location in the worst imaginable locations, and that was going to be a part of it. It became a contest to see how many people would drop on the film or go crazy or have to leave. It really infected us. It went beyond making the film. And you don't stop to think what the easiest solution to your problem is."[17]

"I've worked with a lot of directors who say, 'To hell with it, I'll go with it this way,'" Mark Johnson said. "I've never seen Billy accept anything less than what he asks for. That's really a trademark of his." Considering the costs involved in constructing and then moving and rebuilding the bridge, long treks to locations, housing cast and crew (sometimes in camps they had to build because there were no other accommodations), and unpredictable weather, including a hurricane that, Friedkin said, washed away one of the sets, it is not surprising the budget escalated to over $20 million.

As Bud Smith said, "Billy will keep at it until he gets it right, or he'll throw it out of the movie." In the editing, for example, the four prologues were at one time incorporated into the body of the film as flashbacks, but Friedkin ultimately decided to open the picture with them, according to Smith. In one version, the film began with a shot of camels on a street in Jerusalem. The idea was to put the audience off balance as to time frame, Smith said, and then suddenly we see jeeps roar into the scene. The first prologue in the released film shows Nilo committing a murder in a hotel room in Mexico. "Originally, Nilo was to be the enigma of the group," Green said. "I tried to talk Billy into taking it out of the film."

"The impact of sound is very important to Billy," Smith said. "If he could ever override a visual with the impact of sound, he would do it. When we did *Mayhem on a Sunday Afternoon* for Wolper Productions, he put wireless microphones inside the football pads, and that was back in the early sixties when wireless mikes were hardly heard of."

Buzz Knudsen, the dubbing mixer who won an Academy Award for

The Exorcist and dubbed *Sorcerer* and other Friedkin films, said that even the sound of footsteps has to be absolutely perfect. "Billy can tell if they're a fraction off. If they don't have the right squeak or heaviness, they're out."

"To Billy, film is like a painting," Charles Campbell, the sound effects editor, said. (Campbell, who was nominated for his work on *Sorcerer,* has won Academy Awards for *E.T., Back to the Future,* and *Who Framed Roger Rabbit.*) "And there are all these layers in a painting, and he will not allow any color to be in there that's wrong. In the bridge sequences, for instance, where you are inundated with sounds—creaks, groans, howling winds, thunder—he is so demanding that if you were to unravel any of these things, you'd find there is purity in every sound." In other words, every individual sound is original and unique. Campbell attributes much of his success and expertise to Friedkin's demands. Campbell chuckled and said, "The suggestion was made by Billy initially, and when I say 'suggested,' I mean that's what he ultimately expected, that the trucks have complete characters. 'I want them to have an animal sound,' he said. Our production sound man, Jean-Louis Ducarme, recorded a wealth of material to use as a basic for the trucks. We augmented that with a tiger roar for the *Sorcerer* truck and a cougar growl with the *Lazaro* truck. It didn't stand out, but there was a slow, guttural growling underneath."

Friedkin's use of sound also complements his taste in artwork: both can be appreciated as bizarre, lending themselves to more tension or more insanity. For instance, in the scene in which the liquid nitroglycerin is found to have leaked out of its casing, the sounds Friedkin wanted to hear when the drops of the nitro were shaken from the explosives expert's hand were "miniexplosions."[18] He also wanted pistols to sound like rifles, rifles to sound like shotguns, shotguns to sound like cannon, explosions to sound like atomic bombs. Campbell said that in order to augment various sound effects, "Billy, Ducarme, who is an accomplished musician, and I rented a bass drum, bass fiddle, viola, and cymbals, and kept them on the dub stage. For example, bow draws on the viola were used as part of the various creaks and groans on the bridge. Another time, we weren't getting quite the sound Billy wanted for one of the explosions. So he had me lay over the rim of the bass drum, and then he hit it with all his might." Shaking his head at the memory, Campbell said it made his teeth chatter and his whole body vibrate, but "everything had to be bigger than life. A lot of this stuff was supposed to be in the characters' heads. Sounds to these people were either amplified or muted." Using the French prologue as an example, Campbell explained that Manzon, who is about to be indicted on charges of fraud and bribery, drives through Paris. The shot starts off as a pure sustained music note, and it's tense, like Manzon. The car starts to round a corner, and the sound of a passing motorcycle takes over, bringing him out of his thoughts, back to reality.

Given Friedkin's penchant for "bigger than life," it seemed strange that in the scene in which the two trucks loaded with their volatile cargo depart Porvenir, only a muted music cue and the rumble of the trucks complement the moment, while in the original *Wages of Fear* the trucks blast their horns as they begin their trek. "We found that Billy was dissatisfied with the way he directed that sequence," Campbell said. When any director is unhappy with the film he has shot, the best editing, the most appropriate music, and the most imaginative sound effects *will not* correct or improve that image. But everyone tries to do their best. Campbell explained: "We worked on it for two weeks on the dubbing stage, Buzz Knudsen, Bob Glass, Dick Tyler, Bud Smith, and myself. Billy would come in, listen, and reject everything that we'd done. He said at one point he wanted to hear a symphony of dogs. 'I want to hear mutts, mongrels, big dogs, little dogs, howling and barking.' We had crickets and normal night sounds at that point. We put it together. It was an interesting approach, and it played well. Billy came in, and his then-wife, Jeanne Moreau, was with him, and they sat down and we played it straight through. There was no comment, no waving of arms, no yelling 'stop.' When it was over, he stood up, faced me, and said, 'What the hell is all this dog stuff about?' He keeps you off guard when he chooses to."

And then there are times Friedkin gives you a different surprise, according to Knudsen. "We spent a week mixing the first bridge crossing. We called him over late in the afternoon to look at it, knowing he would come in and shoot it to ribbons because he always has something to say, even if it's one thing, because he spots everything. He walked in, we ran it, he turned around, gave us the thumbs-up, and said, 'Great.' He left us sitting there with our mouths open for about half an hour."

Sorcerer was nominated for an Academy Award for best sound.

Just as sound effects are important to establishing tension and reality in Friedkin's films, so too is music. In the montage creation of the trucks in which we see the two trucks constructed from the junked bodies of a dozen others, Bud Smith said, the "driving rhythm of the sequence came about naturally. I used to race cars. I've torn cars apart and put them back together. Billy understands that mechanical aspect too. It's almost like what I did when I cut the Iraqi sequence of *The Exorcist*. It's a four-beat rhythm. You just get the drive going. In *Sorcerer* it was ratcheting and tightening and pulling and pushing. Then we cross-cut Nilo smoking and the smoke and flames of the oil fire to build tension and time pressure. And when we added in that great music by Tangerine Dream, it just fucking laid in perfectly." (This score was praised as an integral part in capturing the mood and texture of the film. The *Los Angeles Times* appropriately described it as "Latin Anxious."[19] One cannot help but wince, however, at the use of an overture. According to *Time,* Friedkin issued directions to theater managers, insisting house lights be dimmed and the overture played, putting us "into a mood suitable for his work.")[20]

Friedkin states that he heard Tangerine Dream while in Munich, Germany, for the opening of *The Exorcist*. Had he heard them sooner, he'd have asked them to score that film. When he decided to make *Sorcerer*, he sent the three-man group a copy of the script. Months later, "while I was in the middle of the jungle, a big package arrived from Munich. It was ninety minutes of their musical impressions of the story. Out of that ninety minutes, twenty to twenty-five minutes was exactly what I was looking for."[21]

What Universal Studios was looking for was a way to market the film for domestic release. (Paramount Pictures would handle the foreign marketing.) According to Friedkin, "The first thing Sid Sheinberg, president of Universal Studios, said when he saw the advertising for the picture was 'Jesus, can't we get all these Spanish names out of the ad?' I said, 'Yes, I think we could get all these guys to change their names. Let's pay them to do it. How much do you think it would take to get Francisco Rabal to change his name to Frank Robels?' They really didn't know what the hell to make of all these Spanish names and all this other stuff. So they said, 'Let's sell the picture on Bill Friedkin.'"[22] The trailer that ran in theaters, advertising the film, begins with a voice announcing, "William Friedkin, who gave you *The French Connection* and *The Exorcist*, now gives you *Sorcerer*."

Contractually, Friedkin had final cut on *Sorcerer*, which meant no studio executives could take the film away from him and recut it. According to his agent, Tony Fantozzi, "The one thing Billy and I do not have is the luxury of saying, 'Somebody else screwed the film.'" (Beginning with *The Exorcist*, Friedkin has enjoyed the privilege of final cut on all his films.) However, in the case of *Sorcerer*, Friedkin admits that he did not protect himself contractually regarding the foreign release of the film.[23] Bud Smith explained that the foreign distributor did recut the film to the extent that the prologues were shortened and incorporated into the body of the picture and the focus of the story was on the oil well fire and political terrorism, not the four criminals.

"I had the best possible bookings for *Sorcerer*," Friedkin said.[24] "But it came out when *Star Wars* was sweeping the country, and the mood of the moviegoing public had swung away from what I was trying to do with *Sorcerer*."[25] As one disgruntled patron said, "I couldn't get in to see the picture at Mann's Chinese Theater [in Hollywood, California] in its first week because the lines of people were around the block. Everybody thought Friedkin was going to zap them again with this thing called *Sorcerer* after having done *The Exorcist*. But that second week you could've stood at the back door of that theater and cut loose with a six-inch scatter gun, and not hit a soul."

Friedkin admits that the title of the film hurt it "because so many people have told me that they expected another *Exorcist*" and states matter-of-factly, "I tried to be very conscious of the fact that I really didn't want a title that was too close to *The Exorcist.* We had three or four other titles in mind, but none of them seemed significant enough."[26] Neither Friedkin nor Walon Green could recall any of these alternate titles. But Green did say that originally it was going to be entitled *Wages of Fear,* but they dropped it because "it was such a literary title in English. I didn't like the title *Sorcerer* on the heels of *Exorcist,* though. In fact, the most heated creative argument we had was over that title. I said I thought it was a cheap shot."

"The title *Sorcerer* occurred to me to represent several things," Friedkin said. "Each character was a kind of evil wizard, a specialist. One with explosives, another a wheel man, another is a manipulator of people, and the fourth is a trigger man. Then the sorcerer, really, was fate. The concept of this film was that no matter what people do to try to control their lives, even under the most difficult and impossible circumstances, they still lose out in the end. But this is also a film about betrayal. So many of the most profound experiences I've had have ended on a note of betrayal"—he chuckled—"or have resulted in my feeling that no matter what you do, kings don't mean a thing. But fate was the sorcerer. I thought that would be a concept that would be easy enough for people to absorb. I find, having to sit and explain it, that nobody who saw the picture absorbed it."[27] He laughed again. Green said he didn't buy that reasoning then and still doesn't now.

Friedkin is also unequivocal on his casting: "I believe to this day that the same film, with Steve McQueen, would have been a masterpiece." While Green chose not to speculate on the film's success or failure with McQueen's participation, he does believe "McQueen could carry a film about fate because you know that this guy wouldn't stop fighting. You read that in the way he walked. You could believe he could drive that truck across that bridge. That's what got us excited."

There were two incidents concerning the film that got others excited as well. The first concerned Charles Bluhdorn, chairman of the board of Gulf and Western, the parent company of Paramount Pictures. According to Friedkin, in the scene set in the oil company office, "there's a picture of the board of directors of this company that is sending men off to die in the jungle to put out an oil fire. We took that picture out of the Gulf and Western stockholders' report. I understand that when Mr. Charles Bluhdorn saw the film at a private screening in his office, he stopped the movie and held a kind of kangaroo court to determine who it was that gave me that picture. I think Bluhdorn felt I'd committed some kind of treason. But we didn't want to get a whole bunch of guys and put them in business suits and take their picture when we already had this one."[28] (Admittedly, a cost-saving decision on Friedkin's part.)

The second incident took place several thousand miles away, back in the town of Alto Gracia in the Dominican Republic. Green told the story as related to him by a friend: "When they began filming on that location, Billy had an excellent translator, who was also his assistant, named Luis Llosa, a Peruvian leftist journalist, an intelligent, very literate guy. Billy gave this speech that Llosa translated to the people of the town assembled for the riot scene. He said, 'I was told that I couldn't shoot this sequence in the Dominican Republic because I was told you people have no balls. The government has taken them away from you, and you are afraid to come out and riot! You are afraid to demonstrate how you feel against all the injustices that are done to you!' It was an incredible political speech. The people got crazy. You can see the anger in them in that riot scene.

"After the film crew left the Dominican Republic, which had been a virtual dictatorship in which there had been no passage of power in years, an election was held. The rival party, which was a liberal party, beat the party that was in power. The president nullified the election, and a revolution broke out. It started in Alto Gracia with people coming into the center of town and rioting, just like they did in the film. It spread from Alto Gracia through all the towns and finally to the capital, and they forced the president out. The election was upheld. I liked the idea that maybe the riot scene in *Sorcerer* had gotten those people to do that."

Friedkin said that he no longer thinks of *Sorcerer* in terms of success or failure. "It was a terrific challenge to make this picture, and I was enormously pleased with the results, knowing there are many problems with it for audiences."[29] Commercially speaking, he says, "Why should I have a success with *Sorcerer?* I shouldn't link *Sorcerer* and *Citizen Kane* . . . but the only solace I can take is that *Citizen Kane,* the greatest film I've ever seen in my life, was not successful."[30]

The critical reaction to *Sorcerer* was divided. *Cue* magazine said, "Friedkin's updated effort is just another adventure yarn. . . . It all adds up to yet another example of the folly in re-making a story already filmed brilliantly." The New York *Daily News* felt "the movie is severely limited by the fact that the characters are not even remotely defined, making it impossible to care what happens to them." And the harshest review was from the *Village Voice*'s Andrew Sarris, who condemned it as "a visual and aural textbook on everything that is wrong with current movies: no narrative flow, no psychological development of characters, no interaction of performers, no true unity of locale amid the exotic location, no feelings, no build-ups, no structure, not a single line of resonant dialogue, not a single scene with dramatic tension."[31] Some notable critics found merit in *Sorcerer.* Jack Kroll, in *Newsweek,* called it "the toughest, most relentless American film in a long time . . . lean, hard, ruggedly acted. . . ."[32] The *New Republic*'s Stanley Kauffmann said it was "snappily edited and directed."

And Roger Ebert, in the *Chicago Sun-Times*, stated, "It's the most involving thriller since *Jaws*. . . . Roy Scheider comes across here as a surprisingly physical actor, using his face and body to make points so that dialogue isn't needed. . . . The story is told with the directness of narrative classics like *The Treasure of the Sierra Madre*. . . . Friedkin's camera is so much in the midst of the action—so close to the details—that we're almost part of the cargo."[33]

Friedkin said he thought he must be "a pretty good filmmaker," having made *The French Connection* and *The Exorcist* back-to-back.[34] He also believes that a "dangerous position to be in is when you start believing your own press notices and people telling you what a genius you are, and you don't want to hear anything negative about what you're doing." And in a voice filled with frustration, he said, "I wasn't prepared for my success or my failure. I felt like someone totally buffeted by fate without any control over his own destiny. That's one of the themes of *Sorcerer:* No matter how much you struggle, you get blown up."[35] Friedkin calls *Sorcerer* "my favorite of all the films that I've made. . . . It's about revenge, vengeance, betrayal—this is how I feel about life. I feel that life is filled with betrayal and false promises, and that fate is around the corner waiting to kick you in the ass."

"It's just too bad the commercial aspect didn't happen with this picture," Bud Smith said. "Billy said to me, 'You know, Bud, if it had been a success, we'd have gone back to the jungle and tried to make another film there, a better one.'"

II

An accepted axiom in show business states that your peers like to see you fail, and the more spectacularly you fail, the better, because then they can say later that my film didn't do as badly as his film. This axiom applies only to commerciality. Though Friedkin's "classic" has achieved cult status, it is still considered a failure in terms of box office. Yet in light of the obvious problems for audiences—a misleading and most inappropriate title, unredeemed anti-heroes, as well as a phenomenon called *Star Wars*—Friedkin's most personal film is, not surprisingly, his most visually enriched and grimly aberrant. It is therefore worth description in detail.

As the film opens, a high-pitched eerie musical chord wells up, and an image appears to be fading in through a sinister, evil blackness. The title *Sorcerer* suddenly moves across to the center of the screen. The letters look as if they have been painted across a rough wall with a wide brush. As it fades out, that initial image becomes darkly visible—a hideous face with teeth bared, demented eyes wide. It's a face carved in stone, and then it is gone. The face of fate. Primal. Heathen. Terrifying. Friedkin immediately establishes a sense of dread, disorder. In *Paul Crump,* Friedkin dealt with man against the system; in *French Connection,* it was man against man (cop versus criminal); in *The Exorcist,* the conflict was man versus the supernatural. With *Sorcerer,* Friedkin pits man against fate, an intangible enemy, an unseen nemesis.

Walon Green said that Friedkin "sees violence in terms of the insanity of all mankind." In the prologues, each character is presented as responsible for bloody, violent death. Nilo calmly, coldly murders a man in a hotel room overlooking a plaza where a Mexican band gaily plays. A musical sting carries us from Nilo clearing his throat as he exits the hotel to a dusty Jerusalem where Kassem and his comrades blow up a Jewish bank with a satchel charge. Panic, fire, and motionless bodies fill the street. Their terrorist act is quickly dealt with as Israeli commandos storm their apartment building, charging up the stone stairs, the sound of their boots echoing. The scene resonates the fleeing of the robbers in *Crump.* Several terrorists are machine-gunned, one is captured, but Kassem escapes into the enraged crowd that shouts for the blood of his cohort, who is placed in a police truck. Jerusalem, a center of Christian, Jewish, and Moslem faiths, explodes in flame and anger; the world teeters on the edge of anarchy. As the police truck speeds away, sirens blaring, we cut to the pastoral charm of Paris, the sound of a siren fading in the distance. In his elegant apartment, Manzon appears nervous, preoccupied. He finds a birthday gift from his wife in the bathroom. It is a watch with an inscription: *In the tenth year of forever.* Manzon and his business partner, Pascal, have twenty-four hours before they will be arrested on charges of fraud, fifteen million francs' worth. Manzon speaks to Pascal outside a restaurant and asks him to ask his father (who is also Manzon's father-in-law) again to lend them the money to cover the debt. Pascal is rattled. His father already refused once, saying they took the risk and must bear the consequences. As Manzon walks back toward the restaurant, a shot rings out, glass shatters. He turns and races to Pascal's Porsche, the rear window in shards. Peering inside, he sees Pascal has committed suicide, shooting himself through the mouth.

We cut to a sign advertising Bingo Night and pull back to reveal a Catholic church and all the hubbub of a wedding in a New Jersey suburb. It is abrupt, no sound bridge, a cinematic exclamation point. Friedkin whips us from situation to situation, the editing itself utilized to propel the action line. It is also in this New Jersey setting that Friedkin's dark humor surfaces. Four men in a blue sedan double-park opposite the church and enter the sanctuary. In the basement several priests count up thousands of dollars. They wear visors, looking more like Las Vegas dealers than servants of the Lord. Wearing stocking caps and dark glasses, the four men burst in, pistols drawn. Up at the wedding, the priest performing the ceremony states, "Christ abundantly blesses this love." We cut back to the basement as hundreds of dollars are dumped out of canvas sacks and the robbers stuff their pockets. One of the priests asks, "Do you know whose parish this is?" When he makes a move for the door, the burly gang leader shoots him in the leg and kicks him in the face to stop his moaning. Scanlon, one of the robbers, looks on with surprise and concern. Upstairs, the priest intones, "You have strengthened your consent before the Church," and Friedkin pushes in close to the bride and groom. The bride has a black eye. (Apparently, her consent had to be strenthened.) The robbers make their getaway through a warehouse district, Scanlon at the wheel. At the church, the wounded priest's cry of "We've been hit!" rings of underworld exclamation as opposed to heavenly explanation.

An argument erupts in the getaway car. The Irishman in the back puts a gun to the head of the gang leader. Scanlon turns in his seat, taking his eyes from the road. A truck with Meridian Freight painted across its trailer panels pulls out in front of them. Its air horn blasts. The car ricochets off the trailer. A body flies out the back door. The sedan flips over, skids on its roof into a fire hydrant. A bloody body hangs out a window. Water, a symbol of life, shoots up into the air, drenching the dead on the asphalt, mixing with the blood. Quick, startling, yet strangely seductive in its awfulness. (One can almost hear Bacon whisper "vitalizing," with awe.) Scanlon limps away as a crowd and police gather, the sight of money spilling out of the dead men's pockets distracting them.

Two beefy-looking thugs, one with fleshy features and a gold chain around his neck, enter the back room of a restaurant and explain to Carlo Ricci (played by Gus Allegretti, who was Captain Kangaroo's puppeteer for nineteen years, Friedkin said), that though this "punk from Queens" walked away from the accident, he can't make a move. Ricci, dark and chiseled features partially obscured by shadow, tells them with a steely gaze, "He robbed my church. He shot my brother. I don't care where he is or what it costs. I want his ass." The only "spiritual" connotation for the mob is "an eye for an eye."

Indeed, the world of Friedkin's vision is a dangerous, violent, morally bankrupt one where truly there is no God, only fate, at the moment in the guise of tormentor. Meeting his friend Vinnie that night, Scanlon is told he's "on the hit parade" because of who the priest was they "whacked." Even in the shadows of their transient hotel meeting place, Scanlon's "friend" watches cautiously over his shoulder. Vinnie lays out Scanlon's whole problem: "Forget the heat. Ricci himself is out looking for you." Scanlon says, "You know I never carry a pistol." Vinnie asks him if he'd "like to tell Mr. Ricci that in person." Scanlon knows he has to hide out, but where? Vinnie tells Scanlon the two thousand dollars he got from the heist will get him to someplace "nobody wants to go looking." Shaken, Scanlon realizes he has no choice. "I owed you a favor. This is it," his friend says. The loud clatter

Sorcerer. Learning that a prominent mobster has ordered a "hit" on him, Scanlon (Roy Scheider, left) enlists the aid of a friend, Vinnie (Randy Jurgenson, right) to get out of the country.

of an El train roars by as Scanlon, his face bruised and bandaged, absorbs the shock of uncertainty. The soul of fate is chaos.

Throughout these prologues, Friedkin foreshadows the sweltering Latin American perils in store for our criminal quartet, frequently with ironic counterpoint. Nilo leaves the hotel by coming down in a wrought-iron elevator painted green, as are the walls of the hotel. Metaphorically, he is descending into a green hell. As Kassem and his fellow terrorists prepare to depart for safer country, they quickly examine a map. "The short way is dangerous. The long way takes three hours," Kassem's friend tells him. For hunted men, either way is treacherous. When Kassem decides to take "the long way," the inference is far more ironic and complex than he knows. Friedkin establishes a Parisian restaurant with close-ups on a plate of escargot, blood-red wine, and roast pig, all quite appetizing yet strangely unsettling. Manzon, his wife, and a friend of theirs make small talk to which Manzon pays distracted attention regarding second-rate lobster in warm Latin American waters. The truck Scanlon crashes into has a logo, Meridian

Freight. Friedkin's brand of cynical humor may be twofold here. Certainly the longitudinal lines dissecting the globe pass through steamy equatorial countries where Scanlon eventually finds himself, but for purposes of ironic contrast, consider that a meridian is also defined as the highest point of power, prosperity, and splendor. Scanlon careens off a "meridian" in an industrialized section of town, a giant globelike water tower looming overhead, dwarfing the surrounding area. The place he will ultimately find himself is an industrial cesspool of the world. While Vinnie tells Scanlon he does not know where it is Scanlon will be going, Friedkin stages the moment under a bright yellow billboard for Coppertone tanning lotion ("Tan, don't burn"). They pass large colored signs advertising dinette sets, carpeting, and living room furniture for sale—things Scanlon will not see, have, or enjoy again. Even an old junked car sitting in a nearby lot has a grillwork similar to the truck he will soon be driving.

The world of Friedkin's personal vision is as aberrant as it is beautiful. A muted sunrise trying to break through the heavy gray cloud cover over a quiet lush green jungle appears peaceful and tranquil, especially after the deafening racket of the el train climaxing the New Jersey prologue. But Friedkin's jungle has the same exotic appeal turned grotesque as David Lean's jungle in *The Bridge on the River Kwai*. In *Kwai*, we move through the verdant bush to reveal the prisoners of war slaving to lay a railroad track under the sadistic eyes of their Japanese guards. Similarly, the serene beauty of *Sorcerer*'s jungle turns ugly as we cut to various shots of the village of Porvenir awakening. *Porvenir* means "promise of the future." Bony dogs scratch for food. Crabs scramble over a black, decaying mound. A huge oil-storage tank with a monstrous black condor painted on it fills the screen; like a dark deity, the imposing image dwarfs everything around it. A man pulls an open cart; fresh pig carcasses hang in it. Blood runs down another man's back from the severed bull's head he holds by the horns across his shoulders. From a distance, the jungle looks safe, inviting. Pushing in more closely, cankered images of death assault the eyes, yet perversely appeal to the senses. The pig carcasses, for instance, feel "right" somehow in this environment, not glazed and dressed on a silver platter as shown in the classy Parisian restaurant. (In *The Wages of Fear*, the village of Las Piedras looks very much like *Casablanca*'s Casablanca; at the very most, it is run-down but *far* from squalid.)

Friedkin's camera finds Scanlon in the throes of his personal nightmare, his sweat-soaked hand tightly clutching his bedsheet. The images are those of a bloody body hanging out of the car at the New Jersey crash, a window of steel bars like a prison cell, and subliminal cuts of a rooster being killed (an ironic allusion to the dead-canary motif of gangsterism). With the squeal of a pig being slaughtered mixing with his own startled cry, Scanlon bolts upright into frame, awakening from one nightmare into another—the very landscape of mud, sweat, and humidity Friedkin has already established.

Heironymus Bosch evoked visions of hell with beaked demons torturing human souls. Friedkin's hellish vision appears amazingly more maleficent in its environment, more infernal in its corruption. The town buildings—coarse makeshift structures of rotting wood, crumbling adobe, and corrugated iron panels—appear as malignant growths, like cancerous sores erupted from the jungle floor. Torrential rainstorms signaled by thunderclaps cannot cleanse the filth; they mix with the decay, adding to the stench. The encroaching jungle seems held at bay, choking off the sky; low dark clouds hang shroudlike, oppressive. It is as if nature were trying to obscure the oozing wound on its body.

But gangrene has spread, in the form of corruption. Manzon, for example, attempts to buy his way out. He offers the watch, the gift of his wife the last day he saw her, to the town photographer (dozens of black-and-white snapshots are stuck to the walls of his shack). Looking around the room, Manzon sees two cheap paintings that stab at his heart—three kittens watching a parrot on its perch and a mother cuddling her baby. He is told the watch, plus two thousand pesos, will get him out of the country. "I have only the watch," he says stoically. The photographer slowly, contemptuously shakes his head. Kassem cannot afford the corrupt tariffs on plane tickets and false passports either. He has "less than one hundred pesos, all I could save in a year." When Nilo lands at the dirt runway in a plane also carrying goats, supplies, and a blind child, he must bribe his way through customs. But Friedkin has not neglected a cynical sense of humor amid this corrupt environment. Sitting in the El Corsario bar, Scanlon stares at a faded, peeling picture of a young blonde reclining on a beach, her tanned thighs inviting, her hand reaching for a bottle of Coca-Cola—a very phallic symbol as far as Scanlon is concerned. He swallows hard, the longing (mercifully) broken when the bartender (Frederick Ledebur) sets a plate of food in front of him, absently wiping the knife and fork on his grimy shirt before giving them to Scanlon.

Friedkin uses this sequence to open one of the few dialogue scenes in the film, all the while keeping his camera at eye level and in close to effect a boxed-in feeling. Manzon enters and sits at the corner of the bar. Scanlon buys him a drink and mentions that he's heard a "rumor" that the Frenchman "used to be in banking." He indicates the dour barkeep, adding, "Carlos here is an ex-reichsmarschall." "Carlos" gives him a cold look. (The clear indication is that Porvenir has been a haven for the hunted for years.) Manzon asks Scanlon, "What is your profession?" "Ice hockey," he replies dryly, then, "Did you read about this place in the travel brochure?" "I heard it had a healthy climate," Manzon says. "Not what you expected?" Scanlon asks. Manzon answers, "It was *exactly* what I expected."

Tough, cynical talk, interrupted when Manzon stiffens, sitting back on his stool, his movement revealing the chief of police and a deputy who have entered the bar. They roust Scanlon. Manzon quietly rises to leave, and the police demand to know if he and Scanlon are friends. Manzon says, "No." Friendships are obviously tenuous at best. "Every man for himself" has pointed meaning here. Filth and corruption are as inseparable in Porvenir as water from mud, as is demonstrated when the chief demands to see Scanlon's identity card. Scanlon, who has taken the name Dominguez and can't speak Spanish, flippantly tosses the card on the bar, thereby making the chief reach for it. He tells "Dominguez" the card is false, "a violation of the immigration laws." Friedkin's irony is quite funny—as if someone would want to immigrate to this rathole!

The policemen take Scanlon to their headquarters. Several naked bodies lie on the floor behind bars. Presumably, they could not pay extortion money. In the chief's office, a photograph of *El Presidente* hangs on the wall behind his desk, seemingly approving of any and all actions his police take. In this case, Scanlon is told he will now pay a third of his (meager) earnings to them. One need not look for slime oozing through cracks in the walls; it sits grinning behind the desk wearing a badge and uses the cocked hammer of his .45 pistol to open Coke bottles. Scanlon's tough-guy attitude is cowed as he is dismissed with a caustic "Adios, Señor Dominguez." Welcome to Porvenir, residence of the defeated and the damned.

Friedkin's vitiated imagery is rich not only in corruption and squalor but in action. Friedkin cuts from the quiet of police headquarters to the monotonous hum of drilling and a close shot on a steel deck—dirty, caked with ground-in dried mud. We rise away from it through a steel frame. Men wearing steel caps and oil-smeared coveralls with the symbol of the condor stenciled on them make preparations to drill. This oil derrick stands in mechanized defiance to the jungle-covered hills. Small storage tanks and tent bungalows picket the steel tower. A massive mushroomlike rock in the distance dominates the man-made field. Suddenly, an explosion. The ground trembles. Several men on girder platforms fall facedown and watch as a monstrous fireball, like an umbrella opening, roars up and swallows them. Workers scramble, fall, run for cover. Storage tanks ignite in a hot orange apocalypse. Screams of burning men are extinguished by more explosions. Two men dive into a bungalow that explodes in their faces. Injured workers are dragged to safety or crawl. One has lost his arm at the elbow. The oil fire intensifies. A charred body smolders in a ditch. The iron derrick twists and collapses, engulfed in flames. The world has turned into a verdurous hell. Though we discover immediately following this sequence that terrorist guerrillas detonated the Poza Rica oil field, Friedkin's visual onslaught is as though the jungle—nature—enraged at man's encroachment, has unleashed a firestorm of destruction. The aural blast of explosions is fate's convulsive laughter; the creaking fall of the derrick, mankind's sorrowful moan. (In *The Wages of Fear,* no explosion is shown. The oil fire is mentioned only through the convenience of dialogue.)

A charred detonator fills the screen. It sits on a desk in the Corepet oil company offices. Corlette (Ramon Bieri), the stocky foreman, angrily paces, saying, "We'll get it to the capital, maybe we'll get some results." Lartigue (Peter Capell), the Corepet manager, thin, balding, rimless glasses on a bloodless face, says, "The government's been told it's an accident." "What?" Corlette flairs. "In this country, terrorists who blow up American oil wells are patriots," Lartigue calmly responds. Corlette explodes, "We're paying that government to give us *protection!*" Lartigue pours himself a glass of Scotch. "El Presidente," he says, "cannot risk his liberal image by sending his troops to chase patriots." On this last word, Lartigue tips his glass in a toast.

With this scene, Friedkin demonstrates that the manipulation envelops everyone. Corlette's reactions are in direct contrast to Lartigue's calm explanations. Corlette's bearlike physique gives bite to his anger. Lartigue suggests a corporate man, his shirt white and pressed, even in the heat; his demeanor that of a person who has seen this type of situation before; his act of tipping his glass toward Corlette on the fact that El Presidente will not interfere is his way of saying welcome to the real world.

As Lartigue begins reading a telex from the "home office," Corlette fixes his attention on the black-and-white photograph of El Presidente, staunch and proud in his uniform, that hangs on the wall. (Likenesses of El Presidente are painted on the village walls and buildings; his photograph hangs in the El Corsario bar. In other words, his presence can be seen and felt everywhere.) Corlette vents his frustrations at this picture of a man who, like the Corepet board of directors, whose photograph hangs over Lartigue's desk, manipulates from the safety of far, far away. The telex "emphasizes attention immediate supply obligations with minimum concern R and D." Corlette realizes that the company wants the crude oil any way he can get it, period. He sits, and sighs. He has no choice. He lowers his head, defeated. Green said he wrote the scene with a Kafkaesque flavor, that these two men "talk around the subject" of sending others to their possible (probable) deaths. Friedkin's direction, however, allows us to see the anger, frustration, and manipulation hinted at in Green's spare dialogue.

Like portents of death carrying the bodies of the injured and dead, two heavy canopied trucks roll through the stream running along the edge of Porvenir. Women cry, and men wait tensely in the middle of town for word of friends and loved ones. A hand on a machete handle. We move up to reveal a bearded man who shakes his head and waves off a questioner. Armed soldiers stand guard in the truck beds. The people rush the trucks before they stop, wailing, shouting. A woman's scream, and the scorched, bloodied bodies of the living are hastily taken by friends and family. The anger wells up in the crowd. They pound on the trucks. Soldiers fire their weapons into the air to frighten off the mob. The anger spreads. Fists and shouts of "Puta!" fill the air. The man with the machete, still in its scabbard, pulls a tarp off the back of the second truck. A close-up on a charcoal-black body, burned beyond recognition and wrapped in plastic, stares back, mouth frozen open in the moment of death. Another scream of horror, and four men climb into the truck bed, the crowd now silenced. Shock courses through the people as other tarps are cast off and more blackened bodies wrapped in plastic are gently, reverently, lifted out of the truck. They pass over our heads. Black death.

Isolated cries from the crowd suddenly erupt into a riot. Townspeople storm the trucks. The machete is drawn. Soldiers fight hand-to-hand. They are overwhelmed, dragged out into the street, beaten and pummeled. Gasoline splashes on the vehicles. "Fuck the Americans! Kill the Americans!" the people shout in Spanish. A torch ignites a truck canopy. We whirl around. Local police, mounted on horseback, brandishing rifles, charge the crowd. Fire and smoke billow into the air. The mob surrounds the police, who swing their weapons like clubs. They too are pulled down into the muddy street. The trucks burn fiercely.

The man with the machete, now on horseback and seen through surging flames, urges the crowd on, raising his fist in defiance. Rifle shots explode, glass breaks, the mob hurls rocks at a wall plastered with posters of El Presidente proclaiming *Unidos Hacía El Futuro* ("Together to the Future"). The fire rages, framed as to engulf the lie on the wall.

The controlled chaos of the sequence masterfully reflects Friedkin's documentary style—"follow the action," "the screen is out of control."[36] Nature's wrath was fiery and loud. In this riot the anger smolders, flares, stifles, and then erupts with ferocity, violence, and brutality. Yet there is a giddiness at the visceral combination of fear and excitement. Friedkin has thrust us into the grand horror of Isenheimer's Crucifixion, the scream of Bacon's pope. (In *Wages*, the crowd surges around the trucks only to get the injured men. No riot. No anger. Only a few anti–American potshots before the trucks arrive, like "The Yanks never die!" and "They give you a handful of coins, and that's it.")

Friedkin cuts from the angry turmoil of the riot to the still blackness of night. A funeral procession of flickering candles snakes its way through the town, the wails of the women cutting through the darkness like a knife— Friedkin's most chilling moment. As the procession passes Manzon's room, we can see it through his windows, yet he sits with his back to the wall, rigid, afraid to look. On the cut to Scanlon, he stares at his newspaper, but he cannot read it. Friedkin shows us their abject fear; these are men hiding from death and with a parade for the dead just outside their door, their nightmare vision turned too real. Even in this rathole, death is no stranger.

A problem scene follows. When Corlette and Del Rios (Chico Martinez), an explosives expert, examine the dynamite, they discover that the liquid nitroglycerin has seeped out of the sticks and settled in the bottom of the crates. Friedkin sets the scene in a shack, foliage around it so dense they must hack their way to it with the help of a machete-wielding soldier. The incessant buzz of insects adds an irritating edge to the already claustrophobic surroundings, the wet, sticky humidity one can feel pressing down through the green canopy oozing through the three men's clothes. After Del Rios has gently pried open one of the crates, he slides his hand down inside. The suspense mounts with the look of apprehension on his face as he slowly lifts his hand out of the crate, his fingertips wet. Cupping his fingers with his other hand, he slowly backs out the door. If he slips, the liquid nitro could blow his hand off.

Corlette steps aside. The soldier is frozen. Outside, Del Rios squats down, turns his head away and passes his hand over the ground, letting the nitro drip onto the jungle soil. Birds squawk in fright at the sound of the explosions, like automatic weaponsfire, which are *too* loud. Del Rios tells Corlette that the cases have sat too long without being turned; the liquid nitro has leaked out of the sticks and into the bags. "If you give these cases any kind of a bump, they will blow."

While Friedkin masterfully fuses his sense of realism with the sense of sensation (was it the fear in Del Rios's eyes or the humidity of the jungle that makes one's palms sweat?), his use of sound heightens not the tension of the upcoming journey but (unfortunately) the audience's knowledge of the unstable nature of the nitro. Friedkin's wont of "larger than life" has exploded into "bigger than believable." Also, one wonders why Corepet simply doesn't send for other (better) explosives. The only reason seems to point to Friedkin. So committed to an action story line, he apparently sees comment or discussion of such matters as too expository. It is an unfortunate deletion, troubling in its obviousness.

But Friedkin continues to turn the screws visually. When a helicopter pilot explains to Corlette that there's too much turbulence to fly the nitro to the Poza Rica oil fire two hundred miles away, Corlette offers more money. "It's not the money," the pilot says. "You need a suicide jockey." Friedkin cuts to a tubercular-looking man hacking up his guts in an outhouse and Corlette's voice, heard through a megaphone, announcing, "We now need experienced truck drivers. Men who are willing to do a dangerous job." Friedkin uses the visual correlative of a sick and dying man with Corlette forced to call for volunteers for death.

Scanlon, Manzon, Kassem, and his friend "Marquez" (Karl John), who is actually a white-haired old German named Angerman, are chosen to drive the trucks. In a brilliant montage, the trucks are "created" from a graveyard of chassis and parts. Fans, belts, lug nuts, lights, carburetors are cleaned, replaced, refined. Drive shafts turning and pistons pumping are cross-cut with the oil fire spewing thousands of gallons into a fiery end and sinister close-ups of Nilo, smoking a cigarette, mentally sizing up which one of the four he could easily kill. A rhythmic musical pulse, like the ticking of a clock, lies over the montage, mixing with the sounds of ratcheting, grinding, and welding. Operational though they may be, the trucks are battered, dented. One is painted with the legend *Lazaro* across its hood, the other with *Sorcerer* below its doors and a facsimile or a horned devil on its hood. A strange combination of mechanized civilization and primitive superstition. Scanlon and company then swing-load three cases of nitro into the bed of each truck, gently but firmly securing the cases in sand. (In *Wages,* none of the four characters who are hired — Mario, Jo, Luigi, and Bimba — are *shown* to have had any driving experience, though they *say* they do. And the trucks they drive are the oil company's two best. The nitroglycerin is loaded for them. It is not unstable like the dynamite in *Sorcerer.* The truck beds are also equipped with elastic bases to absorb shock.)

Early morning. The blackness of night still hovers like the humidity in the air. Scanlon, Manzon, Kassem, and Corlette make a final check of the trucks. Where's Marquez? Kassem spies Nilo leaning against a post, silhouetted, cigarette smoke curling around his head. Deadly apprehension crosses Kassem's face. He runs to Marquez's room. A fly buzzes. Blood drips. Kassem, revenge in his eyes, attacks Nilo with a switchblade. Nilo deftly throws him into a puddle. The irony of the attack is that Kassem calls Nilo a "Zionist," "a Jew dog." Marquez — a German and, one suspects, a former Nazi because of his friendship with Kassem — was obviously the least likely to give Nilo a fight because of his age. Nilo is already shown to be the most coldhearted of the group. He, after all, is the only individual who kills only for profit.

They need another driver. Obviously, Kassem and Nilo cannot be together, so Scanlon takes Nilo and Manzon goes with Kassem. Just as in *Kwai* and Peckinpah's *The Wild Bunch,* adversaries who do not speak the same language must become comrades. The British prisoners and their Japanese captors ultimately work side by side to build a railroad bridge. A band of American outlaws agree to rob a train for its munitions in return for gold supplied by vicious Mexican federales. As the trek commences in *Sorcerer,* Manzon and Kassem are total strangers to each other, and Scanlon tensely, forcefully, tells Nilo, "I been clocking you every second since you got into this town. If you're going to pick your nose on this truck, you better clear it with me first. Because if you don't, I'm taking you and this nitro right into a ditch." Fear, distrust, anger, suspicion, tension, or paranoia could explode the dynamite as easily as a deep pothole.

Scanlon and Nilo, in *Lazaro,* leave fifteen minutes ahead of *Sorcerer* into the jungle landscape that is fate's playground. And Friedkin gives us a visual signpost to prove it. Early into the trek, *Sorcerer* pulls up a hill. Friedkin pushes in on the truck, and as it passes out of frame, the stone face seen at the very opening of the film emerging from the blackness is revealed—just as terrifying, just as ominous. Fate, presented in a visual naturalistic fashion, appears as part of the geography of a chaotic world where strangers and enemies must rely on each other for survival. While the opening image of *Wages* focuses on a small child with a piece of straw toying with four beetles on a parched patch of earth (an intriguing visual), the theme of manipulation is established but not returned to in such visual terms. Friedkin, however, not only establishes this theme visually (fate emerging from the darkness) but restates it throughout with image and action.

Fate, represented in several guises—the stone face, the black condor logo of the oil company, the oil fire—torments these four men (fate's version of a good time) first by bringing them together in this Third World hellhole where the best they can hope for is to simply exist and then offering them a diabolical avenue of escape. True, they are unsympathetic, unredeemed criminals, responsible for violent deaths. But they are also men with nothing to lose but their lives; men on the edge of the abyss, "without alternatives," as Friedkin says, hiding in "a place nobody wants to go looking," desperately searching for a way out. The artist Francis Bacon has said that "it's only the consciousness of death in life that gives [death] its power."[37] Friedkin's quartet of losers live on borrowed time, constantly on edge. For them, living with death has become a way of life. They are keenly aware of every glance, every new face that appears in town. Suspicion and fear are their intimate companions.

For example, when Nilo stepped off the plane, his white suit and white shoes not only focused immediate attention to his presence, but the hard countenance, pencil-thin mustache, and sunglasses gave him the "look" of someone out of place in Porvenir. Scanlon, who had come to pick up supplies from the plane, watched Nilo as a rabbit watches a fox. In town, Nilo took a room across from Manzon's who peered cautiously through his blinds as Nilo told "Carlos" he'd need it only for a week. Kassem, too, shadowed Nilo's movements through town. Scanlon, Manzon, and Kassem each wore the same expression: Has he come for me? The irony of Nilo is that the hunter has apparently come to hide. Why else would he sit on a case of dynamite for two hundred miles? (The characters in *Wages* seem to have no other function than to stand around looking tough; it is all we see them do. When the time comes to hire drivers, the response of the men is more a reflection of their boredom—let's drive the trucks because it's something to do—rather than an act of desperation. In Friedkin's retelling there is a definite sense of urgency not only to extinguish the fire for the survival of the village, which depends on Corepet for employment, but because of the desperate desire—the *dramatic* impetus—of these men. That lack of urgency in *Wages* greatly reduces the visceral response to the drive.)

Early in the trek, fate and Friedkin use a psychological attack meant to demoralize and confuse. A heavy rain pelts Scanlon and Nilo standing at a fork in the road. They are unsure of their map's route to the oil field. A white road arrow lies in a puddle. An old man in a serape and wide-brimmed hat obscuring deep wrinkles on his face sits by the roadside. "Which road leads to Poza Rica?" Nilo asks in Spanish. "Do you want to go home?" the old man replies. "No, no. Which road leads to Poza Rica?" The old man tells them, "Poza Rica is dead." Of course Scanlon and Nilo want to go home, or anyplace but where they are. Forced to answer no, they are told through extended implication that going to a dead place makes them dead men. Lost men in the middle of the jungle on a lost quest. Nilo tells Scanlon the old man "is loco." One smiles at Friedkin's irony: The old man merely sits in the rain, while Scanlon and Nilo transport unstable nitro on a suicide run.

To the cold cynic, the intent of the journey may be viewed solely as an act of greed. Moments before departure, Scanlon told Corlette that with two trucks it's obvious the company does not believe both vehicles will make it. Manzon, the "financier," smoothly, forcefully, demanded double wages *and* legal residence or they don't drive. In Friedkin's fatalistic view the effort in "living and experiencing [life] on even the most dangerous levels"[38] is the point, the outcome preordained. Regardless of approach, the passage is brutal and courageous filmically and viscerally.

In a sequence as white-knuckling as the chase in *The French Connection*, Scanlon and Nilo confront an impossible obstacle—a sagging bridge made of frayed hemp and rotted wood. A river rages below. Sheets of rain are so heavy, we cannot see the other side of the gorge. They cannot turn back, having just slid down a muddy trail. Most of the roads the trucks must traverse can barely be seen for the heavy undergrowth. (In *Wages*, the trucks travel entirely on wide *graded* roads. The original film feels less perilous; less "classic.") The bridge sways in the howling wind.

Nilo tries to run away. Scanlon chases him back up the hillside, throws him down, then threatens him with a thick branch he holds like a club. "We're going to cross that bridge!" Scanlon commands. "And you're going to guide me 'cause I can't do it alone." Enemies who need each other! Scanlon looks and sounds reminiscent of Humphrey Bogart in *The Treasure of the Sierra Madre* with his battered hat, unshaven face, and tough-guy stance. It was exactly what Friedkin wanted, too, according to Green, who said that the director purposely molded Scheider's performance into the Bogart-type toughness of Fred C. Dobbs, the character Bogart played in

Sierra Madre (one of Friedkin's favorite films). One can easily see the resonances of Dobbs in Scanlon's face as he inches the truck forward across the rickety bridge — tense, fearful, determined. The planks under the weight of the truck splinter. One of the wheels drops into a gap, pulls up and splinters another plank, jolting the truck. The bridge groans. Upriver we can see the concrete towers of a bridge that used to span the gorge. They stand as silent crumbling relics of progress, metaphors of man's failure to control his world, a world nature has thrown into turmoil and unleashed on fate's pawns.

The truck belches and snorts like some primordial beast. Scanlon tries to keep *Lazaro* righted as the bridge sways and moans. The nitro cases, still secure in the damp sand when Scanlon turns a furtive glance toward them, look ironically, chillingly, like cheap coffins.

Out front, Nilo waves his hands, trying to guide, his white coat soiled and drenched. He no longer acts the cool, cold killer — he is *scared*. Looking through the windshield, Scanlon can barely see Nilo's shape squatting on the bridge for all the cascading rain. Scanlon steers *Lazaro* ahead. One can't help but lean and roll with the truck. Unsympathetic criminals, true, but they have blood in their veins. Watching Scanlon seemingly will the truck over the bridge, we glimpse the idea Friedkin had in wanting to cast Steve McQueen. The persona McQueen established as the fast-driving detective in *Bullitt* was, likely, the "baggage" Friedkin was after. But watching Scheider strain and pull, one can see and feel his nerves screeching with every snapping plank and swaying motion. Scheider may have had to act, as Green said, but with his gladiatorial visage, Scheider's Scanlon is believable, gutsy, and, most important, desperately human.

Like a crying animal, the wind howls. *Lazaro* growls, its crooked bumper and round headlights frame the yawning maw of its straining engine. Safely across, Scanlon's mind whirls, his body twitching with excitement as he ploughs through the jungle, confident that "no way they're going to make that bridge . . . we're sitting on double shares." Nilo's reaction reads more realistic — we're still sitting on dynamite.

Friedkin does not allow time to catch one's breath. He cuts back to the bridge — *Sorcerer* lurching across it, Manzon at the wheel, Kassem guiding. The storm has worsened; the bridge sags dangerously. Kassem shouts, "Come on!" He grabs hold of a rope and moves along a plank. A rotting log snaps under his weight, and he disappears from sight. He manages to hold fast to the bridge and pulls himself up, disoriented, dazed. And *Sorcerer* rolls forward. Manzon can't see him: "Where are you?" "Stop! Stop!" Kassem screams. He straddles a wide hole in the treacherously swaying bridge. *Sorcerer* roars nearer, its grillwork an ugly yellow grin, like a leering skull. Manzon stops and stands out on the truck's running board. "Are you all right?" he calls out. Suddenly a high-pitched musical squeal attacks the ears

Sorcerer. Kassem (Amidou) cries out as the nitro-loaded truck driven by Manzon (Bruno Cremer) appears perilously close to tipping over.

as we see the huge tangled mass of a dead gray tree smash into *Sorcerer* and the bridge. Fate (and Friedkin) will stop these two with the painful deathlike grip of these gnarled branches. It is as if a monster has risen up from the depths of the river, as though nature has screamed, "Enough!"

Manzon, machete in hand, hacks away at the tangled grotesqueries holding *Sorcerer* in place. Kassem, with the steel winch line from the front of the truck over his shoulder, drags himself to the end of the bridge and secures the line around a stump. "Come on!" he shouts. The rain torrents down like a million white stingers. The winch line draws taut, and Manzon inches *Sorcerer* forward. One of the bridge support ropes stretches, and its anchor shifts, unknown to Kassem. *Sorcerer* roars and belches exhaust smoke over the top of its cab, like a snorting bull. A loose plank lodges under one of the double rear tires. The support rope beings to unravel. The truck wheels spin against the plank. That musical cue becomes unbearably tense.

The stump with the line around it loosens in the mud. Manzon turns the wheel. The rope support snaps. The bridge sags, the plank dislodges, *Sorcerer* lurches forward, Kassem screams, the bridge collapses, *Sorcerer's* rear wheels are suspended over the watery abyss. We suddenly realize we have been holding our breath. Unfortunately, we can also recall a distant echo from earlier in the film, "Any kind of bump." (In *Wages,* there are no bridge sequences. There is a moment with the truck's having to back out onto a suspension platform to negotiate a turn on a hillside road. Watching it, however, one just sighs, loudly.)

"Action is character," Friedkin says, and in visualizing his fated world, he makes his characters functions of the action, which is the purpose of the plot. Scanlon and Nilo pull to a stop and stare in disbelief at the fallen redwood-size tree blocking the road. Stepping from the truck cab, Nilo begins laughing, loud and hard, at the utter fatalistic absurdity of the situation. Scanlon walks to the tree, Friedkin framing him puny and powerless next to one of nature's toppled giants. He falls to the ground, slamming it with his fist in frustration.

Looking up at the tangled green canopy where sunlight filters through in pale, infrequent shafts, Scanlon gets an idea — cut down eight trees. Grabbing a machete, he sinks waist-deep into the swamp, hacking wildly at the vines hanging like spider webs. Another image depicting man's flailing at fate's hostile playground. Nilo refuses to help, seeing the impossible pointlessness of Scanlon's act. When Scanlon advances threateningly, machete in hand, Nilo pulls his pistol from his pocket and fires several times, purposely missing a startled Scanlon.

Suddenly, Manzon and Kassem appear. Kassem examines the tree, thick branches and vines roped around its solid trunk, and simply says, "I think I can move it." Using tall slender branches cut and shaved by the others — the only time all four work together, Friedkin's visual storytelling a mirror reflection of their actions: quick, efficient, wordless — Kassem rigs a makeshift tripod over the middle of the massive trunk. He suspends a rock from a string he dangles from the tripod. Cutting out one of Nilo's trouser pockets (a tense moment for Nilo since Kassem uses the same knife he tried to kill him with earlier, and the look on Scanlon's and Manzon's faces indicate they don't much care if Kassem "slips"), Kassem fills it with sand and uses it as a counterweight by tying it to the end of the string suspending the rock.

They carefully lift a bag of nitro out of its crate and place it on top of the tree. A black condor cries overhead; fate watches what they do. They back the trucks to safety. Kassem gently punches a hole in the bottom of the bag. Nitro slowly drains out, the rock hanging above. Kassem cuts a hole in the pocket; sand spills out. He bolts for cover. The pocket empties, the rock drops, and the tree explodes, filling the screen with a million pieces of flying bark. It is as if the jungle screamed in pain. The middle of the tree vanishes, splinters the only reminders of its existence. The condor screeches above.

Friedkin says his characters "respond to life with simple solutions, not high-blown ones."[39] Scanlon's actions at the tree are far-fetched, complicated, "high-blown." Kassem, already established as an explosives expert, has the "simple solution": Blow up the tree. Ironic, and significant, it is that he uses his expertise to save life—the town of Porvenir, his own, and his comrade's. (In *Wages*, Bimba, conveniently, suddenly, brightens with the idea of using the nitro to explode a boulder blocking the road. The explosion itself happens offscreen. The scene feels as dull and heavy as the rock sitting in the road. It's set in a mountain pass made up of loose gray rocks. At least Friedkin's jungle is visually interesting. Admittedly, the scene is capped comically with Mario, Luigi, and Bimba urinating on the black spot where the boulder used to be. Jo, ostracized for cowering rather than helping Mario maneuver the truck over the extension platform earlier, says he'll "celebrate alone" and urinates by himself.)

Kassem's action, however, does not go unnoticed. As the group drives off, *Sorcerer* leads the way, a bonus for Manzon and Kassem, who will then be the first to arrive at Poza Rica. Friedkin cuts from a shot of the condor gliding and screeching overhead to an aerial shot of the trucks moving up the crest of a rain-forested mountain range. The condor screeches again, the angle as though it was the condor's point of view—fate's point of view.

In the truck cab, Manzon and Kassem speak of Paris. Showing Kassem the watch his wife gave him the day Pascal killed himself, Manzon tells him that he met his wife in Paris ten years ago and the day she gave him the watch was the last day he saw her. "It's five minutes to nine, in Paris," Manzon says, putting the watch in his shirt pocket. We see a civilized man who attempts to retain his dignity, his manners, amidst the sweat and squalor. Back in Porvenir, he smiled at the weary barmaid, Agrippa (Rosario Almontes), who looks fifty years old but may be only twenty. Her smile back was a genuine bright smile; a moment—fleeting as it was—of lightness, cordiality, between two people in a quagmire.

But Manzon's sentiment and Kassem's act of removing fate's obstacle have marked them in Friedkin's unsentimental vision. A gunshot rings out, and the right front tire explodes. Manzon and Kassem react. In a long shot, *Sorcerer* runs off the high road and down the hillside. The three cases of nitro fly forward, and we cut to the truck exploding with a reverberating *WAUMP!* As Friedkin said, "No matter how much you struggle, you get blown up." So much for sentiment and good deeds.

The explosion of *Sorcerer*—the actual imagery—looks perfunctory, uninteresting, not like the oil well or the tree. In *Wages*, however, no explosion is shown, only visually alluded to with a flash of light and the tobacco in the cigarette Jo rolls suddenly blown off his paper. As *Lazaro* rolls up to the site of the explosion, it appears as if there had been a rock slide. Comparing this scene to its counterpart in *Wages*, *Sorcerer* is sadly lacking. Director Clouzot displayed a remarkable visualist's talent in this sequence. We approach the site of the explosion with the truck. Splintered branches are strewn across the road as we advance through a grove of trees. Suddenly we are bathed in sunlight. A crater slowly fills with thick black oil from the broken pipeline alongside the road. Burned, shattered, arthritic-looking trees stand bare against the sky. There is no trace of truck or drivers, only Bimba's cigarette lighter. The place has an eerie otherworldliness to it.

At the site of the explosion in Friedkin's film, Scanlon and Nilo have a violent confrontation with a band of machine-gun-toting revolutionaries (presumably the same ones who set the detonator on the Poza Rica oil well and shot out the tire on *Sorcerer*). They tell Scanlon they want only the truck; they will let him and Nilo go. The leader of the gang actually plans to kill them in the road. Friedkin injects a bit of black humor into the tension by revealing that none of the terrorists knows how to drive. He again reveals character through action by having Nilo pretending to be ill, and then in a moment of confusion, he draws his pistol and with deadly accuracy, shoots the three terrorists standing in front of the truck—but not before he takes a bullet in the stomach. Scanlon, too, reveals another layer only hinted at in the New Jersey prologue when he told Vinnie that he never carries a pistol. One can draw from his comment that Scanlon has probably never killed anyone. Recall, he reacted with surprise when the priest was shot. Certainly, he's no Robin Hood, but not a murderer either. Grabbing a shovel from the back of the truck where he stands with the gang leader, Scanlon swings and hits him in the neck with the blade. The leader falls. Scanlon raises the shovel over his head and hits him twice more. We hear mushy thunks, but Friedkin does not show us the impaled body, only Scanlon's action—the reaction of a frightened man, a man fighting for his survival.

Considering Scanlon's actions here and back in Porvenir when he attempted to make friends with Manzon, he seems less villainous, less *unlikable* than Mario, his counterpart in *Wages*. Mario (played by French actor Yves Montand, who has the look of "a hard-fisted poet")[40] treats the youthful attractive cantina barmaid Linda (Vera Clouzot, the director's wife) as less than a dog, uncaring of her feelings. For instance, as Mario and Jo are leaving Las Piedras with their truckload of explosives, Linda climbs up on the running board and pleads with Mario not to go. Fed up with her whining, he pushes open the door to knock her off the vehicle. She is nearly crushed under the rear wheels. That's the action of a sympathetic hero? He also purposely runs over Jo's leg with the truck when Jo has slipped in the oil-filled crater trying to guide him through it.

Friedkin balances the next sequence on the edge of twilight, the edge of sanity. Driving through a moonscape environment of twisted barren formations of rock, Scanlon tries to keep a dying Nilo talking, to hold on. "What're you going to do with all that money, you hump?" Scanlon demands to know. A smile spreads across Nilo's face: "Get laid." Scanlon laughs. "Best whore in Managua," Nilo coughs. "Two whores!" Scanlon says, his voice rising, a hint of hysteria. "You do it . . . for me," Nilo gasps. "I'll do it!" Scanlon shouts as Friedkin cuts to the truck winding its way through the grittily surreal geography. His face pale, eyes darting, Scanlon asks aloud, "Where am I going?" We cut to a grainy image from Scanlon's memory—his friend Vinnie telling him to get a train to Baltimore and then to the pier. Friedkin pushes in on Scanlon's eyes, the landscape reflected in the windshield seeming whiter, bleached, skeletal. The truck sounds become low guttural sounds of agony. "Where am I going! What do you mean you don't know?!" The words ring in Scanlon's (and our) ears as hallucinogenic images of panic and death flash on screen—steel bars on windows, the bridge swaying, a bloody body hanging from the car in New Jersey, even Nilo driving the truck gone out of control (Nilo never takes the wheel on the trek). "Where am I going! What do you mean you don't know?!" assaults Scanlon's psyche, and now sharper, clearer images and sounds intrude—*Sorcerer* exploding, a stream of blood pooling around Manzon's watch, the wailing of police sirens. Friedkin visually and aurally strips Scanlon's viscera to paranoid numbness. Scanlon stops the truck—it gasps, but Nilo's cackle rails loud and strong. Scanlon looks down at a dead man. Nilo's eyes are open, a trickle of blood runs out of his closed mouth, yet the cackle grows louder. Scanlon shakes, pulls Nilo's body from the cab, and the truck motor coughs, sputters, and dies. Panicked, Scanlon tries to restart the engine, but all he can hear is a cacophony of derisive laughter. The odometer reads 216.7 miles. (It was set at zero when they left Porvenir, 218 miles from Poza Rica. Scanlon had chalked 218 above the speedometer.) Friedkin angles the shot as though from fate's point of view: looking down on Scanlon and the metal corpse of *Lazaro* in the middle of a no-man's-land, out of place, insignificant, seemingly failed.

Then Friedkin cuts to black, and out of it stumbles Scanlon, vacant-eyed, carrying a case of nitro, uncaring (unaware now?) of the volatility of it. Workmen grab the case from his arms as he turns toward an orange glow. We turn with him to reveal the oil fire. It shoots up into the night, seductive, beckoning, mocking, deadly. Hanging on the iron archway entrance to the field is the Corepet logo, the black condor, silhouetted in the flames. Scanlon staggers and drops unconscious before the fiery image, like a sacrifice to a god.

When Scanlon returns to Porvenir, Friedkin stages the moment as a hero's welcome. Cheering crowds greet the helicopter that delivers him.

He wears the ironic equivalent of a hero's laurel wreath in this climate — a Panama hat and loose white coat. They have replaced his dark clothes and battered fedora. But his walk is slower, the face drawn, the eyes reflecting . . . loss. Friedkin and Scheider have completed the Bogart persona in the way Pauline Kael once described Bogart's performances: ". . . taking the tough guy role to its psychological limits: the man who stands alone goes from depravity through paranoia to total disintegration."[41]

In the El Corsario, Corlette hands Scanlon a check for $40,000. "It's no good to me. . . . Our deal was cash," Scanlon says softly. Corlette says he'll take care of it. The police chief and the deputy who rousted Scanlon enter and take seats on barstools, like vultures perching. Corlette tells Scanlon he told a friend in the capital "you're a first-rate driver." "Not anymore," Scanlon says. Rebirth, redemption, and regeneration are anathema in Friedkin's fated world. Scanlon stares blankly — catatonic, disintegrating; a man at the frayed ends of his physical and emotional tethers. He has survived the flirtation with death, but it has left him juiceless, soulless.

In *Wages,* Mario, the only survivor of the four, happily swerves his truck to and fro across the road on his return to Las Piedras. He has a check for $4,000 in his pocket. The "Blue Danube Waltz" blares on the radio. This is cross-cut with Linda dancing in the cantina, with the rest of the town in celebration of Mario's good fortune. Mario loses control of the truck, and it plunges over a precipice just after Linda suddenly faints. With flames framing the scene, we push into the truck cab to a close-up of Mario, eyes open, blood streaking his face. While many praise the film as an existential testament of its time, Mario simply rides for a cheap fall, while Clouzot drives out with cheap irony. In Friedkin's journey through the heart of darkness, there are no convenient coincidences such as losing control of the truck. Friedkin's vision of fate is much more devious.

With sounds of Charlie Parker's slow jazz version of the lover's lament "I'll Remember April" playing on a radio in the bar (as with Manzon's reminiscences of Paris, this song shall prove an ironic foreshadowing), Scanlon asks Agrippa, the barmaid, to dance. The lines in her craggy face seem frozen, her eyes tired and dulled. They turn slowly in small circles, his light-colored clothes in contrast to the dirtiness of the street outside — another fleeting moment of relief and tenderness, in the tough masculine world Friedkin presents. But fate and Friedkin allow it only as a ruse. We pan outside to a dented blue taxi squealing to a stop. Just as Nilo was introduced in Porvenir stepping off the plane in white shoes, so too another pair of white shoes emerge from the taxi. We pan up to reveal the fleshy features of one of Carlo Ricci's thugs. Behind him, Scanlon's "friend" Vinnie. ("Billy doesn't see betrayal simply as one sleazy crook betraying another. He sees it as a malevolence throughout all human nature," Green said.)

Recognizing Vinnie signals the film's climax—a much more believable climax, rooted in story *and* character, than the ending presented in *Wages*.

True, Friedkin establishes Scanlon and Agrippa dancing close to the open rear exit of the El Corsario (we can plainly see street activity). True, the two policemen and Corlette's assistant who sits with him are wearing holstered pistols. And true, several soldiers holding rifles are at a nearby table. Yet, considering Scanlon's state of mind—and that even though we hear no gunshots, no cries of anguish, not even the sounds of scuffle or shouts of escape—it appears obvious Scanlon will soon be dead.

The most significant visual metaphor, though, Friedkin presents himself: It is fate's point of view, a high-angle shot looking down at the exterior of the El Corsario. Vinnie enters the bar, the thug already inside. Then we see a man pass in front of the El Corsario, blood running down his back from the severed bull's head he carries by its horns across his shoulders—a grotesque image of death that Friedkin revealed earlier as one of the first impressions of Porvenir, the "promise of the future." With this final sharp stabbing at one's already punished viscera, Friedkin visually closes a brutal circle—the powerful grip of fate that no man, no matter where he hides, can evade.

10
The Brink's Job

"Brink's was made because Dino De Laurentiis wanted to pay me half a million dollars. . . .
I can't think of another reason. Seriously."
                                    —William Friedkin

I

Overnight, Friedkin fell from the apex of the cinematic pyramid. In Hollywood vernacular, he went from "hot" into "the toilet." He contends that the "marvelous filmmaking that we respect—that people like David Lean have written the textbook on—there is no audience for that anymore."[1] The scars from his commercial pillorying for *Sorcerer* obviously went deep. One cannot help but wonder, then, if *The Brink's Job* was a kind of penance. (Friedkin had no possessory credit this time.)

"I was eating myself up and burning myself out after *The French Connection, The Exorcist,* and *Sorcerer,*" Friedkin said. "*Brink's* was light, not world-shaking. A human comedy."[2]

Comedy and Friedkin? The voice of Bud Yorkin, coproducer of *Minsky's,* echoes from the past: "I've always thought that comedy is not Bill's forte because he really is heavy."

Originally *The Brink's Job* was to be directed by John Frankenheimer *(The Manchurian Candidate, Black Sunday),* but according to Friedkin's agent, Tony Fantozzi, Frankenheimer was fired by Dino De Laurentiis, whose company was producing the film, and then Friedkin was contacted. "De Laurentiis' gang had already done all the location scouting," Fantozzi said. "It was all set to step into. The attraction at that time was not to have any deep, philosophical thing. It was 'Let's have a little fun with these wacky characters.' It certainly wasn't the idea that he had to have a hit to get back in the good graces of Hollywood. We had no idea if there was going to be an audience for it. Friedkin liked the whole idea of the picture. That kind of decision took us about an hour to make. 'Let's go to Boston and have some fun. We like the pea soup.'"

175

According to Ralph Serpe, producer of *Brink's,* "I'd heard [Friedkin] was a monster, that he wants to write, produce, do everything. But he told me, 'I've learned my lesson. I'm trying to get out of the gray area and into the white.'"[3]

(When Friedkin directed *Minsky's* ten years earlier, he was trying to get out of independent feature filmmaking and into the mainstream of Hollywood. Recall he disliked the "television sensibilities" of the *Minsky's* script and was not successful in getting many changes in it.)

Friedkin hated the various scripts that De Laurentiis had commissioned about the Brink's robbery, which occurred in 1950 when eleven masked men robbed the Brink's Armored Car Company in Boston of $2,700,000. "The approach in the early scripts was just kind of a banal caper film," said Friedkin who brought in Walon Green to write a new screenplay, not about "organized crime and a brilliant caper, but of *disorganized* crime and its farcical forces pitted against the farcical forces of the establishment, which was not only the Brink's Company, but the FBI as well. Their reputation as crimebusters was enhanced by the fact that they broke the Brink's case, but that was a sham; the robbers were known to most of the police officers and wise guys in Boston the day after it happened—but it took the FBI six years to break the case and they spent $29 million on it because J. Edgar Hoover was convinced that it was a conspiracy between the Communist party and organized crime. So they were off in the wrong direction. It's a classic story of misdirection and of things not being as they seem."[4]

"Our inspiration for the film was *Three Penny Opera,* a dark parody of the underworld," Green said, adding that he and Friedkin also believed that filmically the robbers and the robbery were closer in texture to an Italian film entitled *Big Deal on Madonna Street,* a comedy about a bunch of dopes attempting a big money heist. "But the funny thing is that we really couldn't be sillier than the real guys who robbed Brink's. They were more outrageous than the characters on screen. The did hold up gumball factories! That's why Brink's was perfect for these two-bit criminals. It was a cheap company. It was sitting there waiting for these guys to rob it. It called to the lowest echelon of criminals . . . the grotesqueries. Billy's entertained by these grotesque caricatures. When we started meeting the guys involved with Brink's, they were exactly that. Unsophisticated. For example, why should a guy like Tony Pino [the "brains" of the gang] rob Brink's when a guy like 'Slick' Willie Sutton never even looked at it because he figured the alarm system would be the most sophisticated in the world? Because a dumbo like Tony Pino sees a cheap, lousy lock on the door and just figures there must be a cheap, lousy alarm system too."

To write this story about "guys who were just goofs," Green said he relied on Noel Behn's book *Big Stickup at Brink's,* which provided much of the screenplay's structure, and Friedkin, who was the real catalyst. "He makes you examine the subject. You have to be the most expert on it." He interviewed three surviving members of the gang—Vinnie Costa (Pino's brother-in-law), Jazz Maffie, and Sandy Richardson (who were also unofficial technical advisers on the film)—and spent time in Boston getting the feel and flavor of the people and its environs, so that "by the time we finished writing the script, I don't think anybody—even the guys who did the job because they didn't know a lot of the individual things that happened to the others—knew about the robbery, Boston, the police, and everything else at the time of the robbery as well as we did."

Though there were originally eleven members of the gang, Friedkin's style trademark of verisimilitude was overridden by storytelling technique: Keep it simple. "Eleven was too many," Friedkin said. "We eliminated four of [the gang members] completely."[5]

Something Friedkin did not jettison from the script, though, was "establishing character organically," Green said. "It has to belong in the line of action. He wants the character introduced in some memorable fashion. One of his favorite films and mine too, is *Treasure of the Sierra Madre.* The economy of character introduction in that film is sensational. The bar fight between Tim Holt, Bogart, and the foreman perfectly lays out where those two guys are at that point. They beat up the foreman together, take *all* his money, count out what they're owed, and give him back the rest. That tells you that starting out, anyway, these are honest guys. They even pay the bartender out of their money. That's Billy's idea of establishing character."

Green cited visceral examples of both action and dialogue introductions in *Brink's.* "When Sandy Richardson comes into Pino's coffee shop one night and pretends to stick Pino up and then pops a paper bag to scare him, that tells you he's kind of a grinning Irish fuck-off. Now Specky O'Keefe's introduction is all in dialogue, but the dialogue is like action because he's talking about the invasion of Normandy and how *he* set the whole thing up."

(In Friedkin's opinion, the story and characters in *Minsky's* were depthless "one-liners.")

Friedkin did drop the idea of name stars—"the baggage"—believing "*Brink's* didn't need stars." What it needed was precisely what Friedkin had presented in his past films—actors who *looked* the part, from the rubberfaced savagery of Hackman as Popeye Doyle to the guilt-wracked visage of Miller's Damien Karras to Scheider's hollowed tough guy in *Sorcerer.* It is Friedkin's lineage of the street; he *shows* us the kinds of faces that Dickens, Chandler, and in the case of *Brink's,* Damon Runyon, could only write about—the scruffiness of Peter Falk, the moon-shaped pudginess of Allen Goorwitz (usually known as Allen Garfield), the menace Peter Boyle can conjure up, the pathos in Warren Oates's eyes, Paul Sorvino's bemused behemoth, Gerard Murphy's devilish grin, and Kevin O'Connor's sad smile all reflect a place, namely, Boston's North End, circa 1940s.

Friedkin calls the North End "one of the last fabled places in the country"[6] and chose to film there. He enlisted the expertise of Dean Tavoularis, the Academy Award–winning production designer for *The Godfather Part II* (he was also nominated for *Brink's*), to recreate time periods reflecting the 1930s, 1940s, and 1950s. In Friedkin's words, they were "building not only facades, but accents." Parking meters and television antennas were removed, lampposts replaced, billboards repainted, vintage mint automobiles borrowed and aged with dirt and rust.[7] Tavoularis said he examined old blueprints and photographs to reconstruct the old Brink's facilities, which had been turned into a garage. Even Brink's armored trucks (considered dangerous weapons which are supposed to be destroyed when they are retired, according to the *New York Times*)[8] and the original three-foot-thick vault door, discovered at a Mosler Safe Company plant in Idaho, were shipped to Boston for what would be a two-month filming. Scully Square, once known as the Times Square of Boston, was "recreated as it looked in 1942, with six thousand dollars' worth of fruit and vegetables on pushcarts, Red Cross signs — an entire period," Friedkin said.[9]

There was a problem at one point with one of the props. According to Barry Bedig, the prop master, "Billy wanted a horse-drawn beer wagon for a scene. I said, 'We better get a horse in from New York or Hollywood so it won't spook.' Billy said, 'No, there's millions of horses here in Massachusetts.' This was a night scene that took hours to light. So Billy says it would be great to have this horse pull the wagon out, and we pan the car in. Well, there was this arc light staring at this horse. Sure enough, the horse spooked. Billy said, 'Barry, what the fuck is wrong with that horse?' Everybody is silent. I said, 'Billy, I don't know. I can only get the horse. You teach it to act.' He just started laughing. And we got a horse from New York."

Besides Boston itself, the look and feel of 1930s, 1940s, and 1950s movies were other influences on the film, said Bud Smith, the editor, and Mark Johnson, one of the assistant directors. There are some dolly shots but no zooms, Johnson said, because "that wasn't the look we were after." There are also no drastic camera angles, according to Smith. "There's movement of people in the frame but not a lot of frame movement."

But the most significant influence was Edward Hopper, the American realist artist whose paintings have been described as "the quintessential expression of the Great Depression . . . an elegiac downer about loneliness."[10] The Hopper look, "bleak cityscape," as Friedkin calls it,[11] was exactly what he wanted. "The sparseness of Hopper suggests Boston: old bricks and lampposts as well as the way these characters lived. These were cheap boosters [thieves] who simply went out and did this thing."[12]

(Friedkin only borrowed from Hopper; he did not steal as he admitted he did from film director Rouben Mamoulian for *Minsky's*.)

The accents and ambiance of the street also had to be reflected by the extras hired to populate them. The faces in Friedkin's films tell stories; their lines and angles form a geography that becomes as integral to the authenticity of the film as the sets, music, sound effects, even the story itself. As Lou DiGiamo, Friedkin's casting director, points out, "The guys who play the barroom scenes look like they've been drinking for fifty years. The bookies are, no doubt, bookies. The peanut vendor is a peanut vendor, the nun is a nun."[13]

And as Mark Johnson explains, "With Billy, every extra has to know what they're specifically to do. Some directors will say everybody whose names start with these letters walk left to right. The others walk right to left. It looks like people just milling around. We were dealing with people who not only had never worked as extras before but who didn't speak English in many cases." Johnson illustrated his point saying that for one of the major establishing shots of a marketplace they needed carts, horses, buses, and over 400 extras. "We spent hours setting it up. Now the extras had to be told not just to buy fruit from this man and leave but to buy it, walk over, and say 'Hello' to this couple, and then hop on the bus. I had to do this with all four hundred people. Billy was ready to shoot and called for a rehearsal. There was some poor woman who was just standing there, and Billy went straight to her and asked, 'Do you know what you're doing?' She said, 'No, no one told me.' I'd gotten to three hundred eighty-seven people. I had missed this woman and some others. Billy's eye is incredible. You can't get by with him. I thought, 'I busted my ass here and still had to give more.'" Ironically, Friedkin claimed he was not being "a stickler for detail" on *Brink's.*[14] Even so, Johnson said this incident was also indicative of the ways Friedkin "keeps you on edge."

Yet another example came from Randy Jurgensen, whom Friedkin chose to play one of the FBI agents. It was a scene where Jazz Maffie, played by Paul Sorvino, is questioned by the FBI. Jurgensen said, "Our backs were to the camera, which was on Sorvino. In the first take we were rapid firing questions at him: 'Did you do this? Where were you?' He's looking at each of us with a little smile because his answers are there. Afterwards, Billy called me over. He said, 'I want you to say to Paul, "Look, you wop, I know you're lying."' Obviously this was going to do something to Sorvino who is of Italian extraction. Obviously, this is what Billy wanted. He's done this to other actors and to me in other pictures. But I don't want it to sound like he has to stoop to ethnic slurs to get something out of his talent. He does it from a point where it will enhance the actor.

"So we did the scene again. I took the beat when it was my turn, and Sorvino was already looking at me before I asked the question. So I said to him, 'What are you looking at, you wop?' He sat back. The next question came: 'Where were you?' He says, 'Well, I know . . . I . . . I was over there.'

And he kept shooting looks over at me. At dailies that night after both takes were run, Sorvino stood up and said, 'You got me, Billy. I owe you one.' He knew I would never do something like that myself."

Sorvino said, "Billy wants the scene to go a certain way. What he wants is specific. But you learn that as you do it. He's like Warren Beatty, who directed me in *Reds*. He doesn't tell you a damn thing about the scene. You do it until it comes right."

The actor's last statement describes Friedkin's filmmaking in every aspect—and this is no surprise, considering his past films. As they say in Hollywood, "The money is up on the screen." To get *Brink's* "right" cost $12.5 million (an expensive film in 1978 when the average cost of a picture was $5 million).[15] It was reported that Peter Falk's salary was $600,000, that 1,000 extras were paid $100 a day as an average,[16] that over 30 lampposts were temporarily replaced at a cost of $500 apiece, that to restore the original Brink's facility and its Prince Street surroundings cost $250,000.[17] Inconvenienced residents of the area were compensated with $100 and cable television (since antennas had to be removed).[18] Dino De Laurentiis also told NBC *Nightly News* that payoffs to Boston-area mobsters and the hiring of unneeded teamsters to assure smooth production "added one million dollars to the film's cost."[19] Friedkin told the media two days later that De Laurentiis' comment was "a misstatement made in haste. . . . The total cost of the Teamsters from beginning to end from January to August of 1978 was six hundred eighty-one thousand, six hundred twenty dollars. The total cost to the Boston Police Department for crowd control was two hundred twenty three thousand, seven hundred twenty-eight dollars.

"We were not forced to use any Teamsters we did not need. I was closest to this film. I saw what was going on on the set everyday. In fact, the Teamsters made a great many concessions to get this film made in Boston."

When asked about organized-crime figures on the set of the picture, Friedkin said, "I never bother to ask a person where they live, what their sexual preferences are, or whether they have a criminal record. I was unaware that it was a crime in this country to have a criminal record."[20]

(There was also a break-in at the editing rooms of the Boston location, and three armed men stole "fifteen reels of work print" after they "pistol-whipped, bound and gagged the assistant editors," according to Friedkin. A ransom demand of $600,000 was made, lowered to $500,000 and then finally to $25,000. No ransom was paid. The stolen film was reported to be outtakes—film that would not be used in the final picture. Friedkin said the robbers were "obviously crazy brigands.")[21]

However, as far as the actual costs of the film were concerned, Ralph Serpe, the producer, said, "It would have been about half the price to recreate this movie on a Hollywood lot, but you wouldn't have gotten the same atmosphere."[22] Friedkin admits, "It cost a lot of money to do it. I could have done it for less."[23]

Yet, considering all these expenditures, the most significant sum may well be Friedkin's half-million-dollar fee for directing—his personal wages of fear. For the first time in his career, he previewed his film, something he once flatly stated he would never do "as long as I live."[24] Yet he "brought the picture down to Long Beach at two hours and five minutes. Long Beach is a good place to preview because you get a mixed audience instead of the cinema buffs you find in Westwood, which is really an extension of the Lincoln Center Film Society. I knew I was going to cut the film to about one hundred minutes, which I think is about right for a movie like this, but I didn't know *what* I was going to cut. The audience told me."[25]

The Audience. The Public. That's where success is measured in show *business*. The Audience made *The French Connection* a hit and *The Exorcist* one of the top money-grossing films in history. The Audience also resoundingly rejected *Sorcerer*, Friedkin's most personal film. By previewing *Brink's*, Friedkin seems not only to be asking the Audience to tell him what to cut but also asking for their approval. "You could feel the resentment when the picture got serious," Friedkin said. "The audience had been laughing all the way through. Then, after the caper was finished, the picture turned a lot darker, and it was obvious they didn't like it."[26]

According to Bud Smith, after the preview, sequences were not recut, but rather whole scenes came out. The "darkest" moment—the vicious beating of "Gus" Gusciora (Kevin O'Connor) in prison by the FBI in an attempt to make him confess to the Brink's robbery and implicate the others—was excised. [Ironically, this scene *is* in the videotape version of the film.] Smith said, "We also took out exactly fifteen minutes of what I considered to be funny material. Like the relationship between Vinnie and his girlfriend [there is only a brief scene between them after the robbery when they toss the guns away into a lake] and a scene where Specky O'Keefe and his partner, Gus, go to this bar, get drunk, and pick up a couple of hookers after the robbery. These scenes were hilarious, but they diverted from the main story."

Mark Johnson recalled, too, that Friedkin shot several different endings for the film. "There was a modern-day ending that we didn't use. He may have known exactly how it was going to end but wanted some alternates." Johnson added, "I have a feeling Billy was never completely resolved in his own mind what he wanted to do with the film."

Friedkin called making *Brink's* "the most fun experience I've had as a director. It was in a city I love. I was mixing with bookkeepers, basketball players, criminals, cops ... all the wonderful people in the North End of Boston. But it was an ill-conceived project ... I was not deeply committed to the theme of *Brink's*."[27] (Similarly, he said he had "no vision whatsoever" with *Minsky's* either.)

That theme, according to Walon Green, was threefold. "Part of it is the irony of these street guys taking down a legend. And fate, except that fate was a bit of a jester because it played with these guys. It gave them moments when they took their wives out to dinner and bought them fur coats. But it was also about sandlot camaraderie; these were your buddies and you did not let them down. Guys like Jazz Maffie, who could have copped a plea but didn't. Even when they were all offered the world. And O'Keefe, who fell apart. They didn't dislike him for it. He knew he couldn't hold it together, and it was dumb they even took him in the beginning.

"But basically, no matter how it came down or how stupid Pino's moves were, they didn't blame each other or turn on each other. They all took it, went down with it, served their time, and that was it. And they did that on less than a handshake with people they didn't even like."

Friedkin once said, "The lesson in *Minsky's* is, if you can at all possible avoid doing pictures you don't have a strong feeling for, you shouldn't do them."

II

The story goes that in preproduction on *Brink's* Dino De Laurentiis was heard to shout, "Why am I making this picture: no sex, no violence, no action!"[28]

It is easy to perceive why De Laurentiis would question the soundness of making a film devoid of the primary ingredients of his previous productions, which include *Serpico* (1973), *Death Wish* (1974), *Mandingo* (1975), the remake of *King Kong* (1976), and *Orca, the Killer Whale* (1977). One might see *Brink's,* then, as an "arty" risk on his part.

Friedkin, however, is another matter. By his own admission, he was in effect a gun for hire, simply working for a fee. And when he asked the Audience to validate the picture, he invalidated, for all intents and purposes, his own vision. Therefore, *The Brink's Job* is a hack job.

Seeing the film without benefit of the aforementioned knowledge, it was still evident that Friedkin had lost confidence, his beliefs had collapsed, he had surrendered his integrity.

He had also created another hybrid film. Recall, he referred to *Minsky's* with that term because of the myriad directions that picture took: his own dark claustrophobic edge, Norman Lear's television sensibilities, a mishmash of "looks." *Brink's* is definitely a Friedkin film and, thereby, a hybrid of his own making.

Under the influence of Edward Hopper, Friedkin recreated the textures and tones of Boston with monochromatic richness: sharp gray skies, the steel-blue interior of Brink's, dingy yellow billboards, dark brownstone facades, even stained aprons and T-shirts. And like Hopper's most famous painting, "Nighthawks," Friedkin's Boston reflects urban loneliness. "Nighthawks" depicts a late-night diner with three customers sitting at the counter and a blond counterman. None of the four seem to be involved in any interaction, including the man and woman seated next to each other. These are solitary figures. Outside, the street is deserted, cold-looking, a row of vacant windows and storefronts. This is the "bleak cityscape" of Hopper that Friedkin vividly captured not only in night scenes but in daylight sequences as well. But the most significant aspect that Friedkin incorporates throughout *Brink's* is Hopper's use of light. In "Nighthawks," it spills out onto the street. It has been described as a "light which could have been treated as a Rembrandtesque pool of radiance within warm shadows, but is kept hard, flat, uniform, impersonal, relentless—a light at once high keyed and bleak, cold for all its brilliance, devoid of energy or spirit."[29] This is the look of *Brink's*. Tony Pino's (Peter Falk) diner, called Phillie's (the same name as the diner in Hopper's painting), the interior of the Brink's facility, the police lineup room, even a shot of an old car driving down a road with telephone poles receding crookedly into the distance, have this bleak brilliance, by now a trademark of Friedkin's films.

Friedkin also recorded two gut-wrenching moments of human misery, focusing on Specky O'Keefe (Warren Oates, in one of the finest performances of his career). Both scenes take place in prison. After the Brink's robbery, O'Keefe and Gusciora were arrested for unrelated crimes and given outrageously long prison sentences in hopes they would crack and tell what they knew about the Brink's. In the first scene, Jazz Maffie (Paul Sorvino) comes to visit O'Keefe, who believes the other gang members have forgotten him, are spending his share of the dough. His sister is dying of leukemia, and he demands that $2,000 be sent to her for an operation he believes will help her. Friedkin leaves the camera rolling on O'Keefe, who loses his grip. Anger and frustration are clenched in his fists, paranoia about guards stealing his magazines is manifested in a crooked grin, and he leans across the table gritting his teeth, saying "I can't do no more time. . . . I ain't got no more *control!* Can't you understand that?" The eyes reveal both the plea and demand of his statement. In the second scene with O'Keefe, still in prison, the FBI questions him, and he refuses to talk. He tells them, "Doing time don't bother me. I can do time. . . . I know what suffering is. And torture. But I can hold out. Forever. . . . I ain't going to tell you nothing." Tough talk, but tears roll down his cheeks, the lines in his face are like the cracks in an egg shell. O'Keefe's own shell is about to fall apart.

We are in close on O'Keefe for this examination of pain. It is one of the handful of close-ups Friedkin uses in the entire film. The close-up, *the* statement of cinema, allows an audience to peer into the soul. In O'Keefe's, we

"Nighthawks" painted by Edward Hopper. (Courtesy of The Art Institute of Chicago.)

see a spirit broken, nerves numbed, pitiful sadness. (One recalls images of a black man sitting in prison, sobbing, in *Crump* as he recounted a beating he received in a Chicago police station. And Emory, in *Band,* telling his friends about his only true love and how everyone laughed at his "funny secret." Of Karras's scream, denying the devil his body and soul. And Scanlon's drawn stare after his spiritual and physical pummeling. These are men at the limit, on the brink of the abyss. O'Keefe has been the last glimpse of this helpless heroism to date in a Friedkin film.)

But *Brink's,* in Friedkin's own words, was "light . . . a human comedy." Bleak, cold lighting and human misery do not make for "light" comedy. But light comedy *does* appeal to the Audience. They laugh. They tell their friends how funny it is and they *must* see it. But *telling* us it's a comedy is not enough. A poster ad showing cartoon representations of the gang throwing money into the air is not convincing either. The Audience must be *shown* it is funny. And Friedkin does not know how to do that. He would have an easier time holding mercury in his hand. (Reviews were split on *Brink's.* For example, *Time* called it "a crime movie that has been conceived in the antic spirit of a burlesque show,"[30] while the *New York Times* said it is "neither especially comic nor . . . suspenseful.")[31]

Friedkin's strengths lie in dark images of kinetic violence and volatile stress where action generates the drama that feeds the fear. His better films flirt with death. Bits of cynical humor he excels at, such as "Santa Claus" chasing the black dope pusher in *The French Connection.* But in *Brink's* he relies on stringing together sight gags, poor Three Stooges imitations. The film opens with Pino, his brother-in-law Vinnie (Allen Goorwitz), Gus, and Sandy (Gerard Murphy) attempting to rob a meat-packing plant. Uniformed policemen charge up the staircase, and the robbers scramble for cover. Vinnie sprawls across a table stacked with beef shanks; Gus and Sandy slide down a chute into a vat of animal blood; Pino is the only one apprehended because of squawking chickens he's disturbed by trying to hide in the poultry room.

As with *Sorcerer*, Friedkin focuses on criminals. But here he has substituted aberrant behavior with gross stupidity — scene after scene of it. Yes, Friedkin adheres to his action-reveals-character dictum, but the moronic behavior of the characters, from Pino's dumb luck (which applies to both his successful and failed robberies) to J. Edgar Hoover's (Sheldon Leonard) pomposity (he tells the assembled newspapermen when the case is broken, "Crime does not pay," in an attempt to take the onus from the $29 million he spent to investigate it), remains static, uninteresting, uninvolving, one-dimensional. There is nothing to admire or relate to with anyone in the film. It may look real, but the characters exist as unreal cutouts. Obsessions that drove Doyle, Karras, and Scanlon are replaced solely with acts of buffoonery here.

Attempts at witty lines fall flat too. When Pino is released from prison, Vinnie greets him at the prison gates with back issues of *Captain Marvel* comic books. Pino can't believe there's a Captain Marvel, Jr.! Vinnie explains that Lois Lane dumped Superman and "started shackin' up with Captain Marvel." Pino looks at Vinnie and says, "You know the trouble with you? You don't read the comic books. You just look at the pictures." Friedkin has already established these guys as a cross between the Three Stooges and the gang-that-couldn't-shoot-straight. They are not smart enough to be the Marx Brothers.

But, maybe Friedkin hopes that, like Vinnie, the audience will only look at the pictures of this bleak-looking cartoon and simply laugh at Vinnie rolling around on a million gumballs, which spill out of a door marked Do Not Open that he opens anyway. Or Pino, nonchalantly stealing ties from a sidewalk display while Vinnie distracts the vendor. (One gets the impression this is supposed to endear Pino to us as a likable rogue.) Or O'Keefe and Gus, sitting in a diner wearing stolen caps that still have the price tags dangling from them. It does not work because Friedkin has made the film with the bleak eye of the director of *The French Connection*, and this is not conducive to laughter. And neither is stupidity when there is no threat, no conflict, no obstacle to thwart, even by accident. The Audience already *knows* Pino and his gang successfully robbed Brink's. And since Friedkin insists on staying true to the break-in, there is no suspense, no action, no violence. One longs for him to take dramatic license, as he did in *The French Connection* when he had Doyle shoot the hit man in the back. Friedkin

The Brink's Job. **From left, Vinnie Costa (Allen Goorwitz), Tony Pino (Peter Falk), Jazz Maffie (Paul Sorvino) and Stanley Gusciora (Kevin O'Connor) prepare to rob a bubblegum factory.**

confuses the picture with conflicting tones of comedy and corruption, and annoys the Audience in the extreme.

The most damning element of Friedkin's sellout lies in the theme, for it is there that Friedkin, most clearly and painfully, betrays himself. As Green explained, the first part was the irony of these bunglers' stealing millions of dollars from *the* security legend. Since Brink's was portrayed as being an outfit of bunglers, too (cheap locks, cheap alarms, sleeping guards), Friedkin eliminates all respect for both sides of the law. There is a vacuum where any intelligence might lie; the Audience has no one to identify with, no opportunity to become involved on any level with these dolts. And that includes the FBI.

In the second part, fate is represented as a prankster rather than a monster. Fate must have a soft spot for fools, according to this vision.

Finally, the third part represents the antithesis of *Sorcerer*. The code of honor among the crooks in *Brink's* is childlike in its simplicity. Sandlot camaraderie means you do not squeal on your friends, you don't *betray*

The Brink's Job. From left, Joe McGinnis (Peter Boyle), Vinnie Costa (Allen Goorwitz), Sandy Richardson (Gerard Murphy), Tony Pino (Peter Falk), Jazz Maffie (Paul Sorvino), Specs O'Keefe (Warren Oates), and Stanley Gusciora (Kevin O'Connor) prolong the joyous moment of pulling the "crime of the century."

them. That violent malevolence of mankind that Friedkin believed so strongly in and visualized so thoroughly in *Sorcerer* is missing in *Brink's*. Friedkin simply cut it out of the film. (Green said he argued with Friedkin to put O'Keefe's confession *back in* the picture.) In violating his personal vision by eliminating the betrayal and by lifting out the more violent acts in the latter part of the film because the preview audience "didn't like it," Friedkin shows us only stupid people. But these stupid people are crooks. (Even the police and newsmen are shown reaching for stray dollar bills on the floor of Brink's after the robbery.) And Friedkin wanted the Audience for *Sorcerer* to be behind his criminal characters. Since the Audience rejected them, Friedkin attempted to find a visual way to elicit sympathy for his band of boobs here.

He tries it with a fantasy, the final image of the film before the final credits roll. After the grinning Brink's robbers are escorted to jail past throngs of screaming admirers, well-wishers, and the flashbulbs of the press (smiling lawbreakers were also cheered by the masses in *Minsky's*), Friedkin cuts to a long slow-motion shot. To the tune of Glen Miller's lively big-band hit "In the Mood," Friedkin reprises the gang joyously tossing the green cash into the air. Admittedly, there is a whimsy to the image, the dream of waltzing into a bank and waltzing out with as much money as you can carry. By shooting it in slow motion, Friedkin prolongs this one glorious moment for Pino and his gang. And, one believes, Friedkin extends it for the benefit of the Audience by allowing them to share the fantasy. But the dream exploded ninety-eight minutes earlier when we realized that Friedkin told us only stupid people are funny, only stupid people are capable of (or is it susceptible to?) sandlot camaraderie, and, by extension, then, only stupid people (the Audience?!) could be taken in by this film.

11
Cruising

"I condemn you as the worm of worms."
—Arthur Bell, *Village Voice* Columnist
and Gay Activist, to William Friedkin[1]

I

Originally, Steven Spielberg (*Jaws, E.T., Raiders of the Lost Ark*) was going to direct *Cruising*, the story of an undercover cop searching for a murderer in the dark enclaves of New York City's gay community. In 1970, Philip D'Antoni, who had just produced *The French Connection*, secured the rights to Gerald Walker's novel because "it was the spookiest book I'd ever read. It terrified me. I brought little Stevie in right after [he finished his 1971 television movie] *Duel*." D'Antoni believed Spielberg "would be great for *Cruising*. He wanted to do it. There was no question in his mind. I hired him for the same reason I had hired Billy for *French Connection*. The two of them were so much alike it was incredible—young, aggressive, *tremendous* energy.

"But five months later, I decided I did not want to do *Cruising* because I felt there was no way of doing it the way I wanted to have it done and be true to the story." D'Antoni wanted realism and now considered Walker's book, which was inspired by a long series of mutilation murders of homosexuals in New York, too horrific and its implications of a cop losing his identity in a morass of decadence too aberrant to visualize.

By late 1978, Spielberg had two phenomenal successes to his credit, *Jaws* and *Close Encounters of the Third Kind*. D'Antoni had retired comfortably from the movie industry. And Friedkin was returning from a press conference on *Brink's* and was telling former police detective Randy Jurgensen that he had decided next to do a film called *Cruising*. Jurgensen recalled that Friedkin asked him if he knew what it was about. "I told Billy, 'I have an idea.' And then he said to me, 'You did that, didn't you?' I said, 'Yes, Billy.'"

Jurgensen had spent fourteen months in the early 1960s posing as a

189

homosexual in Greenwich Village in an attempt to apprehend "two men
who we believed to be police officers who were extorting money from
homosexuals for being homosexuals. Out of the eleven homosexuals who
came forward to the DA's office with complaints, two were killed. The DA's
office believed police officers were responsible.

"My boss called me in. He said, 'Have you ever had a man suck your
cock? Have you ever had it up the ass?' I said, 'What?' I was told I was going
undercover. I was told I would never pick up my paycheck at the station.
I was being picked because of my record [he had spent six years in undercover narcotics] and my physical looks. The men I was after did not look
like me at all. In fact they were called the Salt and Pepper Team by the
police department because one was black and one was white. It seems that
these two guys, dressed as policemen, would catch homosexuals engaged
in sexual acts and take them to the Charles Street police station. But only
to the outside. One of the guys would walk inside, and the homosexual in
the car would see him talking to the desk sergeant because the station had
a large window. The guy would say to the sergeant, 'Am I going right to get
to the Westside Highway?' The sergeant would say, 'Yeah, just go down the
block.' All the homosexual would see was the sergeant nodding. The guy
would walk back out and say, 'Okay, the sergeant is with us.'

"These two would keep the homosexual all night and then take him
into the back of the court the next morning. One guy would go up to the
bridgeman and ask him some questions. The bridgeman would nod. The
guy would come back and say, 'This is going to cost another five hundred
dollars.'

"So now, to pay off the judge, the sergeant, and themselves, they'd tell
the homosexual it's going to cost one thousand two hundred dollars. They'd
take this victim to the bank, and he would draw out the money.

"At the time I was there in Greenwich Village, all the gays seemed to
be living well. I never saw one on food stamps. Also, in 1962, nobody was
out marching in the street saying, 'I'm gay, and I'm proud.'

"So I searched for these two guys, believing they were police officers.
[He associated with both the leather and mainstream echelons of the gay
community.] In the end, through a lot of luck one day down at the piers,
there they were — Salt and Pepper — going away with a poor victim. I recognized them because they looked so obvious. Nobody else was black and
white in uniform there.

"We went to a grand jury. They were convicted on extortion. Nine and
eleven years, respectively, they were given. There never was an indictment
for murder. Nobody saw the murders. And these were heinous murders.
We had an arm in the water. We had remains outside a meat-packing
house." (He explained that these body parts were classified as CUPPI, Circumstances Undetermined Pending Police Investigation, because without

the cause of death there is no murder. "If you find a body without a head, the medical examiner cannot give you the cause of death because the victim may have been shot in the head before anything else.")

Though there was not enough evidence to connect these murders to the two impostors for a conviction, Jurgensen said there was enough evidence "to confuse the extortion, so we might wind up with a hung jury and those two could walk out the door. You go for the sure one."

Jurgensen said he felt a personal sense of achievement having proved that policemen were not involved in these extortions, and he was promoted from white shield to gold shield detective.

This dark tale, rooted in realism about a cop's obsession to find killers and fears, real and imagined, seemed ideal for the director of *The French Connection, The Exorcist,* and *Sorcerer.*

Friedkin once said, "You don't know what it is that attracts you to a film. My films deal with irrational fear. Also my own fears: bureaucracy, homosexuality. . . . I try to deal with the violence in me through my films."[2] He chose to write the screenplay himself (it was his first feature-film script). He adapted very little from Walker's book—specifically, the title, a couple of character names, and the idea of a rookie cop assigned to catch a killer of homosexuals. Friedkin has called the book "a marvelous murder mystery with a terrific story."[3] Most of the incidents that make up the body of the picture were taken from Jurgensen's experiences while he was searching for the police impostors. Friedkin also examined the files of the New York City District Attorney's Office, Police Homicide Division, and the Medical Examiner's Office, covering two decades of brutal murders involving homosexuals from crimes of passion to the unsolved "bag murders," which involved dismembered body parts discovered wrapped in plastic bags. Articles written by Arthur Bell in the *Village Voice* detailing the vicious slayings of homosexuals were also used, Friedkin said, as part of his research.[4] He began writing and rewriting. Friedkin says he wrote five drafts (not unusual for a motion picture).[5] However, he would continue making changes in *Cruising*—some baffling, some demanded—almost to the day of its release.

When he began filming around Greenwich Village in early July of 1979, Friedkin had a star, Al Pacino *(The Godfather Part I* and *Part II).* Yet, unlike the situation in *Sorcerer,* Friedkin did not believe *Cruising* required a star. He said the role of Steve Burns, the undercover cop, was originally to be filled by Treat Williams (he played a young detective in Sidney Lumet's *Prince of the City).* "I think any good young actor could have come off in the part of Steve Burns," Friedkin said, but he hired Al Pacino, who was thirty-nine years old then. "When he read the script, he said he wanted to do it. He said, 'I gotta do it. I love it and I must do it.' I felt, yeah, then he should do it. Jerry Weintraub [producer of *Nashville, Oh God,* and

Cruising] and I said this is too good to pass up. We'll have to go for it. Warner Bros. was going to make the film, and when we brought Pacino in, it meant we had to pay him two million dollars and they backed off. They said, 'We don't think he's worth it to the picture.' So we made the film with Lorimar." (Already one senses Friedkin is in trouble. Hiring a "star" does not guarantee commercial success.)

Jurgensen recalled that with the signing of Pacino, Friedkin wanted his star "to play the dual role of cop and killer. It was a possibility that the killer could wear glasses and a mustache and the cop would be clean-shaven. Obviously they would be two separate characters. But at the moment of truth, it would be like a fusion. At their confrontation, Billy said, you'd see the killer and the cop facing each other. The cop is dressed like the killer, and they both look like each other. The cop has by now a duplicate of the murder weapon — the knife — so what you'd have on screen is the killer on the left and the cop on the right. The similarity would be mind-boggling: the same dress, physical features, knives. Twins of the same seed." (In Walker's book, the cop and killer are strikingly similar, but they never have a face-to-face confrontation.) Friedkin soon threw out this mirror-image concept, but he would later replace it with something one production supervisor called "vague and ambiguous."

But what weren't vague were Jurgensen's stories, which he had already told Friedkin and then told Pacino, "to make him feel confident," the former detective said. "How I did the investigation made it believable. It would be very easy to be a homosexual cop and do that. What would be hard is not to be a homosexual cop and do that. So I convinced Pacino this is the way we did these things. There were a lot of forerunners in undercover narcotics, a lot of mistakes made, and no two situations were ever the same. But when I did this, there were no forerunners. One of the things I'm always asked is, obviously, if you lived down there for fourteen months, *did* you? My answer is, I was undercover narcotics, and I never stuck a needle in my arm, so when I was undercover homosexual, I never slept with a man."

One of Jurgensen's experiences reflected in Friedkin's film was an incident in which he said he "saw a guy wield a knife and cut a homosexual. I didn't take police action at that point. I went around to all the hospitals because that guy was cut bad enough to die. I later pointed the assailant out to the other cops because I knew who he was. I remember the other cops saying to me, 'For Christ's sake, what are you? Are you some kind of fucking faggot? Why didn't you bring the guy in? Why didn't you go with the guy?' Billy took exactly what those guys did to me and used it to create the scene in the car stakeout between Pacino and myself. When I say to him, 'Why didn't you go with him?' he says back to me, 'I don't know.'" Jurgensen said that was his response to the other policemen. "I didn't go because I thought I was turning homosexual. I just didn't go with the guy. I did not take part as a police officer."

Then there was "the inspector I worked for who was under a tremendous amount of pressure [at that time], and I brought Billy to meet him. He is built exactly like Paul Sorvino, only Paul is almost twenty years younger."

(Sorvino, who plays Captain Edelson, amiably commented that "most people who saw *Cruising* thought I'd degenerated physically. They thought I was fifty-five, fifty-six years old.")

Jurgensen said, "The bar where Burns goes to meet the captain and they have the conversation about some guy owning all those leather bars [a Mafia inference, with Edelson saying he "can't make a move" on Tommy Mancuzzi, also known as Tommy the Joker] is the exact same bar where I met my inspector. That subway station is exactly where I met him and told him, 'I can't do this anymore. I just cannot.' I told him I was afraid of losing my identity, not as a male, but as a cop. I had nothing to remind me of being a cop. There were periods of time that I would forget for days on end that I was a cop. You really have to be a cop to understand that statement. I remember the boss telling me then, 'I'm on the line here. It really looks like a police cover-up. The DA is convinced cops are doing all this.' He said to me, 'We're more than police officer and superior. We're partners. We're in this together.' Billy asked me, 'How could an inspector and a cop become partners?' I told Billy that I thought the guy believed I was the last hope."

Jurgensen also explained that he was the *only* undercover policeman on the case because the police department was also conducting an extensive internal investigation into the murders, not because of media attention but because of pressure from the district attorney's office.

"I was told I would disappear," Jurgensen said, just as Burns is told in the film. But while Burns is told emphatically that "*nobody* can know anything about what you're doing," Jurgensen said that he was only told not to discuss the case with other members of the police department. While Jurgensen followed those orders, he also chose not to tell his grilfriend at that time what he was doing because he simply did not discuss his cases with anyone. One night, Jurgensen said, "I was on my way to this club, and my girlfriend was coming down the street with her brother and some other people. I was going the opposite direction up the street in a leather jacket and with a sparkle star over one eye that this other girl painted on for me. Now what are the odds of this happening? So I'm going to this club, Trudy Heller's, where Mia Farrow, Tiny Tim, Liza Minnelli, and Barbra Streisand would go. My girlfriend looked at me, I looked at her, and you can't believe what was said because I never told her what I was doing. I went on to the club and did what I had to do, and I don't even know what that was.

"We filmed that scene. Karen Allen [who plays Burns's girlfriend,

Nancy] actually sees Pacino, and it was taken out of the film. In the film now it seems everything is A-okay, and in the next scene with her, something is wrong between them.

"In between was the scene where Pacino had some eye makeup on. He comes dragging into his Village apartment, and she's sitting there waiting. By the time he sees her, it's too late. She can't believe what she sees. She says, 'What's going on?' He says, 'I don't want to talk about it. I can't talk now.'"

Jurgensen said he worked this case "seven nights a week, thirty days a month. I took off, maybe two nights in a row. I was not supervised. I overdid my job. So whenever I had an opportunity to get away from that beating, pounding music that I would hear *every* night, I did go for softer-sounding music. Billy took that and used it. When we are in the gay world, it is a driving beat. When Burns is with Nancy, it's soft, slow, dreamlike."

Cultural details and jargon also worked their way into the film. "We'd hang out and listen, just like we did on *French Connection*," Jurgensen said. "The scene where Burns goes in and asks what the different-colored handkerchiefs mean I had done. ["A light blue hankie in your left back pocket means you want a blowjob, right pocket means you give one . . . . A yellow one, left side, means you give golden showers; the right side, you receive . . . ."] That was the actual store. We had a host of those kinds of lines. Billy didn't use them for shock value. He used them where they would fit in. In the final confrontation scene when Burns and Stuart Richards [Richard Cox] are firing lines back and forth, the only thing lacking is the gum chewing—'You want it here?' 'I want it now.' 'Hips or lips?' 'I want to see the world.' It was that kind of banter.

"It was the same thing with the two cops in the beginning of the picture, hassling the transvestites. ["Come up here. I want to show you my nightstick," one cop taunts.] The police department did get complaints from homosexuals about two cops making them go down on them. Billy took that and used it.

"We had a killing many years ago—it had nothing to do with the case I was on—that was described to us in detail by the Medical Examiner's Office. That murder was re-created in the same hotel where it happened." In that scene, a young man, lying nude on his stomach, his wrists pulled behind his back and bound to his ankles by a leather strap, is stabbed repeatedly in the back with a knife. The costume designer, Robert deMora, recalled that Friedkin "wanted to do something with the boots the two men in the scene were wearing. He asked, 'What would be the attraction?' (He's very fascinated when he doesn't completely understand what's going on in certain scenes like that.) Well, it was the attraction of the leather. Lots of people are interested in boots. Billy wanted to start on the boots. I said, 'Have his hand on the boot. Then have his hand move up.' We had long discussions as to how the physical thing would work. Once he got the two guys on the bed and the murder started, that was all his."

Friedkin filmed in the Rambles in Central Park, and, according to Jurgensen, "we duplicated what we saw there. Clubs where we went to film catered to, asked only, was for that leather gay section." One of the more bizarre scenes in the film was what became known as "precinct night." Since deMora knew that milieu very well, he went to Friedkin and "suggested we mix it up a bit. The way it was written, everybody was in uniform with a tie and a badge. I told him it would look absurd, too true, too perfect, though a lot of those functions do look like that. I suggested we use khaki and also have some with ties and shirts off. He bought that."

Another strange scene took place in a police station interrogation room where several detectives (including Jurgensen and Sonny Grosso, who was also a technical adviser on this film) question Burns and the suspected killer whom Burns has led them to when a large, muscled black man walks in wearing only a cowboy hat and an athletic supporter, and slaps Burns out of his chair. Was this credible?

"A scene like that actually happened with another homicide case," Jurgensen said. "It was a double murder. When the suspect told the judge how the confession was extracted from him, the judge sent him to Bellevue for two weeks of observation. The 'pick your feet in Poughkeepsie' scene was real life in *French Connection,* just as that scene in *Cruising* was real. In some parts of the city, confessions were extracted without the hand play, and we told Billy that. Since beatings leave physical marks, smart detectives don't beat confessions out of people. So when you're sitting down talking and a suspect is over on the other side of the room and the door opens with a black man standing there in a cowboy hat and jockstrap and says, 'I know you did this killing, and I'm going to testify' and the suspect says, 'Who is that guy?' and you pay no attention—especially after it happens three or four times—the suspect starts saying, 'Yes, I shot Lincoln.'"

"I believe in exaggeration and distortion," Grosso said. "I don't believe in lies. That scene in *French Connection* where Doyle has killed the FBI man and is so wrapped up in himself that he's reloading his gun to me is a gross exaggeration. But that kind of thing happens. Just like when we went into the bars, I saw things like the golden shower where twenty guys would take a piss on another guy. As far as the interrogation scene goes, there have been victims of police brutality, not as extensive as the movies or Billy would like us to believe, but it does happen. These acts of seeming impossibility do happen. We were showing people scenes that they had never seen before. These scenes become almost incredible."

"We filmed in a section of the city where homosexuals frequent, live," Jurgensen said. "Also, this is where the clubs are. This is where the bars are. This is where the shops are. The people, how they lived and dressed there, that's in the movie. Let's go back to *Brink's*. It happened in the Italian section of Boston. We didn't do it in the black section. *French Connection* happened all around the city. That's exactly where we went. In doing *Cruising*, Billy was not doing anything other than what he'd done in all his other movies."

Except, on *Cruising*, Friedkin and his production had the added pressure of being under siege. The gay community was outraged at what many perceived as an antigay film.

"It was horrendous," Burtt Harris, the production manager said. "We had four hundred cops for crowd control. Shooting in New York, you usually only need ten at most. And did you ever see a star on a cop? We had three-star generals out there. We had two of them down in a bar called the Meat Locker. They said, 'Why can't you do this someplace else?' They wanted us to get out of their jurisdiction. Well, Christopher Street is where it is, and it ain't gonna move.

"During shooting, the noise was incessant. The demonstrators blew whistles and threw eggs."

"And bottles," Jurgensen said. "One hit Jerry Weintraub. He was right out there with Billy on the camera truck. We had one night where probably seven hundred demonstrators were on the street, people in their apartments hanging sheets out, people that joined the demonstration for lack of something else to do."

"Flashbulbs were popping off," Harris said. "You can't shoot at night with flashbulbs going off. Al Pacino never wanted to come out of the trailer. Every time he'd come out, they'd start calling him 'pig' and 'murderer' and 'fag basher.' It was really ugly."

According to one report, late in the filming, "violence erupted when mounted police tried to break up a group of some eight hundred homosexuals who marched in protest."[6] What was Friedkin's reaction to all of this? Harris said, "There was nothing he could do. After the first day, he looked at me, laughed, and said, 'This is insane.' I said, 'It ain't gonna get any easier.' You see, you're allowed to demonstrate one hundred feet from what you're demonstrating against. We get a permit, they get a permit." He added, "Our crew handled it all nicely. We were decent, and that annoyed them."

"Right before we started the film," Weintraub said, "this Arthur Bell fellow from the *Village Voice* got a copy of the script and made a whole thing about nothing. He had a wrong script. He had an early draft."

Bell attacked *Cruising*, saying, "It's almost a road map on how to kill a gay. It's a product of the grossest dreams of a reactionary gay-hater."[7] (By extension, this logic tells us that Hitchcock films are blueprints on how to murder a variety of people.) "First of all," Weintraub said, "in order for this film to be antigay, the filmmaker and the producer would have to be antigay. Nobody can accuse Billy Friedkin or Jerry Weintraub of being antigay."

"I have no particular feelings about the morality or immorality of homosexuals," Friedkin said. "I never set out to make an antigay film.... My personal feeling was that gays felt the film would portray the dirty laundry of the gay world.... Many intelligent and dedicated members of the gay community went completely crazy on the subject of *Cruising.* We became adversaries. I am *not* their adversary. I thought *Cruising* was going to do some good, achieve an understanding about the way a certain group of gay men were being preyed upon in New York City and are to this day."[8]

"We did a murder mystery centered around a certain segment of the gay community," Weintraub said. "The people who got uptight about *Cruising* were the people who were not into the leather scene, not into the bar scene. They thought everybody would think that everybody who is gay was in that world. Does that mean that every time you see a rabbi on the screen that every Jew wears a round black hat? That's silly. It makes no sense. Just like it does not mean that all gays wear leather or give golden showers or whatever else happened in *Cruising.* Like it doesn't mean all heterosexuals do it or don't do it. So if we were to make that film and make it not about gay people, would somebody say it was antiheterosexual. No.

"What we were trying to do was be true to the subject matter, which I guess every good filmmaker tries to do. We were very, very careful to make it accurate. We weren't making anything up, we weren't trying to perpetrate a hoax on the public. Because of that, we felt—not vindicated (yet that's a good word)—but we felt comfortable with the fact that we weren't betraying anybody in the gay community.

"In fact, I felt that it would help because if a kid got off a bus from Duluth, Minnesota, he wouldn't make a beeline for those bars first thing until he learned what the city was all about—the danger. And if he wanted it, wanted to live on the edge, great. I'm all for people doing what they want to do. That's up to them.

"I have a lot of gay people working for me, who were there when we were making the film, who couldn't understand the uproar. The people who thought it was antigay *really* thought it was antigay before they ever saw the film." Weintraub said he was very troubled by the demonstrators because their protests were "in direct violation of the First Amendment. And of all segments of society trying to suppress somebody from doing something, to see the gay population do it is really hard to take because they don't want to be suppressed. They don't want to be prevented from walking down the street holding hands with their lover."

"A lot of people in the gay community were demanding to speak to Billy to talk about the screenplay and whether he should do the movie," Sonny Grosso said. "Billy's attitude was, he didn't have time for that. I believe that's a true attitude."

Grosso further explained that when he served as a technical adviser on *The Godfather*, the Italians tried to exert the same type of pressure on that picture to halt its production. "We do have the freedom in this country to shoot any kind of movie we want. What you have as the buyer is the freedom to refuse to see it. Maybe Billy made a movie nobody wanted to see, and they didn't show at the box office. I believe in that. That's where you can kill us all."

Weintraub said, "They should have waited until the picture opened. I kept saying, 'Wait until you've seen the film. If you feel this way after you've seen it, you have a perfect right to get a sign and march all you want, but don't march around when you don't know what the film is.'

"If you have somebody to talk to about a certain issue, you can get it settled. But when I sat down with the three so-called gay leaders in New York City—who will remain nameless at this point because it really doesn't matter—to have a meeting, nothing was settled. They were going to have a protest meeting in a church in Greenwich Village that night or two nights later, with thousands of people. I said, 'I'm very happy to negotiate with you, talk to you until I'm blue in the face. If we reach some type of agreement, can you stop this meeting in the church?' They said, 'No, we can't.' I said, 'Why can't you?' They said, 'Well, how can we do that?' I said, 'If you're the leaders of the gay community, you're supposed to be able to do that. I can deliver anything I say I'm going to deliver. What can you deliver?' Nothing"—he shrugged—"so there are no leaders in the gay community. We had a whole section of the gay community protesting us and another section protesting them. It was quite a time." Weintraub smiled.

It was reported in the *New York Times* midway through filming that "the National Gay Rights Task Force said . . . that it was withdrawing its demand that the city rescind the permission of Lorimar Productions to film here because, it acknowledged, its actions smacked of censorship. It added, however, that it expected street demonstrations to continue so that 'the question of self-censorship by those making *Cruising* will be kept alive.'"[9]

Other problems plagued the filming as well. The production designer, Bruce Weintraub (no relation to the producer; his credits include the remake of *Cat People*), recalled that certain locations had to be changed because many of the bars refused to give permission to be used. He added that "the Mineshaft, the sleaziest bar in the world, pulled out the day before we were scheduled to shoot there. So we prefabricated an exact duplicate, down to the wall graffiti, right next to it. It was justice."

"There were also times we walked onto sets and had to turn right around and get out because of bomb scares," Barry Bedig, the prop master, said.

Some of the difficulties had a humorous side as well. For example, Robert deMora, the costume designer, recalled that Pacino had to have his hair curled for the part. "He came out looking like Harpo Marx initially. So I tried to explain it to Billy as tactfully and diplomatically as possible. And before I could get it all out, Billy said, 'Are you trying to tell me you fucked up my million-dollar star?' And then he laughed and laughed."

While hundreds of gays protested the film, 1,600 willingly worked on it as extras.[10] Robert Glass, the sound effects mixer on the picture, recalled a story Friedkin told about shooting the "precinct night" sequence. "Billy said that they started shooting that bar scene at nine in the morning. They had the bar serving beer, and I guess everyone was uptight. So Billy said he had to let everything run for three hours or so until the extras had time for a few beers to relax and start hugging and not act so frightened in front of the cameras. He said he didn't deliberately try to get them to do things. He said to them to just pretend this is uniform night. Don't let the fact that we have floodlights on you bother you."

Grosso added that in those scenes when the extras "would be dancing, we'd yell 'Cut!' and they wouldn't. They continued hugging, kissing, dancing, and biting each other's ears."

Friedkin said there were times during the shooting when scenes didn't work. If you get a director's block and the film is costing eight thousand dollars a day, "you do *something*. You go on instinct. There was a scene with Pacino coming up an elevator. I hated it. We had two weeks left, and Pacino said to me, 'Maybe I'm the wrong guy for the part.' I said, 'Maybe you're right, Al.' So I told him to do it naturally."[11]

Burtt Harris recalled another point during the production when "Billy said to me, 'Fuck this catered food. Everybody's had it. How much is it going to cost to get a couple of grills?' (Catered food is okay. Free food is good food.) I said, 'Let me figure it out.' One of the guys on the crew—and it was a small crew—knew a guy in Jersey who had a cow cut up for us. The Teamsters parked their trucks and started cooking. Billy said, 'This is better.'" (When Harris worked with Friedkin eleven years earlier on *Minsky's* as the assistant director, he said, "Billy didn't have a whole lot of free time, so he'd send the prop guy to get pizza. That fucking Friedkin could eat a pizza a day, I swear.")

Considering the constant pressures during the filming, it is astonishing to discover that "the physical cost of the picture," according to Jurgensen, "was three million dollars, not counting Pacino's fee."

"We did the film within the parameters of the money we were allocated, and it's amzing it got done at all," Harris said. "See, Billy had his ass on the line with *Cruising*. He took a deferment and had to make the film in seven or eight weeks. Otherwise it was out of his pocket. And we could only work eight hours a day because of overtime costs. Naturally, the cheaper you make a film, the sooner you're into profit."

Certainly, the publicity generated by the protests and the controversial nature of the film would guarantee strong initial business at the box office. But Bud Smith had to finish editing the raw footage.

Smith said, "After the film has been shot in script form, you take it and throw it up in the air, so to speak. (That's not a lot different from other films I've worked on with Billy or other people.) In the shooting script, Billy established water and the city, morgue, bar, pickup, hotel, killing. After the killing it was back to the morgue, and then he established Burns, who comes into the captain's office. In that scene you understand about Burns's whole life, background, his father and mother, why he's a policeman, and it's all condensed down to the captain's question 'Have you ever had a man smoke your pole?' And then, 'Do you want the job or not?'

"Then we go immediately to the supposed killer and establish his character. As a viewer, not an editor but a viewer, I said, 'Billy, this scene doesn't work because I know who the killer is already.' So we started throwing it up in the air. Let's try this sequence here, a montage there, put him with his girlfriend now. We just kept pushing the killer character further back until we reveal him when Burns looks through the Columbia University yearbook. But you actually do see him briefly in some of the earlier bar scenes."

Friedkin says that though he wrote five drafts of the script, he "changed it in the editing room, going more for ambiguity." He believed this would allow "the audience to take away from the film what they bring to it."[12]

According to Charles Campbell, supervising sound effects editor, changes became numerous. "It was like a jigsaw puzzle. It was juxtaposed constantly. Things that used to be in reel one would end up in reel four and then back again. When we were predubbing the picture, getting our sound effects tracks to match up with the picture, my crew and I had to keep up with the changes. Hundreds of sound effects and Foley units that have to be juxtapositioned. We had thirteen different dupes or versions."

This is an excessive number of dupes for *any* film. Excessive, too, was the looping, the rerecording of the actor's dialogue for a clearer reading or because of unintended background noise. According to Campbell, noisy harassment by the demonstrators resulted in *Cruising*'s "being eighty percent looped. And the sound effects and Foley are just this side of one hundred percent reproduced. I sat down with Billy and one of my associates, and we would listen to *every* single sound effects track and Foley track, one at a time, so Billy could scrutinize them. Every sound—the boots on different surfaces, the leather creak of the boots, the buckle rattles, the hat, the leather jacket—was recorded on separate tracks. There was also a general movement track, so that every time someone raised his arm or made just the slightest move, we had complete dimension."

"For a feature film, a Foley session would book about three days in a Foley stage to record," Robert Glass, the sound effects mixer, said. "For

Cruising, I think it was about six weeks. You just do everything—feet, movement—over and over against the action on screen that they project for you until it's exactly right. And whenever we had the leather squeaks and jingling keys, we played them much louder than they normally would be for someone walking along, especially at the end. We played the jingling keys and leather squeaks a little higher, so you get the feeling it's in Burns's head. It's like there is impending disaster. It adds to the tension and the overall effect of the film. You'd leave the theater feeling drained, like you've never had a moment's rest."

One of the best examples of this came about by accident. At the end of the film, Burns has returned to Nancy's apartment and shaves in the bathroom. She dons Burns's leather hat, jacket, and sunglasses. Burns, his face reflected in the bathroom mirror, apparently watches her. We then hear the sounds of footsteps like the killer's walk, the squeak of leather, and the jingle of keys. Campbell said this was a sound effects idea he and his crew had on the Foley stage. They recorded it but held those effects off as alternates, "so we weren't locked into them. When the time came, I said, 'Billy, see how you like this,' and we played it for him. He said, 'Who is responsible for this?' Now, you never know in that situation if you're going to get a hatchet in the head. Generally speaking, it's his film, and if you do something that takes it down a different path, it may not be what he's looking for. So I said, 'I am.' He said, 'This is probably one of the single finest sound effects contributions I've ever heard.'" (Strangely, these sounds are absent from the videotape cassettes of *Cruising.*)

Ironically, this moment in the filming itself was, as Robert deMora put it, "an invention of the moment. It really stuck in my mind because Billy was going to end this film with this very bizarre picture of the girl now dressed in all this stuff. Billy may have had it stored away in his think tank for months, but it was never mentioned. It happened as it was being filmed."

They only took four weeks to dub *Cruising,* as opposed to *The Exorcist* and *Sorcerer,* which were sixteen weeks in dubbing, Robert Glass said. Again, part of the reason was the restricted budget. "He could have nit-picked further on *Cruising.* Just a stabbing scene you could spend two or three days on, just deciding what you want to do with the levels of music and sound, augmenting with screams or whatever. But maybe he's also a little disillusioned with what audiences put up with in theaters without demanding any more. If you've given them superior products and then watch them flock to see something like *Friday, the 13th,* it must be disheartening."

Campbell recalled that "Billy was there on the stage with us, which is not his normal procedure. We'd call him to look at something after we finished it. He has favorite expressions. If there's an effect he doesn't like, it's 'Take it out, dry clean it and burn it.' Or 'Broom it.' He has a lot of idiosyncrasies. On *Cruising* he developed a new one. If there was an effect or a music cue or piece of dialogue he didn't like, you'd hear him from down in front say, 'Honk!' Then we'd stop, go back, and he'd explain what he'd want. He 'honked' a lot on *Cruising*."

And Friedkin was demanding, as he had been on his past films. But one day on the dub stage, his "on the edge" style of work created a problem. Campbell said, "We'd gotten through about half the picture successfully, and we'd just finished another reel and were feeling pretty good. I was in the coffee klatch, and Billy came in and said something about the next day's work. I said, 'But, Billy, we're almost running dry.' And he said, 'What do you mean, running dry?' I said, 'We have kept up this far, but the changes have—' And he said, 'Ah, I haven't made any changes in two weeks.' I said, 'Billy, we've cut so many versions of this film.' It was something that just kept building. I was tired-out on this movie. I finally just lost my control and said, 'Billy, I hate this fucking picture, and I'm not too crazy about you, either.' He just stared at me for a minute, turned around, and walked away.

"I felt bad about my temper flaring, but I felt he was being unreasonable to push any harder when we had kept up this pace. I certainly wasn't going to let him down, but we had to slow down somehow.

"So I went to lunch. When I came back, Bud came up to me, kind of laughing, and said, 'What the hell did you say to Billy?' I told him, and Bud said, 'Well, Billy came to me and said we're going to have to replace Chuck on this picture. He hates it.' (He didn't say anything about my saying I wasn't too crazy about him. Just the picture.) So Bud said, 'Well, Billy, here's the problem: If Chuck leaves, the whole effects crew will walk.' Billy shook his head and left early that day.

"And for a week, Billy wouldn't speak to me. There would be times I'd hear something that I thought could be done better, and I'd say, 'Billy, that isn't as effective as it could be from my standpoint.' Billy would turn to Buzz Knudsen [the chief mixer] and ask him what he thought. And Buzz would say, 'I kind of agree with Chuck. Let's try it.'" By the end of the week, it had blown over, Campbell said.

There was also one very significant evening Campbell recalled. "After we dubbed the first part of the movie, we ran them along with the rest of the picture. I was sitting up at the mixing console, and Billy was next to me. A little over halfway through the movie, he looked disturbed, turned to me, and said, 'What in the hell ever possessed me to make this picture?' Then he said, 'That's all. We're not running anymore tonight.' And he left."

The six-member board of the Classification and Ratings Administration (CARA) of the Motion Picture Association of America (MPAA) might well have wondered what possessed Friedkin to make *Cruising* as well. But when CARA members vote on a rating on a film, it is not based on personal opinion but on how *parents* would view the contents of the picture. Sex, violence, and language are the most obvious concerns of CARA, and *Cruising* is strong in these areas—strong enough to warrant an *X* rating initially. This meant most theaters would not exhibit it and many newspapers would refuse to advertise it.

According to a report in *Variety,* Richard Heffner, MPAA rating chairman, "suggested Friedkin and Weintraub secure the services of Dr. Aaron Stern, a New York psychiatrist and Heffner's predecessor as . . . chairman, 'for the expressed purpose of editing the film to get an R rating.'

"That is an unusual, if not unprecedented, way to obtain a rating."[13]

According to Bud Smith, "I was requested to go to every rating screening personally, whether I had to sit inside with them or wait outside. I took the print personally." They were still dubbing the film when the rating-board screenings were requested, Smith said, so he took the work print of the picture, not a composite. (The work print is what the editor has originally cut together from dailies. The picture and soundtrack are on separate reels. A composite is the marrying of the two to one piece of film.) A source at CARA, who requested anonymity, said, "It is a common practice of the board to rate a work picture if the dialogue is all intact, if the picture is in color if it is supposed to be in color, and if they are guaranteed that what is in the work picture will also be the same as the finished picture for release."

In Smith's opinion, CARA "has no rules. It's how they feel today. In other words, today, if you shoot someone in the back, that could be an *R.* If you say, 'Fuck, fuck you, fuck everyone' in *All the President's Men,* that's *PG.*

"Now, with *Cruising,* it's subject matter. They say we must have an *X* rating because of three scenes. The first one is the stabbing scene. I admit that's a heavy scene, but we've all seen stabbing scenes before, like *Repulsion,* where someone is cut with a razor blade, and ax murders. So why do they want to give us an *X?* I totally recut the killing. I took out some of the more horrifying footage. There was an over-the-shoulder angle of the killer, showing the knife going straight down into the victim's back. Now you see one quick shot showing the knife go into the back. Another shot I had before shows him pull the knife out, and blood squirts into frame and across the victim's face. I took it out and put in another take, so when he pulls the knife out, you hear the scream and see it from the side angle but you don't see blood squirt into frame. You do see it trickle down his neck but not squirt."

Variety said that "there were a series of contacts, meetings and changes in the film . . . that resulted 'in a removal of two shots as well as several frames from other shots,' according to Friedkin. Among the changes was a shortening of the opening murder scene."[14] A *Los Angeles Times* article examining the rating of *Cruising* states that "according to sources, the ratings board wanted the blood toned down and the repeated stabbing motions eliminated."[15] In the film, blood no longer squirts, and there are three stabbing motions.

"The second thing," Smith said, "was in one of the early bar sequences. Someone was supposed to be way in the background, and it looked like he was giving someone else head because they had their head in someone else's lap. So I had an optical made. We took a pencil and made a traveling matté, thereby giving the effect that a person is walking by a post while the post itself was also moving, and that covered the image. But the board said, 'That's no good because we know what's behind the post.' Now what kind of logic is that? Swear to God." This scene was later darkened. *Variety* reported that "Dr. Stern . . . advised that Heffner would be satisfied with the darkening of three shots; Friedkin produced a letter from Technicolor senior veepee Jay Cipes to prove the darkening occurred."[16] No specific mention was made that this scene was one darkened. The *Los Angeles Times* states that in this bar scene "identified by an outside sign as the Wolf's Den, a pan, or sweeping shot from left to right, shows the bar's inhabitants. In one corner, and in clear view for eight seconds, is a scene of two men engaged in fellatio. The ratings board wanted this scene eliminated entirely."[17] In the film, this scene exists, but the bar is not identified by name, nor is the fellatio scene immediately obvious because of the darkening.

Smith said the third scene of contention involved a sequence known as "precinct night," which "was totally reedited per the board's instruction, but impact-wise it was still heavy." This scene *may* have been included in the *Variety* article as one of the "darkened three shots." Again, no specific mention was made. However, the article does state that "on March 3, two weeks into the pic's release, [Friedkin and Weintraub] stated that a memo from [Albert] Van Shmus [administrative director of the rating administration] requested two additional frame cuts be made. Those deletions involved an inferred scene of fellatio between two men and another shot in [precinct night]." *Variety* goes on to say that Friedkin and Weintraub agreed to make the changes but stated it may "take as long as five weeks." The article says that "during that time period the fellatio scene was darkened and later cut entirely."[18] The *Los Angeles Times* reported that in this bar scene, "which is populated by men dressed in various police uniforms, Friedkin has his camera move around the bar for a total of 86 seconds. . . . There is a variety of sexual acts, real or imagined, taking place in the sequence. The ratings board wanted the bottom of the frame (in effect, the bottom of the screen the audience is watching) moved up, to eliminate the sex in the foreground."[19] In this sequence, as with the previously mentioned fellatio scene, the sexual *activity*, darkened or not, appears simulated. No genitalia are exposed.

Friedkin broke a barrier with *Cruising*, a mainstream Hollywood production. The world of leather gay sadomasochism, a subculture unto itself, had never been presented in such detailed, realistic fashion before. (Paul Schrader's *American Gigolo*, released in late 1979, hinted at it.) Friedkin was not doing anything different in *Cruising* than he had done in *Boys in the Band, The French Connection* and *The Exorcist;* he was melding the familiar with the unfamiliar and thereby presenting something new, a dark freshness. In *Band,* men talk about their sexual relationships—with each other; in *Connection,* good guys chase bad guys, but the cop is a savage and the criminal sophisticated; in *Exorcist,* horror is not the dark shape under the bed at night but a cunning evil in broad daylight. So, too, *Cruising,* where cop and killer meet in a landscape of bars and dancing where aberrance has replaced conformity.

Alterations at the request of CARA in any film may be viewed as censorship or self-regulation by the MPAA. Either way, *Cruising* would seem to have greatly affected the board, for there were several other changes made that did not make headlines. According to Bud Smith, "I took a scene out of the picture in which a uniform cop, DiSimone [Joe Spinell], and his partner are playing cards, and whoever loses the game gets three whacks in the ass with a nightstick. This scene I'm referring to takes place near the end of the movie. Anyway, DiSimone loses the game and says to his partner, 'You owe me three whacks.' The Irish cop says, 'C'mon, I was just kidding.' DiSimone pulls out his gun and says, 'I want the three whacks in the ass.' So he gets the whacks. I cut that scene out, and the board got all over our ass for taking it out. They said, 'We can't give you an *R* rating because you altered the film.' What kind of logic *is* that?"

Two other changes were not in the imagery but in the *sound.* Smith said the sound effect of a whip cracking across someone's back in the "precinct night" sequence CARA wanted toned down. (It is now nonexistent.) And according to Robert Glass, the sound effects mixer, "in the first stabbing sequence, the goriness of the sound (like meat tearing) was a little too much for them."

Regardless of alterations, performed or not, Friedkin's film indeed proved too much for General Cinema Corporation. Less than three weeks before its scheduled opening, executives of one of the nation's largest theater chains canceled the bookings it made for 32 of its 850 theaters to exhibit the film. Senior vice president of General Cinema, Larry Lapidus, said *Cruising* was "unsuitable for our clientele." Shortly after this announcement, David Picker, executive vice president of Lorimar Productions, said those lost bookings were quickly filled.[20]

Two weeks prior to *Cruising*'s release, Friedkin faced the press following a preview screening of his film, which continued the controversy and churned out headlines. Though most of the 350 representatives of the media remained "calm and orderly," Arthur Bell condemned the film, shouting that it "can only cause psychological and physical violence against gays."[21] Bell reportedly waved his cane angrily at Friedkin and called him "the worm of worms." Friedkin answered with "an equally theatrical gesture" and then began reading aloud articles about gay murders written by Bell.[22] He indicated these articles were sources of his research.[23] (Later, Jerry Weintraub would recall that Bell "sent us a bill for using his material. I know we didn't pay it.")

Friedkin also told the press, "If this film helps bring attention to this [violence], the ultimate effect will do more good than harm." When pressed on questions of "responsibility," he only said he and Weintraub "feel an enormous responsibility to the community and to the public at large."[24] (Earlier that same day, the *Los Angeles Times* ran a story that said in part, "If *Cruising* should inspire violence between or against homosexuals, Friedkin says he feels in no way responsible. 'No more so than a newspaper might inspire another hillside strangler by writing articles on the one that's been arrested.'" Friedkin is also quoted as saying, "There's no experience or feeling on the screen in this film that I myself have not felt or undergone."[25] There was no further explanation.)

Press kits were handed out that included numerous articles about violence committed against gays (Bell's included), a statement from United Artists, the film's distributor, that stated in part, "It is the policy of United Artists to encourage a free creative atmosphere and not to act as a public censor," and a biography of Friedkin that states only that "William Friedkin was formerly married but is now paying alimony."

But Friedkin did succeed in stunning the press audience. He said, "All the acts of violence in this film are committed by heterosexuals."[26] He maintained that "in my opinion, the principal killer is not gay. He is a sick person who takes his sickness out on gays." His most baffling statement was "I myself was not sure whether there was one killer or more than one."[27] He insisted, "It's ambiguous."

As one reporter later wrote, "In effect, Friedkin was telling [this audience] that they had not seen on screen what their questions indicated they thought they had seen."[28]

What *had* they seen? What *was* Friedkin doing? Toying with the media? Creating an aura of intrigue? Or confusion?

Reviewers almost uniformly panned the film. Writing in *Newsweek*, David Ansen neatly summed up the critical response with "What Friedkin's film is about is anybody's guess. If he just wanted to make a thriller, he has made a clumsy and unconvincing one. If he wanted to explore the psychology of his characters, he has left out most of the relevant information. If he intended to illuminate the tricky subject of S & M, he hasn't even scratched the surface.... Friedkin isn't interested in explaining his milieu; he merely offers it up as a superficially shocking tableau for the titillation and horror of his audience."

The film opened nationally on February 15, 1980, with the director's third possessory credit reading, "William Friedkin's *Cruising*." ("If it's a film

by somebody instead of *for* somebody, I smell art," Friedkin once said.)²⁹
The protestors and the public lined up for pickets and tickets. It was
reported that the largest demonstrations were in San Francisco and New
York "with roughly 200 protestors counted at single theaters in each city.
Inside the National Theater on Broadway in New York, a dozen protestors
unfurled banners and began chanting as *Cruising* began."³⁰ Outside the
Regent Theater in Westwood, California, one woman carrying a sign urging
patrons not to see the film stood in lone protest on its second day of release.

A protest organizer who saw the film was quoted as saying, "It is more
filthy, more violent, and more offensive than I expected. For straight people, I think it will give an erroneous impression of gay life." Another patron
remarked, "The thing that offended me was the gore. Otherwise, it was kind
of monotonous."³¹ Still another called it "a cinematic herpes blister."

Cruising made more than $5 million in its first five days. At the end of
two weeks, the gross was $10 million. However, the combined totals from
the third and fourth weeks were less than the take from its first five days.³²
Cruising was coasting into commercial obscurity.

"I would have liked to have done a hundred million dollars with *Cruising*," Jerry Weintraub said. "Then I would have been satisfied."

Tony Fantozzi, Friedkin's agent, said, "Billy wanted to show you a slice
of society that you haven't seen. So the question is: Are you interested in
a society that exists today in New York City where we can take you by the
hand and show you those people, those places, those characters? The public
said, 'We dont' give a shit about that.'"

Weintraub didn't believe people were shocked enough. "They didn't
see two naked men making love to each other. I think they thought they
were going to see much more sex, much more than they saw. They wanted
to see a sexual nightmare."

"*Cruising* may be one of the ten worst films of all time," Friedkin said.
"I don't deal in those terms. I'm not affected personally by critics, but I'm
certainly affected commercially. If critics go against a picture, it will probably have trouble with an audience. If they're for it, chances are it will find
an audience."³³

The advertising art for the film centered on the star. "Al Pacino is cruising for a killer," reads the cut line with the actor's face dominating the
poster. The presence of Pacino did not bolster box office receipts. (The
star's previous film, . . . *And Justice for All*, grossed $25 million.)³⁴ Friedkin
said, "I feel in retrospect that the addition of Pacino meant nothing. I felt
he was too old for the part. It's about a rookie, a young kid. The part was
written for somebody who is about twenty-one, twenty-two. And innocence. It's about the corruption of innocence, which Pacino no longer
brings to a part. But I don't blame him for either the success or the failure
of the film."

Cruising soon disappeared from theaters but Friedkin's name remained in the headlines for several more months. Members of the MPAA said the filmmakers had not made the promised changes. Friedkin and Weintraub stated they had complied with all the changes requested by the ratings board in order to obtain an *R* rating.[35] Maybe some prints had the appropriate changes. However, the inclusion or exclusion of simulated violence and sex had little or no effect on the film's acceptance or rejection by audiences.

Friedkin emphatically believes that "there is no subject that is off limits to a filmmaker."[36]

II

He called it "a pretty fucking strong film, one of those experiences you don't forget." Walon Green was talking about *Salo*, Italian director Pier Pasolini's film based on the book *Salo: 120 Days of Sodom* by the Marquis de Sade. (The picture was presented at the 1977 New York Film Festival, considered "the most important of the American international festivals.")[37] Green, his wife, and Friedkin saw the picture together before Friedkin began filming *Cruising*, Green said. "It's about these five degenerate noblemen who go to this castle and for one hundred twenty days indulge themselves in the most perverse acts and finally build themselves up to a final climax where they'll all die, where there's nothing left to do. They kidnap these adolescent boys and girls and these old whores who they isolate with them in this castle.

"Pasolini sets the film in Fascist Italy, and he's very loyal to the story, actually. What makes it so disturbing is that the horror you're seeing on the screen you know is actually being done somewhere. So it takes the taint of fiction off it."

Among the "horrors" on view in *Salo* are penises burned with lighted candles, forced fellatio, men's open mouths urinated in, people forced to eat plates of human feces, and throats slit.

"Billy thought it took enormous courage for a director to do this," Green said. "It's more than just a devastating horrifying film. Billy couldn't get off the subject. He was obsessed."

Green also said he believed Friedkin's desire to make *Cruising* was not unlike Pasolini's when he made *Salo*. "I think they both thought, 'If I go as far as I can into this area, I'll find some kind of spirit there.'" Green added that Friedkin's exploration was a search for truth. "Whether you look on the dark side or the light side, you look for something that will substantiate it." But in Green's opinion, Friedkin "just didn't find anything."

Both *Salo* and *Cruising* are violent films, nightmare visions of sexual and emotional excesses. *Salo* wallows gratuitously in its gritty presentation, the attitude of its director being that sexual torture and excremental frolicking are life-affirming, even fun. The final image shows the five noblemen, arms laced over one another's shoulders, joyfully dancing a high-kick step. (Green believes the rumor is true that Pasolini was murdered by the "freaks and weirdos" he'd begun to associate with while making this, his final film.)

Cruising, however, is an altogether different nightmare. The New York City skyline, a metropolis of glass and steel, floats serenely on the East River, as if the city were drawing relief and strength from life-giving waters. A crewman on a tugboat chugging across the screen suddenly spots something floating in the steel-blue water—a severed arm, stiff and gangrenous. Friedkin does not merely introduce chaos to this tranquil world. He allows a symbol of life (water) and a symbol of death (the arm) to occupy the same space in silent, aberrant harmony. Disease has found solace. It is as if Francis Bacon had been retained to promote New York City tourism.

Friedkin has begun what promised to be his most fatalistic, horrifying, and bizarre film—a reflection of reality, violent yet seductive, vitiated but compelling, in which sex and aggression meld and blur into a nightmare for the soul, where conflict becomes man against himself. However, when Friedkin chose to "go more for ambiguity," he might as well have changed the title from *Cruising* to *Confusing*.

To begin to unravel the mystery, we must return to the shooting of the film. According to Robert deMora, costume designer, "It was to be Richard Cox [who plays Stuart Richards] as the murderer. And I said to Billy, 'I have everything to fit Richard.' He said, 'But I don't want Richard to do that.' When Billy told me that, I got so confused. I said, 'I don't know what you're saying. What do you mean?' He said, 'Oh, you'll understand. The outfit will be the same. The image will be the same. But that mole that one has will be there and then not be there. That's so you shouldn't have a clear-cut killer.'"

"You see, Billy didn't want to show who was the murderer," said Barry Bedig, the prop master. "Each murderer wore sunglasses. It was all set up that way, that everybody had the same look with sunglasses on, even Pacino."

According to deMora, Friedkin's first script had more of the tone of Walker's book in that you really believed the undercover cop does go berserk fearing for his own identity and becomes the killer. With subsequent revisions, "it became much more vague and ambiguous."

Randy Jurgensen said, "The first time I saw that it was not the same killer through the whole picture, I blinked. I honestly did not ask Billy about it. It is Stuart Richards in the porno arcade booth who kills the fashion designer. The hotel killing is not done by Richards. The hotel killer is killed

Cruising. **Steve Burns (Al Pacino, center) mixes into the gay leather subculture.**

in the Rambles by Richards. Why that is, I don't know. It was not in the
script."

So *two* murderers cruise the gay S & M bars, and both look very
much alike. The hotel killer, later identified as Eric Rossman (Larry Atlas),
Stuart Richards, and Steve Burns each walk with a slight hitch in their step,
as well. One can see Friedkin's concept of identities melding and blurring.
But then he does something that completely destroys any hope of coherence
for the audience. According to Randy Jurgensen, the killers speak in the
same voice when they kill, and that voice belongs to Stuart Richards's
father.

At first glance, this appears to be shoddy storytelling on Friedkin's part.
Two different, unrelated murderers speaking in the same voice is absolutely
not a viable example of Slavko Vorkapitch's concept of total immersion,
which Friedkin toyed with in *The Exorcist,* wherein he had Karras reach
down to depress a tape-recorder button with his left hand and in the
close-up on the recorder his right enters the shot. One can also understand
Time's head shaking over "the last-minute injection of a demon who seems
to have drifted in, half-baked, from *The Exorcist.*"[38]

The reference is to a scene late in the film wherein Friedkin establishes Richards's father as hating his son. Meeting in a park, Richards tells his father that all he's ever wanted to do was to please him, but whatever he does is "never good enough." Jack Richards (Leland Starnes) turns to his son and says, "You know what you have to do." (In the hotel, Rossman, speaking in Jack Richards's voice, tells his victim, "I know what I have to do." Near the end of the film, Stuart Richards lies in a hospital bed with a knife wound in his shoulder and, in his father's voice, tells Edelson, "I didn't kill anyone.") Friedkin stages this park scene between father and son in a chillingly surreal fashion. A deadly finality hangs in the air like a shroud, but it's blanched and washed out, an ominous, smothering whiteness unlike any other exterior daytime scenes in the film. We later discover that Richards's father has been dead for ten years. This psychotic fantasy might have been one of the most disturbing and frightening in the film had Friedkin not included subliminal flashbacks to the hotel murder (which Richards did not commit) and then to Rossman (Richards's first victim) while Richards spoke with his father. These flashbacks serve as visuals of confusion, not ambiguity.

During his press conference, Friedkin said that "the principal killer is not gay but a sick person who takes his sickness out on gays." When Richards kills Rossman in the Rambles, they do not engage in sex. In the porno arcade booth, the victim (a bearded fashion designer) prepares to perform fellatio on Richards, who then stabs him repeatedly in the back— the same way the previous two killings were performed. Friedkin also claimed that "all the acts of violence" in his film "were committed by heterosexuals." The filmmaker obviously overlooked Rossman. Prior to the hotel killing, it is implied that the victim and killer engage in sex (they play with each other's boots and then fall into bed). Later, at the morgue, the medical examiner (Barton Heyman) tells Edelson he found a slight rupture above the victim's anus, indicating intercourse, and semen, but no sperm.

Friedkin has contrived to take similar experiences and facts (Jurgensen's story, Walker's book, and unsolved murders) and weave them into a visceral pattern with a common theme. That theme appears to be malevolence somehow passed on from person to person. As brutal as *Cruising* is, it is not the joy of decadence and violence that is *Salo*, but there may be a connection. A line of dialogue from *Salo* states, "There is nothing more infectious than evil." Friedkin may have been influenced by that concept, for certainly the heinous murders committed by the killers in *Cruising* are ugly, evil acts, and with multiple killers, who look and dress similarly but who speak in the same voice, one can recognize the infectious aspect. While the idea has merit, Friedkin's execution lacks coherence. In striving for ambiguity, he fails literally and visually to impart this theme of infectious evil within the reality of the film. Action reveals character, but character absolutely requires explanation because this omnipotent malevolent threat otherwise exists as a muddled, unconvincing gimmick.

True, the gay leather bars have their own dark, dangerous, bizarre aesthetic. One of the articles about these bars written by Arthur Bell, included in the *Cruising* press kit, states, "The indoor playgrounds aren't bars in the traditional sense but backroom battlegrounds, houses of fantasy. . . . Dimly lit chambers where whips crack and urine and Schlitz are often served in the same container. . . . Fantasy becomes reality for a $2 entrance fee. . . . All around you different psychodramas take place. Men indulge in combat sex, in voyeurism, in smoking grass, smelling things, swallowing things, popping things. . . . The atmosphere is not uncomfortable nor is it depressing. It is like a narcotic, and while you are there you are unaware of the world outside."[39] With the notable exception of the urine and beer concoction, Friedkin otherwise introduces both killers in this milieu. For example, the first club is located beneath a meat-packing plant. Iron meathooks hang on overhead runners outside the black-painted building. Friedkin visually establishes a sense of palatable fear and impending doom. We must go down, metaphorically speaking, into the earth to enter the club. There this netherworld exists, where men dressed in black leather and blue jeans drink, dance, and grope each other; where there is nothing friendly or familiar about the music that one critic described as "asserting itself with the anxiousness of a scream in the night";[40] where even the shadows sweat.

Other leather bars feature a huge American flag painted black and white with flashing rows of lights (colors, like familiarity, have been drained from this atmosphere) and sexual alternatives such as nipple pinching or a man inserting his greased fist into another man's anus (this is strongly implied, not shown). These practices, clothes, music, and decor are parts of a modern hedonistic ritual for the daring and inclined. Edelson tells Burns, "It's a world unto itself."

Friedkin's story thrusts Burns into this world, and we are witness to it from Burns's perspective. This aberrant atmosphere—another perception of reality—with its visceral acts of violence, aggression, and sex, is a dream of heady captivation or a nightmare that must be defeated. It's also another aspect in Friedkin's ambiguity of storytelling. He believes that whatever the audience brings to the film they will take away. Specifically, if we believe Burns becomes seduced by the dark dream so that latent homosexual tendencies arise within him and he comes to identify with the killer he pursues thereby becoming a murderer of homosexuals, then we will see evidence in the film to confirm it. If we believe otherwise, then we will find clues to prove those preconceived contentions.

When we meet Burns, his eagerness to investigate the killings has a boyish quality. After explaining the dangers involved, Edelson asks Burns if he wants the assignment. Burns's response of "I love it" rings of naivete, as though he'd just been asked to lunch. One could also infer that response as hiding his excitement, as if the danger were already addictive to him.

In the following scene, Burns lies in bed with his girlfriend, Nancy. He tells her he can't divulge his assignment, but he'll receive a gold detective's shield upon its completion. In the background soft music plays, and when Nancy mentions that his father called, Friedkin cuts to a close-up of Burns, his face darkening, and an ominous music sting fades up. Nancy says to Burns, "I had no idea you were so ambitious." He replies, "There's a lot about me you don't know." Friedkin uses cryptic dialogue and visceral music — *not* action — to establish an apparent rift between Burns and his father. This is *never* followed up in the film. Since we have no idea of what problem may exist between father and son, Burns's reaction becomes pointless. And if Friedkin's point was to attempt a spiritual connection between cop and killer, then Friedkin still retains the storytelling problems David Wolper believed he had twelve years earlier. As for the line "There's a lot about me you don't know," one anticipates Friedkin will *show* us the implications of Burns's taciturn comment.

What Friedkin shows us are initially shocking bar scenes with Burns (and us) moving through them, being cruised (examined, checked out) by men looking for sex or some alternative. This exploration of a strange, different world might have gone from shock to illumination but instead goes from shock to tedium because nothing happens. Friedkin's quest for ambiguity fails here. Burns, and we by extension, become mere voyeurs, not participants. Yes, Burns gets fondled once; yes, he dances with a man; but in neither instance is the individual coming on to Burns either of the killers.

Early in his investigation, Burns stands under an archway in the Rambles at night. Two men cruise him simultaneously. One, DiSimone, a uniformed policeman who earlier harassed two transvestites, hates women because his wife ran out on him. DiSimone, dressed in civilian clothes, and Burns make eye contact in this park scene. Then another man walks by, turns, and makes eye contact with Burns as well. This man we recognize as Rossman from the hotel stabbing, even though he does not wear leather or sunglasses. As he walks away, we see Burns follow him. And then Friedkin fades to black. That's it! No more! DiSimone functions only as a red herring in this murder mystery, and Rossman and Burns — well, who knows?

When Burns and Richards finally confront each other, it is a qualitatively different encounter, unlike the previous murders. (Earlier, Burns had recognized Richards's picture from a set of Columbia University yearbook pages Edelson had given him. Prior to the hotel killing, a professor of the university had been murdered offscreen, and Edelson, groping for *any* leads, told Burns to look at the photographs, "see if you recognize anybody.") The initial murders, with their powerful close-up images of the

Cruising. **Steve Burns (Al Pacino, left) considers following Eric Rossman (Larry Atlas) into the Rambles.**

knife thrust over and over into the victim's back, are gory and unsettling. The killers pose an obvious, deadly, heinous threat.

Apparently, Friedkin decided that blood and gore were not to be functions of the cop-killer confrontation. (Burns now carries a knife like the killer's, the police department having matched up the blade with one of the victim's knife wound X-rays.) Also, Richards knows Burns is aware of who he is since Burns broke into Richards's apartment, left evidence of the break-in, and made sure Richards saw him afterward. That night, they meet in the park. Each wears black leather; each carries a knife in his boot. Burns slips his pants off. "I want to see the world," he says to Richards, who believes Burns wants sex. Richards slips his pants down and reaches for his knife. Both men lunge at each other. We barely see a struggle or a knife implanted. Richards groans facedown on the ground. Burns, breathing heavily, slides to the ground, spent. This moment of truth for Burns—a life-and-death conflict—has resulted in his catching a killer.

But has Burns defeated the nightmare world he has been sucked into, or has he been intoxicated by its dark aberrance? Upon his arrival in Greenwich Village, Burns was befriended by Ted (Don Scardino), who shares the apartment next to Burns's with his jealous lover, Gregory (James Remar),

Cruising. **Steve Burns (Al Pacino, left) begins his come-on with suspected killer Stuart Richards (Richard Cox).**

a dancer who is out of town in a stage play. Burns and Ted talk about gay life, the killings, and Gregory's selfishness. For those inclined to believe Burns finds Ted sexually attractive, fine. For those who see Burns simply responding to another human being as a concerned friend, fine too. Friedkin makes no judgment.

What he does, however, is stage a fight between Burns and Gregory prior to Burns's confronting Richards. (Gregory had returned from the canceled run of his play.) Burns has come by to see Ted, but he is working a night job now. Gregory accuses Burns of being "trash," Burns becomes angry, and they scuffle. Gregory pulls a butcher knife on Burns, who then exits.

After Richards has been arrested, Friedkin cuts to a night scene at Burns's Village apartment building where he had been living under the name of John Forbes. Edelson arrives at Ted's apartment where DiSimone gives him the details of what looks like a lover's quarrel resulting in murder: Ted lies face up on the bathroom floor, multiple stab wounds cover his body, a large butcher knife close by. (Friedkin reportedly used a David

Bowie record album cover that showed the singer "sprawled out, as if in death, on a tile floor" as inspiration for this scene.)[41] DiSimone informs Edelson that they are looking for Ted's roommate, as well as the tenant who lives next door, John Forbes, for questioning. Edelson reacts to the name of Forbes, saying, "Jesus Christ." One can understand Edelson's reaction since earlier Burns had told him he couldn't do this job anymore — "Things are happening to me, and I don't think I can handle it." Edelson may well believe Burns cracked under the stress of the job and killed Ted. To an audience, however, there should be no question that he did *not* kill Ted since there had been no reason whatsoever established for this type of action on Burns's part.

Friedkin reprises a scene from the opening of the film showing a black-leather-clad figure with jingling keys and a slight hitch in his step (recall, both killers and Burns have this attitude) walking toward a bar in the meat-packing area of town. One can infer that this is Burns *or* that Friedkin is trying to point up that these killings are a vicious cycle, an infectious evil. An audience takes away from his film whatever they bring into it. "It's ambiguous," Friedkin says.

Finally, at the end of the film, Burns has returned to Nancy's apartment. Since accepting this assignment, he has seen her several times, each time dressed in leather. Never once has she seemed even curious why he wears these very different clothes. As the scene opens, Nancy enters her apartment to find Burns in the midst of shaving in the bathroom. He says he'll be right out and wants to tell her "all about it." She puts on a record, and the soft lilting melody that played when we first saw them in bed together fills the apartment. (We had heard it again during one of Burns's prior visits with Nancy. In that scene, they are again in bed, Burns on his back. Nancy begins to move down his body, her head disappearing out of frame, apparently to perform fellatio on her boyfriend. Friedkin begins to push in on Burns's face, which contorts. The music playing in the background fades out, and the sounds, voices, and pulsating music of the bars fill his thoughts. Sound becomes character, but the effectiveness is diminished because Friedkin chooses ambiguity as his storytelling reference. Therefore, Burns's reaction may be interpreted as sexual confusion or a strong attraction to that subculture or a nightmare.) Burns continues shaving, and we see Nancy don the leather jacket, cap, and reflective sunglasses she finds in her living room. Burns looks at himself in the mirror and hears the sound of boots approaching, the squeak of leather and jingle of keys. Friedkin dissolves to the city again floating on the water, but this time the water glows brightly, the sun dripping into a late-afternoon haze and a tugboat cruising across the screen.

Has the evil cycle really begun again? Does the brightness of the final image metaphorically mean the infection has been eliminated? Or is the haze an ironic veil for the evil? Has Burns, previously seen throughout the film dressed in dark blacks and blues but now in Nancy's apartment wearing a white sweatshirt and faded blue jeans, conquered the darker impulses and returned to being a loving boyfriend? Is he (our) soul in torment, or has he (have we) bested the nightmare? Does he stare at the mirror because Nancy resembles Richards in the leather and sunglasses, or is he wondering if his shave is close enough?

One can see at least the outline of Friedkin's intentions with *Cruising*. The philosopher Nietzsche may have stated it best in *Beyond Good and Evil* when he wrote, "Whoever battles with monsters had better see that it does not turn him into a monster. And if you gaze long into an abyss, the abyss will gaze back into you." But Friedkin, apparently, got other ideas. Unfortunately, his ambiguities are more confusing than provoking.

Prior to the film's opening, the director gave an interview to the *Los Angeles Times*. The reporter wrote, "The only faults Friedkin sees in *Cruising* are his own inadequacies as a filmmaker."[42]

12
Deal of the Century

"An experience like *Deal of the Century* is like
watching your child rendered grotesque."
—Paul Brickman[1]

I

Friedkin suffered a heart attack while driving to his Burbank Studios office on March 6, 1981. He was forty-two years old. "It was this incredible pain from arm to arm across my chest. I couldn't breathe. I didn't know what was wrong with me . . . I tried to get out of the car and walk, but I couldn't put one foot in front of the other. I was three minutes from the studio. . . . I got to the paramedics' center at the main gate of the studio. I passed out right on the floor. The paramedics immediately tried to revive me. (I was dead for seven seconds, I'm told. What happens when you're dying is, you begin to lose your senses one at a time. The last sense to go is the sense of hearing.) The paramedics threw nitroglycerin pills down my throat, and they were giving me shots. Suddenly the pain was gone, and there was nothing but blackness, and the last words I heard were from this paramedic trying to take my blood pressure. He was saying, 'I'm not getting anything.' I just peacefully died.

"Remember that scene in *All That Jazz* where the guy is traveling through blackness toward a light? I swear to God that is exactly the experience I had. I was moving through blackness toward a light, but it was as though I was on an escalator and no pain.

"The next thing I remember was waking up looking into the lights of the St. Joseph's Hospital emergency room. The pain was back, and I thought I was in hell. I believe at that particular time they didn't want any bad Jews in heaven, so they let me come back here. . . ."[2]

This experience apparently provoked other considerations for Friedkin. He later said, "Every breath I draw is a fucking miracle to me."[3]

But prior to his heart attack, Friedkin was already experiencing radical changes. He turned down a script entitled *Legion,* William Peter Blatty's

218

sequel to *The Exorcist.* "There were some bloody offscreen murders in my script," Blatty explained, "and Billy had just finished *Cruising* and was having an aversion even to implied violence. He didn't want to see any kind of murder with a knife or shears or hatchet or whatever. We had another meeting later, and he was still harping on decapitations and knife murders. . . . Since a year ago, Billy has expressed an aversion to depicting any form of violence on the screen, and I don't know why.

"It seems to me that somehow the criticism that *Cruising* drew as perhaps being excessively graphic in depicting whatever the hell it depicted (I've never seen it) may have made him ultrasensitive on the subject." Pausing for a moment, Blatty then added, "There's nothing more insufferable than a person who has smoked since age six who decided to quit at age sixty. Billy is kicking a long addiction, and presently it's insufferable to me." Blatty laughed good-naturedly.

Reflecting on his career to this point, Friedkin said, "I have inadvertently moved away from films that involve people emotionally. . . . I have not said I'm going to set out and make films about people that nobody gives a shit about, but it has happened. Nobody cares about the people in *Sorcerer, Brink's Job, Cruising.*

"I'm going to try to make films that people care about—that they care about the characters—and fuck the filmmaking. If I fail at that, I'm finished, I'm washed up as a director. I'd have to go on the scrap heap with all the guys who lost track of their audience. . . . There are many talented guys who just went down the fucking tubes, like Billy Wilder, who made films for twenty years that connected with their audiences, who for some reason, lost track about what people care about.

"If you're a film director, you're lucky to stay current for ten years. The last films that Hitchcock made were just awful. They were made on his reputation. . . . I'm coasting on my reputation now. A studio will back me because I've made a couple of hits. That's all."

Ironically, Friedkin's next project was a Broadway play about a violin player who becomes paralyzed and wants to die and the doctor who refuses to allow it. *Duet for One* starred Anne Bancroft and Max von Sydow. It had a short run. However, the aforementioned irony may have had its own methodical twist. Plays cannot rely on cinematic resources for resonance and nuance. They must depend on the *characters* to propel the action. Directing this play may have been Friedkin's way of concentrating on character—not cinematic—development.

With his last three films rejected by the Audience, a brush with death, and serious career reevaluations, one is not surprised the next screenplay he chose to direct was a comedy. One is apprehensive, however, that the director of *Minsky's* (sort of) and *Brink's* was about to try comedy again. The script was *Deal of the Century,* considered among Hollywood insiders as

"the funniest and most erudite screenplay anyone had read since Preston
Sturges."[4] Written by Paul Brickman *(Risky Business)*, the story concerned
the sale and proliferation of military arms—everything from bullets to
rockets. He interviewed arms dealers who, he says, "market the stuff
as though they're selling Oldsmobiles." The script he wrote was also a
satire on American ingenuity. Eddie Muntz, a "cynical arms salesman," has
the opportunity to make the deal of the century by selling a defective drone
(an unmanned fighter plane) called the Peacemaker to the dictator of a
banana republic for $300 million. Muntz's slogan is "Bigger bangs for less
bucks."[5]

Friedkin reportedly "heavily reworked the script." According to the
director, the film "deals with all the bribery and chicanery in the aerospace
industry. Their motto is 'Make the deal at any cost.' Almost every incident
depicted in the film is true. Most of the high-priced advanced weaponry
doesn't work. When a weapon fails, the military simply revises the conditions of the test."[6] He called the military-industrial complex he depicts "a
bizarre world." During location filming, for example, at the Chet Holifield
Federal Building in Orange County, California (originally built by Northrop
Corp. with government funding for the development of the B-1 bomber, but
it has stood virtually uninhabited since the early 1970s),[7] Friedkin staged
the unveiling ceremonies of the Peacemaker, the hopeful corporate salva-
tion of the fictional Luckup Industries. In this scene American flags wave
proudly, mock-ups of Luckup missiles stand erect on a green in place of
garden flowers, and Luckup executive Frank Stryker (Vince Edwards)
delivers his opening remarks to the cheers of the military brass and blue-
suited civilians in the reviewing stand. "A drone does not bleed, die,
become addicted to drugs, shoot his officers or refuse to fight." A buxom
celebrity christens the Peacemaker prototype with a bottle of champagne.
A smiling priest stands at the microphone and comments on the "glorious
moment" and their "sense of mission." Friedkin said, "There is no way to
exaggerate it. We took these remarks from actual opening ceremonies—
even the minister!"

When a reporter asked Friedkin if this film was "*really* intended to be
a comedy," he replied, "Yes, this is the toughest film I've ever done. . . . It's
not slapstick, but more a behavioral comedy. I think audiences will laugh
and then kind of go 'Aghhhhhhhhhhh.'"[8] (Friedkin called *Brink's* a
behavioral comedy while filming it, too. A dreadful gnawing begins in one's
viscera that the ratio of laughter to moans will be grievously disparate.)

After shooting was completed, the film was put into first cut by the
editors, Ned Humphreys and Jere Huggins. Bud Smith had been
unavailable, but after returning from New York where he had edited
Flashdance (for which he would receive an Academy Award nomination),
he stopped in to see Friedkin and the editors, formerly Smith's assistants.

"Billy asked me to take a look at the cut they had of *Deal*," Smith said. "After the screening, I said to Billy, 'I know one thing. I can't hurt it.'"

(Smith explained, "That doesn't mean you can then make it a successful film. It's just that editorially I know I can sharpen the picture up. I know what Billy wants and likes in order to make the film move more quickly.")

Friedkin was preparing to go to Paris, France, to photograph an air show being held there, Smith said, and he wanted to integrate that footage into *Deal*. "Billy was going to be gone a couple of weeks, and he asked me if I would take the film and shake it down, recut, and we'd look at it when he got back. I tightened it up and threw scenes out. Billy came back and basically liked a lot of it but didn't like all of it. So we started recutting it again." They spent four more months tightening, sharpening, and juxtaposing scenes. Air-show footage of state-of-the-art jet planes was added.

There was also one particular scene they needed help with, Smith recalled. It was a sex scene in which Katherine DeVoto (Sigourney Weaver) seduces General Cordosa (William Marquez), dictator of a fictional Latin American country. The point of the seduction is to convince Cordosa to purchase the defective Peacemaker. Smith said the problem with the scene was "we did not have it on film." He explained that Friedkin brought in Robert Towne, the Academy Award–winning writer of *Chinatown* who was also renowned for his uncredited rewriting of scripts, "to look at the film to help us get DeVoto and Cordosa together." Stock footage of military hardware and voice-over dialogue written by Towne were inserted into the picture.

Deal was previewed (!) in Los Angeles, New York, and Boston, Smith said, "and it previewed high."

Critics, however, laid *Deal* and Friedkin low. For example, the *New York Times* review stated that "the total lack of wit apparent in the direction of Mr. Friedkin, whose inability to build a gag to a proper payoff amounts to a major career disability in anyone who wishes to do comedy."[9] *Variety* said, Friedkin "doubtlessly had something important on his mind here he wanted to satirize, but lost sight of it trying to adapt to young comedy standards."[10] The *Los Angeles Times* review began by calling the film "a full-scale disaster."[11] The *Wall Street Journal* simply warned moviegoers, "Keep away from this turkey."[12]

During an interview with the *Wall Street Journal* conducted two months after the film's release, Paul Brickman, credited writer and coexecutive producer of *Deal*, lamented, "Friedkin did not make the movie I wrote, which is a shame because it's the best script I ever had a hand in." By way of example, the *Journal* states that in Brickman's original script arms dealer Eddie Muntz and his moralist partner Ray argue about the arms scam Muntz wants to perpetrate. Ray says, "We're talking about killing people." Muntz responds, "We're talking about a lot of cash and a fair amount of moral degradation." But Muntz's onscreen dialogue goes, "All we're doing is selling a commodity—like Coca-Cola."[13] In a *Playboy* interview, Chevy Chase, who plays Muntz, called the film he made "a piece of shit."[14]

Deal was intended as a black comedy along the line of Stanley Kubrick's *Dr. Strangelove*. In Bud Smith's opinion, they "didn't achieve it. Kubrick's film wasn't slapstick; strange and bizarre, but funny. The actors played their roles straight in *Strangelove*. Chevy Chase can't do that."

Originally, Jack Nicholson was slated to portray Eddie Muntz, but that deal fell through. Smith said, "Billy was forced to cast it with Chase. If it had been cast with Nicholson, it would have been a completely different movie. I was told the studio needed another vehicle for Chase [he had just completed *National Lampoon's Vacation*], that they had him under contract and wanted him to be in this project."

Friedkin was *forced* to cast Chase?

According to Smith, Warner Bros. said "that was the only way Billy could get the project on, and he said it was the best screenplay he'd read at that time." In other words, Friedkin was determined to make this film. "Billy didn't let this film go down lightly," Smith added. "He worked his butt off, as we all did. But not every film works. *Deal* was one of those fluke films. Whether it's casting or execution or how Billy was feeling or whatever, it just didn't come together."

II

Shortly before the filming of *Deal,* Friedkin stated, "Audiences today just want to be entertained. They don't want to have their spirits troubled by anything. A complete escape. A filmmaker who wants to do other than just entertain, to make people laugh or be moved in some very superficial way, has got a lot of problems today. He's got to disguise his themes."[15]

With *Deal,* Friedkin wanted to "just entertain," to "disguise his themes" of arms proliferation madness and the aberration of greed through satire, and thereby hoped "to make people laugh." However, the film he made is, thus far, the *worst* of his career.

Recall the sequence in Steven Spielberg's film *Jaws* in which Quint, the salty shark hunter, crushes a metal beer can to demonstrate his toughness. As counterpoint, the scientist Hooper crushes a styrofoam cup. *Nowhere* in Friedkin's *entire* body of work is there a moment that provokes as much laughter as this scene in *Jaws*. Yet, Friedkin has directed three of the most viscerally compelling American films ever made—*The French Connection, The Exorcist,* and *Sorcerer*—and, astoundingly, he made them back-to-back. The significance of *Deal* is that it demonstrates Friedkin's conflict between the exhilarating darkness of his vision and a misplaced comedic understanding.

As he often does, Friedkin establishes a visual ambiance with his opening imagery. In *Deal*, the word *Luckup*, in large blue letters, fills the screen. Friedkin widens the shot to reveal the Luckup Industries corporate headquarters, a cold, impersonal brown block of a building. *Luckup* is intended as a visual joke, a put-on of the term *fuckup*. The impression is that Friedkin wanted to mix the satiric (Luckup) with the sinister (the building), a provocative chaotic vision. But Friedkin's joke feels juvenile, and he photographs the building flatly, as though it were a dimensionless facade, a cheap cartoon. However, satire is not a cartoon; it's absurdity made real. In *Dr. Strangelove,* for example, Kubrick frames a shot during the attack on Burpleson Air Force Base with a machine-gun barrel blasting away at a building with a sign in front of it reading *Peace Is Our Profession*. Kubrick shoots the attack sequence with documentary-style realism, thereby making the satire all the more absurd for its reality. With *Deal*, Friedkin sacrifices his own documentary action style, apparently believing an audience's desire for "complete escape" means escaping from reality. In his quest to "move people in some superficial way," Friedkin turns the absurd into the puerile and reality into a cartoon.

For example, one of his sight gags has the Peacemaker (which has the appearance of a mutated bat) malfunctioning at its unveiling and blowing up the Luckup Industries water tank sitting atop a hill. The obviousness of the gag renders it unfunny. Another sight gag shows Muntz, wearing a cast from having been shot earlier in the foot, *again* shot in the *same* foot by accident by Katherine DeVoto. Blood gushes and spurts out of the cast, bathing it, Muntz's pant leg, and the carpet in sanguinary red. Is anyone slapping his knee in uncontrollable hysterics over this gag? Is Friedkin?

Scenes at the air show display a remarkable lack of atmosphere combined with an equally remarkable blandness. We see shots of planes, stockpiles of bombs, and isolated groupings of military men looking here and there. The angles for each of these moments are always the same—the repeated shots of planes taking off from runways are right to left, we repeatedly look down at the ordnance, the military perusers stride toward the camera apparently to give the impression of crowdedness. The repetitions become tedious; their inclusion points toward padding. In all its flight sequences the Peacemaker looks like a plastic model on which the glue hasn't dried. When the arms show is destroyed, the fiery bedlam is obviously a smoking miniature, which Friedkin displays from one angle only. The warehouse where Muntz stores his used weapons armory is actually a converted church. The irony is obvious, but Friedkin, again, photographs the church flatly, boringly, neither real nor surreal. By the time he cuts inside, we've lost interest, the irony blunted.

In *The French Connection,* Friedkin presented New York City as a decomposing body. The door to Regan's bedroom became a symbol of fear.

The lush jungle in *Sorcerer* was inviting yet dangerous. Nighttime—black, brutal, seductive—beckoned in *Cruising.* Friedkin adopted an uncharacteristic lack of care with *Deal,* as though he meant it when he said, "Fuck the filmmaking." Not only does he betray his considerable abilities with this attitude; he also insults the Audience.

But Friedkin wants the Audience to laugh, to be entertained, to care about his characters. Prior to *Deal,* Friedkin's name appeared on several other films that could loosely be considered comedies. For *Good Times,* Friedkin pushed the corny aspects of comedy, broad sight gags. In *Minsky's,* Friedkin (and others) tried to present the slapstick of burlesque. With *Brink's* it was unfunny stupidity. But there was also *The Boys in the Band.* As Mart Crowley said, Friedkin concentrated less on the scabrous humor and "gouged at the dark underbelly." *Band* is the best of the group, for it is the most fully realized with respect to Friedkin's cinematic strengths in probing the aberration of human nature. Yet all the humorous bitching and backbiting dialogue of the characters remains intact. And the Audience laughs. In *Deal,* Friedkin tries to do the reverse of what he did with *Band:* Disguise the aberration (darkness) with comedy (lightness). He wants to make the aberrant greed of the characters funny; he wants the Audience to like his characters. But one cannot laugh at what is unfunny or like what is repugnant.

For example, Frank Stryker, top executive of Luckup, ominously informs his advertising minions that they are in a battle to sell the Peacemaker pilotless fighter plane. "And our enemy is now Moscow. Our enemy is Rockwell, Northrop, Lockheed, McDonnell Douglas, Grumman, and the rest of our worthy competitors, foreign and domestic. The corporate well-being of Luckup is on the line." Stryker, tough and hard-driving, sets a maniacal tone. Selling weapons of death for profit resonates with ironic fatalism. But once Stryker delivers his speech, Friedkin allows him no further development or dimension. Even when Stryker attempts to demonstrate the firepower and precision of the Peacemaker in a last-hope effort to sell it at the film's climax, the crazed gleam in his eye seems more script convenience than satiric bent.

Friedkin introduces General Cordosa rehearsing a television spot in which he explains to the citizens of San Miguel that their country must have more weapons. For this "sad necessity" he denounces "the leftist politicians and terrorists, profiteering businessmen, and women for wearing perfume." He then declares it "a crime for female government employees to wear trousers." The intention was to present a villain, a despot of social, political, and economic vulgarity. Instead, Friedkin destroys any sense of reality—be it straightly comedic or absurdly threatening—with this puerile, stupid speech. Later, while visiting the Southern California arms show, Cordosa expresses an interest in seeing "some cultural highlights . . . like female

Deal of the Century. **Arms dealer Eddie Muntz (Chevy Chase) and his partner Catherine DeVoto (Sigourney Weaver) give Central American dictator General Arturo Cordosa (William Marquez) the VIP tour at the International West Coast Arms Show.**

mud wrestling." The director of *The French Connection* seems to be trying to tap into what an audience of adolescents might find funny.

This same criterion is utilized for Eddie Muntz, the "hero" of the film. Sitting in a sleazy bar in San Miguel, Muntz waits to meet with a revolutionary group that wants to purchase his cache of used weapons. He puffs on a cigar and tells us in voice-over he's been there two days, and "I'm ready to hitchhike to Jonestown for a few laughs and a cool drink. This place is hotter than Dolly Parton's minipad." As played by Chevy Chase and directed by Friedkin, Muntz is meant to be a charming but cynical rogue. But by taking Chase's screen persona of wisecracking smirking superiority and combining it with Friedkin's concept of funny, Muntz's meanspirited crassness could *never* be mistaken for likable roguishness or comic relief, dark or otherwise.

Later, Friedkin adds another dimension to Muntz. When Cordosa hesitates to purchase the defective Peacemaker, Muntz asks his girlfriend,

DeVoto, to have sex with the dictator to ensure the sale. While Friedkin gouges into the repellant side of greed, he asks the Audience to "like" and "care" about the hero, now turned pimp. Worse yet, DeVoto readily agrees to Muntz's request. Her only motivation is her avarice, as well. As a character, DeVoto was a nonentity prior to this scene; a sexual decoration with no real function in the film, she now becomes a loathsome sexual decoration.

The man who made *The Exorcist* also tries to promote mirth from the "sex scene" that follows DeVoto entering Cordosa's hotel room. Friedkin cuts to a close-up of a television screen on which there are images of missiles blasting out of their silos. We soon discover this is a videotape Cordosa and DeVoto are watching. Then we hear the voice-over love-making dialogue of Cordosa and DeVoto. Friedkin never shows them in bed; he uses the phallic hardware and specially written Robert Towne dialogue for sexual symbolism and sexual jokes. We hear Cordosa moan, "Oh, Oh!" DeVoto purrs, "Toro, Toro. What an hombre you are." We see multiple minirockets fire rapidly from a jet fighter. DeVoto says, "These films are such a great idea. You are such a great bull." Cordosa moans faster. Rotary cannon, mounted in helicopters, fire their loads. Cannons recoil. Cordosa groans. DeVoto sounds concerned, "No, General, you'll hurt yourself." A rocket suddenly spins out of control. "I don't know what's wrong," Cordosa says, panicky. The rocket crashes. DeVoto consoles him, "You don't have to apologize to me." A jet fighter crashes on a runway, nosedown. Cordosa cries, "How can I make this up to you?" DeVoto answers, "Just sign the contract"—a large rocket on a launching pad topples and explodes—"and you'll always be El Magnifico to me." A B-52 bomber closes its bomb-bay doors. Cordosa sighs, "Okay, Okay."

Long before Alfred Hitchcock ended *North by Northwest* (1959) with Cary Grant leaning down to kiss Eva Marie Saint and then cutting to a shot of the train they are on entering a tunnel, this kind of visual correlative was a sexual cliché.

What Friedkin may have intended as the film's most absurdly dark comedic moment concerns Ray, Muntz's sidekick. He has decided to give his life over to Jesus Christ, to be "born again." But when a Hispanic couple driving a Chevy with a flame paint job dings the fender of his Porsche as he backs out of a parking space, they blame him, complete with epitaphs. Ray decides to apologize to them, accept the blame, pay for damages, and go on with his life. The Hispanic driver takes exception and slashes one of Ray's tires. He then takes a crowbar and smashes all the windows on the Porsche, to the cheers of his girlfriend. Born again or not, this action has gone too far for Ray. In the trunk of his car rests a flamethrower he recently purchased for Muntz. Popping the trunk he fires up the flamethrower and torches the Chevy, claiming he just wants to give that paint job "a little

Director William Friedkin (left) gives instruction to his stars Chevy Chase and
Sigourney Weaver for a scene from *Deal of the Century.*

touch-up." And then Ray goes back to Muntz and agrees to help him make
the sale of the Peacemaker to Cordosa when earlier he was solidly morally
against it.

Audiences have applauded this car sequence. Presumably, Friedkin
has tapped into the fantasy of any motorist ever involved with an irate driver
in a fender bender. But as he presents it, Ray's action serves as a wretchedly
unpleasant moment as well as an unconvincing plot point and character
revelation: Ray abandons his newfound morality because his car is trashed?
This action justifies the selling of a destructive weapon to a dictator?

The man who directed *Sorcerer* also borrows a scene from *The
Treasure of the Sierra Madre,* a classic film about greed. Near the end of that
John Huston picture, the gold dust the three prospectors had sweated and
worked and even killed for blows silently away in the wind. It's one of the
great visual, visceral, and ironic moments in American cinema. In *Deal,*
what begins as a promising scene has Muntz delivering a vanload of arms
to the revolutionaries in San Miguel. They hand him a suitcase full of
money. Suddenly, government helicopters roar in with soldiers armed with

machine guns, who begin blasting away. The action, excitement, and controlled confusion Friedkin does so well explode onscreen. And then Muntz drops the suitcase. A gunner in a helicopter shoots it up. The suitcase pops open (offscreen), and Friedkin, framing the shot from a low angle, shows the money blowing away from us into a creek bed. While watching Muntz's money float off, the only visceral response one feels is disgust that Friedkin has befouled one of the great images of American cinema by associating it with an insufferably greedy, obnoxious, and unlikable "hero," as well as shooting it flatly, like all the other images in his film. It serves as yet another example of Friedkin's "fuck the filmmaking" attitude.

As the credits roll at the end of *Deal,* a card reads, "A William Friedkin Film." At a screening, one patron was heard to grumble, "What's he bragging for?"

Nineteen years after *Minsky's,* nine years after *Brink's,* and four years after *Deal,* Friedkin stated, "If I could direct a comedy, I would, believe me."[16]

13

To Live and Die in L.A.

"Coming off of *Deal*, Billy wanted to make a
statement that hard-hitting filmmaking is his
forte."

— Bud Smith

I

During his days of experimentation at television station WGN in
Chicago in the early 1960s, Friedkin convinced nightclub singer Jean-
Pierre Aumont to sing the song "Where Have All the Flowers Gone?" on
film. According to Paul Hunter, who had worked with Friedkin on several
documentaries for WGN, "We went to this abandoned brickyard to shoot.
Billy intercut World War One footage—French soldiers and buildings being blown apart—and Aumont singing this song. Billy used sound effectively. He added machine-gun fire and bombs going off, and then he'd cut
to dead silence and then to Aumont singing 'Flowers,' referring to all the
young men of France who were killed. . . . Billy would also have close-ups
of Aumont without his mouth moving, but you'd hear him singing. The idea
was that he's thinking this, and then suddenly his lips would start to move,
and he'd pick up the song. We thought it was real hot stuff, very innovative
at that time."

Nearly twenty years later, in April of 1984, Friedkin directed another
song set to pictures. By this time, these visual vignettes were called music
videos. The song was entitled "Self-Control." Laura Brannigan, who performed the song, was featured in the video. As interpreted by Friedkin,
song and imagery mesh into a seductive dream where the night offers a surreal mix of eroticism and danger.

The following year, Friedkin returned to television and directed the
"Nightcrawlers" episode of the resurrected *The Twilight Zone* series.
Friedkin called "Nightcrawlers" a "very powerful, very intense story that
encapsulated the Vietnam experience" for a guilt-ridden veteran.[1] This
filmic short story of a soldier's cowardice and the bloody retribution sought

by the ghosts of his dead comrades was one of the better episodes of that short-lived series.

Other feature-film directors had made music videos, including Brian De Palma, who directed Bruce Springsteen's "Dancing in the Dark." And well-respected filmmakers such as Martin Scorsese, Steven Spielberg, and Clint Eastwood had brought their considerable directorial talents to the world of television with episodes for Spielberg's failed anthology series, *Amazing Stories.*

Considering Friedkin's motion-picture-career quagmire — four films in eight years with little critical or commercial validation — his forays into the medium of television, as well as the stage play he directed, may be construed as his "new" days of experimentation. Or, possibly, as opportunities to work. Sam Peckinpah once said, "If you're a director and you don't get a chance to direct, you start to die a little."[2]

Regardless of the reason, resuscitation arrived in the form of galleys for a new book, *To Live and Die in Los Angeles.* It is a story of murder and obsession, of a Secret Service agent's pursuit of a counterfeiter. Friedkin said, "It intrigued me because it was written by a Secret Service agent [Gerald Petievich], the most decorated agent in the field for fifteen years. He has protected every president from Lyndon Johnson to President Reagan." Petievich also created Secret Service agents "with feet of clay," Friedkin went on. "I met him and asked, 'Are there really agents like this?'" Petievich introduced Friedkin to the men and women he based the characters in his book on — the bureaucratic superiors, the informants, the agents. "This was a peek behind the curtain, and I found that the characters were real," Friedkin said, adding that "all the incidents were grounded in Petievich's experience." He cited an example he used in the film. "There is a guy in the Secret Service who, on a dare, jumped off the Vincent Thomas Bridge [in San Pedro, California]. Twenty guys bet him fifty dollars each that he couldn't do it, wouldn't live to collect it. The guy did it."[3]

Though Friedkin and Petievich cowrote the screenplay, Friedkin added a chase sequence that was not in the book. The director called the concept of the chase "pure cinema. You can't do it in a book, in a play, on canvas. It's the most difficult kind of sequence to think up." It had been twelve years since the nerve-jangling elevated train chase in *The French Connection* (never equaled, in the opinion of many critics) but Friedkin believed he could do a chase sequence in *To Live and Die* "that would keep my attention and the audience's, hopefully. But it would also be different from *French Connection.*"[4]

According to Bud Smith, who served as producer, supervising film editor, and second-unit director on this picture, he and Friedkin studied "all the dynamic car chases we could find. We pulled out *French Connection* and *Bullitt,* and we brought in Buddy Joe Hooker to be our stunt coordinator."

"Most of this chase is illusion," Friedkin said. "There's not one dangerous shot in it. A lot of the time there are only two vehicles moving—the
camera car and the stunt car. The idea is to conceive the shots so they look
dangerous." By way of example, he explained that when one car is chasing
another and they speed past other cars, those other cars are stationary. "It's
creating the illusion of movement when there is none," Friedkin said. He
also experimented again with the Slavko Vorkapitch theory of deep immersion with a spectacular climax in which the driver of a car escapes his pursuers by driving the wrong way against the flow of freeway traffic, and the
freeway traffic is itself reversed, driving on the left side of the freeway, not
the right. In Friedkin's view, "it will still work if the audience is involved."

Friedkin had set a trend with *French Connection,* which he said had a
"macho sensibility" he "did not want to emulate in this film." Keenly aware
of the inevitable comparisons to come between *Connection* and *To Live and
Die,* Friedkin hired Lilly Kilvert, whose television commercial production
designs he admired, as his production designer because he "wanted a
woman's sensibility in the film wherever possible." He also wanted a
cinematographer who had not done a hard-edged action picture. Friedkin
brought in Robby Muller, whose previous work included the introspective
Paris, Texas, and likened him to "a poet with a very soft palate."[5]

However, the inclusion of "other sensibilities" did not preclude
Friedkin's "hard-hitting, uncompromising filmmaking" (to use Bud Smith's
terms). "We stayed far away from Beverly Hills," Friedkin said. "The locations for this film were metaphors to me for Los Angeles....[6] I wanted an
industrial landscape that hovered over ramshackle, chaotic housing."[7] According to Bud Smith, this look of urban decay was influenced by a book
entitled *Twenty-four Hours in Los Angeles.* "The book shows you Los
Angeles from sunrise to sunrise in pictures," he said. "Refineries, punk kids
on the street, Watts imagery, hookers, strippers. It influenced the production design and the locations. Billy did *not* want to use downtown L.A.
because it's used in so many television cop shows. He wanted a different
look ... different visuals than most people are used to seeing." Industrial
places like Wilmington and San Pedro and the dry desolation of the Mojave
Desert were some of the locations Friedkin shot—where red, yellow, and
green color schemes are scarce. "Billy hates red, yellow, and green," Smith
said. "They're too pleasant. They don't put you on edge."

Another consideration, Smith said, was "to go into the streets and make
a cop show that's not already on television. In a film you can take more time
with your visual statement and do more hard hitting with language and
violence. That's reality! Billy had Gerry Petievich as his technical adviser.
He would tell Billy the way things would go down, and not everyone comes
out alive, and if you're going to kill someone, you fucking kill them. You
blow their head off."

There are a number of graphic killings, beatings, and shootings in *To Live and Die*. Evidently, Friedkin lost his aversion to depicting violence. He has also said that he thought his heart attack "would change my life, change my outlook; but it didn't."[8] Willem DaFoe *(Platoon, The Last Temptation of Christ)*, who portrays Rick Masters, the counterfeiter, has several particularly brutal scenes. In one, he shoots a lawyer in the groin; in another, he sticks the barrel of his pistol deep inside the mouth of one of his buyers after a savage fistfight and tells him, "You broke your contract with me, Jeff. Now I don't know whether you're into it, but you're going to have to suck on this until you give me back my paper."

Speaking in an interview with the *Los Angeles Times* one month after the film's release, DaFoe stated that as an actor he gets "annoyed when you are told to be aggressive or sadistic when the character isn't always required to be. I'd suggest a lighter touch, and Billy would say, 'It's inappropriate.' And as I watched the film, there were times when I thought it was stronger than I'd intended playing it, and that made me kind of sick." DaFoe added, "The violence per se doesn't really bother me—it's a violent world—but what does bother me is the kind of latent homosexual violence (in the film) that Billy Friedkin really grooves on."[9] Bud Smith said that "it's obvious" that kind of violence is in the film, but "Billy did it to show that character as a little weird." Friedkin later sued the *Los Angeles Times* in a $15-million libel suit, charging that the interview "portrayed him as a sadist with a bent toward homosexual violence." Friedkin also "demanded a retraction, which the *Times* will not print."[10] At the time of this writing, the situation remains unresolved.

"I believe films today contain too much sex and violence," Friedkin said shortly after the film opened. "A lot more restraint needs to be shown by myself and others. Seriously. You sometimes come late to that realization." He cited a scene from *Indiscreet*, a 1958 film starring Cary Grant and Ingrid Bergman, in which Grant kisses Bergman goodnight outside her apartment. He leaves but then turns back to see her door open. Grant enters her apartment, the door closes, and the camera holds on the door. Friedkin called it "the most beautiful love scene I've ever not seen. I haven't reached that maturity as a filmmaker to do that."

As far as his directing of the sex scenes in *To Live and Die*, Friedkin said he let the actors improvise their scenes, and "the moment they came together I just cut. . . . I've seen a man shot, but I have no real interest in watching two people make love."[11]

Friedkin also did some improvising during the shooting of the film. Bud Smith recalled that the opening sequence was to be a montage of images under the main titles. "But in the film the two agents talk about their job—protecting the president. Well, we never see that. We just see these two cowboy cops. Billy realized it and said, 'I gotta shoot that scene.'" Now the picture opens with a presidential motorcade arriving at the Century Plaza Hotel in Century City, California, and the two agents, Chance and Hart, thwarting an assassination attempt on the president by an Arab terrorist.

Also, the climax of the film was changed, Smith said. In the script, Chance (played by William L. Peterson) and his new partner, Vukovich (played by John Pankow), meet Masters in a gym locker room where they plan to arrest Masters in a sting operation by trading real money for his counterfeit currency. Suddenly, guns are drawn, shots fired, and Vukovich is killed. "Billy came out of the locker room where we were shooting this scene and asked me, 'What do you think if we switch and shoot Chance instead of Vukovich?' I said, 'Jesus Christ, I never thought of that. That's a big fucking deal.' But we decided, fuck it, why not? That was Billy's idea on the spot; a different twist."

Another "different twist" came in the shape of a new ending requested by SLM, the production company financing the film. They didn't like the fact that *either* agent gets killed, Smith said. Irving R. Levin, the producer, "convinced Billy to go shoot another ending, with Chance and Vukovich alive up in Alaska in a cabin. We shot it, cut it, previewed it, and threw it out." Friedkin said that the positive ending previewed higher than the other ending, but he still didn't use it "because I didn't like it. I felt [my original] ending was inevitable, and with what I was driving at, it had to end this way." He further explained that Alan Ladd, Jr., head of MGM studios (the distributor of the film), "did not want Chance to live and encouraged me to go this way." There was also a clear contractual deal with his partners at SLM, Friedkin said. "They were in charge of the money. I was in charge of the picture."[12]

And being "in charge of the picture" not only meant who would live and die in the film and how it would end but whom Friedkin would preview it for and whom he wouldn't. For example, part of a preview audience who saw the film at MGM studios prior to its release included students from the University of Southern California School of Cinema. A preview audience it did not include was the Secret Service. Friedkin said he refused their request to prescreen the film on First Amendment grounds. "They said, 'We want to see the picture because we think you've used actual photographs of people who have threatened the president of the United States.' (Every photograph in the film is staged.) I said, 'Tell me what photographs I'm using of someone who threatened the president, and I'll take them out of the picture.' They said, 'No, we want to see the film.' I said, 'There are no photographs of anyone who tried to threaten the president.' Then they said the film was a textbook for counterfeiting money and they wanted to prescreen it with an eye toward editing that sequence."[13]

(Originally, the counterfeit money shown printed in the film was to be printed only on one side, according to Lou Edemann, supervising sound effects editor, who was present on the dubbing stage where many of the confrontations between Friedkin and agents of the Secret Service took place. "Gerald Petievich supplied Billy with the printing plates," Edemann explained, "and Billy decided to print on both sides of double-thick paper because he had scenes where the money would be thrown around.")

Friedkin said that the Secret Service "interviewed everybody on my film; the editor twelve times, the property master six times. I interviewed with them once for three hours." He continued to refuse their request for a screening. "I said, 'If you can get a United States attorney to give you a subpoena, I'll resist the subpoena.' I sent a formal letter to the head of MGM, saying don't you dare screen this picture for these guys until it's released." Friedkin said the United States Attorney's office denied the Secret Service's request for a subpoena. Again, agents returned and requested a screening. "I said, 'Look, I'll screen the film for the secretary of the treasury, who is your boss, and if he tells me that there's anything in it that endangers national security or something then I'll cut it.' That was the last I heard from them."[14]

But there were other things Friedkin heard that he liked and things he did not like. He liked the music of the two British musicians, Jack Hues and Nick Feldman, better known as Wang Chung. He gave them a copy of the script and a sense of what the film was about, and asked them "to record their impressions."[15] Like Tangerine Dream, whom Friedkin had asked to perform the same task on *Sorcerer*, Wang Chung had never written music for a film before. Also like Tangerine Dream, Wang Chung was asked to write their music and mail it to him because he did not want them to score the picture. He told them he wanted "to be inspired by the music. I want the editing to be inspired by the music. Write raw meat. Nothing romantic, nothing sentimental, and don't write a title song. I don't want one, and I don't think you can put this title into a lyric. They recorded about sixty minutes of music and mailed it to me. I took what I liked and cut it into the film."

Friedkin said the two musicians saw the film during its postproduction phase and were pleased. "Then the lead writer wrote a title song based on the feeling he got from the film. I liked it and shoehorned it into the beginning. Three days before we finished mixing the picture, they came in with another song called 'Lullaby.' I liked it and found a place for it in the scene where Chance is driving to [his girlfriend] Ruth's house. They wrote more songs, and I told them I didn't have any more room for them in the film."[16]

According to Bud Smith, Friedkin redesigned the sound mix for the film by isolating certain pieces of the music; for example, by using them for effects and playing them louder. "Billy would say, 'I want the music to blow my brains out.'"

Friedkin also liked the gunshot sound effects Lou Edemann (who won an Academy Award for his sound effects editing on *Who Framed Roger Rabbit?*) and his crew recorded. "Billy wanted them harsh and staunch; they had to be bigger and better than before," Edemann said. "We recorded thundercracks under the gunshots. We fired guns off under a corrugated aluminum top usually used for shade, but the resulting sound was like a slap. Billy loved that." But a gunshot effect Friedkin used throughout the film was the one Edemann recorded in a canyon, resulting in an echoing effect. Originally it was only to be used in an early scene where Chance's first partner, Hart (Michael Greene), is killed up at Masters's desert warehouse. "But then Billy wanted it everywhere—inside, outside," Edemann said. "And it works. We used it when Chance is killed in the locker room. That sound became part of the whole effect of the picture."

Visceral, edgy effectiveness is what Friedkin's best films are about, and there were mistakes in *To Live and Die* that were preconceived, such as wrong-way traffic flow in the freeway chase, and some that were not. For example, Edemann recalled that in the scene where Chance and Vukovich interrogate a suspected diamond smuggler under a bridge near a railroad yard, the smuggler kicks Chance in the leg, knocking him to the ground. "He hit a microphone cord when he did it, and there was this haywire noise through Vukovich's dialogue. I told Billy we'd have to rerecord that. Billy said, 'I can't do that. I'll never get that performance again.' Most directors believe once they get something on film that is stupendous, why would they even want to *think* about doing it over again. But this line was awful. Billy said, 'Leave it alone.' We did put a train screech going by over it. I still think we should have fixed it.

"But Billy's totally unpredictable. We went way over our dubbing schedule on this film. Billy thought we'd dub it in four or five weeks. We took ten weeks. He won't let anything go. He's fanatical.

"Billy thought the cars we recorded sounded too anemic. We recorded the cars they drove, but they weren't bigger than life," Edemann said. So they detached the mufflers, recorded that sound, and even miked the sound inside the muffler. "Billy didn't want a hot rod, but he did want something big and powerful."

During the chase, cars race along on top of railroad ties, but "that actual sound is a lot of noise with no definition," Friedkin said. Edemann and his crew went on a Foley stage and recorded the sound of a basektball bouncing across wooden slats. Friedkin said he augmented that sound effect "by scraping a hammer over a washboard."[17] Another effect Friedkin came up with while on the dubbing stage was used during the chase whenever a car went under a bridge, Edemann said. "Billy wanted an ominous sound. He punched a pencil hole in the bottom of a styrofoam cup and blew into it. The sound was eerie. He liked it. We used it."

Something Friedkin did not like was Edemann's taking a week's vacation during the dubbing of the picture. Edemann had made his family vacation plans based on the original dubbing schedule. When the picture went over schedule, it was too late to change them. According to Edemann, Friedkin was in New York for the week. Bud Smith told Edemann not to call Friedkin; everything would be fine. When Edemann returned from his week away, he was told there had been no problems. "Then I saw Billy, who asked, 'How can you take a vacation in the middle of dubbing a show?' I explained that I'd had plans. Billy said, 'I'm holding you personally responsible for this fucking mess.' I said, 'I heard it all went great.' 'Well, it *didn't*,' Billy said, and stormed off.

"I went back and quizzed everybody. No problems. I saw Bud, who suggested I go talk to Billy. I went to see him and said, 'Billy, I don't know what to say. Bud and I discussed it. My editors were here to handle it.' He said, 'I'm holding you personally responsible.' I said, 'What does that mean to me?' He said, 'I don't know yet! Just go back and get this picture dubbed.'" At this point in retelling the story, Edemann laughed and said he did not believe Friedkin acted this way intentionally. "Billy's not happy with *anything* until everything is just right."

As an example, Edemann said that in the riot scene that takes place in a prison yard, a guard in a tower fires four shots, and then we cut and see two ricochets on the ground. "I had six shots cut in. That's the way it should be. Billy said, 'Goddamnit, no. I only want four shots.' I said, 'Well, there's the ricochets.' 'I only want four shots.' 'But—' 'I don't care. Four shots.' I fixed it and cut out two shots." But there was a problem. Edemann said they had predubbed the scene so six shots were recorded on the master tape. Edemann's corrected sound track with four shots and the master tape were somehow cross-patched on the mixing console.

"We ran the scene, and six shots came up," Edemann continued. "Billy looked at me and said, 'Lou, I only want four shots.' 'I know. I cut two of them out.' 'Well, I heard six.' Bob Glass, the sound effects mixer, did not know he'd cross-patched, but he thought he knew what had happened. We ran it again, and six shots came up. Billy was just livid. He shouted at me, and I said, 'Billy, I don't need this bullshit! I cut out two shots!' He said, 'I always hear six!' Back and forth we went, and I said, 'I don't need it' and walked off the stage.

"I was told later that the mixers and Billy tried it again. They heard six shots, and Billy picked up a cup of coffee, threw it in the air, and was yelling, 'I can't believe this!' The coffee splashed on the mixers. I was outside, thinking to myself that Billy won't let me back on the show and I don't even want to *be* on the show now. Then out walked the three mixers, saying, 'We don't need this. We don't need this at all.' We later talked with Billy. He apologized, and we went back to work."

To Live and Die in L.A. opened on November 1, 1985, to mixed reviews. The trade papers were split. *Variety* said the film "looks like a rich man's *Miami Vice*.... Film is very commercially intended, but the intense vulgarity of the characters and virtuoso stylistic overkill will, like that of *Year of the Dragon*, turn off mainstream audiences."[18] The *Hollywood Reporter* stated that "some will be appalled by its rapacious violence, others will be thrilled by its searing action. Certainly William Friedkin's [film] travels the meanest streets of film noir, and genre buffs will be blown away."[19] Writing in the *New York Times*, Vincent Canby began by calling Friedkin's film "not a very satisfying melodrama, but, even when it turns wildly, improbably stupid, it's never boring as it could be. . . . It hooks you at the start and, long after you've told yourself that what you're watching is utter nonsense, it holds the attention. . . ." He went on to say that one stays with the film "not because what happens is especially affecting or even surprising, but because you've been hooked by its rhythmical audio-visual beat." Canby praised the "slick" photography and "irresistible" score but attacked the plot as being "of such literalness that it becomes impossible to react to it viscerally. . . . Mr. Friedkin, who once set trends, is now desperately following them."[20] But Michael Wilmington stated in the *Los Angeles Times* that Friedkin is "obviously trying to top *The French Connection*" by "grabbing at the lightning of the past." He then writes, "The shock is that he very nearly gets it. Coming off a decade of flawed or misfiring projects, and working against the memory of an endlessly copied film, Friedkin seems reborn, galvanized into life."[21]

Ironically, each review attests, admiringly or grudgingly, to the fact that indeed, as the advertising line on the film stated, "The director of *The French Connection* is on the streets again."

II

Violent, disturbing, and ruthless, *To Live and Die in L.A.* pushes the thriller genre into a nihilistic dance of corruption, vengeance, and death. Friedkin compels us to the edge of a hell where darkness is light, cop is criminal, and aberration is normal. He has envisioned a world not in chaos (for that implies an attainable stability) but thriving because of chaos; a world where nothing is what it appears to be.

Ironically, the two primary characters — Chance, the agent; Masters, the counterfeiter — are the personifications of their names. Friedkin allows their actions to tell us exactly who they are. For Chance, the single most important action is defying death. Early in the film he leaps off the Vincent Thomas Bridge, which rises hundreds of feet above Long Beach harbor. The opening line in Bob Fosse's *All That Jazz* (1979) states, "Being on the wire is life; the rest is waiting." Fosse illustrates the statement by showing us Joe Gideon walking a tightrope. Friedkin takes Chance a step further. Chance isn't on the line; he's attached to it. It's the risk, the ultimate chance. During the car chase, Friedkin goes from a close-up on Chance driving his car to a subliminal cut of him jumping off the bridge. His elation at making the jump parallels the excitement of escaping his pursuers. And his reaction to surviving the plunge is the same as ultimately evading capture in the chase: laughter, an explosion of joy and excitement at teetering on the brink, his life at stake. Chance's first partner, Hart, calls him "a hot dog" and warns him that he's "pushing too hard." Chance laughs it off. As appropriate in a Friedkin film, living on the edge makes for a fuller, more intense life.

In Masters, Friedkin finds an artist. The portraits he paints have a repellent yet haunting quality. The twenty-dollar bills he prints are done with the same laborious attention to detail. Indeed, a tribute to his cunning and craft is that he has never been apprehended ("You're not the first agents to get close to Masters," Chance's and Vukovich's superior tells them) and his funny money is considered the best ("I had your last shipment sold within a week," one of Masters's contacts tells him. "I had people *begging* for some of them twenties").

Friedkin presents Masters's counterfeiting artistry in his own remarkable documentary style. Masters blows on the aluminum plate he has just photographed against four negatives of twenty-dollar bills, his breath fogging on the plate revealing the positive images. He mixes the paint and starts the presses. The rhythmic chugging sounds of the press, the blank paper rolling through the printer and then dropping into a catch tray with four perfect images of green twenties on each, are combined with the hard-driving beat of Wang Chung's music, Friedkin's moving camera, and Bud Smith's excellent editing, giving the sequence a quickening pulse. Masters adds more ink to the rollers and runs the newly printed money through the press again, this time with new serial numbers appearing in the lower left and upper right corners of the bills. The rhythmic beat continues as Masters carefully cuts the excess paper from his funny money and then tosses piles of bills into a dryer, along with rags and poker chips to give the phony currency the proper texture.

But Friedkin takes the concept of counterfeiting—that nothing is what it seems—beyond Masters's lab. For example, when Chance jumps off the bridge, it looks as if he's committing suicide until we plainly see the lifeline trailing out from his pant leg. When Masters meets his girlfriend in the dressing room of the avant-garde theater where she performs, it appears as though it's actually a man he kisses passionately on the mouth until Friedkin reverses the angle. Masters breaks the kiss, and his friend removes a short dark wig, revealing that he is a she with a mane of rich red hair. Chance

To Live and Die in L.A. Counterfeiter Eric Masters (Willem DaFoe) carefully prepares to manufacture a fresh batch of twenty-dollar bills at his secret workshop somewhere in the California desert.

and his new partner, Vukovich, pose as corrupt bankers in order to entrap Masters in a direct buy of his counterfeit money. We watch Masters and his girlfriend, Bianca (Debra Feuer), make love, and then Friedkin cuts to another angle, revealing Masters and Bianca watching a videotape of their lovemaking. Friedkin's imagery suggests that neither love nor money is "real."

And what may be the most bizarre example of nothing being what it appears to be triggers the car chase. Chance and Vukovich need $30,000 to run their scam on Masters, $20,000 more than their department will allocate. Chance's girlfriend, Ruth (Darlanne Fluegel), who is also his informant (again, love is not "real"), tells him about a bagman for corrupt diamond brokers who she knows is coming into town by train. He'll be carrying $50,000. Chance convinces a reluctant Vukovich to help him "take this guy down," who's "breaking the law anyway." The bagman, Ling (Michael Chong), turns out to be an FBI agent working undercover, who is shot and killed by accident by one of his own agents. A dozen cars try to chase down

To Live and Die in L.A. **Agents Vukovich (John Pankow, center) and Chance
(William Petersen, right) put their careers on the line by robbing a fence (Michael
Chong, left) to finance a renegade undercover operation of their own design.**

Chance and Vukovich as they swerve and careen through the Los Angeles
River basin, truck loading docks, and the wrong way on the freeway. They
do not know who was chasing and shooting at them (Vukovich shot back)
until the next day in a morning Secret Service briefing scene. The report
of the incident from the FBI says the undercover agent's abductors killed
him. In reality, the Secret Service stole from the FBI, who in turn chased
the Secret Service agents. Both sides believe they are battling bad guys.

   More so than with Doyle in *The French Connection*, Friedkin has imbued Chance with a motive for arresting Masters. Revenge has become
Chance's mission in life. (As played by William L. Petersen, Chance has the
determined expression of Steve McQueen without the charisma.) Watching
Chance's obsession turn to aberration is fascinating; however, it lacks the
involvement of Doyle's comical outrageous savagery or even Scanlon's test
of endurance. All of Chance's energies are focused on catching Masters, to
the point of justifying breaking the law, namely, stealing money from the
bagman. In comparison, Doyle would never plant drugs on a suspect in

To Live and Die in L.A. U.S. Secret Service agent Richard Chance (William Petersen) unscrupulously forces ex-convict Ruth Lanier (Darlanne Fluegel) to become his lover and informant by threatening to revoke her parole.

order to bust him. Doyle has his pride. He likes the chase because it is his job; he's a professional. Chance is a maverick. It's an attitude expressed right down to the clothes he wears: cowboy boots and blue jeans. He's the first one through the door, gun drawn, when a score of agents descend on Masters's desert printing lab. As Hart warned him early in the film, "You push too hard. You take it too personally. You're never going to reach retirement." True, Doyle pushes himself hard, but it is still just a job, and once he catches Frog I, he'll go on to the next assignment. Chance sees the job as a vendetta. Doyle picks up an anonymous girl for a one-night stand because he likes her boots. Chance's "love" interest, Ruth, supplies him with information; otherwise, he threatens to revoke her parole. For Doyle it's obsession born of pride; to Chance, it's obsession born of aberration.

Friedkin allows aberration to reach into the texture of his images as well. Decay was the look of New York City in *French Connection*. In *Cruising*, the city had a harsh monochromatic look, except at night when it took on a slick surreal tone. A uniformed cop in that film says, "One day this whole city's going to explode." In *To Live and Die,* Friedkin presents Los Angeles as a city that has already exploded. It's shattered, fragmented. Friedkin cuts sharply from Masters's white art deco house with its many windows, giving it an expansive appearance, to the ugly industrialized Long Beach harbor of steel girders, cranes, and tankers. There are Masters's portraits with their grotesque appeal (not unlike the works of Francis Bacon, Edvard Munch, and Gerald Scarfe — all artists Friedkin admires) and Hart's head turned to a bloody pulp by a close-range shotgun blast. Ruth's bungalow home looks as though furnished by Goodwill Industries, while lawyers' offices are rich woods and veneers. Masters drives a sinister-looking black Ferrari; Chance four-wheels a Dodge Ram. To Friedkin, an auto graveyard is as fascinating and representative an image of L.A. style as a white-bricked courthouse plaza with rows of palm trees evenly spaced.

Friedkin, who called Los Angeles "the most inorganic city I have ever seen,"[22] has taken the dark underbelly that has so fascinated him and exposed it to light — hot and bright — with this film. For example, the Pasadena office of Max Waxman (Christopher Allport), an attorney who passes Masters's funny money, is a combination of green and red rooms. As Bud Smith points out, red, green, and yellow are colors Friedkin doesn't care for because they "don't put you on edge." Allowing the color scheme into the film, Friedkin uses it as counterpoint. For example, the pleasant greens and reds of Waxman's offices become the backdrop for a vicious fight between Masters and Waxman, who has stolen Masters's money. The scene climaxes with Masters shooting Waxman in the groin and then in the head (implied by a point-of-view angle). The yellow walls of Ruth's home are faded, stained, and dirty. They reflect Ruth herself, her blond hair hanging limp, her face sad, almost hard-looking; the house, like Ruth, no longer cared for. What appears to be blood drips down onto a silver printing plate in Masters's lab, but we quickly realize it is actually red ink. Friedkin uses bright red and lime-green colors for his main title logo, reflecting simultaneously a garishness coupled with boldness. And then, as an exclamation mark, he adds another counterpoint with a red blotch next to the title. It splatters, like a drop of blood, and a red trail runs down the length of the logo. Suddenly, the bloody mark becomes recognizable — a grotesque facsimile of a palm tree. The title alone is keenly existential; the bloody illustration adds fascination to the fatalism.

Unfortunately, the film does not open with this main title but with the introduction of agents Chance and Hart, arriving at the Century Plaza Hotel as part of President Reagan's bodyguard. That night on the roof of the hotel, Chance discovers a murdered policeman and a terrorist, who has wrapped himself with sticks of dynamite, standing at roof's edge. The terrorist claims he is ready to die to kill all enemies of Islam. Chance wants to talk him down and then sees Hart (who has climbed up from a balcony below) yank the terrorist backward off the roof. The terrorist screams, pulling the pin on his explosives. The resulting explosion has a strangely muted sound, considering the numerous sticks of dynamite involved. The hotel is unrattled, and, oddly, Hart is unharmed since the explosion was instantaneous and he was, from the angles shown, next to the falling body. It is an unfortunate prologue because it seems wary on Friedkin's part—something uncharacteristic. In many of his previous films he draws the audience into the story— the aberration—like the murder in *French Connection*, Merrin's facing the demon in *The Exorcist*, or the dismembered arm floating serenely in *Cruising*.

But this was not the only seeming inattention to detail on Friedkin's part. When Chance and Vukovich snatch Ling at Union Station, they take him to a bridge underpass to rob him. Believing the money to be in Ling's carrying case, Chance repeatedly smacks the locked case against a wall. Chance's sunglasses fly off his face, and he does not retrieve them. Ling is then accidentally killed. After Chance and Vukovich leave the scene, the glasses are still there on the ground close to Ling's body. The glasses would have Chance's fingerprints on them. So did the FBI miss them later, or was Friedkin hoping we wouldn't notice? One other discrepancy occurs toward the end of the film when Masters is burning down his downtown warehouse printing lab. His black Ferrari is inside the warehouse. Masters dies inside. Flames are dangerously close to the vehicle. Later in the film, we see Bianca and her girlfriend drive off in the black Ferrari. How did the car get from the burning warehouse back to Masters's home? These may seem like nitpicking details, but they are *obvious* details. It is true that thrillers are far-fetched at times, which may be inherent in their lure, but in these instances, Friedkin has fetched too far. Though these moments prevent this picture from being on a par with Friedkin's best films, *To Live and Die* is still a visceral film of aberrations and obsessions—a Friedkin film.

It is also about bonding and honor. Chance, of course, is loyal and honorbound to Hart; therefore his obsession with catching Masters. Chance also exhibits loyalty to Vukovich when he tells him he wouldn't have taken evidence—Waxman's dealers' code book—from the scene of a crime if he didn't believe he could trust his partner. Just as Doyle and Russo are partners, and Edelson tells Burns they are partners, so too Chance and Vukovich—men who must trust and depend on each other.

There is the example of Chance's trying to convince Cody (John Turturro), one of Masters's couriers whom Chance had busted earlier at the airport passing counterfeit currency, to testify against Masters. Cody, serving time in prison, had just been attacked out in the prison yard, a "hit" arranged by Masters. Even though he realizes Masters was responsible, Cody refuses to roll over on his friend. Chance responds, "Anybody who would is a piece of shit." But then he reminds Cody that his "friend" had just tried to have him killed. Therefore, all bets should be off. (Ironically, Cody agrees and then escapes from Chance when he convinces him to stop at a hospital where he says his little girl is a patient. This is the one time in the film where Chance shows a modicum of compassion—which results in betrayal. Note, too, that Chance had called ahead to the hospital, inquiring whether a woman named Roseanne Brown, the name Cody gave him, was a patient there. Yes, a Roseanne Brown is a patient, but she turns out to be the wife of an inmate Cody knew.)

Vukovich also displays loyalty and honor. Troubled by his conscience after the robbery and death of Ling, Vukovich goes to an attorney named Grimes (another appropriate personification and played as such by Dean Stockwell), who is also Masters's counsel but doesn't like Masters's pushing him around anymore, and tells him what happened. Grimes tells the agent the only recourse he has is to testify against his partner in open court. Because Vukovich will have to serve some time in prison, Grimes assures him he will get the sentence reduced—and it will cost Vukovich $50,000, the very amount they took from Ling. Vukovich refuses to betray his partner.

Masters has a similar belief in the sanctity of loyalty and honor. He visits Cody in prison, promising to do all he can to help, but when he detects weakness in Cody's moral strength (he thinks Cody will roll over), he contracts with Jeff (Steve James), one of his buyers who has prison contacts, to have him murdered. When the job is bungled, Masters calmly asks Jeff for the return of his payment. It's a point of honor. When Jeff refuses and threatens him with a knife, Masters reacts with cool deadliness by sticking his pistol down Jeff's throat.

Honor and loyalty are Chance's, Vukovich's, and Masters's positive traits. Ironically, these terms are also associated with money, currency. One honors debts with money, and loyalty is synonymous with trust, as in the motto inscribed on coins and printed on paper currency: *In God We Trust*.

But it is in the climax and epilogue of the film that Friedkin fuses honor, life, death, and betrayal into an aberrant circle of normalcy. Chance and Vukovich have just placed Masters and his bodyguard, Jack (Jack Hoar), under arrest in the gym locker room. Pistol drawn, Chance spins Masters into the lockers, sticking his pistol into Masters's neck. "This is from Jimmy Hart in the desert," Chance says, showing him a poker chip he found in the dryer of Masters's desert printing lab. "Suck on this awhile." Vukovich moves to handcuff Jack, who suddenly produces a shotgun from a locker. Jack and Chance shoot at each other, and both fall dead, Chance shot in the face. Masters bolts from the room while Vukovich begs Chance not to die. Chance, the "hot dog," had told Hart that he wasn't concerned about making it to retirement, only "bagging Masters." Chance lives to "bag" Masters but dies before retirement. Vukovich, refusing to let his partner down, drives to Masters's downtown printing lab, a warehouse with a large white Chinese figure painted on a red door. (He had been told of the lab earlier by a local artist who admired Masters's portraits.) Inside, red and yellow mix with smoke as Masters sits calmly while the fire he lit engulfs his printing equipment.

Vukovich knocks Masters to the ground. Masters gets up and strikes Vukovich repeatedly with a two-by-four. The agent lies unmoving. Masters covers him with shredded paper and lights a torch to burn him. Vukovich rises, pistol extended, and fires point-blank. Masters drops his torch and is suddenly engulfed in flames. But we see a beatific expression on Masters's face, revealing ecstasy, relief. (At the top of the film, Friedkin had shown Masters burning an unfinished painting. Friedkin framed Masters bracketed by the flames as he watched the canvas consumed by the fire.) A tortured sadness has been inherent in Masters's eyes throughout, especially noticeable when he burned his portrait. Now, in his lab, the flames arching up around him, his eyes show joy and serenity.

At Masters's now empty home several days later, Grimes speaks to Bianca, asking why she stayed with Masters for so long. She asks him the same question. "Just business," he replies. Her facial expression implies that her reason was identical. She walks outside to the waiting black Ferrari and climbs in next to Serena (Jane Leaves), another dancer at the avant-garde theater, who is now Bianca's lover. But Masters didn't mind. In fact, he gave Serena to Bianca as a "surprise" the night he was killed. One could interpret Masters's idea of eroticism as divorced from love but not from aesthetic pleasure. But to Bianca, it was all business, and she and Serena roar off down the street.

Friedkin cuts to Ruth in her bungalow. Boxes are stacked in the center of the room. She is moving. And then a bruised and scarred Vukovich arrives. He calmly informs her that he and Chance figured out that she had set them up with Ling. She knew all along he was FBI. Vukovich wants the $20,000 Chance left with her from the Ling robbery. She claims part of the money was owed to her and she was "ripped off for the rest." Vukovich asks her not to "shine me on" because now they have a relationship. "What?" she asks incredulously. "You're working for me now," he says evenly.

We hold on her face, the Vincent Thomas Bridge rising in the background seen through her window like an ever-present reminder of Chance, whom we then see in a subliminal cut as Ruth realizes she must now be an informant and sexual slave to Chance's partner. Vukovich now wears the same style of sunglasses, jeans, and cowboy boots Chance did. He even exhibits Chance's arrogant cockiness. Before, Vukovich had wanted only to operate by the rules. After the chase, he wailed, "What are we going to do!?" while Chance laughed and howled, "We did it!" Vukovich, meta-phorically speaking, had the lifeline attached when he became Chance's partner. He had been seduced by the aberrant excitement, his loyalty to his partner. And now, with Ruth, he is picking up where his partner left off. Ruth, the betrayer, cannot break the aberrant circle that is Friedkin's vision of normalcy, of life and death in a world where chaos is the rule.

14
Rampage

"The films I make are kind of awestruck at the
violence in our society; the casual, everyday,
unexpected violence that everyone of us has
to live with."
— William Friedkin[1]

Friedkin says he cannot forget witnessing the execution of Vincent
Ciucci in the electric chair. Ciucci, who had asked Friedkin to be one of
the witnesses, was Paul Crump's cellmate.[2] Friedkin, who said he had
always been "dead-set against capital punishment," made *The People Versus
Paul Crump* "to save a man from the electric chair." His astonishing
documentary, made in 1962, accomplished that end. "Paul Crump is still in
prison," Friedkin said. "He has been in prison longer than any other person
in the United States."[3] When Friedkin made this statement in November
of 1987, Crump had been incarcerated for thirty-four years. Friedkin has remained in contact with Crump over the years, helping to finance his appeals
and appearing at his parole hearings.

However, Friedkin's attitude on the death penalty has changed. "Now
I think there are instances when capital punishment would be justified.
When I was against capital punishment, I never thought about the victim
or the relatives of a victim. Now I identify more in that direction. . . . I do
not believe it is right for society to take a life. Neither do I feel prisons are
adequate to house killers. Nothing is served. What is the answer? I don't
know." When asked exactly how he felt about capital punishment, Friedkin
answered, "At this point in my life, my feelings are ambivalent."

Following another foray into television, this time with two lackluster
movies for television about a special antiterrorist team (*C.A.T. Squad I* and
II) and another musical video ("Somewhere" sung by Barbra Streisand),
Friedkin returned to the big screen to reexamine the death penalty in *Rampage,* which he wrote and directed.

Ironically, neither *Crump* nor *Rampage* ever played to the audiences
for which they were intended because of legal problems. *Crump* was considered too libelous and inflammatory. At the time of this writing, *Rampage*

247

is immersed in undisclosed litigation, and individuals contacted for discussion of the film have declined any comment. Also ironic is the fact that both *Crump* and *Rampage* screened at film festivals; *Crump* in San Francisco, and *Rampage* in Boston. At the Boston Festival, *Rampage* was reviewed by *Weekly Variety*, which praised the film as a "forceful drama."[4]

This, the twelfth feature film in Friedkin's career, was supposed to be released in December of 1987 or January of 1988, the director said at a symposium held at the University of Southern California on November 19, 1987. *Rampage* was screened for the symposium, and afterward Friedkin said his film was based on an actual case that took place in the late 1970s in Sacramento, California, the trial of a serial killer. (A book by Thomas P. Wood is also credited.) "There were certain things I was trying to get at very crudely in an hour and a half. One of the things was: Lawyers are interchangeable in this system. [Both the prosecutor and defense attorney, played by Michael Biehn and Nicholas Campbell, respectively, look very much alike, even down to the part in their hair.] A defense attorney is not necessarily an impassioned advocate. . . . His feelings may or may not be strongly with the accused. He's doing a job. The prosecutor in this case starts out, as I did, against capital punishment. In the course of the story, he comes to believe that this [killer], according to the letter of the law, was guilty and sane.

"The springboard for me was two cases that occurred over the last few years. One was the John Hinckley case; the other was the case of John Wayne Gacy in Chicago. Gacy killed thirty-eight young men that we know about. Hinckley shot at the president but didn't kill anybody."

According to Friedkin, Dr. Jim Cavanaugh, who operates a rehabilitation program for serial killers at the Rush Presbyterian St. Luke's Medical Center in Chicago, was one of several psychiatrists called upon to testify in both cases. "Cavanaugh's testimony in the Hinckley case was that Hinckley was insane and therefore not guilty by reason of insanity. In the Gacy case, he testified that Gacy was sane. That's how the jury found him—sane, guilty, and going to the electric chair. . . . Gacy killed thirty-eight people, and he's sane. Hinckley killed nobody, but he's insane. It seems to me a serious blip in the system." He also stated, "I think the notion of the insanity plea has gotten way out of hand."

A factual story about a serial killer, the insanity plea, and the death penalty. The ingredients seemed ideal for Friedkin, who admitted that "very few studios would even consider the subject matter." However, Friedkin said that Dino De Laurentiis (who Friedkin believes has "always been very courageous") asked him to make another film for him. Nine years earlier, they had worked together on *Brink's*. "I told Mr. De Laurentiis that I wanted to make this very risky, very uncommercial subject." De Laurentiis had just produced *Blue Velvet*, David Lynch's strange, violent, black comedy about small-town life, and, Friedkin said, De Laurentiis told him, "Fine, go ahead."

Shooting *Rampage* in a very fast twenty-six days, Friedkin said that though it may have been a mistake, he "tried to make the film without style . . . no discernable visual style." He explained that "most films today are all style and no content. . . . There's an MTV culture. One of the impetuses for this film was anti that. Paintings and still photographs are about composition. Films are about their subject matter. *To Live and Die in L.A.* is much too much style for the way I presently feel about filmmaking." (Recall that, for example, Vincent Canby, in his review of *To Live and Die*, criticized the film, calling it "nastily trendy," a "perfect example of . . . today's 'new' movie, which has its origins in music videos and which attempts to work not through reason or identification with characters but poetically, through style. . . .")

Friedkin also kept the cost of the picture to just under $5 million, citing the substantially low cost as being one of the reasons he made it.

And he also said he does not know what he wanted to say with *Rampage*. "I did know when I started to make it, but as I see it, I'm not sure it's clear at all. I was trying to take on an important subject. . . . People are either for or against the death penalty."

Except Friedkin, who says he's "ambivalent" on the subject. And just as his striving for ambiguity in *Cruising* rendered that film nearly incoherent, Friedkin's ambivalence toward the death penalty severely mars *Rampage*.

Friedkin has stated that there are only three major reasons to make films: to make people laugh, cry, or frighten them.[5] In his book *Trivializing America*, Norman Corwin considered Friedkin's statement and added that "possibly he did not include a fourth reason—to make them think—because in some circles that is the same as frightening them."[6] Watching *Rampage*, the only frightening aspect to ponder is what has happened to William Friedkin's passion?

Friedkin has said, "The gift to a filmmaker is that he is permitted to serve the audience."[7] Enthusiastic audiences stood in long lines for the white-knuckled ride of *The French Connection* and the electrifying fear and fascination of *The Exorcist*. But no one, it seemed, could be coerced into theaters showing *Sorcerer*, one of the most muscular action films ever made. Rejected by the Audience, Friedkin's choice of projects since 1977 has not equaled the passion inherent in every frame of his three finest films. For Friedkin, that passion is synonymous with his vision—a dark, tragic hopelessness where Popeye Doyle still attacked with an obsessive, outrageous savagery; where Scanlon veritably willed his truck across a rickety bridge in a battle with fate. The struggle was the crux of Friedkin's bleak outlook, living on the edge of the abyss. That Charnier escaped from

Doyle, that Karras died, that Scanlon was betrayed, are the realities of the reflection of life Friedkin offers up for the audience to consider. And this reflection, his unique vision—fatalistic, violent, realistic—is so viscerally realized in his compelling visual style that *The French Connection, The Exorcist,* and *Sorcerer* shall retain their gut-level intensity as classics of their genres.

Friedkin followed with two comedies, *Brink's* and *Deal,* finally realizing he was out of his element, and two dramas—*Cruising,* misdirected into ambiguity, and *To Live and Die in L.A.,* a return to the action film with his own aberrant twist. And the aberrance of human nature is the key to his vision and therefore his passion; the desire to visualize the obsessions and fears that propel his characters toward the edge where death enhances life. Doyle was a target for an assassin's bullet, Karras's soul was the devil's desire, Scanlon was a worthy opponent in fate's game. For Chance, physical danger was an integral part of the pursuit, and Burns is set out as prey for a monster.

Friedkin's early documentary *The People Versus Paul Crump* was absolutely a study in aberration—a man's life slowly ticks away toward a date of execution. Friedkin made the film to save Crump's life. It had a point of view. In *The French Connection,* beleaguered cops battle a million-dollar drug trade. *The Exorcist* was about redemption. *Sorcerer* was about fate. Even *Deal* dealt with the insanity of arms proliferation. The problem with *Cruising* was that he decided to make a statement about ambiguity and apparently cut the heart out of the film and left it in the editing room. But with *Rampage,* the absence of passion has resulted in a deeper wound.

Under the opening titles we see a dark moving specter on a dirt road, cutting through the orderliness of an orchard that appears to extend into infinity. We circle high above in a slow aerial shot, and then Friedkin pushes us in closer, revealing this black shadow under a midday sun as Reece (Alex McArthur). Wearing blue jeans and cowboy boots, he walks with a purposeful, lanky gait. We occasionally catch a glimpse of his blissful countenance, bisected by wraparound dark glasses and framed with long straight dark hair. Yet there is something unnerving about this young man. Suddenly, Friedkin intercuts his ethereal angles with low ones skimming, hurtling just above this orchard. Fear, like a cold sweat, dampens our palms.

Visually, Friedkin has connected Reece's look of contentment with the fast, ominous, riveting low-angle shots; they are like Reece's thoughts bolting ahead, undirected, lethal. Is this a visualization of insanity? Something gnaws at our viscera. Reece's expression and stride remain transfixed, unchanged. Friedkin seems to be asking us which is more frightening, the face of sanity or that of insanity? Which does Reece possess? Or is Friedkin attempting to take us beyond aberration to a plane where the calm and chaotic harmonize? Friedkin poses these questions with imagery underscored by a strangely haunting Ennio Morricone musical theme. It is as though we are moving beyond good and evil into a brightly lit abyss. Friedkin has seduced us with this dichotomy. Thus far, his ambivalence and "no style" are eerily mesmerizing.

But soon afterward, Friedkin shows us the blood. Reece has calmly, deliberately entered a house and murdered the two women inside. Friedkin does not show us Reece, knife in hand, carving up the bodies. Instead we see the aftermath—blood-spattered body parts in extreme close-up only. The screen looks barely able to contain all the dark rich red blood the body organs float in. But of what value is shock if its sole purpose is gratuitous? Heinous crime, horrific image, yes. But when Friedkin cuts to these quick subliminal flashes (one has barely a moment to be cognizant of the image), the visceral point seems designed only to jolt. Aberrant images in Friedkin's films—such as Regan's masturbating with the crucifix, the vicious stabbings in *Cruising,* and Hart's head turned into a bloody pulp by a shotgun blast— are shocking and revolting, but (until this picture) they also served as visual manifestations of a threat, resulting in dramatic revelations pivotal to the unfolding of the story.

In *Rampage,* Friedkin could easily have left the description of Reece's acts in dialogue form without showing us the gory aftermath since he elected to make the film with "no discernable visual style." He said he shot scenes as if he had "just happened to show up" when the action was taking place.[8] No, the film does not look like a home movie, but neither does it have the feel of a news-camera or a follow-the-action documentary. During one of the murder sequences, Friedkin cuts to an exterior shot of a pleasant white house where Reece is butchering. Children play in the yard. Friedkin pushes the camera in toward a curtained second-floor bedroom window. The idea is explicit—the world appears as a sunny, blue sky, anyday in anytown. But a beast is loose and can strike anytime. It's the kind of imagery that was effective in Hitchcock films of the 1950s but in the late 1980s it feels trite.

One could also argue that Friedkin sets the butchery in a daylight nightmare where the inexplicably horrific is happening. However, unlike *The Exorcist,* another daylight nightmare of equally inexplicable horror, *Rampage* fails to *involve* the audience. We are not participants. In *The Exorcist,* we experience a sense of dread, palatable fear, every time Friedkin takes us toward Regan's bedroom because we are emotionally and viscerally involved with the characters, and especially through Friedkin's *style,* which makes us participants by enclosing us in the bedroom, in the horror. In *Rampage,* Friedkin's choice of no style is akin to pushing the audience away from the action, the movement, the aberration—the *soul* of his abilities and best work.

The "anytown" look is crisply photographed by Robert D. Yoeman, but

Friedkin's "no style" style appears synonymous with dullness, as though the director set up the camera, had the actors say their lines, and then everybody went home. One would never have expected to describe a Friedkin film as "dull," but it succinctly fits *Rampage*. For example, when Reece is captured by the police at a gas station where he works, Friedkin keeps us at bay from the action. Reece tries to escape down the street, and the police surround him, telling him to get down flat. Recall the controlled chaos of the bank explosion in *Sorcerer*, Doyle dressed as Santa Claus chasing the pusher, and the robbers escaping down the staircase in *Crump*. Friedkin made us *participants*, involved us. Films may be about their subject to Friedkin, but to negate style and composition is to present content without form. The courtroom scenes, too, have an uninvolving feel. The dark woods of the walls fail to infuse the drama with any tonal atmosphere of shadowy apprehension. But neither are these scenes coldly antiseptic or imbued with the flinty blue steel coloring Friedkin used so effectively in *The Exorcist, Sorcerer,* and even *Brink's*.

Friedkin's ambivalence about his subject has resulted in ambivalent filmmaking. His conflicting feelings appear to have made him adopt neither a real nor surreal approach, which results in ninety-five minutes of the dull and the bland.

Characters as written by Friedkin also fail to compel. The prosecuting attorney, Fraser, harboring guilt over the death of his daughter, at first refuses to argue for the death penalty he is adamantly against. Political aspirations and pressures finally convince him to reconsider. When his wife, Kate (Deborah Van Valkenburgh), tells him halfway through the film that their marriage is failing, Friedkin sets the scene with Kate's approaching Fraser on a boardwalk. Fraser does not face his wife. Roughly, her dialogue in the scene is "I think we should split up." His response is "Yeah." End of scene. Episodic television programs frequently use these sorts of broad brushstrokes to establish their stock guest-star characters.

Friedkin keeps the aberration that is Reece ambiguous. The character has almost no dialogue. Action reveals character, or should. Friedkin explained that in his research, he was "struck by the normalcy of these serial killers up to the moment when they snapped."[9] By extension, then, we, the audience, are the jury. We are aware of his horrible actions. Well into the film, Friedkin gives us another look at the aberration. Reece escapes from custody while being driven back to jail. He slashes the throat of one of his guards. That night, he is recaptured in a church, where he is discovered nude, having painted himself with white paint and blood. A terrifying sight, but its inclusion feels like an afterthought for the sake of action. During the courtroom scenes, Reece sits quietly, calmly, as though he were a spectator, not the accused. But is he sane or insane? By the legal definition, does Reece understand the difference between right and wrong? Friedkin leaves the character enigmatic. Reece may know full well what he did, and he may not.

It is not that Reece is an enigma that presents difficulty, however. It is what an ambivalent Friedkin does with him. After the attorneys have delivered their closing statements and the jury retires to deliberate, Friedkin cuts to Reece's jail cell. Lying motionless on his cot, his lips chalky white with dried saliva, the killer has killed himself—apparently, the authorities believe, with poison slipped to him by his mother. Suicide!? Why did Friedkin even *bother* to explore the insanity plea and the death penalty? He has twisted his ambivalence into wretched irony. That he provokes an angry visceral reaction is not a compliment. If Friedkin wanted to "frighten" the audience into "thinking," it should have been about something other than the aberration he ultimately displays, namely, the emasculation of his own film.

Passion was the core of *Crump*. Guilt or innocence was not the issue to Friedkin. The focus was saving Crump from the electric chair. Friedkin demonstrated an unflinching understanding of human suffering and frailty and regeneration. Crump's story was a shout of indignation and a sob of hopelessness wanting hope. In *Rampage*, Friedkin raises important, volatile issues and resolves them timidly.

15
The Guardian

"None of my films are perfect."
— William Friedkin[1]

In the mid-1970s, Coppola, Scorsese, Kubrick, and Friedkin were the star directors; their names on a film were as much a guarantee of box office success as Redford, Streisand, Pacino, and Eastwood. Because of the phenomenon called *The Exorcist,* Friedkin was offered and accepted a contract to make three motion pictures for Universal Studios. Soon afterward, *Sorcerer* was in preproduction, and Friedkin was trying to develop another horror film. He asked Walon Green, who had just completed the screenplay for *Sorcerer,* to write the script. The story was about a movie director who was hired to make a horror film about horror films, "but things would start to go wrong for this guy," Green recalled. "His own life would start reflecting greater horrors than he was seeing in his film. Finally, he wouldn't be able to distinguish one from the other. . . . Billy wanted to call it *A Safe Darkness,* which refers to the movie theater where you can watch frightening films and indulge in abject fear and yet you're in this safe darkness." But after the commercial disaster of *Sorcerer,* Green said, "Universal was not in a mood to have Billy do anything else, nor was he in a mood to do anything else for them."

However ironically, sixteen years later, Friedkin did make a horror film for Universal. Entitled *The Guardian,* the film is Friedkin's return to a genre for which he admits a special affinity: "If I could find a film in this genre all the time, this is probably all I would do. . . ."[2]

Originally, Dan Greenburg adapted his novel *The Nanny* to screenplay form for producer Joe Wizan, who then hired Steven Volk, who wrote Ken Russell's *Gothic,* to do the second rewrite. Then Wizan gave the script to his longtime friend Friedkin.

The story concerns a parent's worst nightmare. As Friedkin, a father himself, states it, "The idea that the person who comes into your home to take care of your most precious commodity—your child—is very often someone whom you don't know at all. They put on a good front . . . and then

254

certain things start to happen."[3] In other words, real-life nanny horror stories, which Friedkin knows of firsthand because of his young son, Jack. "My wife [at that time actress Lesley-Anne Down] and I went away for two days, and we came back to this girl [their English nanny] and her girlfriend who'd picked up three guys in a bar and brought them back to our house. . . . Here's this girl, sweet and demure, well educated, great family background—and she winds up getting rolled by Hell's Angels in my bed with my son there. . . ."[4]

This kind of reality in a film was deemed "too real, too disturbing" by Universal, Friedkin said, and they persuaded him to add a "supernatural element," which "in a story like this or *The Exorcist* gives the audience a chance to distance themselves from the horror. . . ."[5] To emphasize this "supernatural element," Friedkin, in "creative collaboration"[6] with Wizan, added a "hideous, ancient tree—a sort of demon-god, which sustains itself on babies sacrificed to it by the nanny."[7]

But Friedkin's intention was not to make a "monster movie," and it was reported that the original three-quarter-scale tree built by Peter Chesney's Image Engineering "was abandoned when Friedkin deemed video tests of the effects too reminiscent of a Godzilla movie." Friedkin shut down the production for three weeks and had the mechanical effects redesigned by Phil Corey. The result: a three-story-high, twelve-foot-diameter tree made of wood and urethane foam, with hydraulics capable of violent and realistic sucker punches. (The delay was expensive, Friedkin told the *Los Angeles Times*, but "the studio has been totally supportive. They realize everything is for the betterment of the picture." The *Times* added that "Universal executives declined to answer questions about Friedkin's track record or the current film.")[8]

There were also certain performances that presented Friedkin with problems, specifically the wolves that protect the nanny. "Every wolf, like every human being, has a personality," Friedkin said. "Some wolves cannot growl. Others can. Others charge; some can't. Friedkin learned this only later—after he fired the wolf trainer. "I was going to go the rest of the way with dogs, and Joe [Wizan] convinced me not to do that. . . . It dawned on me that what a director must do at all times with his cast is adjust to their strengths and play down their weaknesses. As I get older, I sometimes forget that. Mr. Wizan reminded me of that on this occasion, and I brought this brilliant wolf trainer back on the film."[9]

And there was also the unexpected, which, in at least one instance, Friedkin said, "wasn't difficult for me to deal with at all." In the first take of an early sequence in the film, Jenny Seagrove (who plays the nanny) held up the baby to the tree, and as she prepared to recite her incantation, "the baby wee-weed right in her face."[10]

Filming was completed in September of 1989. Editing, preview

Director William Friedkin on the set of *The Guardian.*

screenings, and final mixing took another six months. When Friedkin sub-
mitted his "realistic story about unexplainable events"[11] to the MPAA
Ratings Board, he anticipated the worst. After all, the film shows wolves
devouring human bodies, and at its climax, the tree spews blood. But
Friedkin could not recall the board's requesting any cuts. However, he said,
"I never thought it would get out as it is now."[12]

The $12-million film[13] (originally budgeted at $10 million)[14] premiered
April 19, 1990, as the opening feature of the American Film Institute/Los
Angeles International Film Festival, where it reportedly received a
"dismissive reaction."[15] When it opened nationally a week later, a paying
audience in a Los Angeles theater laughed at it. During the free Universal
Studios employee screening the following day, the laughter was louder.
And this was not the "nervous laughter" that Friedkin says occurs "when
people find themselves seeing a film that is too much to take."[16] It was the
derisive chortling and guffawing of an audience reacting to a film that critics
were calling "a tree bites man tale"[17] and "primally silly,"[18] with characters
that are "boring . . . dullards" in "a plot that doesn't work at all."[19]

Friedkin expressed his thoughts on critics and horror films a few days
before *The Guardian* opened, before the reviews were out. "What critics
usually do with [horror films]," Friedkin said, "is try to describe the plot, and
the minute you try to do that, you're lost because most of these films don't
make a lot of plot sense. They move you on different levels. It's more about
feelings and sensations and a cold hand on the back of your neck. If that
happens to you, it's a successful horror film . . . ."[20]

The image that opens *The Guardian* is an owl, simultaneously frightening and serene. But the uncanny eyes of this owl—deep black pupils sur-
rounded by the bright yellow of the iris—and their hypnotic gaze truly
unsettle. Friedkin immediately and visually establishes a feeling of
foreboding that is both natural and unnatural.

In reemphasizing this atmospheric dichotomy throughout the film,
Friedkin maintains a sense of chaos with nature. Great blowing winds whip
through heavily wooded areas in the dead of night. And stumbling out of
this darkness at one point comes a terrified, bloodied figure pursued by
snarling wolves. Inside the architectural gem of a house where Phil (Dwier
Brown) and Kate (Carey Lowell) live with their newborn son, Jake, ar-
rangements of pink, white, yellow, and purple flowers—from single buds
in vases to large bouquets in baskets—are neatly framed within shots of the
art deco off-white interior of the home. These delicate blossoms act as a
kind of unthreatening reality in direct conflict with the thick green foliage
outside the windows that appears to surround the house. One gets the feeling of being comfortably trapped while a bad dream lurks just outside.

But the nightmare that is the real monster of nature is actually deep
in the woods beyond the house: that hulking, leafless, gnarled, dead-looking

The Guardian. **Beneath her charming demeanor, Camilla (Jenny Seagrove) hides a terrifying secret.**

tree protruding with the faces of the babies the nanny, Camilla (Jenny Seagrove), has bloodlessly sacrificed to it. (When she holds a child up to the tree, the baby suddenly disappears from her hands — spirited away — and its image appears frozen in the bark.) And this deadly tree is no passive aberration of nature.

At one point, three punks (Hell's Angel types) terrorize Camilla, who attempts to hide herself and little Jake at the base of the tree. One of the punks strikes Camilla, knocking her down, and then slices her abdomen with his knife. She screams, and the tree attacks by nearly decapitating one punk with its powerful limb, digesting another within its trunk, and impaling the third with a thick spiked root after ripping off the punk's leg with a tentaclelike root. Fire then consumes the body.

Note carefully, though, that all that has been described are *moments* of dread, *details* of premonition, and *isolated* scenes that shock. Back in 1984, Universal had released a film called *Terror in the Aisles,* a compilation of scenes from horror films. The problem was that these scenes of horror, such as the famous shower murder from *Psycho, totally* lost their effectiveness because they had been taken *out of context,* out of the narrative, the story, the plot, that led up to the moment of realization, of horror. The examples described here from *The Guardian* are no different: a cinematic collage that may elicit "feelings and sensations"; collectively, however, they do *not* make for a successful or even coherent horror film.

Friedkin continued his statement regarding critics and horror films, saying, "The story has to be somewhat coherent, but not necessarily. Some of the best [horror] films I've ever seen, you don't go to for the story; you go there for the feelings they can produce and trigger off in you." Friedkin had earlier cited *Diabolique, Psycho, Rosemary's Baby,* and *Alien* as his favorite horror films.[21] What he did not mention was that these are four excellent examples of strong tight story structure. Horror films are melodrama; the genre *demands* plot. To conclude his statement, Friedkin searched for an example to illustrate his "story-somewhat-coherent-but-not-necessarily" theory, and, strangely, he presented a contradiction. He said, "The only reason *The Exorcist* works is because of [William Peter] Blatty's story and screenplay. No question about that."[22]

Conversely, story problems with *The Guardian* nullify its nuances and resonances as well as the visceral impact Friedkin believed would be "produced and triggered off."

Introductory cards at the top of the film tell us that the Druids worshipped trees, "sometimes sacrificing human beings to them," and they believed "every tree has its guardian spirit" and some of these spirits "embody powers of evil." Friedkin then introduces a fairy-tale ambience with a little boy reading "Hansel and Gretel" to his month-old baby sister, Leah. (The director said he "tried to do a contemporary resetting, not retelling, but resetting of the 'Hansel and Gretel' story" because "these stories gave children throughout their later lives great courage and hope from the fact that [they] could overcome the powers of evil.")[23] Mr. and Mrs. Sheridan, the parents of these two children, leave for a weekend vacation, entrusting their nanny, Camilla, working here under the name of Julia, with the children's safety. At one month, Leah is the perfect age for Camilla's evil purpose. The nanny steals the child and sacrifices her to the tree. Threat established.

A year later, Camilla is hired by Phil and Kate, a working yuppie couple, to care for their newborn son, Jake. One night, a small earth tremor rattles the house, and Phil goes to check on his little boy. He discovers Camilla and Jake in the bathtub. She is not at all embarrassed to be seen nude by Phil, who appears slightly startled at her uninhibitedness. Phil also has a dream in which Camilla makes violent love to him. Illicit erotic potential established.

When the punks terrorize Camilla and Jake, Friedkin begins the sequence in a pastoral meadow not far from Phil and Kate's home. Holding

Jake in her arms, Camilla runs through the woods, across a stream, and deep
into thicker woods to the tree. The winded punks find her, and the tree
viciously kills them. Another threat established.

Then the problems begin.

Ned (Brad Hall), a friend who lives up the street from Phil and Kate,
has taken a liking to the attractive Camilla. She leaves for a walk one night.
Ned drops by unexpectedly with roses, and Kate tells him to go after her.
Ned calls to Camilla, who has gone off into the woods. The wind howls. He
follows her and witnesses her idyll with the tree. She stretches out naked
on a limb, the branches stroke her, and she, well, *molts* into the tree. Wolves
appear and growl at Ned. He runs away, scared to death. Reaching his
house, he telephones the police, who are skeptical at his insistence that
coyotes are prowling in his yard. Ned calls Phil's house and gets the answer-
ing machine. With fear in his voice, he leaves this message: "I saw
something tonight. I can't *believe* what I've seen! Camilla—don't let that
woman back in your house!" The wolves get into Ned's house and kill him.
Camilla is there too. With a wave of her hand, she makes Ned's mauled body
and the bloodstains on his telephone vanish. Note Camilla's powers.

The next morning, Phil listens to his phone messages. The first is from
Mrs. Sheridan (remember her from the beginning of the film), who tearfully
tells Phil (though they've never met) she needs to talk to him. Camilla
overhears this. Then Ned's message starts. She also hears this and interrupts
Phil, who stops the tape.

Phil goes to see Mrs. Sheridan, who tells him her little baby, Leah, was
taken away by their nanny, Julia. Mrs. Sheridan describes her to a rightly
confused Phil, but the only connection he perceives is circumstantial: Both
women are "attractive" with "English accents." However, he does not
believe Julia and Camilla are one and the same—until he sees Mrs.
Sheridan's son, Scott, whom we saw reading "Hansel and Gretel" to little
Leah earlier. Phil looks at the fairy-tale book and recognizes it from his
earlier dream. Scott also tells Phil that Julia had a purple birthmark on her
stomach. Phil recalls seeing that birthmark on Camilla's stomach in his
dream, too. *Suddenly,* Phil is convinced!

We, however, are convinced this is a contrivance. He confronts
Camilla immediately, telling her he checked all her references and they are
fake. He accuses her of taking the Sheridan baby, and then he plays back
Ned's frightened message. Camilla *heard* Mrs. Sheridan's message *and*
Ned's voice on the tape. In the hours between that time and Phil's return,
she *never* listens to the tape? And with the powers she demonstrated at
Ned's house, she couldn't have erased that tape?

Phil tells Camilla to get out, and then Kate says something is wrong
with Jake. At the hospital, the doctor isn't sure why Jake won't respond. The
baby is put into an incubator. Kate prays, and Jake revives. Phil goes out

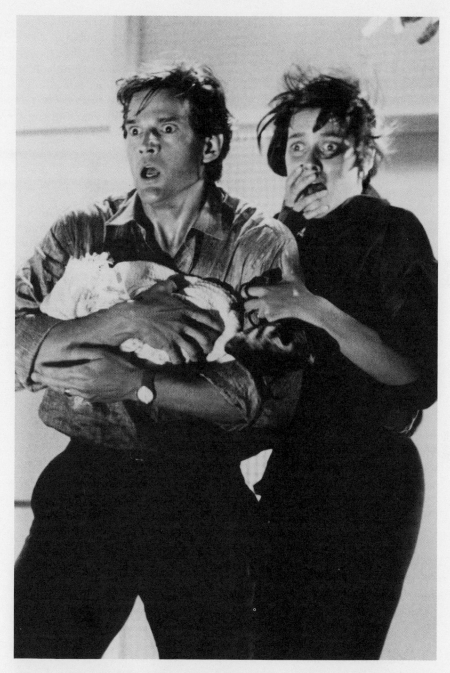

The Guardian. Phil (Dwier Brown) and Kate (Carey Lowell) try to protect their baby from its mysterious new nanny.

to get the doctor. Camilla appears from behind a curtain. As she advances, Kate says, "What are you doing here?" Camilla opens the incubator. Kate says, "He doesn't need you, stay away." Camilla gently pulls off Jake's heart-rate pads. Kate says, "The doctor is coming. Leave him alone." Camilla lifts Jake out of the incubator. Kate says, "Leave him alone. Don't move him." Camilla heads for the door, and Kate *never makes a move to stop her.*

This inaction on Kate's part is totally unbelievable. Phil comes in, grabs Jake, and punches out Camilla. Then Phil and Kate run out of the hospital. Do they think the hospital staff is going to hurt them?

Just a reminder: Phil and Kate are unaware of Camilla's powers. And the illicit erotic potential established earlier has apparently been dropped.

Arriving back home that night, Phil and Kate find their home under wolf attack. Kate screams, "They want the baby!" How does she know that? Neither she nor Phil have ever *seen* the wolves before this. She slips inside the house to get the Jeep keys and yells to Phil, who holds Jake, "I'll meet you at the entrance to the woods." One can only surmise that the reason for this statement is that it's written in the script.

Phil runs into the woods. He turns and sees Camilla chasing him — but she has levitated — flying! This black silhouette moves inexorably above the trees in pursuit of Phil. Because it is so unexpected, it is initially effective and chilling, but then we immediately wonder why she didn't use this power to escape the punks.

Camilla's powers are inconsistent. They appear (or do not) only for pur-poses of story convenience. Therefore, when Camilla corners Phil and Jake at the tree (that Phil's pell-mell run through the woods leads him there is an amazing coincidence), we are not surprised that she does not levitate when Kate hits her head-on with the Jeep. After all, if Camilla hasn't the sense to erase an incriminating telephone message, she certainly can't be expected to dodge an oncoming vehicle.

So, with Camilla's broken body lying at the base of the tree, Phil notices three faces of babies protruding from the tree trunk. (We saw them when Camilla sacrificed Leah.)

The next morning, Phil and Kate have told their tale to the police, who understandably have difficulty believing them. Phil asks the detective (Xander Berkeley) if he saw the babies. The detective says he saw the carv-ings. "They're *not* carvings," Phil insists. He says he is *sure* they are the vic-tims of Camilla. Phil's deductive reasoning, based on his conversation with Mrs. Sheridan and seeing those faces in the bark one time at night, is far too ludicrous a stretch.

Phil and Kate tell the detective they are going home to pack and leave town. Once home, Kate sits in her bedroom holding Jake while Phil goes to the backyard, picks up a chain saw, and marches off into the woods,

The Guardian. Phil (Dwier Brown) attempts to shield his infant son.

obviously to cut down the tree. We no longer wonder why these characters do illogical things because we already know why: It's in the script.

At the tree, Phil starts sawing. Blood gushes out, and a mighty limb decks him. One expects the wolves to appear, but maybe they are too tired from terrorizing Phil and Kate the night before.

At home, Kate is confronted by Camilla, who has begun to molt again; bark has grown on her skin. She demands Jake. Kate clutches him tightly and dashes into the nursery.

Phil battles the tree, which has a root wrapped around his leg. But the tree misses impaling Phil on its wooden spike. It's gotten sluggish.

Camilla breaks down the nursery door, telling Kate she needs the child. Kate tries to open the window to escape. We notice the wall, however. It has been changing throughout the film. First, Kate painted a light forest scene on it. Later it has become a dark jungle motif with large brightly colored flowers in the foreground and animal faces with yellow eyes peering up at the crib. And then in another scene it's the forest painting, and now it's the jungle. Maybe Friedkin is testing the "total-immersion" theory again as he did in *The Exorcist* with Karras's hands and in *To Live and Die in L.A.* with the traffic on the wrong side of the road.

But at this point in *The Guardian*, we are reeling from plot blunders, gaffes in logic, and inane character motivation. We don't *care* about the wall. We also don't care whether Friedkin's grown-up versions of Hansel and Gretel destroy the tree and the witch. The roller coaster of *The French Connection* has derailed, the electricity of *The Exorcist* has short-circuited, the muscle that is *Sorcerer* has turned flabby.

What has happened to Friedkin may be what he said has happened to many filmmakers: "There are talented guys who just went down the fucking tubes."

In September 1980, Friedkin said, "I'm coasting on my reputation now. A studio will back me because I've made a couple of hits, that's all." Regrettably, this statement remains too true.

Indeed, concluding this study on a note of despair was not intentional. But it may be appropriate for a filmmaker who sees the world in hopeless terms, whose films, good and bad, reflect this . . . ideal. This term is not used loosely, for in Friedkin's iconography, "no hope"[24] functions as irony, a purging into a fuller, richer, and exhilarating view of life lived on the edge of a razor or a shard of glass.

Friedkin's imagery is about compelling visceral reaction. It is about the chilling fear of Merrin standing in the shaft of light thrown from Regan's closed window, a man of goodness dressed in black come to save a little girl from evil forces. It is Popeye Doyle's maniacally funny obsession in which he busts drug pushers "for those three bags" and "for picking your feet in Poughkeepsie." It is Scanlon's awakening from a nightmare only to find himself battling fate in a green hell. Crump's holding on to his sanity as he holds fast to the bars of his cell, hoping that he "won't just slip away and, and be no more." Stanley at his birthday party, giggling grotesquely, driven over the edge by his own irrational fears. The boys in the band, who understand, as Harold says, that "life is a goddamn laff-riot" and accept their homosexuality, and those, like Michael, who "don't understand any of it."

It's Chance charging through an airport security system announcing himself as a Secret Service agent. Klaxons blare, a policeman races after Chance who chases Cody who bolts past passengers in the crowded terminal, shouting, "Out of my way!" It's Frog I, waving "bye-bye" to Doyle at the subway station after an elusive cat-and-mouse game and Doyle later returning the cute wave when Charnier and Boca screech to a halt at Doyle's roadblock. It's Karras, lying face down in a pool of blood at the bottom of the M Street stairs, squeezing Father Dyer's hand with his torn and bloody fingers.

Friedkin's successes are resounding, his failures astounding. "Electrifying," "innovative," "controversial," "flawed," and "nearly unwatchable" are terms that convey the extreme spectrum of Friedkin's films. He has said that "the more experienced you get, the harder it gets." "Not every film works" goes the saying in Hollywood. One hopes to see again in his future films the talent, the ability, the passion he has visualized so masterfully in the aberrance of his images—darkly seductive, violently beautiful—combined with characters full of the courage and doubt, intensity and fear, that compose the soul of Friedkin's cinematic reality.

Notes

Except as noted, all interviews were conducted by the author.

The People Versus Paul Crump

1. *Dialogue on Film,* William Friedkin Seminar, Vol. 3 & 4, February/ March 1974, p. 13.
2. Ibid., p. 28.
3. Interview with William Friedkin, Seminar on *The French Connection,* University of Southern California, 3 March 1982.
4. *Francis Bacon Recent Paintings 1968–1974,* The Metropolitan Museum of Art, New York, 1975; edited by Henry Geldzahler, p. 14.
5. Ibid., p. 15.
6. Ibid., p. 6.

A Year with Wolper, and a Moment with Hitchcock

1. McCarthy, John, and Brian Kelleher, *"Alfred Hitchcock Presents": An Illustrated Guide to the Ten Year Television Career of the Master of Suspense,* St. Martin's Press, New York, 1985, pp. 314–15.

Good Times

1. Friedkin, William, *Good Times* liner notes, soundtrack album, Atco Records, a Division of Atlantic Recording Corp., 1967.

The Night They Raided Minsky's

1. Applebaum, Ralph, "Tense Situations," *Films and Filming,* March 1979, Vol. 25, No. 6, Issue No. 294, p. 19.
2. Friedkin, William, acceptance speech for *The Exorcist,* The Academy of Science Fiction, Fantasy and Horror Awards Ceremony at the University of Southern California, 11 June 1981.
3. *Dialogue on Film,* William Friedkin Seminar, Vol. 3 & 4, February/March 1974, p. 34.
4. Rosenblum, Ralph, and Robert Karen, *When the Shooting Stops . . . the Cutting Begins,* Viking Press, New York, 1979, p. 12.
5. Ibid.
6. Ibid., p. 14.
7. Ibid., p. 13.
8. Ibid., pp. 29, 30.

9. Ibid., p. 30.

10. Ibid., p. 14.

11. Ibid., p. 25.

12. Ibid., p. 27.

13. Applebaum, Ralph, p. 19.

14. *The Night They Raided Minsky's* review, *Playboy*, March 1969, Vol. 16, No. 3, p. 28.

15. Thomas, Kevin, "*Minsky's* Due Wednesday," *Los Angeles Times*, Calendar, 15 December 1968, p. 1.

16. Kauffmann, Stanley, *The Night They Raided Minsky's* review, *New Republic*, 18 January 1969.

17. Rosenblum, Ralph, and Robert Karen, p. 28.

18. Ibid.

19. Ibid., p. 24.

The Birthday Party

1. *Dialogue on Film*, William Friedkin Seminar, Vol. 3 & 4, February/ March 1974, p. 33.

2. Ibid.

3. Applebaum, Ralph, "Tense Situations," *Films and Filming*, March 1979, Vol. 25, No. 6, Issue No. 294, pp. 18, 19.

4. *Dialogue on Film*, p. 33.

5. Ibid., p. 16.

6. Ibid., p. 17.

7. Ibid.

8. Weiler, A. H., "Murderers 'Beyond Belief,'" *New York Times*, Section II, 15 December 1968, p. 25.

9. Geldzahler, Henry, *Francis Bacon Recent Paintings 1968–1974*, The Metropolitan Museum of Art, New York, 1975, p. 15.

The Boys in the Band

1. Wolf, William, "Surefooted Friedkin Riding Tide of Success," *Los Angeles Times*, Calendar, 15 October 1972, p. 76.

2. Kael, Pauline, *The Boys in the Band* review, *New Yorker*, 21 March 1970, pp. 166–67.

3. *Variety*, *The Boys in the Band* review, 16 March 1970, p. 3.

4. Champlin, Charles, "Motion Picture Review: *The Boys in the Band*," *Los Angeles Times*, View, 29 March 1970, pp. 1, 4.

5. *Time*, "Shades of Lavender," 30 March 1970, p. 97.

6. Wilson, William, "Francis Bacon's Vision of Isolation," *Los Angeles Times*, Calendar, 27 October 1985, p. 3.

7. Kael, Pauline, p. 167.

8. Wilson, William, p. 3.

The French Connection

1. *Dialogue on Film*, William Friedkin Seminar, Vol. 3 & 4, February/March 1974, pp. 30, 31.

2. Friedkin, William, *The French Connection* Symposium, The University of Southern California, 15 March 1982.

3. *Dialogue on Film,* p. 16.

4. Wolf, William, "Surefooted Friedkin Riding Tide of Success," *Los Angeles Times,* Calendar, 15 October 1972, p. 76.

5. Friedkin, William, *The French Connection* Symposium.

6. Tusher, Will, "Friedkin Says *Connection* Calculated to Make a Killing," *Hollywood Reporter,* 24 March 1972, p. 12.

7. Friedkin, William, *The French Connection* Symposium.

8. Ibid.

9. *Dialogue on Film,* p. 19.

10. Ibid.

11. Ibid.

12. Ibid.

13. *Playboy,* Interview with Roy Scheider, September 1980, Vol. 27, No. 9, p. 84.

14. Ibid.

15. *Dialogue on Film,* p. 18.

16. *Playboy,* p. 74.

17. Friedkin, William, *The French Connection* Symposium.

18. Friedkin, William, Archives Interview for Director's Guild of America, 9 June 1982.

19. Friedkin, William, *The French Connection* Symposium.

20. Ibid.

21. *Dialogue on Film,* p. 20.

22. Schickel, Richard, "A Real Look at a Tough Cop," *Life,* 19 November 1971, p. 13.

23. Friedkin, William, *The French Connection* Symposium.

24. *Dialogue on Film,* p. 7.

25. Ibid., p. 12.

26. Friedkin, William, *The French Connection* Symposium.

27. *Dialogue on Film,* p. 29.

28. Ibid., pp. 28, 29.

The Exorcist

1. Cameron, Sue, "Behind the Glitter of Oscar Night," *TV Guide,* 23 March 1985, Vol. 33, No. 12, p. 8.

2. Bartholomew, David, "*The Exorcist:* The Book, the Movie, the Phenomenon," *Cinefantastique,* Winter 1974, Vol. 3, No. 4, p. 9.

3. Ibid., p. 10.

4. Ibid., pp. 12–13.

5. Ibid., p. 13.

6. Ibid.

7. Winogura, Dale, Interview with William Friedkin, *Cinefantastique,* Winter 1974, Vol. 3, No. 4, p. 15.

8. Blatty, William Peter, *William Peter Blatty on* The Exorcist *from Novel to Film,* New York: Bantam Books, June 1974, p. 39.

9. Bartholomew, David, p. 9.

10. Blatty, William Peter, p. 40.

11. Ibid., p. 41.

12. Friedkin, William, *The Exorcist* Symposium with William Peter Blatty, Sherwood Oaks Experimental College, Hollywood, California, 24 September 1980.

13. Chase, Chris, "*The Exorcist:* Everyone's Reading It, Billy Friedkin's Filming It," *New York Times*, Section II, 27 August 1972, p. D9.

14. Blatty, William Peter, p. 273.

15. Haber, Joyce, "The Midas Touch of William Friedkin," *Los Angeles Times*, Calendar, 24 October 1974, p. 19.

16. Blatty, William Peter, p. 274.

17. Friedkin, William, acceptance speech for *The Exorcist*, The Academy of Science Fiction, Fantasy and Horror Awards Ceremony at the University of Southern California, 11 June 1981.

18. Reed, Rex, "Filming *The Exorcist*—It Was Hell," *Los Angeles Times*, Calendar, 24 March 1974, p. 19.

19. *Dialogue on Film*, p. 10.

20. Friedkin, William, *The Exorcist* Symposium.

21. *Dialogue on Film*, p. 10.

22. Friedkin, William, *The Exorcist* Symposium.

23. Ibid.

24. Friedkin, William, Archives Interview for Director's Guild of America, 9 June 1982.

25. Bartholomew, David, p. 12.

26. *Dialogue on Film*, p. 11.

27. Ibid.

28. Friedkin, William, *The Exorcist* Symposium.

29. Winogura, Dale, p. 16.

30. Friedkin, William, *The Exorcist* Symposium.

31. *Dialogue on Film*, p. 8.

32. Reed, Rex, p. 19.

33. *Dialogue on Film*, p. 5.

34. Ibid., pp. 7–8.

35. Ibid., p. 8.

36. Friedkin, William, *The Exorcist* Symposium.

37. Friedkin, William. *The French Connection* Symposium, The University of Southern California, 15 March 1982.

38. Winogura, Dale, p. 17.

39. *Dialogue on Film*, p. 26.

40. Friedkin, William, *The Exorcist* Symposium.

41. *Dialogue on Film*, p. 26.

42. Winogura, Dale, p. 17.

43. *Dialogue on Film*, p. 6.

44. Reed, Rex, p. 19.

45. Friedkin, William, *The Exorcist* Symposium.

46. *Dialogue on Film*, p. 36.

47. Ibid.

48. Blatty, William Peter, p. 24.

49. Friedkin, William, acceptance speech for *The Exorcist*.

50. *Dialogue on Film*, p. 9.

51. Bartholomew, David, p. 11.

52. Friedkin, William, acceptance speech for *The Exorcist*.

53. Winogura, Dale, p. 16.

54. Friedkin, William, *The Exorcist* Symposium.

55. Winogura, Dale, p. 16.

56. Friedkin, William, *The Exorcist* Symposium.

57. *Dialogue on Film*, p. 21.

58. Friedkin, William, *Sorcerer* Symposium, Director's Guild of America, 6 June 1978.

59. Blatty, William Peter, p. 282.

60. Ibid., p. 281.

61. *Dialogue on Film*, p. 27.

62. Ibid., p. 23.

63. Ibid., p. 24.

64. Ibid.

65. Blatty, William Peter, p. 275.

66. Ibid., p. 279.

67. Friedkin, William, *The Exorcist* Symposium.

68. Winogura, Dale, p. 17.

69. Canby, Vincent, "Why the Devil Do They Dig *The Exorcist?*" *New York Times*, Section II, 13 January 1974, p. 1.

70. Kael, Pauline, "Back to the Ouija Board," *New Yorker*, 7 January 1974, p. 59.

71. Friedkin, William, *The Exorcist* Symposium.

72. Winogura, Dale, p. 17.

73. Goldman, William, *Adventures in the Screen Trade*, Warner Books, Inc., New York, 1983, p. 39.

74. Bartholomew, David, pp. 10–11.

75. *Dialogue on Film*, p. 31.

76. Chase, Chris, p. D9.

77. Bartholomew, David, p. 11.

78. Friedkin, William, *The Exorcist* Symposium.

79. Geldzahler, Henry, *Francis Bacon Recent Paintings 1968–1974*, The Metropolitan Museum of Art, New York, 1975, p. 13.

80. Ibid., p. 6.

81. *Dialogue on Film*, p. 4.

82. Cocks, Jay, "Beat the Devil," *Time*, 14 January 1974, p. 38.

83. Woodward, Kenneth L., "The Exorcism Frenzy," *Newsweek*, 11 February 1974, p. 61.

84. Friedkin, William, *The French Connection* Symposium.

85. Geldzahler, Henry, p. 16.

Sorcerer

1. Champlin, Charles, "The Friedkin Connection," *Los Angeles Times*, View, 2 April 1976, p. 1.

2. Ellison, Bob, "On Top of the World," *Today's Filmmaker*, May 1973, Vol. 2, No. 2, p. 22.

3. Friedkin, William, *Sorcerer* Symposium, Director's Guild of America, 6 June 1978.

4. Champlin, Charles, p. 1.

5. Friedkin, William, Archives Interview for Director's Guild of America, 9 June 1982.

6. Friedkin, William, *Sorcerer* Symposium.

7. Wolf, William, "Surefooted Friedkin Riding Tide of Success," *Los Angeles Times*, Calendar, 15 October 1972, p. 76.

8. Friedkin, William, *Sorcerer* Symposium.

9. Ibid.

10. Schickel, Richard, "Where Did All the Magic Go?" *Time*, 11 June 1977, p. 55.

11. Corliss, Richard, "The New Hollywood: Dead or Alive?" *Time*, 30 March 1981, p. 68.

12. Friedkin, William, *Sorcerer* Symposium.

13. Ibid.

14. Ibid.

15. Ibid.

16. Ibid.

17. Ibid.

18. *Sorcerer,* Sound effects spotting sessions, courtesy of Charles Campbell.

19. Champlin, Charles, "Sitting on a Keg of Nitro," *Los Angeles Times*, View, 24 June 1977, p. 1.

20. Schickel, Richard, p. 55.

21. Friedkin, William, *Sorcerer* liner notes, soundtrack album, MCA Records, Inc., 1977.

22. Friedkin, William, *Sorcerer* Symposium.

23. Friedkin, William, *To Live and Die in L.A.* Symposium, The University of Southern California, 7 November 1985.

24. Friedkin, William, *Sorcerer* Symposium.

25. Applebaum, Ralph, "Tense Situations," *Films and Filming*, March 1979, Vol. 25, No. 6, Issue No. 294, p. 14.

26. Friedkin, William, *Sorcerer* Symposium.

27. Ibid.

28. Ibid.

29. Ibid.

30. Friedkin, William, *To Live and Die in L.A.* Symposium.

31. *Filmfacts,* edited by Ernest Parmentier; a publication of the Division of Cinema of the University of Southern California, Vol. XX, No. 13, 1977, p. 300.

32. Kroll, Jack, "No Exit," *Newsweek*, 4 July 1977, p. 77.

33. *Filmfacts*, p. 300.

34. Friedkin, William, Archives Interview for Director's Guild of America.

35. Friedkin, William, *Sorcerer* Symposium.

36. Friedkin, William, *The French Connection* Symposium.

37. Geldzahler, Henry, *Francis Bacon Recent Paintings 1968–1974*, The Metropolitan Museum of Art, New York, 1975, p. 15.

38. Champlin, Charles, "The Friedkin Connection," p. 1.

39. Ibid.

40. Kroll, Jack, p. 77.

41. Kael, Pauline, *Kiss Kiss Bang Bang,* New York, Bantam Books, 1969, p. 455.

The Brink's Job

1. Friedkin, William, *Sorcerer* Symposium, Director's Guild of America, 6 June 1978.

2. Friedkin, William, Archives Interview for Director's Guild of America, 9 June 1982.

3. Taylor, Clarke, "Filming with the Men Who Broke the Brink's," *Los Angeles Times*, Calendar, 4 June 1978, p. 51.

4. Applebaum, Ralph, "Tense Situations," *Films and Filming*, March 1979, Vol. 25, No. 6, Issue No. 294, p. 13.

5. Buckley, Tom, "Some Last-Minute Shifts in Friedkin's *Brink's* Caper," *New York Times*, 15 December 1978, p. C8.

6. Drew, Bernard, "Doing a Job on Brink's," *American Film*, November 1978, p. 46.

7. Ibid.

8. McMillan, Nancy Pomerene, "Brink's Is Robbed in Boston Again," *New York Times*, Section II, 2 July 1978, p. D12.

9. Drew, Bernard, p. 46.

10. Wilson, William, "Edward Hopper, Eternal Onlooker," *Los Angeles Times*, Calendar, 16 November 1980, p. 99.

11. Drew, Bernard, p. 43.

12. Taylor, Clarke, p. 51.

13. McMillan, Nancy Pomerene, p. D12.

14. Ibid., p. D11.

15. Steinburg, Cobbett, *Reel Facts*, Vintage Books, New York, February 1982, p. 50.

16. McMillan, Nancy Pomerene, p. D12.

17. Taylor, Clarke, p. 48.

18. McMillan, Nancy Pomerene, p. D12.

19. *Variety*, "De Laurentiis Tells NBC Payoffs Cost *Brink's Job* $1 Mil," 14 December 1978, pp. 1, 4.

20. *Los Angeles Times*, "Movie's Director Denies Report of Payoffs to Mob," 16 December 1978, p. 14.

21. Applebaum, Ralph, p. 16.

22. McMillan, Nancy Pomerene, p. D12.

23. Friedkin, William, Archives Interview for Director's Guild of America.

24. *Dialogue on Film*, William Friedkin Seminar, Vol. 3 & 4, February/March 1974, p. 29.

25. Buckley, Tom, p. C8.

26. Ibid.

27. Friedkin, William, Archives Interview for Director's Guild of America.

28. Taylor, Clarke, p. 48.

29. Canaday, John, "The Solo Voyage of Edward Hopper, American Realist," *Smithsonian*, September 1980, p. 130.

30. Rich, Frank, "Light Work," *Time*, 11 December 1978, p. 109.

31. Canby, Vincent, "Dream Caper," *New York Times*, 8 December 1978, p. C13.

Cruising

1. Kilday, Greg, "*Cruising* Pleads the First," *Los Angeles Herald Examiner*, 8 June 1980, p. B9.

2. Friedkin, William, *The French Connection* Symposium, The University of Southern California, 15 March 1982.

3. Pollock, Dale, "Friedkin Film 'Cruising' into a Storm of Protest," *Los Angeles Times*, 4 February 1980, p. 8.

4. Taylor, Clarke, "Friedkin Faces the N.Y. Press," *Los Angeles Times*, Part IV, 6 February 1980, p. 2.

5. Friedkin, William, *The French Connection* Symposium.

6. Breakstone, Linda, "Expected War Over *Cruising* Heats Up as Exhibitor Drops It," *Los Angeles Herald-Examiner*, 1 February 1980, p. A1.

7. Ibid.

8. Friedkin, William, Archives Interview for Director's Guild of America, 9 June 1982.

9. Ferretti, Fred, "Filming of *Cruising* Goes More Calmly," *New York Times*, 7 August 1979, p. C7.

10. Pollock, Dale, p. 8.

11. Friedkin, William, *The French Connection* Symposium.

12. Ibid.

13. Ginsberg, Steven, "Friedkin and Weintraub Defend *Cruising* Against MPAA's Rating Charges," *Variety*, 18 June 1980, p. 6.

14. Ibid.

15. Pollock, Dale, "R-Rated *Cruising:* The MPAA Seal of Disapproval," *Los Angeles Times*, Calendar, 4 May 1980, p. 7.

16. Ginsberg, Steven, p. 6.

17. Pollock, Dale, "R-Rated *Cruising:* The MPAA Seal of Disapproval," p. 7.

18. Ginsberg, Steven, p. 6.

19. Pollock, Dale, "R-Rated *Cruising:* The MPAA's Seal of Disapproval," p. 7.

20. Breakstone, Linda, p. A1.

21. Taylor, Clarke, p. 2.

22. Kilday, Greg, p. B9.

23. Taylor, Clarke, p. 2.

24. Ibid.

25. Pollock, Dale, "Friedkin Film 'Cruising' into a Storm of Protest," p. 1.

26. Taylor, Clarke, p. 2.

27. Kilday, Greg, p. B9.

28. Taylor, Clarke, p. 2.

29. Chase, Chris, "*The Exorcist:* Everyone's Reading It, Billy Friedkin's Filming It," *New York Times*, Section II, 27 August 1972, p. D9.

30. Pollock, Dale, "*Cruising:* Protests on the Picket Lines," *Los Angeles Times*, Calendar, 18 February 1980, p. 1.

31. Ibid.

32. Pollock, Dale, "*Cruising* Tails Off," *Los Angeles Times*, Calendar, 16 March 1980, p. 3.

33. Friedkin, William, Archives Interview for Director's Guild of America.

34. Pollock, Dale, "*Cruising* Tails Off," p. 3.

35. Ginsberg, Steven, p. 1.

36. Friedkin, William, Archives Interview for Director's Guild of America.

37. Steinberg, Cobbett, *Reel Facts*, Vintage Books, New York, February 1982, p. 113.

38. Rich, Frank, "Cop-Out in a Dark Demimonde," *Time*, 18 February 1980, p. 67.

39. Bell, Arthur, "Looking for Mr. Gaybar," *Village Voice*, 24 January 1977, pp. 19, 20.

40. Hilburn, Robert, "Jack Nitzche: Battling the *Cruising* Backlash," *Los Angeles Times*, Calendar, 27 April 1980, p. 7.

41. Ferretti, Fred, "Filming of *Cruising* Goes More Calmly," p. C7.

42. Pollock, Dale, "Friedkin Film 'Cruising' into a Storm of Protest," p. 8.

Deal of the Century

1. Rickey, Carrie, "Has Success Spoiled Paul Brickman?" *Wall Street Journal*, 4 January 1984, p. 20.

2. Friedkin, William, *To Live and Die in L.A.* Symposium, The University of Southern California, 7 November 1985.

3. Friedkin, William, *The French Connection* Symposium, 15 March 1982.

4. Rickey, Carrie, p. 20.

5. Ibid.

6. Harmetz, Aljean, "5 Films with Political Statements Due in Fall," *New York Times,* Arts and Entertainment, 10 September 1983, p. 11.

7. Caufield, Deborah, *"Deal of the Century* Parallels Events of 1982," *Los Angeles Times,* Calendar, 22 December 1982, pp. 1, 8.

8. Ibid., p. 8.

9. Canby, Vincent, "Arms Race Satire," *New York Times,* 4 November 1983, p. C13.

10. *Variety, Deal of the Century* review, 20 October 1983, p. 3.

11. Benson, Sheila, "Chase's *Deal* Misfires as a Comedy," *Los Angeles Times,* Part V, 5 November 1983, p. 4.

12. Salamon, Julie, "Quiet View of Nuclear Horror," *Wall Street Journal,* 3 November 1983, p. 20.

13. Rickey, Carrie, p. 20.

14. *Playboy,* Interview with Chevy Chase, June 1988, Vol. 35, No. 6, p. 56.

15. Friedkin, William, Archives Interview for Director's Guild of America, 9 June 1982.

16. Friedkin, William, *Rampage* Symposium, The University of Southern California, 19 November 1987.

To Live and Die in L.A.

1. Friedkin, William, *Rampage* Symposium, The University of Southern California, 19 November 1987.

2. *Take One,* "Sam Peckinpah Lets It All Hang Out," Vol. 2, No. 3, January–February 1969, p. 20.

3. Friedkin, William, *To Live and Die in L.A.* Symposium, The University of Southern California, 7 November 1985.

4. Ibid.

5. Ibid.

6. Mann, Roderick, "The Director Behind the Crime," *Los Angeles Times,* Calendar, 27 October 1985, p. 15.

7. Friedkin, William, *To Live and Die in L.A.* Symposium.

8. Ibid.

9. Taylor, Clarke, "DaFoe Is Good at Being Evil," *Los Angeles Times,* Part V, 30 November 1985, p. 6.

10. *Variety,* "William Friedkin Sues L.A. Times," 19 February 1986, p. 49.

11. Friedkin, William, *To Live and Die in L.A.* Symposium.

12. Ibid.

13. Ibid.

14. Ibid.

15. Mann, Roderick, p. 15.

16. Friedkin, William, *To Live and Die in L.A.* Symposium.

17. Ibid.

18. Byrge, Duane. *"To Live and Die in L.A.,"* review, *Hollywood Reporter,* 28 October 1985, p. 3.

19. Ibid.

20. Canby, Vincent, "How *Live and Die* Hooks Its Viewers," *New York Times,* Section II, 17 November 1985, pp. 17, 19.
21. Wilmington, Michael, *"Live and Die* Chasing *French Connection," Los Angeles Times,* Part VI, 1 November 1985, p. 4.
22. Friedkin, William, *To Live and Die in L.A.* Symposium.

Rampage

1. Friedkin, William, *Rampage* Symposium, The University of Southern California, 19 November 1987.
2. Mann, Roderick, "The Director Behind the Crime," *Los Angeles Times,* Calendar, 27 October 1985, p. 15.
3. Friedkin, William, *Rampage* Symposium.
4. *Weekly Variety, Rampage* review, 30 September 1987, p. 20.
5. *Dialogue on Film,* William Friedkin Seminar, Vol. 3 & 4, February/March 1974, p. 27.
6. Corwin, Norman, *Trivializing America,* Lyle Stuart, New Jersey, 1983, p. 97.
7. *Dialogue on Film,* p. 31.
8. Friedkin, William, *Rampage* Symposium.
9. Ibid.

The Guardian

1. Friedkin, William, *Rampage* Symposium, The University of Southern California, 19 November 1987.
2. Biodrowski, Steve, "The Guardian," *Cinefantastique,* Vol. 20, No. 4, March 1990, p. 7.
3. Friedkin, William, *The Guardian* Symposium, The Academy of Science Fiction, Fantasy and Horror screening at the University of Southern California, 22 April 1990.
4. O'Toole, Lawrence, "The Fright Stuff," *Entertainment Weekly,* No. 11, 27 April 1990, p. 50.
5. Weinstein, Steve, "The Exorcisms of William Friedkin," *Los Angeles Times,* Calendar, 19 November 1989, p. 107.
6. Friedkin, William, *The Guardian* Symposium.
7. Biodrowski, Steve, "The Story of How Director William Friedkin Got Out of His Tree," *Cinefantastique,* Vol. 20, No. 5, May 1990, p. 12.
8. Weinstein, Steve, p. 107.
9. Friedkin, William, *The Guardian* Symposium.
10. Ibid.
11. Biodrowski, Steve, "The Guardian," p. 6.
12. Friedkin, William, *The Guardian* Symposium.
13. Ibid.
14. Weinstein, Steve, p. 107.
15. Byrge, Duane, *The Guardian* review, *Hollywood Reporter,* 23 April 1990, p. 24.
16. Biodrowski, Steve, "The Guardian," p. 7.
17. Bril, *The Guardian* review, *Variety,* 23 April 1990, p. 2.
18. Rainer, Peter, *"Guardian:* Unintentionally a Real Scream," *Los Angeles Times,* 27 April 1990, p. F4.

19. Siskel, Gene, "Siskel & Ebert," Buena Vista Television, aired 29 April 1990.

20. Friedkin, William, *The Guardian* Symposium.

21. Ibid.

22. Ibid.

23. Ibid.

24. Friedkin, William, Archives Interview for Director's Guild of America, 9 June 1982.

Author's Interviews

Bedig, Barry (27 April 1982)
Blair, Linda (16 January 1982)
Blatty, William Peter (4 October 1981)
Bono, Sonny (18 August 1981)
Bush, Dick (12 June 1982)
Butler, Bill (7 July 1981, 15 August 1981)
Campbell, Charles (17 January 1982)
Combs, Frederick (10 March 1982)
Crowley, Mart (20 May 1981)
Daniels, Danny (12 January 1982)
D'Antoni, Philip (19 July 1982)
De Mora, Robert (20 April 1982)
Edemann, Louis (13 April 1989)
Ekhart, William and Jean (25 October 1981)
Fantozzi, Tony (11 March 1982)
Francis, Harry (26 September 1981)
Friedkin, William (4, 9, 11 September 1980)
Gardner, Gerald (18 September 1984)
Gavin, John (14 June 1982)
Gerrity, William C. (17 November 1981)
Glass, Robert (17 September 1981)
Green, Walon (9, 10 March 1982)
Grosso, Sonny (11 December 1981)
Harris, Burtt (8 June 1982)
Hunter, Paul (12 December 1981)
Johnson, Mark (13 July 1981)

Johnstone, Anna Hill (3 January 1982)
Jurgensen, Randy (2 December 1981, 7 May 1982, 2, 3 June 1982)
Kaplan, Fred (4 June 1982)
Knudsen, Buzz (1 September 1981)
Lazslo, Andrew (31 March 1982)
Parsons, Lindsley (31 March 1982)
Quinlan, Red (19 December 1981)
Rand, "Fat" Thomas (9 March 1982, 3 June 1982)
Roizman, Owen (17 August 1981)
Salven, David (14 March 1982)
Sherick, Edgar (30 January 1982)
Shultz, Gaylin (25 August 1981)
Smith, Bud (2 June 1981, 6 July 1981, 21 August 1981, 17 April 1989)
Sorvino, Paul (29 April 1982)
Tavoularis, Dean (10 October 1982)
Tidyman, Ernest (24 September 1981)
Vercoutere, Marcel (3 September 1981)
Weintraub, Bruce (22 April 1982)
Weintraub, Jerry (1 July 1981)
White, Peter (14 September 1981)
Wisdom, Norman (15 June 1982)
Wizan, Joe (13 November 1981)
Wolper, David (28 June 1982)
Yorkin, Bud (7 December 1981)

Bibliography

Ansen, David. "Hell Bent for Leather." *Newsweek,* 18 February 1980, p. 92.

Applebaum, Ralph. "Tense Situations." *Films and Filming,* March 1979, Vol. 25, No. 6, Issue No. 294, pp. 13, 14, 18, 19.

Bartholomew, David. "*The Exorcist:* The Book, the Movie, the Phenomenon." *Cinefantastique,* Winter 1974, Vol. 3, No. 4, pp. 9–13.

Bell, Arthur. "Looking for Mr. Gaybar." *Village Voice,* 24 January 1977, pp. 19, 20.

Benson, Sheila. "Chase's *Deal* Misfires as a Comedy." *Los Angeles Times,* Part V, 5 November 1983, p. 4.

Biodrowski, Steve. "The Guardian." *Cinefantastique,* Vol. 20, No. 4, March 1990, pp. 6, 7, 59.

————. "The Story of How Director William Friedkin Got Out of His Tree." *Cinefantastique,* Vol. 20, No. 5, May 1990, p. 12.

Blatty, William Peter. *William Peter Blatty on* The Exorcist *from Novel to Film.* New York, Bantam Books, June 1974, pp. 10, 11, 12, 24, 37–39, 273, 274, 275.

Breakstone, Linda. "Expected War Over *Cruising* Heats Up as Exhibitor Drops It." *Los Angeles Herald-Examiner,* 1 February 1980, p. A1.

Bril. *The Guardian* review. *Variety,* 23 April 1990, pp. 2, 23.

Buckley, Tom. "Some Last-Minute Shifts in Friedkin's *Brink's* Caper." *New York Times,* 15 December 1978, p. C8.

————. *The Guardian* review. *Hollywood Reporter,* 23 April 1990, pp. 3, 24.

Byrge, Duane. *To Live and Die in L.A.* review. *Hollywood Reporter,* 28 October 1985, pp. 3, 21.

Cameron, Sue. "Behind the Glitter of Oscar Night." *TV Guide,* 23 March 1985, Vol. 33, No. 12, p. 8.

Canaday, John. "The Solo Voyage of Edward Hopper, American Realist." *Smithsonian,* September 1980, pp. 126–33.

Canby, Vincent. "Arms Race Satire." *New York Times,* 4 November 1983, p. C13.

————. "How *Live and Die* Hooks Its Viewers." *New York Times,* Section II, 17 November 1985, pp. 17, 19.

————. "Why the Devil Do They Dig *The Exorcist?*" *New York Times,* Section II, 13 January 1974, p. 1.

Caufield, Deborah. "*Deal of the Century* Parallels Events of 1982." *Los Angeles Times,* Calendar, 22 December 1982, pp. 1, 8.

Champlin, Charles. "The Friedkin Connection." *Los Angeles Times* View, 2 April 1976, p. 1.

————. "Motion Picture Review: *The Boys in the Band.*" *Los Angeles Times* View, 29 March 1970, pp. 1, 4.

————. "Sitting on a Keg of Nitro." *Los Angeles Times* View, 24 June 1977, p. 1.

Chase, Chris. "*The Exorcist:* Everyone's Reading It, Billy Friedkin's Filming It." *New York Times,* Section II, 27 August 1972, p. D9.

Cocks, Jay. "Beat the Devil." *Time,* 14 January 1974, pp. 38, 39.

Corliss, Richard. "The New Hollywood: Dead or Alive?" *Time,* 30 March 1981, p. 68.

Corwin, Norman. *Trivializing America.* Lyle Stuart Inc., New Jersey, 1983, p. 97.

Daniell, Tina. *Deal of the Century* review. *Hollywood Reporter,* 24 October 1983, p. 3.

Dialogue on Film. William Friedkin Seminar. Vol. 3 & 4, February/March 1974, pp. 3, 5, 7, 9–13, 16–21, 23, 24, 26–31, 33–35.

Drew, Bernard. "Doing a Job on Brink's." *American Film,* November 1978, pp. 43, 44, 46.

Ellison, Bob. "On Top of the World." *Today's Filmmaker,* May 1973, Vol. 2, No. 2, pp. 21–23, 49–54.

Ferretti, Fred. "Filming of *Cruising* Goes More Calmly." *New York Times,* 7 August 1979, p. C7.

Filmfacts. Edited by Ernest Parmentier. A publication of the Division of Cinema of the University of Southern California, Vol. XX, No. 13, 1977, pp. 298–301.

Friedkin, William. Acceptance Speech for *The Exorcist.* The Academy of Science Fiction, Fantasy and Horror Awards Ceremony at the University of Southern California, 11 June 1981.

————. Archives Interview for Director's Guild of America, 9 June 1982.

————. *The Exorcist* symposium with William Peter Blatty. Sherwood Oaks Experimental College, Hollywood, California, 24 September 1980.

————. *The French Connection* symposium. The University of Southern California, 15 March 1982.

————. *Good Times* liner notes, soundtrack album. Atco Records, a Division of Atlantic Recording Corp, 1967.

————. *The Guardian* symposium. The Academy of Science Fiction, Fantasy and Horror screening at the University of Southern California, 22 April 1990.

————. *Rampage* symposium. The University of Southern California, 19 November 1987.

————. *Sorcerer* liner notes, soundtrack album. MCA Records, Inc., 1977.

————. *Sorcerer* symposium. Director's Guild of America, 6 June 1978.

————. *To Live and Die in L.A.* symposium. The University of Southern California, 7 November 1985.

Geldzahler, Henry. *Francis Bacon Recent Paintings 1968–1974.* The Metropolitan Museum of Art, New York, 1975, pp. 6–8, 12–16.

Ginsberg, Steven. "Friedkin and Weintraub Defend *Cruising* Against MPAA's Rating Charges." *Variety,* 18 June 1980, pp. 1, 6.

Goldman, William. *Adventures in the Screen Trade.* Warner Books, Inc., New York, 1983, p. 39.

Haber, Joyce. "The Midas Touch of William Friedkin." *Los Angeles Times,* Calendar, 24 October 1974, pp. 19, 75.

Harmetz, Aljean. "5 Films with Political Statements Due in Fall." *New York Times,* Arts and Entertainment, 10 September 1983, p. 11.

Hilburn, Robert. "Jack Nitzche: Battling the *Cruising* Backlash." *Los Angeles Times,* Calendar, 27 April 1980, p. 7.

Kael, Pauline. "Back to the Ouija Board." *New Yorker,* 7 January 1974, pp. 59–62.

————. *Boys in the Band* review. *New Yorker,* 21 March 1970, pp. 166–67.

————. *Kiss Kiss Bang Bang.* New York, Bantam Books, 1969, p. 455.

Kauffmann, Stanley. *The Birthday Party* review. *New Republic,* 4 January 1969.

————. *Deal of the Century* review. *New Republic,* 28 October 1983.

————. *The Night They Raided Minsky's* review. *New Republic,* 18 January 1969.

Kilday, Greg. "*Cruising* Pleads the First." *Los Angeles Herald-Examiner,* 8 June 1980, pp. B1, B9.

Kroll, Jack. "No Exit." *Newsweek,* 4 July 1977, p. 77.

Los Angeles Times. "Movie's Director Denies Report of Payoffs to Mob." 16 December 1978, p. 14.

McCarthy, John, and Brian Kelleher. *"Alfred Hitchcock Presents:" An Illustrated Guide to the Ten Year Television Career of the Master of Suspense.* St. Martin's Press, New York, 1985, pp. 314–15.

McMillan, Nancy Pomerene. "Brink's Is Robbed in Boston Again." *New York Times,* Section II, 2 July 1978, pp. D11, 12.

Mahoney, John. *The Birthday Party* review. *Hollywood Reporter,* 17 December 1968, pp. 3, 28.

————. *Good Times* review. *Hollywood Reporter,* 13 April 1967, p. 3.

Mann, Roderick. "The Director Behind the Crime." *Los Angeles Times,* Calendar, 27 October 1985, p. 15.

O'Toole, Lawrence. "The Fright Stuff." *Entertainment Weekly,* No. 11, 27 April 1990, pp. 48–51.

Playboy. The Birthday Party review. February 1969, Vol. 16, No. 2, pp. 28, 30.

————. Interview with Chevy Chase. June 1988, Vol. 35, No. 6, p. 56.

————. Interview with Orson Welles. March 1967, Vol. 14, No. 3, p. 60.

————. Interview with Roy Scheider. September 1980, Vol. 27, No. 9, pp. 74, 77, 79, 84.

————. *The Night They Raided Minsky's* review. March 1969, Vol. 16, No. 3, p. 28.

Pollock, Dale. *"Cruising:* Protests on the Picket Lines." *Los Angeles Times,* Calendar, 18 February 1980, p. 1.

————. *"Cruising* Tails Off." *Los Angeles Times* Calendar, 16 March 1980, p. 3.

————. "Friedkin Film 'Cruising' into a Storm of Protest." *Los Angeles Times,* 4 February 1980, pp. 1, 8.

————. "R-Rated *Cruising:* The MPAA Seal of Disapproval." *Los Angeles Times,* Calendar, 4 May 1980, p. 7.

Rainer, Peter. *"Guardian:* Unintentionally a Real Scream." *Los Angeles Times,* 27 April 1990, p. F4.

Reed, Rex. "Filming *The Exorcist*—It Was Hell." *Los Angeles Times,* Calendar, 24 March 1974, p. 19.

Rich, Frank. "Cop-Out in a Dark Demimonde." *Time,* 18 February 1980, p. 67.

————. "Light Work." *Time,* 11 December 1978, p. 109.

Rickey, Carrie. "Has Success Spoiled Paul Brickman?" *Wall Street Journal,* 4 January 1984, p. 20.

Rosenblum, Ralph and Robert Karen. *When the Shooting Stops ... the Cutting Begins.* The Viking Press, New York, 1979, pp. 12, 13, 14, 25, 27, 29, 30.

Salamon, Julie. "Quiet View of Nuclear Horror." *Wall Street Journal,* 3 November 1983, p. 20.

Schickel, Richard. "A Real Look at a Tough Cop." *Life,* 19 November 1971, p. 13.

————. "Where Did All the Magic Go?" *Time,* 11 June 1977, p. 55.

Siskel, Gene. "Siskel & Ebert." Buena Vista Television, aired 29 April 1990.

Sorcerer. Sound effects spotting sessions. Courtesy of Charles Campbell.

Steinberg, Cobbett. *Reel Facts.* Vintage Books, New York, 1982, February, 1982, p. 50.

Take One. "Sam Peckinpah Lets It All Hang Out." Vol. 2, No. 3, January–February 1969, p. 20.

Taylor, Clarke. "DaFoe Is Good at Being Evil." *Los Angeles Times,* Part V, 30 November 1985, pp. 1, 6.

————. "Filming with the Men Who Broke the Brink's." *Los Angeles Times,* Calendar, 4 June 1978, pp. 1, 48, 50, 51, 53.

————. "Friedkin Faces the N.Y. Press." *Los Angeles Times,* Part IV, 6 February 1980, p. 2.

Thomas, Kevin. *"Minsky's* Due Wednesday." *Los Angeles Times,* Calendar, 15 December 1968, p. 1.

Time. "Shades of Lavender." 30 March 1970, p. 97.

Tusher, Will. "Friedkin Says *Connection* Calculated to Make a Killing." *Hollywood Reporter,* 24 March 1972, pp. 12, 27.

Variety. The Birthday Party review. 17 February 1970, pp. 3, 6.

————. *The Boys in the Band* review. 16 March 1970, pp. 3, 28.

————. *Deal of the Century* review. 20 October 1983, p. 3.

————. "De Laurentiis Tells NBC Payoffs Cost *Brink's Job* $1 Mil." 14 December 1978, pp. 1, 4.

————. "William Friedkin Sues *L.A. Times.*" 19 February 1986, p. 49.

Weekly Variety. Rampage review. 30 September 1987, p. 20.

Weiler, A. H. "Murderers 'Beyond Belief.'" *New York Times,* Section II, 15 December 1968, p. 25.

Weinstein, Steve. "The Exorcisms of William Friedkin." *Los Angeles Times* Calendar, 19 November 1989, pp. 8, 107.

Wilmington, Michael. *"Live and Die* Chasing *French Connection." Los Angeles Times,* Part VI, 1 November 1985, p. 4.

Wilson, William. "Edward Hopper, Eternal Onlooker." *Los Angeles Times* Calendar, 16 November 1980, p. 99.

————. "Francis Bacon's Vision of Isolation." *Los Angeles Times* Calendar, 27 October 1985, p. 3.

Winogura, Dale. Interview with William Friedkin. *Cinefantastique,* Winter 1974, Vol. 3, No. 4, pp. 14–17.

Wolf, William. "Surefooted Friedkin Riding Tide of Success." *Los Angeles Times* Calendar, 15 October 1972, pp. 1, 76, 79.

Woodward, Kenneth L. "The Exorcism Frenzy." *Newsweek,* 11 February 1974, p. 61.

Filmography

The People Versus Paul Crump
1962. Black and white. 16mm. Print not available.

The Bold Men
The Thin Blue Line
Pro Football: Mayhem on a Sunday Afternoon
Wolper Productions. 1965. Black and white. 16mm. Prints not available.

The Alfred Hitchcock Hour
"Off Season." Universal Productions, 1965. Black and white. Print not available.

Good Times
A Steve Broidy Production for Columbia Pictures, 1967. Color. Running time: 91 minutes.
    Credits: *Director* William Friedkin, *Producer* Lindsley Parsons, *Executive Producer* Steve Broidy, *Screenplay* Tony Barrett, *Story* Nicholas Hyams, *Cinematography* Robert Wyckoff, *Production Manager* Arthur Broidy, *Editor* Melvin Shapiro, *Special Consultant on Musical Sequences* Wilmer Butler, *Art Direction* Hal Pereira, Arthur Lonergan, *Set Decoration* Arthur Krams, *Assistant Editor* Richard Wahrman, *Sound Effects* Delmore Harris, Carl Lodato, *Costumes* Leah Rhodes, *Makeup* Edwin Butterworth, S.M.A., *Hair Stylist* Hedwig Mjorud, *Sound Recording* Harold Lewis, *Wardrobe* Forrest T. Butler, *Assistant Director* David Salven, *Script Supervision* Marvin Weldon, *Choreography* Andre Tayir, *Process Photography* Farciot Edouart, A.S.C., *Music* Sonny Bono, *Arranged by* Harold R. Battiste, Jr. Jungle sequences photographed at AFRICA, U.S.A., Inc.
    Cast: *Sonny and Cher* Themselves, *Mordicus* George Sanders, *Warren* Norman Alden, *Smith* Larry Duran, *Tough Hombre* Kelly Thordsen, *Garth* Lenny Weinrib, *Brandon* Peter Robbins, *Mordicus' Girls* Edy Williams, China Lee, Diane Haggerty, *Lieutenant* James Flavin, *Solly* Phil Arnold, *Kid* Hank Worden, *Proprietor* Morris Buchanan, *Telegrapher* Charles Smith, *Gangster* John Cliff, *Wrestlers* Herk Reardon, Bruce Tegner, *Peddler* Richard Collier, *Old Timer* Howard Wright, *Bartender* Joe Devlin, *Deputy* Mike Kopach.

The Night They Raided Minsky's
A Tandem Production for United Artists, 1968. Color. Running time: 100 minutes.
    Credits: *Director* William Friedkin, *Producer* Norman Lear, *Screenplay* Arnold

Schulman, Sidney Michaels, Norman Lear (based on the book by Rowland Barber), *Cinematography* Andrew Laszlo, *Production Design* William, Jean Eckart, *Art Direction* John Robert Lloyd, *Set Decoration* John Godfrey, *Visual Consultant/2nd Unit Director* Pablo Ferro, *Dances, Musical Numbers, Sketches Staged by* Danny Daniels, *Costumes* Anna Hill Johnstone, *Music* Charles Strause, *Lyrics* Lee Adams, *Editor* Ralph Rosenblum, *Assistant Director* Burtt Harris, *Set Decorator* John Godfrey, *Set Dress* Richard Adee, *Second Assistant Director* J. Alan Hopkins, *Camera Operator* Richard Kratina, *Production Mixer* Dennis L. Maitland, *Script Supervisor* Marguerite James Powell, *Assistant to Producer,* William Giorgio, *Sound Editor* Jack Fitzstephans, *Dances Arranger* Richard De Benedictis, *Assistant Choreographer* Anne Wallace, *Re-recording Mixer* Richard Vorisek, *Assistant Editor* Michael Breddan, *Assistant Cameraman* Vincent Gerardo, *Still Photographer* Josh Weiner, *Property Master* Donald Holtzman, *Gaffer* William Meyerhoff, *Technical Advisor* Morton Minsky, *Key Grip* Michael Mahony, *Set Construction* Edward Swanson, Walter Way, *Chief Scenic Artists* Edward Garzero, *Wardrobe* George Newman, Florence Transfield, *Makeup* Irving Buchman, *Hairdresser* Robert Grimaldi, *Casting* Marion Dougherty, *Extra Casting* Bernie Styles, *Production Secretary* Shirley Marcus, *Costumes* Eaves, *Opticals* The Optical House, N.Y.C.

Cast: *Raymond Paine* Jason Robards, *Rachel Schpitendavel* Britt Ekland, *Chick Williams* Norman Wisdom, *Trim Houlihan* Forrest Tucker, *Jacob Schpitendavel* Harry Andrews, *Louis Minsky* Joseph Wiseman, *Vance Fowler* Denholm Elliot, *Billy Minsky* Elliot Gould, *Candy Butcher* Jack Burns, *Professor Spats* Bert Lahr, *Mae Harris* Gloria LeRoy, *Scratch* Eddie Lawrence, *Duffy* Dexter Maitland, *Singer in Speakeasy* Lillian Hayman, *Pockets* Dick Libertini, *Mother Anne* Judith Lowery, *Clyde* Will B. Able, *Immigration Officer #1* Mike Elias, *Immigration Officer #2* Frank Shaw, *Valerie* Chanin Hale, *The Minsky Girls* Ernestine Barrett, Kelsey Collins, Marilyn D'Monau, Kathryn Doby, JoAnn Lehmann, Dorothea MacFarland, Billie Mahoney, Carolyn Morris, June Eve Story, Helen Wood, *Opening Narration* Rudy Vallee.

The Birthday Party

An Edgar J. Sherick Production for Palomar Pictures, U.K., 1968. Color. Running time: 124 minutes.

Credits: *Director* William Friedkin, *Producers* Max Rosenberg, Milton Subotsky, *Executive Producer* Edgar J. Sherick, *Screenplay* Harold Pinter (based on his play), *Cinematography* Denys Coop, *Production Design* Edward Marshall, *Sound* Norman Bolland, *Editor* Anthony Gibbs, *Assistant Director* Andrew Grieve.

Cast: *Stanley* Robert Shaw, *McCann* Patrick McGee, *Meg* Dandy Nichols, *Goldberg* Sydney Tafler, *Petey* Moultrie Kelsall, *Lulu* Helen Frazer.

The Boys in the Band

A Leo Productions, Ltd. Production, a Cinema Center Films for National General Pictures, 1970. Running time: 117 minutes.

Credits: *Director* William Friedkin, *Producer* Mart Crowley, *Screenplay* Mart Crowley (from his off–Broadway play), *Executive Producers* Dominick Dunne, Robert Jiras, *Cinematographer* Arthur J. Ornitz, *Sound* Jack Jacobsen, *Supervision Editor* Carl Lerner, *Editor* Jerry Greenberg, *Production Designer* John Robert Lloyd, *Set Decorator* Phil Smith, *Associate Producer* Ken Utt, *Production Manager* Paul Ganapoler, *Assistant Director* William C. Gerrity, *Property Master* Joe Caracciolo,

Hairdressing Verne Caruso, *Wardrobe* Joe Dehn, *Costume Designer* Robert LaVine, *Script Supervisor* Nancy Norman.

Cast: *Michael* Kenneth Nelson, *Harold* Leonard Frey, *Emory* Cliff Gorman, *Bernard* Reuben Greene, *Cowboy* Robert La Tourneaux, *Hank* Laurence Luckinbill, *Donald* Frederick Combs, *Larry* Keith Prentice, *Alan* Peter White.

The French Connection

A Philip D'Antoni Production in association with Schine-Moore Productions for Twentieth Century–Fox, 1971. Running time: 104 minutes.

Credits: *Director* William Friedkin, *Producer* Philip D'Antoni, *Screenplay* Ernest Tidyman (based on the book by Robin Moore), *Music* Don Ellis, *Cinematography* Owen Roizman, *Art Direction* Ben Kazaskow, *Set Director* Ed Garzero, *Editor* Jerry Greenberg, *Assistant Directors* William C. Gerrity, Terry Donnelly, *Sound* Chris Newman, Theodore Soderberg *Technical Consultants* Eddie Egan, Sonny Grosso, *Chief Electrician* Billy Ward, *Associate Editor* Norman Gay, *Unit Production Manager* Paul Ganapozer, *Special Effects* Sass Bedig, *Key Grip* Robert Ward, *Stunt Coordinator* Bill Hickman, *Property Master* Tom Wright, *Location Consultant* Fat Thomas, *Makeup Artist* Irving Muchman, *Wardrobe* Joseph W. Dean, Florence Foy, *Costumes* Joseph Fretwell III, *Casting* Robert Weiner.

Cast: *Jimmy Doyle* Gene Hackman, *Alan Charnier* Fernando Rey, *Buddy Russo* Roy Scheider, *Sal Boca* Tony Lo Bianco, *Pierre Nicoli* Marcel Bozzuffi, *Devereaux* Frederick de Pasquale, *Mulderig* Bill Hickman, *Marie Charnier* Anne Rebbot, *Weinstock* Harold Gary, *Angie Boca* Arlene Farber, *Simonson* Eddie Egan, *La Valle* Andre Erotte, *Klein* Sonny Grosso, *Lou Boca* Benny Marino, *Chemist* Pat McDermott, *Pusher* Alan Weeks, *Informant* Al Fann, *Police Mechanic* Irving Abrahams, *Police Sergeant* Randy Jurgensen, *Motorman* William Coke, *The Three Degrees* The Three Degrees.

The Exorcist

A Hoya Production for Warner Bros., 1973. Color. Running time: 120 minutes.

Credits: *Director* William Friedkin, *Producer* William Peter Blatty, *Screenplay* William Peter Blatty (based on his novel), *Executive Producer* Noel Marshall, *Associate Producer* David Salven, *Cinematography* Owen Roizman, *Makeup Artist* Dick Smith, *Special Effects* Marcel Vercoutere, *Production Design* Bill Malley, *First Assistant Director* Terrence A. Donnelly, *Set Decorator* Jerry Wunderlich.

Music: Krzysztof Penderecki. "Kanon for Orchestra and Tape, Cello Concerto," Courtesy of Angel Records; "String Quartet" (1960), Courtesy of Candid/Vox Productions, Inc.; "Polymorphia" (Orchestra of the Cracow Philarmonia, Henryk Czyz, Conductor), Courtesy of Philips Records; "The Devils of Loudon" (Hamburg State Opera, Marek Janowski, Conductor), Courtesy of Philips Records; Hans Werner Henze, "Fantasia for Strings," Courtesy of Deutsche Grammophon; George Crumb "(Tutti) Threnody 1: Night of the Electric Insects," Courtesy of Composers Recordings, Inc.; Anton Webern, "Fliessend, Ausserts Zart from Five Pieces for Orchestra, Op. 10," Courtesy of Angel Records; "BEGINNINGS, From the Wind Harp," Courtesy of United Artists Records; Mike Oldfield, "Tubular Bells," Courtesy of Virgin Records; David Borden, "Study No. 1/Study No. 2"; Additional Music Composed by Jack Nitzsche.

Iraq Sequence: *Cinematography* Billy Williams, *Production Manager* William Kaplan, *Sound* Jean-Louis Ducarme, *Editor* Bud Smith, *Assistant Editor* Ross Levy,

Supervising Editor Jordan Leondopoulos, *Editors* Evan Lottman, Norman Gay, *Assistant Editors* Michael Goldman, Craig McKay, Jonathan Pontell, *Sound* Chris Newman, *Dubbing Mixer* Buzz Knudson, *Sound Effects Editors* Fred Brown, Ross Taylor, *Special Sound Effects* Ron Nagle, Doc Siegel, Gonzalo Gavira, Bob Fine, *Sound Consultant* Hal Landaker, *Music Editor* Gene Marks, *Gaffer* Dick Quinlan, *Key Grip* Eddie Quinn, *Property Master* Joe Caracciolo, *Script Supervisor* Nick Sgarro, *Costume Designer* Joe Fretwell, *Hair Stylist* Bill Farley, *Administrative Assistant* Albert Shapiro, *Casting* Nessa Hyams, Juliet Taylor, Louis DiGiamo, *Still Photographer* Josh Weiner, *Second Assistant Director* Alan Green, *Ladies' Wardrobe* Florence Foy, *Men's Wardrobe* Bill Beattie, *Production Office Coordinator* Anne Mooney, *Master Scenic Artist* Eddie Garzero, *Technical Advisers* Rev. John Nicola, S.J., Rev. Thomas Bermingham, S.J., Rev. William O'Malley, S.J., Norman E. Chase, M.D.; Professor of Radiology, New York University Medical Center, Herbert E. Walker, M.D., Arthur I. Snyder, M.D., *Optical Effects* Marv Ystrom, *Title Design* Dan Perri, *Color* Metrocolor, *Color Consultant* Robert M. McMillan, *Photographic Equipment* Panavision, *Jewelry Design* Aldo Cipullo for Cartier, New York, *Furs* Revillon.

Cast: *Chris MacNeil* Ellen Burstyn, *Father Merrin* Max von Sydow, *Lieutenant Kinderman* Lee J. Cobb, *Sharon* Kitty Winn, *Burke Dennings* Jack MacGowran, *Father Karras* Jason Miller, *Regan* Linda Blair, *Father Dyer* Rev. William O'Malley, S.J., *Karras' Mother* Vasiliki Maliaros, *Karras' Uncle* Titos Vandis; Barton Heyman, Pete Masterson, Rudolf Schundler, Gina Petrushka, Robert Symonds, Arthur Storch, Rev. Thomas Bermingham, S.J., Wallace Rooney, Ron Faber, Donna Mitchell, Roy Cooper, Robert Gerringer, Mercedes MacCambridge.

Sorcerer

A William Friedkin Production for Film Properties International. A Paramount/ Universal Picture, 1977. Color. Running time: 121 minutes.

Credits: *Director and Producer* William Friedkin, *Screenplay* Walon Green (based on the novel *The Wages of Fear* by Georges Arnaud), *Editor and Associate Producer* Bud Smith, *Cinematography* John M. Stephens, Dick Bush, B.S.C., *Production Designer* John Box, *Sound* Jean-Louis Ducarme, *Music Composed and Performed by* Tangerine Dream, *Art Director* Roy Walker, *Draftsman* Lesley W. Tomkins, *First Assistant Director* Newton Arnold, *Second Assistant Directors* Miguel Gil, Mark Johnson, Albert Shapiro, *Production Manager* Roberto Bakker, *Unit Manager* Gerard E. Murphy, *Production Secretary* Nanette Siegert, *Dubbing Mixer* Buzz Knudsen, *Re-recording* Bob Glass, Dick Tyler, *Key Grip* Gaylin Schultz, *Grips* Bernie Schwartz, George Resler, Bill Kenney, Jim Sheppherd, *Stunt Coordinator* Bud Ekins, *Lighting Gaffer* Patrick R. Blymyer, *Best Boy* Mike Weathers, *Costume Designer* Anthony Powell, *Property Master* Barry Bedig, *Casting Director* Louis DiGiamo, *Construction* Ken Pattenden, Doug Millet, *Technical Advisor* Marvin Peck, *Editor/Music Editor* Robert K. Lambert, A.C.E., *Sound Effects Editor* Charles L. Campbell, *Assistant Editors* Ned Humphreys, Jere Huggins, *Makeup* Ben Nye, Jr., Bob Norin, John Norin, *Assistant Property Manager* Gene Anderson, *Hairdresser* Verne Caruso, *Script Supervisor* John Franco, *Transportation Coordinator* Whitey Ellison, *Helicopter Pilot* Richard B. Holley, *Production Accountant* Charles A. Ogle, *Assistant Production Accountant* Paul Roedl, *Assistant to the Producer* Luis Llosa, *Secretary to the Director* Toni St. Clair Lilly, *Titles* Jean Guy Jacques, *Special Sound* Ron Nagle, Scott Mathews.

Charlie Parker, "I'll Remember April," Courtesy Verve Records. Keith Jarrett, "Hymns/Spheres," Courtesy Polydor Records. Miles Davis, "So What," Courtesy Columbia Records.

Cast: *Scanlon/"Dominguez"* Roy Scheider, *Victor Manzon/"Serrano"* Bruno Cremer, *Nilo* Francisco Rabal, *Kassem/"Martinez"* Amidou, *Corlette* Ramon Bieri, *Latigue* Peter Capell, *"Marquez"* Karl John, *"Carlos"* Frederick Ledebur, *Bobby Del Rios* Chico Martinez, *Spider* Joe Spinell, *Agrippa* Rosario Almontes, *Billy White* Richard Holley, *Blanche* Anne Marie Descott, *Pascal* Jean-Luc Bideau, *Lefevre* Jacques Francois, *Guillot* Andre Falcon, *Donnelly* Gerard E. Murphy, *Boyle* Desmond Crofton, *Murray* Henry Diamond, *Ben* Ray Dittrich, *Marty* Frank Gio, *Vinnie* Randy Jurgensen, *Carlo Ricci* Gus Allegretti, *Father Ricci* Nick Discenza.

The Brink's Job

A Dino De Laurentiis Production for Universal Pictures, 1978. Color. Running time: 103 minutes.
  Credits: *Director* William Friedkin, *Producer* Ralph Serpe, *Screenplay* Walon Green (based on the book *Big Stick-Up at Brink's* by Noel Behn), *Cinematography* A. Norman Leigh, *Production Design* Dean Tavoularis, *Editors* Bud Smith, Robert K. Lambert, *Production Manager* Jonathan Sanger, *First Assistant Director* Terence A. Donnelly, *Second Assistant Director* Mark Johnson, *Music* Richard Rodney Bennett, *Conducted by* Angela Morley, *Casting Director* Louis DiGiamo, *Sound Recordists* Buzz Knudson, Bob Glass, Don MacDougall, *Dubbing Supervisor* Charles L. Campbell, *Supervising Sound Editors* Gordon Ecker, Jr., M.P.S.E., Lou Edemann, *Costume Designer* Ruth Morley, *Set Decorators* George R. Nelson, Bruce Kay, *Art Director* Angelo Graham, *Cameraman* Enrique Bravo, *Assistant Cameramen* Hank Muller, Jr., Garry Muller, Michael Green, *Additional Photography* James Contner, *Sound* Jeff Wexler, *Music Editor* Richard Luckey, *Assistant Editors* Ned Humphreys, Jere Huggins, Scott Smith, *Makeup* Bob Norin, *Assistant Costumer Designer* Gloria Gresham, *Hair Stylist* Verne Caruso, *Property Master* Barry Bedig, *Second Property Master* Gene Anderson, *Rigger-Gaffer* Lou Tobin, *Key Grip* Gaylin Schultz, *Special Effects* Larry Cavanaugh, *Construction Coordinator* John Casacandra, *Construction Foreman* Bob Scaife, *Costumer* Tony Scarano, *Production Services* Sonny Grosso, Randy Jurgensen, *Transportation Coordinator* William C. Bratton, *Location Manager* Carmine Foresta, *Electric Department Supervisor* John DeBlau, *Painter* Roger Deitz, *Boom Man* Don Coufal, *Script Supervisor* Catalina Lawrence, *Production Office Coordinator* Nanette Siegert, *Secretary to the Director* Toni St. Clair Lilly, *Negative Cutting* Donah Bassett, *Stills* Josh Weiner, *Color Timer* Larry Rovetti.
  "Accentuate the Positive" sung by Bing Crosby and the Andrews Sisters, Courtesy of MCA Records, Inc.
  With special thanks to Brink's Incorporated for its cooperation. Since 1859, nobody has ever lost a penny entrusting their valuables to Brink's.
  Cast: *Tony Pino* Peter Falk, *Joe McGinnis* Peter Boyle, *Vinnie Costa* Allen Goorwitz, *Specs O'Keefe* Warren Oates, *Mary Pino* Gena Rowlands, *Jazz Maffie* Paul Sorvino, *J. Edgar Hoover* Sheldon Leonard, *Sandy Richardson* Gerard Murphy, *Stanley Gusciora* Kevin O'Connor, *Gladys* Claudia Peluso, *H. H. Rightmire* Patrick Hines, *Mutt Murphy* Malachy McCourt, *Daniels* Walter Klavun, *F.B.I. Agents* Randy Jurgensen, John Brandon, Earl Hindman, John Farrel.

Cruising

A Lorimar GmbH Production for United Artists, 1980. Color. Running time: 106 minutes.
  Credits: *Director and Screenplay* William Friedkin, *Producer* Jerry Weintraub

(based upon the novel by Gerald Walker), *Cinematography* James Contner, *Production Designer* Bruce Weintraub, *Art Director* Edward Pisoni, *Costume Designer* Robert deMora, *Editor* Bud Smith, *Music* Jack Nitzsche, *Performed by* The Cripples, Willy DeVille, Germs—G.I., John Hiatt (Courtesy MCA Records), Mutiny (Courtesy MCA Records), Rough Trade, Madelyn Von Ritz, Egberto Gismonti; "Three Day Moon" performed by Barre Phillips, "Herbal Scent" performed by Tom Brown (Courtesy Arista Records), *Production Executive* Mark Johnson, *Associate Producer/ Production Manager* Burtt Harris, *First Assistant Director* Alan Hopkins, *Second Assistant Director* Robert Warren, *Camera Operator* Enrique Bravo, *Assistant Cameramen* Hank Muller, Jr., Gary Muller, *Property Masters* Barry Bedig, James Raitt, *Assistant Property Master* Gene Anderson, *Gaffer* Gene Engels, *Key Grip* William Miller, *Technical Advisors* Randy Jurgensen, Sonny Grosso, *Sound Recording* Robert Knudson, Robert Glass, Christopher Jenkins, *Makeup Artist* Allan Weisinger, *Special Makeup Effects* Robert Norin, *Supervising Sound Editor* Charles L. Campbell, *Sound Editors* Louis L. Edemann, David A. Pettijohn, Paul Bruce Richardson, *Assistant Sound Editor* Rick Franklin, *Dialogue Editor* Norman Schwartz, *Set Decorator* Robert Drumheller, *Casting Director* Louis DiGiamo, *Assistant Editors* Ned Humphreys, Jere Huggins, *Music Engineer* Bill Evans, *Hair Stylist* Robert Grimaldi, *Location Manager* Carmine Foresta, *Wardrobe Supervisors* Michael Dennison, Dean Jackson, *Script Supervisor* Sidney Gecker, *Production Office Coordinator* Jennifer Ogden, *Still Photographer* Josh Weiner, *Auditor* Lucille Weiner, *Teamster Captain* Edward Iacobelli, *Production Assistant* Michael Weintraub, *Secretary to the Producer* George Davis, *Secretary to the Director* Toni St. Clair Lilly, *Sound Mixer* Kim Ornitz, *ADR Mixer* Athan Gigiakos/The Sound Shop, New York City, *Color Timer* Larry Rovetti, *Negative Cutter* Donah Bassett, *Construction Coordinator* Carlos Quiles, Jr., *Scenic Artists* Bruno Robotti, Stanley Graham.

   Cast: *Steve Burns* Al Pacino, *Capt. Edelson* Paul Sorvino, *Nancy* Karen Allen, *Stuart Richards* Richard Cox, *Ted Bailey* Don Scardino, *Patrolman DiSimone* Joe Spinell, *Skip Lee* Jay Acovone, *Det. Lefransky* Randy Jurgensen, *Dr. Rifkin* Barton Heyman, *DaVinci* Gene Davis, *Loren Lukas* Arnaldo Santana, *Eric Rossman* Larry Atlas, *Chief of Detectives* Alan Miller, *Det. Blasio* Sonny Grosso, *Det. Schreiber* Edward O'Neil, *Det. Davis* Michael Aronin, *Gregory* James Remar, *Paul Gaines* William Russ, *Patrolman Desher* Mike Starr, *Martino* Steve Inwood, *Joey* Keith Prentice, *Jack Richards* Leland Starnes, *DaVinci's Friend* Robert Pope, *Water Sport* Leo Burmester, *Dancer* Bruce Levine, *3 Card Monte* Charles Dunlap, *Hankie Salesman* Powers Boothe, *Voice of Jack* James Sutorius, *Spotter* Richard Jamieson, *Seller* James Ray Weeks, *Bouncer* David Winnie Hayes, *Bartender* Carmine Stipo, *Cockpit Coke Man* James Hayden, *Tugboat Mate* Todd Winters, *and* Robert Carnegie, Dennis Shea, Larry Silvestri, Lawrence Lust, Penny Gumeny, Ray Vitte, Joseph Catucci, Dan Sturkie, Sylvia Gassell, Henry Judd Baker, Kevin Johnson, Louie Grenier, Burr DeBenning, Mike Barbera, Robert Duggan, Linda Gary.

Deal of the Century

A Steve Tisch–John Avnet Production in association with Bud Yorkin Productions for Warner Bros., 1985. Color. Running time: 99 minutes.
   Credits: *Director* William Friedkin, *Screenplay* Paul Brickman, *Producer* Bud Yorkin, *Executive Producers* Jon Avnet, Steve Tisch, Paul Brickman, *Cinematography* Richard H. Kline, A.S.C., *Production Designer* Bill Malley, *Supervising Editor* Bud Smith, *Editors* Ned Humphreys, Jere Huggins, *Associate Producer* David

Salven, *Music* Arthur B. Rubinstein, *Casting* Nancy Klopper, *Costumes* Rita Riggs, *Unit Production Manager* David Salven, *1st Assistant Director* Terrence A. Donnelly, *2nd Assistant Director* James Freitag, *Set Decorator* Richard Goddard, *Supervising Sound Effects Editor* Stephen Hunter Flick, *Supervising Dialogue Editor* J. Paul Huntsman, *Sound Effects Editors* Warren Hamilton, Jr., Mark Mangini, *Dialogue Editor* Andrew Patterson, *Music Editor* Abby Treloggen, *Production Mixer* Willie Burton, *Re-Recording Mixers* Robert "Buzz" Knudson, Christopher Jenkins, Robert Glass, Don Digirolamo, *Script Supervisor* Betty Abbott Griffin, *Location Managers* Bill Bowling, David Salven, Jr., *Camera Operator* Al Bettcher, *Panaglide (R) Operator* Dan Lerner, *Assistant Cameraman* Jud Kehl, *2nd Assistant Cameraman* Kevin Jewison, *Property Master* Barry Bedig, *Assistant Property Master* Stan Cockerell, *Assistant Film Editors* Craig Bassett, Seth Flaum, *Video Coordinator* Rick Whitfield, *Negative Cutter* Donah Bassett, *Color Timer* Aubrey Head, *Orchestration* Mark Hoder, *Special Effects* Chuck Gaspar, Joe Day, *DGA Trainee* Linca Rockstroh, *Production Associate* Tim Chisholm, *Production Secretary* Nanette Siegert, *Assistant to the Producer* Dolores Hyams, *Men's Costumer* Laurie Riley, *Women's Costumer* Liza Stewart, *Makeup Artist* Frank Griffin, *Hairstylist* Kaye Pownall, *2nd Unit Director in Charge of Optical Effects* Bruce Logan, *Motion Control Photography by* Dream Quest Images, *Motion Control Supervisors* Scott Squires, Hoyt Yeatman, *Motion Control Technicians* David Hardberger, Thomas Hollister, Robert Hollister, Fred Iguchi, Bess Wiley, *Motion Control Assistant* William Reilly, *Computer* Michael Bigelow, *Motion Control Gaffer* Robert Thomas, *Motion Control Grip* Eric Stoner, *Production Coordinator* Keith Shartle, *Front Projection System by* Zoptic, Inc., *Consultant* Zoran Perisic, *Zoptic Operator* Allen Blaisdell, *Zoptic Projectionist* Norman Markowitz, *Rear Projection Coordinator* Bill Hansard, *Visual Effects Editor* Michael Kelly, *Visual Effects Assistant Editor* Jane C. Lang, *Supervisor Visual Effects Enhancements* Kerry Colonna, *Special Miniature Effects by* Coast Special Effects, *Matté Paintings by* Dream Quest Images, *Matté Artist* Rocco Gioffre, *Titles by* Pacific Title.

"Someone to Watch Over Me" sung by Nikka Costa (Courtesy of Renquet Records); "Shine" (Music by Arthur B. Rubinstein, Lyrics by Cynthia Morrow) sung by Maxine Waters, Julia Waters and Clydene Jackson.

Cast: *Eddie Muntz* Chevy Chase, *Mrs. DeVoto* Sigourney Weaver, *Ray Kasternak* Gregory Hines, *Frank Stryker* Vince Edwards, *Gen. Cordosa* William Marquez, *Col. Salgado* Eduardo Ricard, *Lyle* Richard Herd, *Babers* Graham Jarvis, *Harold DeVoto* Wallace Shawn, *Ms. Della Rosa* Randi Brooks, *Bob* Ebbe Roe Smith, *Masaggi* Richard Libertini, *Will* J. W. Smith, *Woman Singer* Carmen Moreno, *Dr. Rechtin* Charles Levin, *Vardis* Pepe Serna, *Rojas* Wilfredo Hernandez, *Pilot on Screen* John Davey, *Molino* Miguel Piñero, *Frenchman* Maurice Marsac, *Russian Translator* Joe Ross, *Gaylord* Jonathan Terry, *Huddleston* Robert Cornthwaite, *Rev. Borman* Gwil Richards, *Newscaster* Kelly Lange, *Sen. Bryce* Ken Letner, *Baptist #1* Jomaire Payton, *Chicano Man* Tony Plana, *Baptist #2* Betty Cole, *Baptist Minister* John Hancock, *Baptist #3* Helen Martin, *Bagman* Eddie Hice, *Rockwell Official* David Haskell, *Charlie Simbo* Ray Manzarek, *Rick Penido* David Hall, *Street Robber* Alex Colón, *Swain* John Reilly, *JWT Assoc* James Staley, *Promoter* Stephen Keep, *Freddie Muntz* Louis Giambalvo, *Man from Grumman* Robert Alan Browne, *Man from McDonnell Douglas* Brad English, *Masaggi's Aide #1* Jim Ishida, *Masaggi's Aide #2* Michael Yama, *Luckup Hostess #1* Judy Baldwin, *Luckup Hostess #2* Jan McGill, *Station Wagon Driver* Frank Lugo, *Chicano Woman* Loyda Ramos, *Freddie's Wife* Wendy Soloman, *Helicopter Reporter* John Stinson, *Woman in Commercial* Janet Louise Smith, *Accordionist* Jesus Carmona.

To Live and Die in L.A.

New Century Productions Ltd. and SLM, Inc., present an Irving H. Levin Production for MGM/UA, 1985. Color. Running time: 116 minutes.

Credits: *Director* William Friedkin, *Producer* Irving H. Levin, *Screenplay* William Friedkin, Gerald Petievich (based on the novel by Gerald Petievich), *Cinematographer* Robby Muller, *Co-Producer* Bud Smith, *Music Composed and Performed by* Wang Chung, *Casting* Bob Weiner, *Consultants* Pablo Ferro, Barry Bedig, *Supervising Editor* Bud Smith, *Editor* Scott Smith, *Production Designer* Lilly Kilvert, *Executive Producer* Samuel Schulman, *Second Unit Director* Bud Smith, *Unit Production Manager* John J. Smith, *1st Assistant Director* Charles Myers, *2nd Assistant Director* Bob Roe, *Stunt Coordinator (Flight Sequences)* Pat E. Johnson, *Stunt Coordinator (Driving & Chase Sequence)* Buddy Joe Hooker, *Second Unit Photography* Robert Yeoman, *Re-recording Mixers* Christopher Jenkins, Robert Glass, Gary Alexander, *Re-recorded by* Todd-AO, *Sound Effects Editors* Louis L. Edemann, Michael Dobie, Jeff Bushelman, *Dialogue Editor* J. Paul Huntsman, *Additional Editing* Jere Huggins, *Assistant Editors* Sonny Baskin, Joseph Mosca, Jill Smith, *Special Effects* Phil Corey, *Art Director* Buddy Cone, *Set Decorator* Crickett Rowland, *Production Coordinator* Dianne Lisa Cheek, *Head Makeup Artist* Jefferson Dawn, *Costume Designer* Linda Bass, *Casting Associate* Gary M. Zuckerbrod, *Sound Recordists* Jean-Louis DuCarme, Rodger Pardee, *Script Supervisor* Jackie Saunders, *Assistant Set Decorators* Richard Hummel, Portia Iverson, *Set Dressers* John Stadelman, Jon Hutman, *Still Photographer* Jane O'Neal, *Location Manager* Michael Healy, *Assistant Location Manager* Michael Helfand, *Painter* Amanda Flick, *Assistant Art Director* Dins Danielson, *Construction Coordinator* Frank Viviano, *Carpenters* Raymond Camaioni, Dennis Hoerter, William Jones, Gavin McCune, *Costume Supervisor* Susie DeSanto, *Hair Stylist* Peter Tothpal, *Negative Cutter* Donah Bassett, *Chief Lighting Technician* Greg Gardiner, *Best Boy Electric* Scott Guthrie, *Electricians* Robert Field, Kevin Galbraith, *Key Grip* Robert Feldman, *Best Boy Grip* Lesley Percy, *Grips* Bill Guerre, Timothy Moore, *Transportation Coordinator* Jeffrey Renfro, *Transportation Captains* Richard Brasic, Olivia Varnado, *Production Secretary* Betsy Oliver Luhrsen, *Assistants to William Friedkin* Adele Joseph, Cindy Chvatal, *Assistant to the Producer* Michele Troxell, *Prison Institutional Coordinator* Gil Miller, *Prison Technical Advisor* Woody Wilcoxan, *Extra Casting* The Atmosphere Agency, *Post Production Auditor* Diana Gold, *Completion Guarantee Provided by* Film Finances, Inc., *Insurance Provided by* Bob Jellen/Albert G. Ruben & Co., Inc., *Menswear Furnished by* Rick Pollack, Sherman Oaks, CA, *Christian Dior Bed Linens by* Wamsutta, *Masters' Paintings by* Reiner Fetting, *Payroll Services Provided by* TPI/EPPI, *Optical Effects* Movie Magic, *Dialogue Re-recorded by* The Sound Shop, *Lab Consultant* Larry Rovetti, *Color Timers* Dick Ritchie, Aubrey Head, *Dolby Consultant* Jim Fitzpatrick.

"Cold Day in Hell" performed by Otis Rush (Courtesy of Delmark Records); "Lookin' Good" performed by Magic Sam (Courtesy of Delmark Records); "Good Morning School Girl" performed by Junior Wells (Courtesy of Delmark Records); "Laudy! Laudy!" performed by Junior Wells (Courtesy of Delmark Records); "Independent Intavenshan" performed by Linton Kwesi Johnson (Courtesy of Island Records); "Uphill Climb to the Bottom" performed by Walter Jackson; "L.A. L.A." performed by AM-FX (Lyrics by Jerry Leiber, Music by Jed Leiber, Produced by Jerry Leiber & Jed Leiber); "Wait" performed by Wang Chung (Courtesy of Geffen Records), "Dance Hall Day" performed by Wang Chung (Produced by Chris Hughes & Ross Collum, Courtesy of Geffen Records); "Wake Up Stop Dreaming" performed by Wang Chung (Produced by Wang Chung, Assisted by David Motion,

Courtesy of Geffen Records); "To Live and Die in L.A." performed by Wang Chung (Produced by Tony Swain & Steve Jolley, Courtesy of Geffen Records); "Lullaby" performed by Wang Chung (Produced by Wang Chung, Courtesy of Geffen Records); "The Conductor Wore Black" performed by Rank & File (Courtesy of Slash Records/Warner Bros. Records, Inc.); "Rank & File" performed by Rank & File (Courtesy of Slash Records/Warner Bros. Records, Inc.); "Red Rose" performed by The Blasters (Courtesy of Slash Records/Warner Bros. Records, Inc.); "Coyote" performed by Rank & File (Courtesy of Slash Records/Warner Bros. Records, Inc.).

Choreographer Leslie Linka Glatter, *Dancers* Jane Leaves, Cherise Bate, Michael W. Higgins, Chris Lattanzoi, Shaun Earl.

Cast: *Richard Chance* William L. Petersen, *Eric Masters* Willem DaFoe, *John Vukovich* John Pankow, *Bianca Torres* Debra Feuer, *Carl Cody* John Turturro, *Ruth Lanier* Darlanne Fluegel, *Bob Grimes* Dean Stockwell, *Jeff Rice* Steve James, *Thomas Bateman* Robert Downey, *Jim Hart* Michael Greene, *Max Waxman* Christopher Allport, *Jack* Jack Hoar, *Judge Filo Cedillo* Val DeVargas, *Doctor* Dwier Brown *Thomas Ling* Michael Chong, *Claudia Leith* Jackely Giroux, *Terrorist* Michael Zand, *FBI Agents* Bobby Bass, Dar Allen Robinson, *Nurse* Anne Betancourt, *Ticket Agent* Katherine M. Louie, *Airport Guard* Edward Harrell, *Utro's Bartender* Gilbert Espinoza, *Agents* John Petievich, Zarko Petievich, Rick Dalton, Richard L. Lane, Jack Cota, *Airline Passenger* Shirley J. White, *Visiting Room Guard* Gerald H. Brownlee, *Tower Guard* David M. DuFriend, *Inmate Ruben* Ruben Garcia, *Prison Guard* Joe Duran, *Prison Assailants* Buford McClerkins, Gregg Dandridge, *Rice's Friends* Donny Williams, Earnest Hart, Jr., *Second Suspect* Thomas F. Duffy, *Special Agent* Gerry Petievich, *Mark Gash* Mark Gash, *Criminal* Pat McGroarty, *Tourist* Brian Bradley, *Serena* Jane Leaves, *Stunt Players* Jeb Adams, Carl L. Anderson, Bobby Bass, Billy Bates, Ken Bates, Jophrey Brown, Bobby Andrew Burns, Bill Burton, David Carlton, John Casino, Phil Chong, Carl Ciarfalio, Ray Colbert, Clarke Coleman, Jim Connors, Wally Crowder, Tim Culbertson, Jay C. Currin, Jeffrey J. Dashnaw, Steve M. Davison, Tim A. Davison, Justin DeRosa, Eddy Donno, Doc Duhame, David R. Ellis, Richard M. Ellis, Kenny Endoso, Tony Epper, Erik Felix, Gloria Fioramanti, Pat Green, James M. Halty, Orwin C. Harvey, Steve Holladay, Larry E. Holt, Bill (Hank) Hooker, Buddy Joe Hooker, Hugh M. Hooker, Richard Hooker, Thomas J. Huff, Gary Hymes, Lamont Jackson, Loren Janes, Matt Johnson, Donna M. Keegan, Henry Kingi, Billy D. Lucas, Pat McGroarty, Gary McLarty, Pat J. McNamara, John C. Meier, Charly Marie Morgan, Jimmy Nickerson, Manuel Perry, Jon Pochron, Chad Randall, Cynthia Lee Rice, Jean Riddel, Vernon Rieta, Dar Allen Robinson, Danny Rogers, Patrick Romano, R. A. Rondell, Ronald Rondell, Debby Lynn Ross, Mike Runyard, Ray Saniger, Dennis R. Scott, Keith Tellez, David H. Welch, Scott Wilder, Dick Ziker.

Rampage

A De Laurentiis Entertainment Group Presentation, 1987. Color. Running time: 97 minutes.

Credits: *Director* William Friedkin, *Producer* David Salven, *Screenplay* William Friedkin (based on the novel by William P. Wood), *Cinematography* Robert D. Yeoman, *Editor* Jere Huggins, *Music* Ennio Morricone, *Production Design* Buddy Cone, *Art Director* Carol Clements, *Set Decoration* Nancy Nye, *Sound* David MacMillan, *Casting* Rick Montgomery, *Assistant Directors* Michael Daves, Regina Gordon.

Cast: *Anthony Fraser* Michael Biehn, *Charles Reece* Alex McArthur, *Albert*

Morse Nicholas Campbell, *Kate Fraser* Deborah Van Valkenburgh, *Dr. Keddie* John Harkins, *Mel Sanderson* Art Lefleur, *Judge McKinsey* Billy Greenbush, *Gene Tippets* Royce D. Applegate, *Naomi Reece* Grace Zabriskie.
(No other production credits available.)

The Guardian

A Joe Wizan Production for Universal Pictures, 1990. Color. Running time: 90 minutes.

Credits: *Director* William Friedkin, *Producer* Joe Wizan, *Screenplay* Steven Volk, Dan Greenburg, William Friedkin (based on *The Nanny* by Dan Greenburg), *Executive Producer* David Salven, *Cinematography* John A. Alonzo, A.S.C., *Production Designer* Gregg Fonseca, *Editor* Seth Flaum, *Co-Producers* Todd Black, Mickey Borofsky, Dan Greenburg, *Music* Jack Hughes, *Casting Director* Louis DiGiamo, *Production Manager* David Salven, *First Assistant Director* Newton Dennis Arnold, *Second Assistant Director* Christopher Stoia, *Special Effects* Phil Cory, *Special Makeup Effects* Matthew W. Mungle, *Sound Effects*, Mark Mangini, *Supervising Re-recording Mixer* Mark Berger, *Effects Mixer* David Parker, *Music Mixer* Todd Boekelheide, *Re-recording Facility* The Saul Zaentz Film Center, Berkeley, CA, *Stunt Coordinator* Buddy Joe Hooker, *Property Master* Barry Bedig, *Assistant Editors* Rob Dean, Mary Jo Markey, *Gaffer* Rick West, *Camera Operator* Don Reddy, *First Assistant Camera* Gary Jay, *Second Assistant Camera* Jeffrey Greeley, Michael Sofronski, *Still Photographer* Luke Wynne, *Sculptor* Daniel Miller, *Art Director* Bruce Miller, *Art Department Coordinator* Vivienne Radkoff, *Set Decorator* Sarah Burdick, *Lead Persons* Laura Settlemeier, Greg Oehler, *Swing Gang* Gregory Zemgals, Louis Floyd, *Storyboards* Doug Lefler, *Construction Coordinator* John Samson, *Construction Foreman* David Cunningham, *Standby Painter* Andrew Reidenbaugh, *Special Effects* Ray Svedin, Hans Metz, *Assistant Props* Stan Cockerell, *Assistant Sculptor* Steve Petruzates, *Sound Mixers* James R. Alexander, Tom Causey, *Key Makeup* Teresa M. Austin, *Makeup Artist* Janeen Schreyer, *Key Hair Stylist* Jennifer Bell, *Assistant Special Makeup Effects* Edward French, *Costume Supervisor* Renee Alaina Sacks, *Costumer* Zoe Hale, *Location Manager* David M. Salven, *Second Second Assistant Director* Ira Rosenstein, *Additional Casting* Rick Montgomery, *Assistant Location Manager* Ted Regopoulos, *Script Supervisors* Judi Townsend, Betty Abbott-Griffin, *Production Accountant* Nava Levin, *Assistant Accountants* Tal Mierson, Carolyn Mock, *Production Coordinator* Paula Benson-Himes, *Production Secretary* Cynthia Boyler, *Assistant to Mr. Wizan* Betty Gumm, *Assistant to Mr. Friedkin* Adele Curcuruto, *Studio Teacher* Rikki Muccia, *Nurse* Barbara Yarbrough, *Transportation Coordinator* Tommy Tancharoen, *Transportation Captain* Lee Garibaldi, *Animal Trainers* Gary Gero, Bobbi Gaddy, Gayle Phelps, Steve Martin, *Production Assistants* Peter J. Novak, Larry Felix, John Barnette, *Special Sound Effects* John P., *Sound Effects Recording* Ezra Dweck, *Sound Editors* David Bartlett, M.P.S.E.; John Dunn; Warren Hamilton, Jr., M.P.S.E.; David Stone, M.P.S.E.; Ron Bartlett; Teresa Eckton; *Foley Editor* Christopher Flick, *Second Foley Editor* Solange Schwalbe Boisseau, *ADR Editor* Alan Nineberg, M.P.S.E., *Second ADR Editor* Stephen Purvis, *Sound Effects Assistants* Sonny Pettijohn, Oscar Mitt, Josie Nericcio, *Foley by* Ellen Heuer, John Roesch, *Negative Cutter* Donah Bassett, *Color Timing* Bob Raring, *Title & Optical Design* Pablo Ferro, *Title & Optical Effects* Cinema Research Corporation, *String Music by* The Greene String Quartet, *Piano Background* Tony Cobb.

"Palau" (Music by Not Drowning, Waving; Lyrics by David Bridie; Performed by Not Drowning, Waving; Courtesy of Mighty Boy Records); "While the City Sleeps" (Written and Performed by Roger Eno; Courtesy of Opal Records); "Wide Open Road" (Written by David McComb; Performed by The Triffids; Courtesy of Rough Trade Records); "Waltz for Debby" (Written by Bill Evans & Gene Lees; Performed by Bill Evans, Scott LaFaro & Paul Motian; Courtesy of Fantasy, Inc.); "Incidental Groove" (Written, Performed and Produced by Joseph A. White, Stephen Sea & Roy Blumenfeld).

Cast: *Camilla* Jenny Seagrove, *Phil* Dwier Brown, *Kate* Carey Lowell, *Ned Runcie* Brad Hall, *Ralph Hess* Miguel Ferrer, *Molly Sheridan* Natalia Nogulich, *Gail Krasno* Pamela Brull, *Allan Sheridan* Gary Swanson, *Punks* Jack David Walker, Willy Parsons, Frank Noon, *Arlene Russell* Therese Randle, *Detective* Xander Berkeley, *Dr. Klein* Ray Reinhardt, *Scotty* Jacob Gelman, *Mrs. Horniman* Iris Bath, *Rosaria* Rita Gomez, *Dr. at Birth* Dr. Barry Herman, *Older Woman* Bonnie Snyder, *Baby Jake* Chris Nemeth, Craig Nemeth, Aaron Fischman, Josh Fischman, *Stunts* Simone Boisseree, Donna Evans, Bill Hooker, Tracy Lyn Keehn, Steve Earl Martin, Lee Janet Orcutt, Cris Palomino, Gary Price, Kristyn Randall, Patrick Romano, Debby Lynn Ross, Anthony G. Schmidt, Charles A. Tamburo, Kim Washington.

Index

297